Then those who feared the LORD talked with each other, and the LORD listened and heard.

MALACHI 3:16

THE COMPLETE

Bible
Discussion
Guide

GROUP DISCUSSION
QUESTIONS FOR EVERY CHAPTER
IN THE BIBLE

IN TWO VOLUMES:
NEW TESTAMENT • OLD TESTAMENT & TOPICAL INDEX

MACK THOMAS

THE COMPLETE
BIBLE DISCUSSION GUIDE
Volume One (Old Testament): © 1993 by Questar Publishers, Inc.
Volume Two (New Testament): © 1992 by Questar Publishers, Inc.

Multnomah Books is a part of the Questar publishing family.

Printed in the United States of America

International Standard Book Numbers:
Volume One (Old Testament & Topical Guide): 0-945564-54-6
Volume Two (New Testament): 0-945564-55-4

93 94 95 96 97 98 99 00 01 — 10 9 8 7 6 5 4 3 2 1

to
Howard G. Hendricks

STUDENT OF GOD'S WORD
TEACHER OF TEACHERS

FIND THESE HELPFUL FEATURES IN THE BACK OF THIS BOOK:

➤ *A GUIDE TO TOPICAL BIBLE STUDIES*
   for personal and group Bible study by topics.

➤ *A STUDY SCHEDULE for the entire Old Testament*

AND IN THE BACK OF VOLUME TWO:

➤ *HELPFUL GROUP GUIDELINES for greater*
   effectiveness in your Bible study discussion group

➤ *PRAYERS AND PROMISES from the Scriptures*
   to pray and believe as you study the Bible,
   as a group or on your own

CONTENTS

QUESTIONS TO ASK AS YOU STUDY <u>EACH CHAPTER</u>:

➤ Since the ultimate aim of Bible study is *to know God better,*
   what does this chapter tell me about God's character and personality?

➤ Since God has given me the Bible to change my life, what needed corrections or adjustments in my habits or character come to mind as I explore this chapter?

➤ In this chapter, what are...
>   the key verses, the key phrases, the key words?
>   the key points or principles—*and how do they*
>>   *work in my life?*

➤ In this chapter, do I see any...
>   commands to obey?
>   promises to claim?
>   standards to live by?
>   examples to learn from?

➤ What three-to-six word title could I give to this chapter,
   to help me remember its teaching?

EVERYONE'S BEST PREPARATION
for Discussing Each Chapter:
Read the chapter...reread it...and reread it again.

QUESTIONS TO ASK AS YOU BEGIN YOUR STUDY OF <u>EACH BOOK</u>:

➤ If you're already familiar with this book, which passages are your favorite parts of it?

➤ If this were the only book in the Bible you knew about or had access to, what things could you still find out about God?

➤ As you scan this book, what *types* of Bible literature does it appear to contain? (You may want to review together the different types, such as those listed here:)
   • poetry
   • historical or biographical narrative (a record of people and events)
   • teaching or sermons
   • laws or covenant agreements
   • parables (short stories and word pictures with a moral point)
   • proverbs (short, wise sayings)
   • prophecy (statements from God about the present and future)

➤ What appear to be the main divisions in this book?

➤ From what you understand about this book, *who* wrote it (and when), and for what *original audience* was it written?

➤ From what you see in looking over this book, what would you say the author was trying most to accomplish?

➤ Which chapter in this book would you say is the key chapter, the one that best summarizes or reflects or unlocks the meaning of the entire book?

➤ From what you see in looking over this book, what kinds of answers and guidelines and solutions in life do you think we can reasonably expect to find in this book?

➤ What four- to six-word title would you give to this book, to best summarize its content and significance?

➤ When you get to heaven, if you asked God, "Why did You include this book in the Bible?" how do you think He would answer?

Genesis

OVERVIEW

(Discuss these OVERVIEW questions both at the beginning of your study of Genesis, then again after you've studied all fifty chapters. Your answers may change significantly once you've looked more closely at the entire book.)

Startup: Talk together about times when you felt you had a "fresh start" or "new beginning" in your life. What was it that gave you this feeling?

SEEING WHAT'S THERE

1. Before launching into a closer look at Genesis, how would you summarize what you already know about this book?

2. Look at the following verses, and describe what they tell you about how the book of Genesis is put together: 2:4, 5:1, 6:9, 10:1, 11:10, 11:27, 25:12, 25:19, 36:1, 36:9, and 37:2.

3. Look also at the list of "Questions to Ask as You Begin Your Study of Each Book" on page 9.

4. Since Genesis is known as the "Book of Beginnings," scan through the book to see where you find the first city; the first sorrow; the first fear; the first rainbow; the first rain; the first murder; the first grandchild.

CAPTURE THE ESSENCE

5. What action on God's part is repeated in each of the following verses — 9:9, 15:18, 17:7, and 17:19? What clues does this offer about the central message of Genesis?

FOR LIFE TODAY

6. Genesis has been called "the indispensable introduction to the entire Bible," "the foundation for understanding all Scripture," "the story of God's purpose and plan for His creation," and "the great introduction to the drama of redemption." With that reputation for this book, what kinds of answers and guidelines and solutions would you like to gain as you examine it more closely?

7. When you get to heaven, if you have a long talk with Moses (the author of this book) and he asks you, "What was most helpful to you in Genesis?" how would you like to be able to answer him?

8. From what you see in God's words to Abraham in 17:1, what would be a good personal prayer to offer to God as you study this book?

9. As you think first about *who God is,* and second about *what the Bible is,* how strongly would you rate your present desire to understand better the book of Genesis? Use a scale of one to ten (one = "no desire at all," ten = "extremely intense desire") to help you decide.

GENESIS 1

Startup: What are the most important "beginnings" you've experienced in your adult life?

SEEING WHAT'S THERE

1. Read this chapter aloud in your group, with everyone taking turns reading. Switch to a different reader each time you come to the end of one of the "days" in that first creation week. (You may also want to continue into the first three verses in chapter 2, which complete the account in chapter 1.)

2. Review carefully the words in this chapter, and decide how much God says about (a) *how* He made everything in our universe, (b) *how long* it took Him to make the universe, and (c) *why* He made it.

3. Look again at the ten words in verse 1. Repeat this majestic statement to yourself. Then, in light of what you know about the rest of the Bible, discuss how much you agree or disagree with this conclusion: The Scriptures never try to *argue* for the existence of God; from the very start they simply *assume* God's powerful and sovereign existence.

4. How many times in this chapter do you see a combined reference to evening and morning?

5. As you survey the order and arrangement of God's creative work, what does Day One have in common with Day Four? Day Two with Day Five? And Day Three with Day Six?

6. What are the strongest impressions or images which this chapter leaves in your mind?

7. Look also on page 8 at the list of "Questions to Ask as You Study Each Chapter." You may want to look again at this list for each chapter in Genesis.

CAPTURE THE ESSENCE

8. If Genesis is the "foundation" for the message of the entire Bible, what important "building blocks" in that foundation would you say are added in this chapter?

9. From what you see in this chapter, what would you say God wants us most to know and believe about His character and personality?

10. Suppose you were telling the story of creation from Genesis 1 to a child. How would the child asked you, "Who made God?"

11. From what this chapter teaches, what are the most important facts about who *you* are?

12. How would you define what the word "beginning" means in verse 1? Would you say that it means the same thing here that it does in John 1:1?

13. What would you say is the best definition for the word "good" as it is used in this chapter?

14. Review again verses 26-30. What would you say are the most important ways in which we are made in God's image?

15. In what ways does this chapter reveal God's orderliness?

16. Discuss how much you agree or disagree with this statement: When it comes to the *origins* of both matter and life in our universe, the creation account in Genesis rules out any possibility of either "accident" or "evolution."

17. Bible teachers have stated that the book of Genesis focuses especially on *God, man,* and *land.* What evidence, if any, do you see for such a focus in chapter 1?

18. From what you see in this chapter, would you say that God wants to be considered *primarily* as the God of His people Israel, or the God of the whole earth? Explain your answer.

19. This chapter tells what happens "in the beginning." What does God want us to understand about what happens "in the end"? Does every beginning have to have an end?

20. From what you've seen in this chapter (as well as in the created world around you), how accurate is it to say that God is an *artist?*

21. Proverbs 2:1-5 tells about the sincere person who truly longs for wisdom and understanding, and who searches the Scriptures for it—as if it were buried treasure. That person, Solomon says, will come to understand the fear of the Lord, and discover the knowledge of God. As you begin exploring the book of Genesis, what "buried treasure" would you like God to help you find—to show you what God and His wisdom are really like? If you have this desire, how would you express it in your own words?

FOR LIFE TODAY

22. What does it mean to you *personally* that you are made in God's image? What does it mean specifically in regard to your own *body,* your own *mind,* and your own *spirit?*

23. What do you feel are the most important ways in which we are to carry out God's instructions to mankind in verse 28?

24. Look at the guidelines for our thought-life given in Philippians 4:8—"Whatever is true, whatever is noble, whatever is

right, whatever is pure, whatever is love-ly, whatever is admirable—if anything is excellent or praiseworthy—*think about such things.*" What food for thought can you find in this chapter that especially strikes you as being *true,* or *noble,* or *right,* or *pure,* or *lovely,* or *admirable,* or *excellent,* or *praiseworthy?*

FOR GOING DEEPER

Notice the first mention of God's Spirit in the Bible, in verse 2 of this chapter. To see more of the Spirit's creative work, what can you discover in Job 33:4, Psalm 104:27-30, and John 3:5-8?

GENESIS 2

SEEING WHAT'S THERE

1. In this chapter, what things do you see God providing for man?

2. What evidence do you see in the first two chapters of Genesis of God's great *concern* for human beings?

3. From what you see in this chapter, what conclusions can you make about God's intended purpose for human beings?

4. What evidence do you see in this chapter that God was directly and personally present in Adam's life?

5. In what ways would you say that verses 23 and 24 serve as a fitting climax to all that has happened so far in the book of Genesis?

6. EYE FOR DETAIL— *From what you re-call seeing in chapters 1 and 2, try answer-ing the following question without looking in your Bible:* What did God create on the fifth day? (See 1:20-23.)

CAPTURE THE ESSENCE

7. Look again at verse 3. In your own words, what do you think it means that God "blessed" the seventh day and "sanctified" it or "made it holy"?

8. In verse 9, what would you say is the sig-nificance of the names of the two trees in the middle of the garden?

9. From what you see in verses 18-25, what did God have in mind when He estab-lished marriage?

10. Look together at Matthew 19:3-6 and Ephesians 5:28-33. How would you say Jesus and Paul interpret the teaching in Genesis 2:24 about marriage?

11. What evidence do you find in this chap-ter for the equality of man and woman?

12. What are the most important things this chapter reveals to us about God?

13. How does the gospel of Christ fit into all that has happened so far in Genesis? Would you say that the gospel represents God's *best* for mankind, or only His *sec-ond best*? Was it God's "Plan A," or only His "Plan B"? What biblical evidence can you give for your answers?

FOR LIFE TODAY

14. If God had written this chapter only for *you,* which words or phrases do you think He would have underlined?

15. From all that you've seen so far in Gene-sis, what are you most *thankful* for?

16. What similarities and what differences do you see between God's presence with us today, and His presence with Adam in this chapter?

17. If Genesis 1 and 2 were not in our Bibles, and there was no other way of discovering the truths that are presented there, what difference would that make in our lives? What would be missing?

FOR GOING DEEPER

Look again at the statement in verse 2 that God "finished" the work He had been doing, and compare it with John 5:17. What would you say is God's work today?

GENESIS 3

Startup: When you get to heaven, and you meet Adam and Eve, what's the first ques-tion you'd like to ask them?

SEEING WHAT'S THERE

1. What exactly does the serpent say to the woman in this chapter?

2. What are the most important decisions and choices that are made in this chap-ter, and how would you analyze each one?

3. Summarize the story of the fall of Adam and Eve as presented here in this chapter, keeping in mind that no historical account can include *every* detail of the events it describes. What are the most important details which *are* included here? What kinds of details are left out, details which might otherwise be quite interesting to us? What does this selection process tell you about what God wants us to understand most from this story?

4. Reflect on the events in verses 21-24 from Adam and Eve's perspectives. At this point, what do you think they expected their future to be like? What are the biggest problems and challenges facing them in the future?

CAPTURE THE ESSENCE

5. How would you summarize what Adam and Eve learn most in this chapter about God, about Satan, and about themselves?

6. Review again what God says and does in verses 16-19, and in verse 23. How much do you think it *hurt* God to administer this punishment to the man and woman He had created with His own hands?

7. In understanding God's words in verses 17-19, what help do you find in Romans 8:20?

8. Verse 15 has been called "the first Messianic promise." How does this verse relate to Christ?

9. Discuss how much you agree or disagree with this statement: The pattern of Satan's temptation of Eve in Genesis 3 appears to be the basic pattern in all of the devil's temptation of human beings.

10. Also discuss how much you agree or disagree with this statement: From the middle of Genesis 3 onward through the end of Revelation, the principle focus of Scripture is God's work to restore His original plan and purpose for all His creation. (Use your knowledge of the rest of the Bible to help you answer.)

11. Imagine yourself being present in the temple in Jerusalem as the twelve-year-old Jesus hears this chapter read and dis-

cussed by the rabbis there. In Luke 2:46 we read that He was listening to these teachers and asking them questions. What verses from this chapter do you think would most impress the boy Jesus, and what questions or comments do you suppose He might have spoken?

FOR LIFE TODAY

12. Which verse in this chapter do you think God wants you to understand best?

13. Discuss how much you agree or disagree with this statement: We today are much more prone to temptation than Adam and Eve were.

14. Think again about the way Eve was "taken in" by the serpent's words. Why are Satan's temptations so appealing to us?

FOR GOING DEEPER

Compare the way Eve was tempted in verses 1-6 (notice especially verse 6) with the way Satan tempted Jesus in Luke 4:1-13. What similarities and differences stand out to you? Also compare Genesis 1:6 with the three forms of worldliness mentioned in 1 John 2:16.

GENESIS 4

SEEING WHAT'S THERE

1. Humanly speaking, what would you say is the best thing anybody does in this chapter?

2. What is the worst or most questionable thing anybody does in this chapter?

3. What are the most important decisions and choices that are made in this chapter, and how would you analyze each one?

4. How many words does Abel speak in this chapter? (After answering that question, look ahead to the statement at the end of Hebrews 11:4.)

5. How many times does Cain do something wrong in this chapter?

6. Review the story of Cain and Abel, once again keeping in mind that no historical account can include *every* detail of the events it describes. What are the most important details which *are* included

here? And what kinds of details are left out, details which might otherwise be quite interesting to us? What does this selection process tell you about what God wants us to understand most from this story?

CAPTURE THE ESSENCE

7. Considering all that has happened in Genesis so far, in what ways would you say that the statements in verses 25-26 are especially appropriate at this point in the story?

8. How would you summarize what Cain learns most about God in this chapter?

9. As this chapter closes, how do you think Adam and Eve would answer this question: What are your deepest hurts these days, and what are your greatest joys?

FOR LIFE TODAY

10. If God had written this chapter only for *you,* which words or phrases do you think He would have underlined?

FOR GOING DEEPER

How do you think the apostle Paul would answer the question "Am I my brother's keeper?" To help you answer, use the principles in Ephesians 4:1-6 and Colossians 3:12-17.

GENESIS 5

SEEING WHAT'S THERE

1. What important truths about creation are repeated in this chapter?

2. EYE FOR DETAIL— *From what you recall seeing in chapters 3—5, try answering the following question without looking in your Bible:* What were the names of Adam and Eve's first two grandsons (the son of Seth and the son of Cain)? (See 4:17 and 4:26.)

FOR LIFE TODAY

3. Look again at the indication of Enoch's relationship with God in verses 22 and 24. If someone wrote down those same words about you—that you "walked with God"— what exactly would you want them to mean by that term?

GENESIS 6

Startup: When you get to heaven, and you meet Noah, what's the first question you'd like to ask him?

SEEING WHAT'S THERE

1. In this chapter and chapter 7, how many times is mention made of God's intention to destroy the earth?

2. In your own words, how would you restate as fully as possible God's *reason* for destroying the earth?

3. What specific commands does God give Noah in the last half of this chapter?

4. What are the most important decisions and choices that are made in this chapter, and how would you analyze each one?

CAPTURE THE ESSENCE

5. What are the biggest problems or challenges that Noah is facing now?

6. Bible teachers have stated that the book of Genesis focuses especially on *God, man,* and *land.* What evidence, if any, do you see for such a focus in chapter 6?

FOR LIFE TODAY

7. If God had written this chapter only for *you,* which words or phrases do you think He might have underlined, and why?

GENESIS 7

SEEING WHAT'S THERE

1. What specific commands does God give Noah as this chapter begins?

2. How many times in this chapter is mention made of someone entering the ark?

3. How many times in this chapter is mention made of the floodwaters?

4. How many times in this chapter is mention made in some way of the death of all living things on the land?

CAPTURE THE ESSENCE

5. How much do you think it *hurt* God to administer this extreme punishment to people He had created?

6. How much do you think it hurt God to bring such destruction upon the earth He had created?

FOR LIFE TODAY

7. Of all that you see in this chapter, what one truth are you most *thankful* for, because of its personal significance to you?

GENESIS 8

SEEING WHAT'S THERE

1. How many times in this chapter is mention made of the floodwaters going down?

2. In your own words, how would you describe the *beauty* of this chapter? What is it that makes this passage so appealing?

3. What has impressed you most about Noah in this book?

4. EYE FOR DETAIL— *From what you recall seeing in chapters 6—8, try answering the following question without looking in your Bible:* After sending out a dove the first time from the ark, how many days did Noah wait before sending it out again? (See 8:10.)

CAPTURE THE ESSENCE

5. Think back on the many details in the flood story which are repeated. What do you think is the purpose for this repetition?

6. After leaving the ark, what do you think would be the greatest adjustments Noah and his family would have to make?

FOR LIFE TODAY

7. Of all that you see in this chapter, what one truth are you most *thankful* for, because of its personal significance to you?

GENESIS 9

Startup: How long have you known about the story of Noah and the ark? What are some of the earliest impressions this story left with you?

SEEING WHAT'S THERE

1. Summarize what God says in verses 4-6 about the significance of blood.

2. What *specifically* does God promise Noah in the covenant stated in verses 8-17?

3. What important word is repeated most often in verses 9-17? What does this word mean?

4. Humanly speaking, what would you say is the best thing anybody does in this chapter?

5. What is the worst or most questionable thing anybody does in this chapter?

CAPTURE THE ESSENCE

6. How would you summarize what Noah learns most about God in this chapter?

7. If you were responsible for giving Noah a job performance review (for his service to God), what comments would you make to him?

8. Recall again the view of some Bible teachers that the book of Genesis focuses especially on *God, man,* and *land.* What evidence, if any, do you see for such a focus in chapter 9?

9. Again, imagine yourself being present in the temple in Jerusalem as the twelve-year-old Jesus hears this chapter read and discussed by the Jewish teachers. What verses in this chapter do you think would most impress Him, and what questions or comments do you suppose He might have spoken?

FOR LIFE TODAY

10. If you've gained a better understanding of the truths in this chapter, in what ways does it deepen your convictions about the sacredness of life?

11. If it's true that *the past is a lesson for the future,* then what would you say are the most important lessons for God's people today to learn from the story of Noah?

Look again at what God says in verses 4-6 about the significance of blood. How do you see this significance expressed also in Leviticus 17:11-12, Deuteronomy 12:23-25, and especially in Hebrews 9:22?

Genesis 10

SEEING WHAT'S THERE

1. Look over the names listed in this chapter. Which of these people have you seen mentioned in other parts of Genesis?

Genesis 11

SEEING WHAT'S THERE

1. With the beginning of the story of Abraham, we come to a major division in the book of Genesis. In only a few sentences, how would you summarize the most important things that have happened so far in this book?

2. What do you think might be most surprising in Genesis to a new Christian reading it for the first time?

3. According to this chapter, what was the *reason* for the planned construction of the Tower of Babel?

4. Summarize the story of the Tower of Babel, once again keeping in mind that no historical account can include *every* detail of the events it describes. What are the most important details which *are* included here? And what kinds of details are left out, details which might otherwise be quite interesting to us? What does this selection process tell you about what God wants us to understand most from this story?

5. EYE FOR DETAIL— *From what you recall seeing in chapters 9—11, try answering the following question without looking in your Bible:* What construction materials were used on the Tower of Babel? (See 11:3.)

CAPTURE THE ESSENCE

6. Notice the sentence that includes the word *name* in verse 4. Then look ahead to see the sentence that uses the same word used in 12:2. From what you know of the story of Babel and the story of Abraham, what lesson can you draw from comparing these two verses?

7. As you think about the overall story unfolding in the book of Genesis, what important step in that unfolding is played by this story of the Tower of Babel? What strategic *purpose* do you think this account might serve in the larger picture?

8. Discuss how much you agree or disagree with this statement: In light of man's sinful tendencies, it is foolish and unrealistic to strive toward world peace and harmony.

FOR LIFE TODAY

9. In verse 4, notice again the motive of the builders of the Tower of Babel. In what ways, if any, is it like any of *your* motives for what you have done or are doing in life?

10. What truths from the first eleven chapters of Genesis are the most relevant to an accurate understanding of our current world situation?

FOR GOING DEEPER

How does the scene in Revelation 7:9-12 compare with what you've seen so far in Genesis, especially here in chapter 11?

Genesis 12

Startup: In the way we read and study the Bible, what kind of old mental habits or faulty assumptions can most easily block this book of Genesis from coming alive in our minds and hearts?

SEEING WHAT'S THERE

1. Chapter 12 has been called the key to the book of Genesis. What does this chapter include that could make it this significant?

2. How many specific promises are included in the words God speaks to Abram in verses 2-3? Is one of them more important than the others? If so, what is it?

3. What are the most important decisions and choices that are made in this chapter, and how would you analyze each one?

4. Look at verses 11 and 14. From your own imagination, what physical description could you give of Sarai? What do you think she might have looked like?

5. As you review the events in verses 10-20, in what ways can you see them foreshadowing the later experience of the nation of Israel in Egypt?

6. From what you see in this chapter, would you say that God wants to be considered *primarily* as the God of His people Israel (the descendants of Abraham), or as the God of the whole earth? Explain your answer.

7. In light of how you're doing spiritually in your life today, which verse in this chapter do you think is the most important at this time—and why?

Look especially at the promise God makes in verse 7. In the following passages, trace the fulfillment of this promise through the Bible, and decide how God wants us to think about it today—Exodus 6:6-8, Deuteronomy 1:6-8 and 8:10-11, Joshua 1:1-4 and 23:12-16, 2 Kings 25, and Ezekiel 11:16-17.

Look also at how Genesis 12 is seen from the perspective of New Testament faith in Hebrews 11:8-10. What did Abraham have most in common with us today?

GENESIS 13

1. What are the most important decisions and choices that are made in this chapter, and how would you analyze each one?

2. What does this chapter reveal about the character of both Abraham and Lot?

3. If you could go back in time, and God brought you into the events of this chapter to act as a personal counselor to Lot,

what kind of counsel would you give him, and how would you express it?

4. What aspect of Abraham's example in this chapter do you think God wants you to understand most?

GENESIS 14

1. Summarize the story of Abram's rescue of Lot, once again keeping in mind that no historical account can include *every* detail of the events it describes. What are the most important details which *are* included here? And what kinds of details are left out, details which might otherwise be quite interesting to us? What does this selection process tell you about what God wants us to understand most from this story?

2. As this chapter concludes, what would you say are the greatest challenges or potential dangers facing Abram at this time in his life?

3. EYE FOR DETAIL—*From what you recall seeing in chapters 12—14, try answering the following question without looking in your Bible:* The king and priest named Melchizedek gave a gift and a blessing to Abraham. Of what area was Melchizedek the king? (See 14:18.)

4. Notice again how Abraham's character is revealed in this chapter. What aspects of his character would you most like to see in your own life?

Genesis 15

Startup: What are some of the most "impossible" things you have believed God for?

SEEING WHAT'S THERE

1. What *specifically* does God promise Abraham in this chapter?

2. In verse 1, why do you think God told Abraham not to be afraid? What might Abraham be fearful of at this time?

3. What has impressed you most about Abraham in this book?

CAPTURE THE ESSENCE

4. Recall again the view of some Bible teachers that the book of Genesis focuses especially on *God, man,* and *land.* What evidence do you see for such a focus in chapter 15?

5. How would you summarize what Abraham learns most about God in this chapter?

FOR LIFE TODAY

6. Imagine that you saw earlier today a message written in fire in the sky. It was addressed to you by name, then continued with these words: *Thus saith the Lord: "Read Genesis 15, for I have something for you there."* Which verse or verses in this chapter do you think He most likely would be referring to?

FOR GOING DEEPER

Think again about what God says to Abram in this chapter, and look back also at His words to Abram in verses 12:2-3 and 12:7. Then look ahead to the words of Jesus in John 8:56. What was God showing to Abram, and why was Abram able to "see" it?

What was Abraham's chief reputation in the New Testament? Find out by discovering what Abraham is called in Romans 4:11 and 4:18, Galatians 3:9, and James 2:23

Genesis 16

SEEING WHAT'S THERE

1. Humanly speaking, what would you say is the best thing anybody does in this chapter?

2. What is the worst or most questionable thing anybody does in this chapter?

3. What are the most important decisions and choices that are made in this chapter, and how would you analyze each one?

4. As this chapter concludes, what would you say are the greatest challenges or potential dangers facing Abram and his family at this time?

CAPTURE THE ESSENCE

5. If you could go back in time, and God brought you into the events of this chapter to act as a personal counselor to both Hagar and Sarah, what kind of counsel would you give each of them, and how would you express it?

6. How would you summarize what Hagar learns most about God in this chapter?

FOR LIFE TODAY

7. As you consider your own life, how much ownership can you claim to the statements Hagar makes in verse 13? Is this a picture of your life as well?

Genesis 17

SEEING WHAT'S THERE

1. How many times do you see the word *covenant* used in this chapter? And what can you learn from this chapter about the biblical meaning of this word?

2. What *specifically* does God promise Abraham in this chapter?

3. What do we learn in this chapter about the meaning of circumcision, from God's point of view?

4. EYE FOR DETAIL— *From what you recall seeing in chapters 15—17, try answering the following question without looking in your Bible:* How old was Abraham when he was circumcised? (See 17:23-24.)

5. As you think about the overall story unfolding in the book of Genesis, what important step in that unfolding is played by this chapter? What strategic *purpose* do you think this account might serve in the larger picture?

6. How would you summarize what Abraham learns most about God in this chapter?

7. As this chapter closes, how do you think Abraham and Sarah would answer this question: What are your deepest hurts these days, and what are your greatest joys?

FOR LIFE TODAY

8. In verses 7-8, how much of God's promise to Abraham would you say applies also to *you?*

9. From what you see in this chapter, discuss together how you would complete this sentence: *What God really wants from me is…*

FOR GOING DEEPER

In verse 1, the words "God Almighty" are the English translation of the name *El Shaddai.* Look at how this name is used also in 28:2-3, 35:10-12, 43:13-14, and 48:3-4. How do these passages help you understand the fuller meaning of this name?

In verses 7-8, focus again on the Lord's promise to *be God* to Abraham and His descendants. Then use the following passages to trace this theme through the entire Bible, and to see its fulfillment—Exodus 6:6-8 and 20:1-2, Deuteronomy 29:12-13, 2 Samuel 7:24, and Revelation 21:6-7. How does God want us to view this promise today?

GENESIS 18

Startup: When you get to heaven, and you meet Abraham and Sarah, what's the first question you'd like to ask each of them?

SEEING WHAT'S THERE

1. Who are the most important people in this chapter, and what are the most important things that happen to them?

CAPTURE THE ESSENCE

2. How would you summarize what Sarah learns most about God in this chapter?

3. From what you see in Abraham's words in verses 22-33, what are the most important things he understands about God's personality and character?

FOR LIFE TODAY

4. If it's true that "you *become* what you *think,*" then what are the most important thoughts from this chapter to plant firmly in your mind?

GENESIS 19

SEEING WHAT'S THERE

1. What are the biggest problems and challenges facing Lot in this chapter?

2. What are the biggest problems and challenges facing the two angels?

3. What are the most important decisions and choices that are made in this chapter, and how would you analyze each one?

4. In verses 36-38, notice the names of the two nations descended from Lot. What do you learn about these nations in Deuteronomy 23:3-4, 1 Samuel 14:47, and 2 Chronicles 20:1-4?

CAPTURE THE ESSENCE

5. If you could go back in time, and God brought you into the events of this chapter to act as a personal counselor to Lot and his family, what kind of counsel would you give them, and how would you express it?

6. How would you summarize what Lot learns most about God in this chapter?

7. Think again about what God did in this chapter to remove Lot and his family from danger. What are some memorable ways in which God has rescued you from danger?

GENESIS 20

SEEING WHAT'S THERE

1. Take a "walk" together through the incidents that happen in this chapter: Using your imagination, talk about the kinds of sights, smells, sounds, and feelings you might experience.

2. From what you see in verse 6, what conclusions can we make about God?

3. From what you see in this chapter, what assessment would you make of Abraham's character?

CAPTURE THE ESSENCE

4. If you were responsible for giving Abraham a job performance review (in his positions as a husband and as a servant of God), what comments would you make to him, based on what you've seen so far in this book?

5. EYE FOR DETAIL— *From what you recall seeing in chapters 18—20, try answering the following question without looking in your Bible:* In 20:7 we see the first instance in the Bible of someone being called a prophet. Who was this prophet, and who called this person by that title? (See 20:1-7.)

FOR LIFE TODAY

6. Think again about Abraham's actions in this chapter. In what kind of circumstances today are you most tempted to respond in a similar way?

GENESIS 21

Startup: Picture yourself as one of Abraham's servants at the time of Isaac's birth. What big changes do you think his birth might bring for you and for others in Abraham's household?

SEEING WHAT'S THERE

1. Humanly speaking, what would you say is the best thing anybody does in this chapter? And what is the worst or most questionable thing anybody does in this chapter?

2. As this chapter concludes, what would you say are the greatest challenges or potential dangers facing Abraham at this time in his life?

FOR LIFE TODAY

3. As you consider your own life, how much ownership can you claim to the statement Sarah makes in verse 6? Is this a picture of your life as well? How much laughter has God given you?

GENESIS 22

SEEING WHAT'S THERE

1. What *specifically* does God promise Abraham in verses 15-18?

2. From what you see in verse 8, how would you analyze Abraham's faith?

3. Take a "walk" through the incidents that happen in this chapter: Using your imagination, talk about the kinds of sights, smells, sounds, and feelings you might experience.

4. From what you've read so far in the story of Abraham, what do you think might be most surprising to a new Christian reading it for the first time?

CAPTURE THE ESSENCE

5. How would you summarize what Abraham learns most about God in this chapter?

6. What emotions do you think God Himself may have been experiencing during the events of this chapter?

7. In how many ways do you see this chapter pointing to Jesus the Savior?

8. Again, imagine yourself being present in the temple in Jerusalem as the twelve-year-old Jesus hears this chapter read and discussed by the Jewish teachers. What verses in this chapter do you think would most impress Him, and what questions or comments do you suppose He might have spoken?

9. From what you see in this chapter, would you say that God wants to be considered *primarily* as the God of His people Israel (the descendants of Abraham), or as the God of the whole earth? Explain your answer.

10. EYE FOR DETAIL—*From what you recall seeing in chapters 21 and 22, try answering the following question without looking in your Bible:* As they journeyed to Moriah to offer a sacrifice, what did Abraham carry, and what did his son Isaac carry? (See 22:6.)

FOR LIFE TODAY

11. Choose one of these sentences, and complete it as fully and candidly as you would like: (a) What I see and understand in this chapter is important to my life because… OR: (b) What I see and understand in this chapter does NOT seem important to my life at this time, because…

12. From what you see in this chapter, discuss together how you would complete this sentence: *What God really wants from me is…*

13. Consider how strongly you desire to know God better, then ask yourself this question: What are the truths revealed about Him in this chapter which He may want me to understand more deeply at this time in my life?

FOR GOING DEEPER

Notice again the oath God swears in verses 16-18. How is this meaning of this oath intensified and expanded in Exodus 6:6-8 and Hebrews 6:12-20?

Look closely at Hebrews 11:17-19, and compare it with what you've seen in Genesis 22. How does each one of these passages help us to interpret the other?

GENESIS 23

Startup: What's the earliest experience in your childhood in which you can recall learning about death?

SEEING WHAT'S THERE

1. Notice in this chapter how Abraham procured the land to bury Sarah. Since God had promised to give this entire country to Abraham, why did Abraham go ahead and pay for this land?

CAPTURE THE ESSENCE

2. Keeping in mind the lessons she may have learned, suppose Sarah was allowed to live her life over again. What, if anything, do you think she would most want to change, and how?

GENESIS 24

SEEING WHAT'S THERE

1. What are the most important decisions and choices that are made in this chapter, and how would you analyze each one?

2. EYE FOR DETAIL—*From what you recall seeing in chapters 23 and 24, try answering the following question without looking in your Bible:* How old was Sarah when she died? (See 23:1.)

CAPTURE THE ESSENCE

3. How would you summarize what Abraham's servant learns most about God in this chapter?

FOR LIFE TODAY

4. From the example of Abraham's servant in this chapter, what can you learn about prayer?

5. In Romans 15:4, Paul reminds us that the Old Testament Scriptures can give us patience and perseverance on one hand, as well as comfort and encouragement on the other. In your own life, how do you see this book of Genesis living up to Paul's description? In what ways, if any, is it meeting your personal needs for both *perseverance* and *encouragement?*

GENESIS 25

Startup: Look at how Abraham is described in verse 8. What other people have you known who fit that description?

SEEING WHAT'S THERE

1. What does this chapter reveal most about the character of Isaac, the character of Esau, and the character of Jacob?

2. As this chapter concludes, what would you say are the greatest challenges or potential dangers facing Esau and Jacob at this time in their lives?

CAPTURE THE ESSENCE

3. Keeping in mind the lessons he may have learned, suppose Abraham was allowed to live his life over again. What, if anything, do you think he would most want to change, and how?

4. In Isaiah 55:10-11, God reminds us that He sends rain and snow from the sky to water the earth and to nurture life. In the same way, God says that He sends His words to accomplish specific purposes. From your study so far, what would you suggest as *God's* primary purposes for the book of Genesis in the lives of Christians today?

FOR LIFE TODAY

5. If it's true that *the past is a lesson for the future,* then what would you say are the most important lessons for God's people today to learn from the story of Abraham?

FOR GOING DEEPER

What does God say about Jacob and Esau in Malachi 1:2-3? And what conclusions are made from this in Romans 9:10-13 ?

GENESIS 26

SEEING WHAT'S THERE

1. What are the most important decisions and choices that are made in this chapter, and how would you analyze each one?

2. What specifically does God promise Isaac in verses 3-5 and in verse 24?

3. What *reason* does God give Isaac for keeping His promises in verses 5 and 24?

4. What reason for Isaac's prosperity is given in verse 12?

5. EYE FOR DETAIL—*From what you recall seeing in chapters 25 and 26, try answering the following question without looking in your Bible:* How old was Abraham when he died? (See 25:7.)

CAPTURE THE ESSENCE

6. If you could go back in time, and God brought you into the events of this chapter to act as a personal counselor to Isaac, what kind of counsel would you give him, and how would you express it?

7. In verse 24, why do you think God told Isaac not to be afraid? What might Isaac be fearful of at this time?

8. What does this chapter reveal about Isaac's character?

FOR LIFE TODAY

9. How much of God's promise to Isaac in verse 24 is also His promise to you?

GENESIS 27

Startup: What kind of pictures come to your mind when you think of the word *blessing?*

SEEING WHAT'S THERE

1. What are the most important decisions and choices that are made in this chapter, and how would you analyze each one?

2. What are the chief elements of Isaac's blessing upon Jacob in verses 28-29?

3. What are the chief elements of Isaac's pronouncement upon Esau in verses 39-40?

4. From what you see in this chapter, how would you analyze the *motives* of each member of Isaac's family—Isaac, Rebekah, Esau, and Jacob?

5. If you could go back in time, and God brought you into the events of this chapter to act as a personal counselor to Isaac and Rebekah and their two sons, what kind of counsel would you give them, and how would you express it?

6. How do the events of this chapter relate to the exchange between Jacob and Esau in 25:29-34?

FOR LIFE TODAY

7. In the area of family relationships, what would you say are the best lessons to learn from this chapter?

FOR GOING DEEPER

What conclusions from Esau's story are made in Hebrews 12:16-17?

GENESIS 28

SEEING WHAT'S THERE

1. What further words of blessing does Isaac give to Jacob in verses 3-4?

2. What specifically does God promise Jacob in verses 13-15?

3. What commitment does Jacob make in verses 20-22?

4. EYE FOR DETAIL—*From what you recall seeing in chapters 27 and 28, try answering the following question without looking in your Bible:* What did Jacob call the place where he dreamed and saw the stairway ascending to heaven? (See verses 17-19.)

CAPTURE THE ESSENCE

5. Why was Jacob's dream in this chapter so important to his spiritual development?

6. How would you summarize what Jacob learns most about God in this chapter?

7. Remember again the view of some Bible teachers that the book of Genesis focuses especially on *God, man,* and *land.* What evidence do you see for such a focus in chapter 28?

8. Again, imagine yourself being present in the temple in Jerusalem as the twelve-year-old Jesus hears this chapter read and discussed by the Jewish teachers. What verses in this chapter do you think would most impress Him, and what questions or comments do you suppose He might have spoken?

FOR LIFE TODAY

9. How much of God's promise to Jacob in verses 13-15 is also His promise to you?

GENESIS 29

Startup: What have been some of your most memorable experiences in moving away from the home of your childhood?

SEEING WHAT'S THERE

1. What does this chapter reveal most about Jacob's character? What does it reveal about Laban's character?

2. How do you see God's sovereign power at work in this chapter?

FOR LIFE TODAY

3. If God had written this chapter only for *you,* which words or phrases do you think He might have underlined, and why?

GENESIS 30

SEEING WHAT'S THERE

1. How many more children are born to Jacob in this chapter?

2. Summarize the story in verses 25-43 of how Jacob's flocks increased, once again keeping in mind that no historical account can include *every* detail of the events it describes. What are the most important details which *are* included here? And what kinds of details are left out, details which might otherwise be quite interesting to us? What does this selection process tell you about what God wants us to understand most from this story?

3. From what you see in this chapter, how would you analyze the character of each of these people at this stage in their lives: Jacob, Rachel, Leah, and Laban?

4. EYE FOR DETAIL— *From what you recall seeing in chapters 29 and 30, try answering the following question without looking in your Bible:* What were the names of Jacob's four oldest sons, in the order of their birth? (See 29:31-35.)

CAPTURE THE ESSENCE

5. If you could go back in time, and God brought you into the events of this chapter to act as a personal counselor to Rachel and Leah, what kind of counsel would you give them, and how would you express it?

6. As this chapter closes, how do you think Jacob would answer this question: What are your deepest hurts these days, and what are your greatest joys?

GENESIS 31

Startup: When you get to heaven, and you meet Jacob, what's the first question you'd like to ask him?

SEEING WHAT'S THERE

1. Based on what you see in this chapter alone, which character do you like most, and which character do you like least?

2. What specifically does God promise Jacob in verse 3?

3. From what you see in this chapter, how would you analyze the *motives* of each of these people—Jacob, Rachel, and Laban?

4. How would you summarize Jacob's work ethic, according to what you see in verses 38-42?

FOR LIFE TODAY

5. How would you say your own work ethic measures up to that of Jacob in verses 38-42?

GENESIS 32

SEEING WHAT'S THERE

1. What are the most important decisions and choices that are made in this chapter, and how would you analyze each one?

2. Look at Jacob's prayer in verse 9. When was the last time in this book that you can recall Jacob praying about something?

3. Why was Jacob given the name Israel, according to verse 28?

4. In your own words, how would you describe the *power* of verses 22-32? What is it that makes this passage so gripping?

5. What has impressed you most about Jacob in this book?

CAPTURE THE ESSENCE

6. From what you see in Jacob's prayer in verses 9-12, what are the most important things he understands about God's personality and character?

7. Notice what happens in verses 24-30. Why do you think God chose to engage Jacob in a wrestling match at this time?

8. How would you summarize what Jacob learns most about God in verses 22-32?

9. As you think about the overall story unfolding in the book of Genesis, what important step in that unfolding is played by this chapter? What strategic *purpose* do you think this account might serve in the larger picture?

10. Once more, imagine yourself being present in the temple in Jerusalem as the twelve-year-old Jesus hears this chapter read and discussed by the Jewish teachers. What verses in this chapter do you think would most impress Him, and what questions or comments do you suppose He might have spoken?

FOR LIFE TODAY

11. Look again at the new name Jacob was given in verse 28, in recognition of who Jacob had become. If God were to give you a new name (something in English, just as Jacob's new name was in *his* language) that reflected your own spiritual giftedness and maturity at this time in

your life, what name do you think that might be?

GENESIS 33

SEEING WHAT'S THERE

1. From what you've read so far in the story of Jacob, what do you think might be most surprising to a new Christian reading it for the first time?

2. From what you see in this chapter, how would you describe Esau's character at this stage in his life? And how would you describe Jacob's character?

3. What does this chapter reveal about Jacob's character?

4. As this chapter concludes, what would you say are the greatest challenges or potential dangers facing Jacob at this time in his life?

5. EYE FOR DETAIL— *From what you recall seeing in chapters 31—33, try answering the following question without looking in your Bible:* How many men came with Esau to meet Jacob? (See 32:6 and 33:1.)

CAPTURE THE ESSENCE

6. As you see the healing in the relationship between Esau and Jacob in this chapter, what factors would you say were most important in bringing about that healing?

7. If you were responsible for giving Jacob a job performance review (in his work as a husband and father and as a servant of God), what comments would you make to him, based on what you've seen so far in this book?

FOR LIFE TODAY

8. What useful principles can you find in this chapter for relationships in your own life?

GENESIS 34

Startup: What kind of people would you say are the easiest to keep your promises to? What kind of people are the hardest?

SEEING WHAT'S THERE

1. How many times in this chapter do you see some reference to God?

2. How many times in this chapter do you see something that was morally or spiritually wrong?

3. Humanly speaking, what would you say is the best thing anybody does in this chapter?

4. What is the worst or most questionable thing anybody does in this chapter?

CAPTURE THE ESSENCE

5. If you could go back in time, and God brought you into the events of this chapter to act as a personal counselor to the sons of Jacob, what kind of counsel would you give them, and how would you express it?

6. What would you say is the major point God is making by including this chapter in the Bible?

FOR LIFE TODAY

7. What would you say are the most important lessons to learn from the mistakes in this chapter?

GENESIS 35

SEEING WHAT'S THERE

1. Take a "walk" together through the incidents that happen in this chapter: Using your imagination, talk about the kinds of sights, smells, sounds, and feelings you might experience.

2. What specifically does God promise Jacob in verses 9-13?

CAPTURE THE ESSENCE

3. Keeping in mind the lessons they may have learned, suppose Isaac and Rachel were allowed to live their lives over again. What, if anything, do you think they would most want to change, and how?

4. In this chapter, what evidence do you see of the author's focus on *God, man,* and *land?*

FOR LIFE TODAY

5. If it's true that *the past is a lesson for the future,* then what would you say are the most important lessons for God's people today to learn from the story of Jacob?

FOR GOING DEEPER

With verse 12 in mind, look also at Jeremiah 27:4-5. How well do you think people today still remember this fact about God's sovereignty?

Look also at Hosea 12:2-5. From the way this prophet remembered him, what were the most important events in Jacob's life?

GENESIS 36

SEEING WHAT'S THERE

1. Look over the names listed in this chapter. Which of these people have you seen mentioned in other parts of Genesis?

2. With the beginning of the story of Joseph in the next chapter, we come to another major division in the book of Genesis. In only a few sentences, how would you summarize the most important things that have happened in this book since the birth of Abraham at the end of chapter 11?

3. EYE FOR DETAIL— *From what you recall seeing in chapters 34—36, try answering the following question without looking in your Bible:* How old was Isaac when he died? (See 35:28.)

GENESIS 37

Startup: In what ways, if any, have you literally seen dreams come true in your life?

SEEING WHAT'S THERE

1. What are the most important decisions and choices that are made in this chapter, and how would you analyze each one?

2. What do you learn in this chapter about Jacob's character and about Joseph's character?

3. How does Judah show himself the leader among his brothers in this chapter, even though he was only the fourth oldest?

4. From their words and actions in this chapter, how would you describe the motives of both Reuben and Judah?

5. As this chapter concludes, what would you say are the greatest challenges or potential dangers facing Joseph at this time in his life?

CAPTURE THE ESSENCE

6. What does this chapter teach us about jealousy?

FOR LIFE TODAY

7. In the area of family relationships, what would you say are the best lessons to learn from this chapter?

GENESIS 38

SEEING WHAT'S THERE

1. Humanly speaking, what would you say is the best thing anybody does in this chapter? And what is the worst or most questionable thing anybody does in this chapter?

2. EYE FOR DETAIL— *From what you recall seeing in chapters 37 and 38, try answering the following question without looking in your Bible:* How old was Joseph when the Bible introduces his story? (See 37:2.)

CAPTURE THE ESSENCE

3. How would you describe Judah's character, from what you see in this chapter?

4. If you could go back in time, and God brought you into the events of this chap-

ter to act as a personal counselor to Judah, what kind of counsel would you give him, and how would you express it?

5. What would you say is the major point God is making by including this chapter in the Bible?

FOR LIFE TODAY

6. What would you say are the most important lessons to learn from the mistakes in this chapter?

GENESIS 39

Startup: How long have you known about the story of Joseph being sold by his brothers, and ending up in Egypt? What are some of the earliest impressions this story left with you?

SEEING WHAT'S THERE

1. What are the most important decisions and choices that are made in this chapter, and how would you analyze each one?

2. Look at the last line in verse 6. From your own imagination, what details could you add to this physical description of Joseph? What do you think he might have looked like?

3. How would you describe Joseph's inward character at this stage in his life?

FOR LIFE TODAY

4. In Jeremiah 23:29, God says that His Word is like fire, and like a hammer. He can use the Scriptures to burn away unclean thoughts and desires in our hearts. He can also use Scripture to hit hard like a hammer, with the power to crush our spiritual hardness. From your study in this book of Genesis, how do you most want to see the "fire-and-hammer" power of God's Word at work in your own life?

GENESIS 40

SEEING WHAT'S THERE

1. What impresses you most about Joseph in this chapter?

FOR LIFE TODAY

2. In verse 8, notice Joseph's quick acknowledgment of God. In what typical situations in your own life could his example be put to good use?

GENESIS 41

SEEING WHAT'S THERE

1. What are the most important decisions and choices that are made in this chapter, and how would you analyze each one?

2. How many times and in what different ways does Joseph acknowledge God in this chapter?

3. What gifts of leadership does Joseph demonstrate in this chapter?

4. EYE FOR DETAIL— *From what you recall seeing in chapters 39—41, try answering the following question without looking in your Bible:* When Pharaoh sent for Joseph in prison, what did Joseph do first before going to see him? (See 41:14.)

CAPTURE THE ESSENCE

5. In what ways would you say the events of Joseph's life so far in Egypt are a foreshadowing of the later experiences there of the Hebrew people?

6. How does this chapter demonstrate both the power and the purpose of God?

7. In the ways God used them, how are Noah and Joseph alike?

8. As this chapter closes, how do you think Joseph would answer this question: What are your deepest hurts these days, and what are your greatest joys?

FOR GOING DEEPER

How is Joseph's strategic life summarized in Psalm 105:16-22? Do you see any details emphasized in Psalms which you don't see emphasized in Genesis?

GENESIS 42

Startup: When you get to heaven, and you meet Joseph, what's the first question you'd like to ask him?

SEEING WHAT'S THERE

1. By putting together the details in 37:2, 41:46 and 41:53-54, about how old would Joseph be as this chapter begins? Approximately how long had it been since he had seen his father and brothers?

2. Notice the thoughts Joseph had in verse 8. How are his dreams in chapter 37 beginning to come true?

3. What do you learn in this chapter about the character of Joseph, the character of his oldest brother Reuben, and the character of their father Jacob?

CAPTURE THE ESSENCE

4. Why do you think Joseph chose not to immediately reveal himself to his brothers?

GENESIS 43

SEEING WHAT'S THERE

1. In this chapter, how does Judah demonstrate his leadership among his brothers?

2. EYE FOR DETAIL— *From what you recall seeing in chapters 42 and 43, try answering the following question without looking in your Bible:* When Joseph's brothers first came to him in Egypt, for how many days did he keep them in his custody before letting them go home? (See 42:17-18.)

GENESIS 44

Startup: What is the most interesting thing you've read in the Bible in the past week?

SEEING WHAT'S THERE

1. Again in this chapter, how does Judah demonstrate his family leadership?

2. What *risks* would you say Judah is taking by what he does and says in verses 18-34?

3. How would you describe Judah's character at this stage in his life?

CAPTURE THE ESSENCE

4. Notice Judah's statement in the last sentence of this chapter, then look back to 37:33-35. If Joseph had sent his brothers back once more to Canaan but held Benjamin in Egypt, how do you think their father Jacob would have reacted?

FOR LIFE TODAY

5. Think about the growth in character that you've witnessed in the lives of Jacob, Judah, and Joseph—three very different individuals. In what one or two areas do you most want to see character growth in your own life in the next five to ten years?

GENESIS 45

SEEING WHAT'S THERE

1. In your own words, how would you describe the *power* of this chapter? What is it that makes this passage so gripping?

2. As the chapter begins, why do you think Joseph chose this particular moment to reveal himself to his brothers?

3. What does this chapter reveal both about Judah's character, and Joseph's character?

4. In verse 26, notice Jacob's initial disbelief about Joseph. Why would this news be so hard for him to believe?

5. Imagine that you are one of Joseph's favorite Egyptian servants, and that Joseph has taught you the Hebrew language. As you passed by the doorway to the room where Joseph and his brothers were, you overheard some of the conversation mentioned at the end of verse 15. What words do you think you might hear, especially from Joseph's brothers?

6. EYE FOR DETAIL— *From what you recall seeing in chapters 44 and 45, try answering the following question without looking in your Bible:* When Joseph sent his brothers to Canaan to bring back their father, what gifts did he send along to Jacob? (See 45:23.)

CAPTURE THE ESSENCE

7. How does this chapter demonstrate both the power and the purpose of God?

8. What emotions do you think God Himself may have been experiencing during the events of this chapter?

9. As this chapter closes, how do you think Jacob would answer this question: What are your deepest hurts these days, and what are your greatest joys?

FOR LIFE TODAY

10. What can you learn about forgiveness from Joseph's example in this chapter?

GENESIS 46

Startup: Typically speaking, what kind of fears would you say tend to increase as we grow older, and what kind of fears tend to diminish?

SEEING WHAT'S THERE

1. What specifically does God promise Jacob in verses 3-4?

2. What was the total number of people in Jacob's family at this time, as indicated in verses 26-27?

3. Look again at verses 28-30. Imagine again that you are a trusted servant of Joseph's, and that Joseph has asked you to drive his chariot as he goes out to meet his father. On the way there, what things do you think Joseph might talk with you about? After you met up with Jacob, what kinds of sights, sounds, and feelings do you think you might experience?

CAPTURE THE ESSENCE

4. In verse 3, why do you think God told Jacob not to be afraid? What particular fears do you think Jacob might be experiencing at this time?

GENESIS 47

SEEING WHAT'S THERE

1. From what you've read so far in the story of Joseph, what do you think might be most surprising to a new Christian reading it for the first time?

2. What do verses 28-31 reveal about the relationship between Jacob and Joseph?

3. EYE FOR DETAIL— *From what you recall seeing in chapters 46 and 47, try answering the following question without looking in your Bible:* How many of his brothers did Joseph present before Pharaoh? (See 47:2.)

CAPTURE THE ESSENCE

4. If you were Pharaoh, and you were giving Joseph a job performance review for his administrative work in Egypt, what comments would you make to him, based on what you've seen so far in this book?

GENESIS 48

Startup: What do you expect to be your greatest opportunities in the coming year?

SEEING WHAT'S THERE

1. What do you learn about Jacob's character in this chapter?

2. What do verses 15-16 reveal about Jacob's understanding and experience of God?

3. In verses 19-20, how do you think Jacob happen to learn these things about the sons of Joseph and their descendants?

GENESIS 49

SEEING WHAT'S THERE

1. Look carefully at verse 1. What is it that Jacob wants his sons to understand?

2. Which of his sons receive the most positive words from Jacob in this chapter, and which receive the most negative?

3. In verse 18, look at the brief prayer Jacob utters in the middle of his statements about his sons. Why do you think Jacob spoke this prayer at this time?

4. In what ways do you see this chapter as an outline of Israel's future history as a nation?

CAPTURE THE ESSENCE

5. Why was it important for Jacob's sons to hear and understand the things Jacob tells them in this chapter?

6. In what ways would you say this chapter represents a major turning point or significant "hinge" in the history of God's people?

FOR GOING DEEPER

How is this chapter viewed from the New Testament perspective of faith in Hebrews 11:21?

GENESIS 50

SEEING WHAT'S THERE

1. What impresses you most about Joseph in this chapter?

2. EYE FOR DETAIL— *From what you recall seeing in chapters 48—50, try answering the following question without looking in your Bible:* Which one of Jacob's sons is compared to a lion? (See 49:9.)

CAPTURE THE ESSENCE

3. Keeping in mind the lessons he may have learned, suppose Jacob was allowed to live his life over again. What, if anything, do you think he would most want to change, and how?

4. From what you've seen in the story of Joseph, would you say that God wants to be considered *primarily* as the God of His people Israel, or as the God of the whole earth? Explain your answer.

FOR LIFE TODAY

5. If it's true that *the past is a lesson for the future,* then what would you say are the most important lessons for God's people today to learn from the story of Joseph?

FOR GOING DEEPER

How was Joseph like Jesus? Look up the following paired passages to assist your discovery—Genesis 37:28 with Matthew 26:14-15; Genesis 41:46 with Luke 3:23; Genesis 39:20 with Matthew 27:2; Genesis 41:41 with Matthew 28:18; and Genesis 45:7 with Matthew 1:21. What other parallels in their lives can you think of?

GENESIS:
THE BIG PICTURE

(Discuss again the questions in the "Overview," plus the questions below.)

1. Who would you name as the seven most important people appearing in the book of Genesis?

2. Imagine that you were helping to produce a film based on the book of Genesis. Describe the kinds of scenery, supporting characters, background music, lighting effects, etc., which you would use to help portray the central message of this book.

3. Look together at each of these passages, and discuss which one you believe is the best candidate for "KEY VERSE" in the book of Genesis — the one which brings into sharpest focus what this book is most about: 1:1, 1:27, 3:15, or 12:2-3.

4. What would you say is the main theme (or themes) in the book of Genesis?

5. SEARCH FOR THE SAVIOR—What words, images, or themes in Genesis have reminded you most of Jesus?

6. What to you personally is the strongest example in this book of someone doing what was right and good?

7. What to you personally is the strongest example in this book of someone doing what was wrong?

8. If Genesis were the only book in the Old Testament, in what ways would it still make a good introduction to the message of Jesus in the New Testament?

9. Based especially on your own experience, complete this statement in the way that's most meaningful to you: I believe it's important for Christians to read and explore the book of Genesis because...

Exodus

OVERVIEW

(Discuss these OVERVIEW questions both at the beginning of your study of Exodus, then again after you've studied all forty chapters. Your answers may change significantly once you've looked more closely at the entire book.)

Startup: When have you felt "trapped" or especially limited in your life? What was it that gave you this feeling?

SEEING WHAT'S THERE

1. Before launching into a closer look at Exodus, how would you summarize what you already know about this book?

2. Find the phrase that reoccurs in the following verses, and then restate this phrase in your own words—6:7, 7:5 and 7:17, 10:2, 14:4 and 14:18, 16:12, 29:46, and 31:13. What clues does this phrase offer about the central message of Exodus?

3. What important conclusions are made about the man Moses in these passages —Numbers 12:3, Deuteronomy 34:10-12, and Hebrews 11:24-28.

4. Look also at the list of "Questions to Ask as You Begin Your Study of Each Book" on page 9.

CAPTURE THE ESSENCE

5. What would you say is the most helpful information in the book of Genesis for understanding the book of Exodus?

FOR LIFE TODAY

6. Exodus has been called "The Book of Redemption," "God's Way Out," and "The Exciting Story of God's Guidance." It has been said that "the entire book is typical of the person and work of Christ," and that it contains "some of the richest, foundational theology of all the books in the Old Testament." With that reputation for this book, what kinds of answers and guidelines and solutions would you like to gain as you examine it more closely?

7. When you get to heaven, if you have a long talk with Moses (the author of this book) and he asks you, "What was most helpful to you in Exodus?" how would you like to be able to answer him?

8. From what you see in the words of the song of Moses in 15:2, what would be a good personal prayer to offer to God as you study this book?

9. As you think first about *who God is,* and second about *what the Bible is,* how strongly would you rate your present desire to understand better the book of Exodus? Use a scale of one to ten (one = "no desire at all," ten = "extremely intense desire") to help you decide.

EXODUS 1

SEEING WHAT'S THERE

1. Look carefully at the first seven verses in this chapter. In how many ways can you see these verses linking the book of Exodus to the book of Genesis?

2. From what you see in this chapter, why did the Egyptians make slaves of the Hebrews?

3. In verses 17 and 21, what reason is stated for why the Hebrew midwives did what they did, and for why God rewarded them?

4. Look also on page 8 at the list of "Questions to Ask as You Study Each Chapter." You may want to look again at this list for each chapter in Exodus.

5. How does this chapter show God already at work on His plan to redeem Israel?

6. If the book of Genesis had somehow been lost before our day, how would that lessen the impact of verse 7 here in Exodus 1?

FOR LIFE TODAY

7. Proverbs 2:1-5 tells about the sincere person who truly longs for wisdom and understanding, and who searches the Scriptures for it—as if it were buried treasure. That person, Solomon says, will come to understand the fear of the Lord, and discover the knowledge of God. As you begin exploring the book of Exodus, what "buried treasure" would you like God to help you find here—to show you what God and His wisdom are really like? If you have this desire, how would you express it in your own words?

EXODUS 2

SEEING WHAT'S THERE

1. What are the most important decisions and choices that are made in this chapter, and how would you analyze each one?

2. Take a "walk" together through the incidents that happen in this chapter: Using your imagination, talk about the kinds of sights, smells, sounds, and feelings you might experience.

3. In your own words, how would you describe the *beauty* of verses 1-10? What is it that makes this passage so appealing?

4. As you look at the people in this chapter, what emotions and moods do you see expressed?

5. What would you do if you were in Moses' place in verses 11-14?

6. For helpful background on the covenant mentioned in verse 24, look at Genesis 15:17-18, 17:6-8, 26:2-5, 26:24, and 28:13-15. What exactly had God promised Abraham and Isaac and Jacob in those passages?

7. EYE FOR DETAIL— *From what you recall seeing in chapters 1 and 2, try answering the following question without looking in your Bible:* How many of the twelve sons of Jacob are listed in chapter 1? (See 1:1-5.)

CAPTURE THE ESSENCE

8. What was the larger answer to the first question asked by the Hebrew man in verse 14?

9. Does verse 24 imply that God had earlier forgotten His promise to Abraham? Explain your answer.

10. Look again at verses 23-24. What would you say were the most important reasons for God allowing His people to experience this suffering?

11. If you were asked to give a character reference for Moses at this time, what would you say about him?

12. From only the evidence you've seen so far in this book, how would you describe Moses' relationship with God at this time?

FOR LIFE TODAY

13. Which verse in this chapter do you think God would like you to understand best?

FOR GOING DEEPER

In what ways would you say God's "remembering" of Abraham and his family in verse 24 was similar to His "remembering" in Genesis 8:1? And in what ways was it most different? Look also at God's promise to "remember" something in Genesis 9:15, and His "remembering" someone in Genesis 30:22. From what you see in these passages, what is the best biblical definition for this word?

EXODUS 3

Startup: When you get to heaven, and you meet Moses, what's the first question you'd like to ask him?

SEEING WHAT'S THERE

1. What specific promises does God make to Moses in this chapter?

2. In verses 13-15, how many answers does God give to the question Moses asks? And how would you restate God's response in your own words?

CAPTURE THE ESSENCE

3. What would you state as the most significant problems and challenges that Moses wrestles with in this chapter?

4. Look again at verses 13-15. Why would it be important for the people of Israel to know God's name? And from God's point of view, why was it important for Him to let them know His name?

5. Think once more about the possible question from the Israelites which Moses passes on to God in verse 13. Bible scholars and teachers point out that the essence of this question is more "What is God's *character?*" rather than "What name does this God go by?" or "Who is this God, anyway?" What evidence do you see in this chapter for such a conclusion?

6. From what you see in His words to Moses, how concerned is God with His *reputation?*

7. How would you summarize what Moses learns most about God in this chapter?

8. Imagine yourself being present in the temple in Jerusalem as the twelve-year-old Jesus hears this chapter read and discussed by the rabbis there. In Luke 2:46 we read that He was listening to these teachers and asking them questions. What verses from this chapter do you think would most impress the boy Jesus, and what questions or comments do you suppose He might have spoken?

FOR LIFE TODAY

9. What is it that you most want to know about God's *character,* as it affects your life today?

10. Consider how strongly you desire to know God better, then ask yourself this question: What are the truths revealed about Him in this chapter which He may want me to understand more deeply at this time in my life?

FOR GOING DEEPER

Look at how Jesus used the Lord God's "I Am" name in John 8:56-59, and how His listeners responded. Look also at how Jesus used this name in John 6:35, 8:12, 10:7, 10:11, 11:25, 14:6, and 15:1. In each of these places where Jesus uses the name, evaluate whether He is saying something *new* about the character of God, or instead simply repeating and echoing what was already revealed about God's character in the Old Testament.

EXODUS 4

SEEING WHAT'S THERE

1. What in this chapter do you think might be most surprising to a new Christian reading it for the first time?

2. What are the most important decisions and choices that are made in this chapter, and how would you analyze each one?

3. What three signs does God give Moses in this chapter, and how would you explain the significance of each one?

4. Notice in verses 29-31 what the leaders of the Hebrew people did when they first heard what God had said to Moses. How would you characterize their spiritual health at this time?

5. Look at what God says He intends to do to Pharaoh in verse 21. Why was it right for God to do this to Pharaoh?

6. From what you see so far in this book, how do you think Moses would answer this question: What is one significant area in which you want to grow personally in the immediate future?

CAPTURE THE ESSENCE

7. Look at what God calls Israel in verse 22. What are the rights, privileges, and responsibilities that go along with this position?

8. In your own words, how would you explain what happens in verses 24-26?

9. What would you say are the biggest *risks* Moses is taking by what he says in this chapter?

10. How would you summarize what Moses learns most about God in this chapter?

FOR LIFE TODAY

11. Look again in verse 21 at what God says He intends to do to Pharaoh. Do you think God sometimes does this same thing to rulers and leaders today? Why or why not?

12. If God had written this chapter only for you, which words or phrases do you think He might have underlined, and why?

FOR GOING DEEPER

Look again at what God calls Israel in verse 22. Explore the following verses, then decide what are the most important aspects of this relationship—Deuteronomy 8:5, Proverbs 3:11-12, Romans 8:14-15, and Hebrews 12:5-11.

EXODUS 5

SEEING WHAT'S THERE

1. Once again, take a "walk" together through the incidents that happen in this chapter. Using your imagination, talk about the kinds of sights, smells, sounds, and feelings you might experience.

2. As you look at Pharaoh's response to the request he received from Moses and Aaron, how would you analyze his personality?

CAPTURE THE ESSENCE

3. What was the correct answer to Pharaoh's question in verse 2?

4. What do the Hebrew work leaders show about their understanding of God in verse 21?

5. What were the correct answers to the two questions Moses asked in verse 22?

FOR LIFE TODAY

6. If it's true that "you become what you think," then what are the most important thoughts from this chapter to plant firmly in your mind?

EXODUS 6

SEEING WHAT'S THERE

1. How many times do you see the phrase "I am the Lord" in this chapter?

2. How many promises does God make to His people in verses 6-8? Which, if any, of these promises do you think would be perceived by the Israelites as more important than all the others?

3. Look at God's reference to His sworn oath in verse 8. What can you discover about this from Genesis 22:15-17?

4. In verse 9, look at the response of the Israelites to God's promises. Do you think this response was justifiable? Why or why not?

5. EYE FOR DETAIL—*From what you recall seeing in chapters 3—6, try answering the following question without looking in your Bible:* What is the first thing in this book that God tells Aaron to do? (See 4:27.)

CAPTURE THE ESSENCE

6. From looking carefully at verses 2-8, what conclusions can you make about God's character and personality?

7. Notice again what God says in verse 3. Why do you think God chose this particular point in Israel's history to reveal so much more about Himself?

FOR LIFE TODAY

8. Which of the promises in verses 6-8 has the greatest personal meaning for you?

9. Look again at verse 9. In what ways, if any, has your response to God's promises been similar to that of the Israelites, and for similar reasons?

FOR GOING DEEPER

Notice again God's reference to His sworn oath in verse 8. How is this meaning of this oath expanded in Hebrews 6:12-20?

Exodus 7

Startup: When you get to heaven, and you meet Aaron, what's the first question you'd like to ask him?

SEEING WHAT'S THERE

1. Glance over chapters 7—10. What two or three words would you use to best summarize what these chapters seem to be most about?

2. Here in chapter 7, what specifically does God say He will do in verses 3-5?

3. What are the most important decisions and choices that are made in this chapter, and how would you analyze each one?

CAPTURE THE ESSENCE

4. Look at how God describes Moses in verse 1. How would you explain this in your own words?

5. How would you summarize what Moses learns most about God in this chapter?

FOR LIFE TODAY

6. Have there been any times in your life when your own heart toward God seemed to be hardened, as Pharaoh's was? If so, what enabled you to get beyond that hardening?

Exodus 8

SEEING WHAT'S THERE

1. Once again, take a "walk" together through the incidents that happen in this chapter. Using your imagination, talk about the kinds of sights, smells, sounds, and feelings you might experience.

2. How many warnings does Pharaoh receive in this chapter?

3. Which plague in this chapter comes without any warning to Pharaoh?

CAPTURE THE ESSENCE

4. As you think about Pharaoh's hardness of heart, how would you explain the difference between the positive quality of *persistence* or *perseverance,* and the negative quality of *stubbornness?*

FOR LIFE TODAY

5. In verse 19, look again at the phrase which Pharaoh's magicians used to described God's working. What is the biggest evidence you have seen of "the finger of God" at work?

FOR GOING DEEPER

Look in verse 22 at the name of the region where the Hebrews lived. What do you discover about this area in Genesis 47:5-6?

Exodus 9

SEEING WHAT'S THERE

1. Once more, take a "walk" together through the incidents that happen in this chapter. Using your imagination, talk about the kinds of sights, smells, sounds, and feelings you might experience.

2. How many warnings does Pharaoh receive in this chapter?

3. Which plague in this chapter comes without any warning to Pharaoh?

4. Notice Pharaoh's words in verses 27-28. What differences do you see in him in this chapter, compared to earlier chapters?

CAPTURE THE ESSENCE

5. Look at God's message to Pharaoh in verses 15-16. Why do you think God chose this particular time to tell Pharaoh this?

FOR LIFE TODAY

6. Compare Pharaoh's words in verse 28 with the what you see about him in verse 34. As a practical guide for your own life, what spiritual insight or principle could you draw from these verses?

Exodus 10

SEEING WHAT'S THERE

1. In verses 1-2, what specific reasons does God give for all that He is now doing in Egypt?

2. How many warnings does Pharaoh receive in this chapter?

3. Which plague in this chapter comes without any warning to Pharaoh?

4. EYE FOR DETAIL—*From what you recall seeing in chapters 7—10, try answering the following question without looking in your Bible:* Where did the locusts go after they were finished devouring Egypt? (See 10:19.)

CAPTURE THE ESSENCE

5. As this chapter closes, compare the situation now with the situation when Moses first returned to Egypt. What are the most important changes that have taken place? And what are the most important things that *could* have changed, but have not?

6. In what ways was Pharaoh's stubborn oppression of the Hebrews a tragic mistake for Egypt?

7. What was God's intended purpose for the plagues upon Egypt, and how well was that purpose accomplished?

Exodus 11

Startup: What are the biggest miracles from God that you've seen in your own life?

SEEING WHAT'S THERE

1. In verse 9, what *reason* does God give for what He is doing in Pharaoh's heart?

CAPTURE THE ESSENCE

2. In your own words, how would you summarize the significance of what Moses tells Pharaoh in verse 7?

Exodus 12

SEEING WHAT'S THERE

1. Chapter 12 has been called the key to the book of Genesis. What does this chapter include that could make it this significant?

2. From the instructions God gives about the Passover in verses 1-20, what is it that He most wants the people of Israel to understand about *redemption?*

3. What requirement for the sacrificial animals do you see in verse 5?

4. What specific promises does God make in verses 12-13?

5. In verse 32, what personal request did Pharaoh make to Moses and Aaron after commanding Israel to leave Egypt? What would you say is the significance of this request?

6. What was the mood among the people of Egypt at this time? (See especially verse 33.)

7. Who might the people be who are mentioned in verse 38?

8. What action of God is mentioned in verse 42, and how would you explain this in your own words?

9. EYE FOR DETAIL—*From what you recall seeing in chapters 11 and 12, try answering the following question without looking in your Bible:* At what time of day was the Passover lamb to be slain? (See 12:6.)

CAPTURE THE ESSENCE

10. What would you say is the significance of the command God gives in verse 2?

11. Look at what God says in verses 14 and 17. Why did God place so much emphasis on the Passover?

12. In how many ways can you see the Passover as a picture of the salvation that comes through Jesus Christ?

13. From the way the Passover is set up, would you say that God intended for it to be thought of more as a *national* holiday, or a *family* holiday?

14. How would you summarize what the people of Israel learn most about God in this chapter?

15. Again, imagine yourself being present in the temple in Jerusalem as the twelve-year-old Jesus hears this chapter read and discussed by the Jewish teachers. What verses in this chapter do you think would most impress Him, and what questions or comments do you suppose He might have spoken?

FOR LIFE TODAY

16. If it's true that *the past is a lesson for the future,* then what would you say are the most important lessons for God's people today to learn from Exodus 1—12?

17. Of all that you see in this chapter, what one truth are you most thankful for, because of its personal significance to you?

FOR GOING DEEPER

Look together at how the Passover regulation in verse 46 is prophetically quoted in John 19:36. What does this imply about the relation of Jesus Christ to the Passover?

Notice also the wording of John 1:29 and 1 Corinthians 5:7. What do these passages confirm about the ultimate meaning of Passover?

EXODUS 13

Startup: How long have you known about the story of Moses and the Israelites crossing the sea? What are some of the earliest impressions this story made on you?

SEEING WHAT'S THERE

1. After reading through this chapter, which words or phrases or sentences here would you most like to understand better?

2. What's the strongest impression or image which this chapter leaves in your mind?

3. If this chapter was the only Scripture portion you had ever known, what would you conclude from it about God?

CAPTURE THE ESSENCE

4. What is the fullest meaning you can find in this chapter for the word "sanctify" (or "consecrate") that begins verse 2?

5. What would you say is the major point God is making by including this chapter in the Bible?

6. From what you've seen so far in Exodus, would you say that God wants to be considered *primarily* as the God of His people Israel, or as the God of the whole earth? Explain your answer.

FOR LIFE TODAY

7. If God had written this chapter only for you, which words or phrases do you think He might have underlined, and why?

EXODUS 14

SEEING WHAT'S THERE

1. What are the greatest challenges facing Moses in this chapter?

2. In your own words, how would you describe the *power* of this chapter? What is it that makes this passage so gripping?

3. What specific promises does God make in verse 4?

4. In verse 14, what does Moses say God will do for His people?

5. What major result of the events in this chapter do you see in verse 31?

6. Summarize the story of how Israel crossed the sea, keeping in mind that no historical account can include *every* detail of the events it describes. What are the most important details which *are* included here? What kinds of details are left out, details which might otherwise be quite interesting to us? What does this selection process tell you about what God wants us to understand most from this story?

CAPTURE THE ESSENCE

7. How justified were the people in their response in verses 10-12?

8. From all that you've seen so far in Exodus, how concerned would you say God is about *reputation*? How would you explain this in your own words?

9. In what ways, if any, would you say that this chapter represents a major turning point or significant "hinge" in the history of God's people?

10. Egypt has been portrayed by Bible teachers as the "womb" out of which the new

nation of Israel was delivered at the time of the Exodus (the nation's actual "birth"). Going along with this analogy, what would be represented by the child's growth inside the womb? What would be represented by the labor pains? And what would be represented by the blood accompanying the birth?

11. Suppose that at this time in history you were an Egyptian official in charge of the royal archives. You have been given orders to write a brief, official account of the Hebrews' departure from Egypt, but you have been asked to do it in a way that does not openly discredit Pharaoh or the Egyptian gods and idols. How would you word this account?

FOR LIFE TODAY

12. Give an answer in ten words or less to each of these questions: What is God's reputation with you personally? What is God's reputation with your family? And what is God's reputation with your church?

13. What are the best lessons in leadership to learn from Moses in this chapter?

EXODUS 15

SEEING WHAT'S THERE

1. From what you see in verses 1-18, what are the most important things that Moses and the people of Israel understand about God's personality and character?

2. From what you see in verses 13-17, what do Moses and the people of Israel understand about God's specific plan and purpose for them?

3. What does God say about Himself in verse 26?

4. EYE FOR DETAIL—*From what you recall seeing in chapters 13—15, try answering the following question without looking in your Bible:* After being parted so that the Hebrews could cross over, at what time of day did the sea waters go back to their place? (See 14:27.)

CAPTURE THE ESSENCE

5. In what ways would you say this chapter serves as a fitting climax to all that has happened in Exodus so far?

6. Songs are often a way to express and release deep emotions. What emotions would you say are behind the song of Moses in verses 1-18 and the song of Miriam in verse 21?

7. If both Moses and Miriam knew at this point that they would never set foot in God's promised land in Canaan, do you think their songs in this chapter would be worded any differently?

8. Look at what God says in verse 26. How would Israel *know* what was right in God's eyes, in order to do it?

9. Suppose a band of armed terrorists stormed into the room where you're now meeting, and took you as hostages in a captivity that was likely to last for days or weeks. Just before they confiscated your Bibles, they allowed you to take one last look at the chapter open before you. Which verse in this chapter would you most try to fix in mind before your Bible was snatched away, and why?

FOR LIFE TODAY

10. Look again at verse 11. In what ways, if any, can you say that you have recognized these character attributes of God in what has happened in your own life?

11. Discuss how much you agree or disagree with this statement: We cannot achieve permanent faith and faithfulness simply by witnessing one miracle of God, no matter how impressive and powerful that single miracle is.

12. Consider how strongly you desire to know God better, then ask yourself this question: What are the truths revealed about Him in this chapter which He may want me to understand more deeply at this time in my life?

FOR GOING DEEPER

Look at how the major events are seen from the perspective of New Testament faith in Hebrews 11:23-29. What did Moses and the Hebrew people have most in common with us today?

EXODUS 16

Startup: What is the most memorable instance you can recall of God providing supernaturally for your needs?

SEEING WHAT'S THERE

1. Look back at God's promises to Abraham in Genesis 12:2-3. How many of these promises have already been accomplished by this point in Exodus? Which of the promises were not yet fulfilled at this time?

2. Verse 23 includes the first occurrence of the word *Sabbath* in Scripture. What does this verse tell us about the purpose of the Sabbath?

CAPTURE THE ESSENCE

3. What emotions do you think God Himself may have been experiencing during the events of this chapter?

4. What does God want most for His people to learn about Him in this chapter?

FOR LIFE TODAY

5. Choose one of these sentences, and complete it as fully and candidly as you would like: (a) What I see and understand in this chapter is important to my life because… OR: (b) What I see and understand in this chapter does NOT seem important to my life at this time, because…

FOR GOING DEEPER

How is Jesus like the manna for God's people in the wilderness? Look at what the manna is called in verse 4, then hear what Jesus calls Himself in John 6:32-33, 6:35, and 6:48-51. What are some of the ways in which Jesus is like this bread mentioned here in Exodus 16?

EXODUS 17

SEEING WHAT'S THERE

1. How many *miracles* have you seen so far in the book of Exodus?

2. Who are the most important people in this chapter?

3. Humanly speaking, what would you say is the best thing anybody does in this chapter? And what is the worst or most questionable thing anybody does in this chapter?

4. Why does God say what He says about Joshua in verse 14?

CAPTURE THE ESSENCE

5. What does God want most for His people to learn about Him in this chapter?

6. Discuss how much you agree or disagree with this statement: During Israel's journey away from Egypt, God could have kept the people from complaining if He had provided for their needs more abundantly.

FOR LIFE TODAY

7. In light of how you're doing spiritually in your life today, which verse in this chapter do you think is the most important at this time—and why?

FOR GOING DEEPER

Compare the incident in verses 1-7 with what Paul writes in 1 Corinthians 10:1-5, especially verse 4. What do you think is Paul's reason for the conclusion he makes about the rock?

EXODUS 18

SEEING WHAT'S THERE

1. After being reunited with his father-in-law Jethro, what does Moses tell him first? (See verses 7-8.)

2. What does God receive from Jethro after Jethro hears Moses' news? (See verses 10-12.)

3. EYE FOR DETAIL— *From what you recall seeing in chapters 16—18, try answering the following question without looking in your Bible:* Who were the two men who held up Moses' hands during the

fighting against the Amalekites? (See 17:12.)

4. From the evidence you see in this chapter, how would you describe Jethro's relationship with God?

5. What does this chapter reveal about the character and personality of Moses, and the character and personality of Jethro?

6. As you think about the overall story unfolding in the book of Exodus, what important step in that unfolding is played by the story of Jethro's advice to Moses? What strategic *purpose* does this account serve in the larger picture?

FOR LIFE TODAY

7. Think back on all that has happened to the people of Israel since they left Egypt. If it's true that *the past is a lesson for the future,* then what would you say are the most important lessons for God's people today to learn from these events?

FOR GOING DEEPER

What further information about Jethro do you gain in Judges 1:16?

EXODUS 19

Startup: In the way we read and study the Bible, what kind of old mental habits or faulty assumptions can most easily block this book of Exodus from coming alive in our minds and hearts?

SEEING WHAT'S THERE

1. What specific promises does God make to Israel in verses 5-6? How fully can you explain what these promises mean?

2. What in this chapter do you think might be most refreshing to someone who was learning about God for the first time?

3. With chapter 19, we come to a major division in the book of Exodus. In only a few sentences, how would you summarize the most important things that have happened so far in this book?

CAPTURE THE ESSENCE

4. Why do you think God makes reference to owning all the earth (or land) at the end of verse 6? How does that fit with

everything else that is going on at Mount Sinai?

5. How would you summarize what the people of Israel learn most about God in this chapter?

6. From what you see in this chapter, would you say that God wants to be considered *primarily* as the God of His people Israel, or as the God of the whole earth? Explain your answer.

FOR LIFE TODAY

7. Imagine yourself personally meeting Jesus sometime tonight, and the words He speaks to you are something from this chapter. Which words can you most easily imagine Him speaking to you?

FOR GOING DEEPER

Look again at God's promise to Israel in verses 5-6. How do you see the fulfillment of these promises in 1 Peter 2:9?

EXODUS 20

SEEING WHAT'S THERE

1. With what words does God introduce the Ten Commandments in verse 2? What might this imply about the nature and purpose of the Ten Commandments?

2. Which of the Ten Commandments deal primarily with the people's relationship with God, and which deal primarily with the people's relationships with one another?

3. In Romans 7:12, Paul says that God's commandments are "holy, righteous and good." What specific evidence for that assessment do you see in this chapter?

4. EYE FOR DETAIL— *From what you recall seeing in chapters 19 and 20, try answering the following question without looking in your Bible:* What was the promised signal from God for Moses and the people to approach Mount Sinai? (See 19:13 and 19:16.)

CAPTURE THE ESSENCE

5. In your own words, what would you say is revealed most about God's character and personality in verses 1-6?

6. If you were one of the Hebrews listening to Moses tell about the Ten Commandments, how do you think you would respond? Would you have a strong desire to keep these commands from God? What would be your deepest *motive* for obeying these laws?

7. Which of these Ten Commandments would you say are the easiest for God's people to obey? And which would you say are the most difficult?

8. Which one of these statements would you say best describes the Ten Commandments: (a) the guidelines for Israel to follow in order to remain God's chosen people; (b) the eternal moral principles of the holy God; or (c) a Hebrew version of the law codes that were common throughout the ancient Middle East.

9. Suppose that at the end of this chapter, Moses added this line: "If you remember only one thing from this chapter, let it be this:..." How do you think he would complete that sentence?

10. Once more, imagine yourself being present in the temple in Jerusalem as the twelve-year-old Jesus hears this chapter read and discussed by the Jewish teachers. What verses in this chapter do you think would most impress Him, and what questions or comments do you suppose He might have spoken?

11. In what ways would you say chapters 19 and 20 serve as a climax to all that has happened in the Bible so far—from Genesis through Exodus?

FOR LIFE TODAY

12. Paul says in Romans 6:14 that we are no longer "under" law, but "under" grace. Discuss how much you agree or disagree with this statement: Being no longer "under" the law means that the law no longer has any spiritual or practical benefit for Christians today.

13. Consider how strongly you desire to know God better, then ask yourself this question: *What are the truths revealed about Him in this chapter which He may want me to understand more deeply at this time in my life?*

FOR GOING DEEPER

How did Jesus view the Ten Commandments? Use the following references in the four Gospels to help you decide—Matthew 4:10, 5:21-22, 5:27-28, 5:33-35, and 15:3-6; Mark 2:27-28; Luke 12:15 and 16:13; and John 8:55. For each passage, tell which one of the Ten Commandments can be linked to what Jesus says, and whether that commandments is *reinforced* or *weakened* by His words.

Also, compare the major teachings you remember from Jesus' "Sermon on the Mount" (Matthew 5—7) with what God teaches here in the Ten Commandments. Then decide which of the following statements is the most accurate: (a) The Sermon on the Mount *replaces* the Ten Commandments; (b) The Sermon on the Mount *negates* the Ten Commandments; (c) The Sermon on the Mount *reflects and parallels* the Ten Commandments; (d) The Sermon on the Mount *deepens* the Ten Commandments.

Exodus 21

Startup: Which problem, if either, do you think is worse among Christians today—*legalism,* or *looseness?*

SEEING WHAT'S THERE

1. Glance over chapters 21—23. What two or three words would you use to best summarize what these chapters seem to be about?

2. Which of the Ten Commandments would you say form the foundation for the ethical and practical guidelines given in this chapter?

CAPTURE THE ESSENCE

3. Look at the famous words that begin verse 24. Then consider them in light of the larger context given in verses 19-27. Then discuss how much you agree or disagree with this statement: The concept of "eye for eye" is primarily a guarantee for Israel's people that there will be equal justice for everyone.

4. Recall again Paul's statement in Romans 7:12 that God's commandments are "holy, righteous and good." What specif-

ic evidence for that assessment do you see in this chapter?

5. Discuss how much you agree or disagree with this statement: God designed His laws in Exodus not as a *means* to salvation, but as a *reflection* or *demonstration* of salvation.

FOR LIFE TODAY

6. In what way, if any, would you say that the words of Jesus in John 14:15 and John 14:21 have a bearing on the laws of God which we see in the book of Exodus?

7. In Isaiah 55:10-11, God reminds us that He sends rain and snow from the sky to water the earth and to nurture life. In the same way, God says that He sends His words to accomplish specific purposes. From your study so far, what would you suggest as *God's* primary purposes for the book of Exodus in the lives of Christians today?

EXODUS 22

SEEING WHAT'S THERE

1. Which of the Ten Commandments would you say form the foundation for the ethical and practical guidelines given in this chapter?

CAPTURE THE ESSENCE

2. Discuss how much you agree or disagree with this statement: There was no distinction between religious laws and civil laws in the laws God gave His people, because every aspect of Israel's life as a nation was to be a reflection of her special relationship with God.

3. Once more, remember Paul's statement in Romans 7:12 that God's commandments are "holy, righteous and good." What specific evidence for that assessment do you see in this chapter?

FOR LIFE TODAY

4. Which commands in this chapter would you say are the most important for Christians today to remember and obey?

5. If all our lawmakers and government officials today fully understood these laws in Exodus and the principles behind

them, what differences do you think it would make in the way they do their job? And what difference do you think it would make in our society at large?

6. Jesus says in Matthew 5:17-18 that not the least portion of God's law will disappear until "all is accomplished" or "all be fulfilled." What do you think God's laws are meant to accomplish or fulfill? How much, if any, has already been done? How much, if any, is still unfinished?

EXODUS 23

SEEING WHAT'S THERE

1. What specific promises does God make to Israel in verses 20-33?

2. Which of the Ten Commandments would you say form the foundation for the ethical and practical guidelines given in this chapter?

3. EYE FOR DETAIL— *From what you recall seeing in chapters 21—23, try answering the following question without looking in your Bible:* What was the punishment for a person if a stolen animal was found alive in his possession? (See 22:4.)

CAPTURE THE ESSENCE

4. In Matthew 23:23, Jesus said the most important aspects of the law are "justice, mercy, and faithfulness." How do you see these important aspects reflected in the laws presented in Exodus?

5. Suppose that joining you here today was a Pharisee from the time of Jesus. You tell him you are now studying the middle chapters in Exodus, and you ask his opinion about what is most important in these chapters. How do you think he might answer?

6. Suppose also that the apostle Paul was here with you today, and you asked him the same question you asked the Pharisee. How do you think Paul would answer?

FOR LIFE TODAY

7. Which commands in this chapter would you say are the most important for Christians today to remember and obey?

8. In Romans 15:4, Paul reminds us that the Old Testament Scriptures can give us patience and perseverance on one hand, as well as comfort and encouragement on the other. In your own life, how do you see this book of Exodus living up to Paul's description? In what ways, if any, is it meeting your personal needs for both *perseverance* and *encouragement?*

EXODUS 24

Startup: Talk together about times in your life when you have most needed to understand God's faithful commitment to you.

SEEING WHAT'S THERE

1. In verse 3, how do the people respond to hearing God's laws?

2. In verse 17, what did God's glory look like to His people?

3. From what you see in this chapter, how would you describe the spiritual health of God's people at this time? Use a scale of one to ten (one = "much weaker than ever," ten = "much stronger than ever") to help you decide.

4. What in this chapter do you think might be most interesting to someone who was reading the Bible for the first time?

CAPTURE THE ESSENCE

5. From the way God confirms and seals His covenant with Israel in this chapter, what would you say He most wants the people to understand about *redemption?*

6. How would you summarize what Moses learns most about God in this chapter?

7. From what you've seen so far in Exodus, how would you summarize the *expectations* God has of His people?

8. Suppose that at the end of this chapter, Moses added this line: "If you remember only one thing from this chapter, let it be this:…" How do you think he would complete that sentence?

FOR LIFE TODAY

9. Notice again in verses 9-11 how Moses and the elders saw God. How much do you think God wants *you* to see Him at this time in your life? Is it as much or more as Moses and the Hebrews elders did?

10. How would you describe the current spiritual health of your church? Use a scale of one to ten (one = "much weaker than ever," ten – "much stronger than ever") to help you decide.

11. How would you describe your own current spiritual health? Use a scale of one to ten (one = "much weaker than ever," ten = "much stronger than ever") to help you decide.

EXODUS 25

SEEING WHAT'S THERE

1. Glance over chapters 25 — 27. What two or three words would you use to best summarize what these chapters seem to be most about?

2. After reading through chapter 25, which words or phrases or sentences here would you most like to understand better?

CAPTURE THE ESSENCE

3. What do you think was symbolized by the bread in verse 30?

4. If this chapter was the only Scripture portion you had ever known, what would you conclude from it about worshiping God?

FOR GOING DEEPER

Notice God's amazing promise and commitment to His people in verse 8. Then use the following passages to trace this theme through the entire Bible, and to see its fulfillment — Exodus 29:44-46, Leviticus 26:11-12, Numbers 35:34, Ezekiel 37:26-28, John 1:14, and Revelation 21:3. How does God want us to view this promise and commitment today?

Exodus 26

SEEING WHAT'S THERE

1. In verses 33-34, what name is given to the innermost room in the tabernacle? What separates this room from the rest of the tabernacle, and is included inside this room?

CAPTURE THE ESSENCE

2. It's often said that a person's home is a reflection of his personality. From what you see in this chapter, how would the tabernacle be a reflection of God's personality?

FOR LIFE TODAY

3. In light of your present relationship with God, what do you think He wants you to understand most about the tabernacle?

FOR GOING DEEPER

Look again in verses 33-34 at the description of the innermost room in the tabernacle. Explore together how this same inner room was configured and furnished in the temple of Solomon—in 1 Kings 6:16, 6:23-28, 8:6-9, and Hebrews 9:3-5. Look also in Ezekiel 41:3-4 and 41:21-23 to see how this room is described in the temple which Ezekiel saw in his vision from God. For both Solomon's temple and Ezekiel's, tell what differences you see from the description of the inner room here in Exodus.

This inner room was also included in the temple which Herod built in Jerusalem, and which was there at the time of Jesus' ministry. Look at Matthew 27:50-51 to see what happened to the curtain that separated the Most Holy Place in this temple.

Finally, review Hebrews 9:3-9 and 10:19-22 to see how God's people today are to view this innermost room in God's dwelling place.

In the Old Testament setup of this room in both the tabernacle and the temple, would you say it was meant more to represent God's *nearness* to His people, or God's *holy distance* from them? Explain your answer.

Exodus 27

SEEING WHAT'S THERE

1. From what you have seen in chapters 25—27, how would you describe the *beauty* of the tabernacle?

2. EYE FOR DETAIL— *From what you recall seeing in chapters 24—27, try answering the following question without looking in your Bible:* How many lamps were to shine from the lampstand to be set up inside the tabernacle? (See 25:37.)

CAPTURE THE ESSENCE

3. In the description of the tabernacle and its furnishings in chapters 25—27, what is the best evidence you see of God's holiness? And what is the best evidence you see of His love and faithfulness?

4. Suppose you were one of the Israelites who had come out of Egypt with Moses. You have heard Moses describe all the instructions from God for building and furnishing the tabernacle. Then you approached Moses and said, "This tabernacle will certainly cost us a lot in time and energy and money; why are we doing this, anyway? Will it really be worth it?" How do you think Moses would answer?

Exodus 28

Startup: Talk together about times in your life when you've especially enjoyed worshiping God. What were the circumstances that brought this about?

SEEING WHAT'S THERE

5. Glance over chapters 28—30. What two or three words would you use to best summarize what these chapters seem to be most about?

6. After reading through chapter 28, which words or phrases or sentences here would you most like to understand better?

7. What was the high priest Aaron to wear on his shoulders, according to verses 9-12? What do you think was symbolized by this?

8. What words were to be inscribed on Aaron's head covering, according to verses 36-38, and what explanation for this is given?

9. In the description of the priestly garments in this chapter, what is the best evidence you see of God's holiness? And what is the best evidence you see of His love and faithfulness?

Exodus 29

SEEING WHAT'S THERE

1. What guarantees does God give to Israel in verses 42-46?

CAPTURE THE ESSENCE

2. What do you think were God's *reasons* for taking the priests through the actions described in this chapter?

3. In your own words, what would you say is revealed most about God's character and personality in verses 45-46?

FOR LIFE TODAY

4. In the New Testament we learn that Christians today are called to be God's royal priests (1 Peter 2:9). In light of your present relationship with God, what do you think He wants you to understand most about the passages in Exodus concerning the Old Testament priesthood?

Exodus 30

SEEING WHAT'S THERE

1. To review, retrace your way through the last several chapters. What are the most important things that have happened since the Israelites left Egypt?

2. What regular assignments was the high priest Aaron given in verses 7-10?

3. What regular requirements were given to Aaron and his sons in verses 19-21?

CAPTURE THE ESSENCE

4. From all that you've seen in chapters 25-30 about the arrangements for the Hebrews to worship God, discuss how much you agree or disagree with this statement: It is impossible to truly worship God without an understanding of His holy character.

Exodus 31

SEEING WHAT'S THERE

1. In verses 1-6, what exactly does God say He has given to Bezalel, Oholiab, and the other craftsmen?

2. According to what you see in verses 12-17, what are the right *reasons* for observing the Sabbath?

3. What did God give to Moses in verse 18?

4. EYE FOR DETAIL— *From what you recall seeing in chapters 28—31, try answering the following question without looking in your Bible:* How many days was the ordination ceremony for Aaron and his sons to last? (See 29:35.)

CAPTURE THE ESSENCE

5. In your own words, how would you summarize what is revealed about God's character and personality in verse 13?

FOR LIFE TODAY

6. In verses 1-6, notice again what God says about His gifts to those who were to build the tabernacle. What gifts has God provided for the work He wants *you* to do?

FOR GOING DEEPER

Look again at verses 12-17, then explore together what God says about the Sabbath in Genesis 2:2-3; Exodus 20:8-11 and 35:2-3; Jeremiah 17:19-27; and Mark 2:27-28. What does God most want us to understand about the Sabbath, and what does He want us to do about it?

Exodus 32

Startup: How long have you known about the story of the golden calf? What are some of the earliest impressions this story made on you?

SEEING WHAT'S THERE

1. Humanly speaking, what would you say is the best thing anybody does in this chapter? And what is the worst or most questionable thing anybody does in this chapter?

2. Summarize the story of the golden calf, once again keeping in mind that no his-

torical account can include *every* detail of the events it describes. What are the most important details which *are* included here? And what kinds of details are left out, details which might otherwise be quite interesting to us? What does this selection process tell you about what God wants us to understand most from this story?

3. In your own words, how would you explain God's response first in verses 9-10, and then in verse 14?

4. How would you explain Moses' first response in verses 19-20?

5. What does this chapter reveal most about the character of Aaron?

6. What does this chapter reveal most about the character of Moses?

7. What does this chapter reveal most about God's attitude toward sin?

8. As this chapter closes, how do you think Moses would answer this question: What are your deepest hurts these days, and what are your greatest joys?

CAPTURE THE ESSENCE

9. What emotions do you think God Himself may have been experiencing during the events of this chapter?

10. If you could go back in time, and God brought you into the events of this chapter to act as a personal counselor to Aaron, what kind of counsel would you give him, and how would you express it?

11. Would you say that Aaron has had an easy life? Why or why not?

12. Look again at verses 30-32. When Moses offered to have his own name blotted out of God's book, if there was otherwise no forgiveness for Israel's sin, why do you think God did not accept that offer?

13. What would you say is the most important thing Aaron learns in this chapter? What is the most important thing Moses learns? And what is the most important thing the people of Israel learn?

FOR LIFE TODAY

14. What do you think are the most important lessons God wants us to learn from this chapter about sin and disobedience?

15. If God had written this chapter only for you, which words or phrases do you think He might have underlined, and why?

FOR GOING DEEPER

On a fateful day many centuries in the future, the man Stephen in Jerusalem would recite much of Israel's history recorded in the book of Exodus. Look at Stephen's remarks in Acts 7:17-44. In this passage, how many events and details can you recognize as being from Exodus?

EXODUS 33

SEEING WHAT'S THERE

1. What change in plans does God indicate in verses 1-3?

2. What reason for this change does God give in verse 5?

3. How does Moses respond to this change in verses 15-16? Why do you think Moses responds in this way?

4. Notice how quickly God agrees with Moses in verse 17. What reasons for this does God give in this verse?

5. What promises does God make to Moses in verses 19-23? And what does God indicate about His character and personality in these verses?

CAPTURE THE ESSENCE

6. Why did the people respond as they did in verse 4?

7. Look again at what God says about Himself in verse 19. How closely does this match what God says about Himself in 3:14-15?

8. What would you say is Moses' strongest motive in this chapter?

9. How would you summarize what Moses learns most about God in this chapter?

FOR LIFE TODAY

10. Think back on all that has happened to the people of Israel since they came to Mount Sinai in Exodus 19. If it's true that *the past is a lesson for the future,* then what would you say are the most important lessons for God's people today to learn from these events?

EXODUS 34

1. What does God reveal about His personality and character in verses 5-7?

2. What does verse 7 reveal about God's attitude toward sin?

3. What specific promises does God make to Israel in verses 10-11?

4. EYE FOR DETAIL—*From what you recall seeing in chapters 32—34, try answering the following question without looking in your Bible:* From what articles of jewelry did Aaron make the golden calf? (See 32:2-4.)

CAPTURE THE ESSENCE

5. Suppose that at the end of this chapter, Moses added this line: "If you remember only one thing from this chapter, let it be this:…" How do you think he would complete that sentence?

6. How fully would you explain the radiance on Moses' face, as described in verses 29-35?

7. How would you evaluate what Moses learns most about God in this chapter?

8. From the evidence you've seen so far in this book, how would you define Moses' personality strengths and weaknesses?

FOR LIFE TODAY

9. If this was the last Bible chapter you read before you died, which verses from it would you most like to be lingering in your mind as you said goodbye to this earth?

10. In Jeremiah 23:29, God says that His Word is like fire, and like a hammer. He can use the Scriptures to burn away unclean thoughts and desires in our hearts. He can also use Scripture to hit hard like a hammer, with the power to crush our spiritual hardness. From your study in this book of Exodus, how do you most want to see the "fire-and-hammer" power of God's Word at work in your own life?

EXODUS 35

Startup: If you were asked to design a church building, what goals and guidelines and principles would you follow?

SEEING WHAT'S THERE

1. Why do you think Moses reminds the people again about the Sabbath at this time?

2. What specific commands from God does Moses pass along to the people in the first half of this chapter?

CAPTURE THE ESSENCE

3. How would you explain the people's positive response to these commands, especially in light of their weaknesses and sinful tendencies that are so evident in other chapters of this book?

FOR LIFE TODAY

4. What would you say are the most useful and important lessons to learn from the example of the Israelites in verses 20-29?

EXODUS 36

SEEING WHAT'S THERE

1. Glance over chapters 36—40. What two or three words would you use to best summarize what these chapters seem to be most about?

2. From what you've seen in Exodus, how accurate is it to say that God is an *artist?*

3. Compare what you see in verses 8-38 with the instructions for the tabernacle given in chapter 26. How well are God's instructions followed?

EXODUS 37

SEEING WHAT'S THERE

1. Compare what you see in this chapter with the instructions for the tabernacle furnishings given in chapters 25 and 30. How well are God's instructions followed?

EXODUS 38

SEEING WHAT'S THERE

1. Compare what you see in this chapter with the instructions for the altar and courtyard given in chapter 27. How well are God's instructions followed?

EXODUS 39

SEEING WHAT'S THERE

1. Compare what you see in verses 1-31 with the instructions for the priestly garments given in chapter 28. How well are God's instructions followed?

CAPTURE THE ESSENCE

2. Look at verses 42-43. What do you think was involved in Moses' blessing in this verse?

3. If you were responsible for giving Moses a job performance review (in his position as the leader of God's people), what comments would you make to him, based on what you have seen so far in this book?

4. At this time in his life, how do you think Moses would answer this question: What three things are you most thankful for these days?

5. Would you say that Moses has had an easy life so far? Why or why not?

EXODUS 40

SEEING WHAT'S THERE

1. To review, retrace your way through the last several chapters. What are the most important things that have happened since God gave Moses the two stone tablets on Mount Sinai (at the end of chapter 31)?

2. What impresses you most about Moses in this chapter?

3. How many times in this chapter do you see a reference to how Moses obeyed God?

4. Look carefully at verses 36-38. How closely does this follow the description of the cloud and fire in 13:21-22?

5. EYE FOR DETAIL— *From what you recall seeing in chapters 35—40, try answering the following question without looking in your Bible:* What man made the ark of the covenant? (See 37:1.)

CAPTURE THE ESSENCE

6. Imagine yourself being present to witness what is described in verses 34-35. How do you think it would affect you?

7. In what ways do you think the tabernacle would help the Israelites to *glorify* God? In what ways do you think it would help the Israelites to *enjoy* God?

8. What is the best evidence you've seen in this book that God truly loves His people?

9. In what ways, if any, would you say that this chapter represents a major turning point or significant "hinge" in the history of God's people?

10. As this book concludes, what would you say are the greatest challenges or potential dangers facing the people of Israel at this time?

11. Keeping in mind all that you've seen in Exodus, imagine yourself asking Moses this question: *How is it possible for a holy God to have a relationship with sinful people, and to enjoy their true worship?* How do you think Moses would answer?

FOR LIFE TODAY

12. If God had written this chapter only for you, which words or phrases do you

think He might have underlined, and why?

FOR GOING DEEPER

In Acts 7:17-44, look together at the story of the life and ministry of Moses which Stephen tells. What details does Stephen emphasize in this story? Look also at the much briefer account of Moses in Hebrews 11:23-29. What details are emphasized here?

EXODUS:
THE BIG PICTURE

(Discuss again the questions in the "Overview," plus the questions below.)

1. Imagine that you were helping to produce a film based on the book of Exodus. Describe the kinds of scenery, supporting characters, background music, lighting effects, etc., which you would use to help portray the central message of this book.

2. Look together at each of these passages, and discuss which one you believe is the best candidate for "KEY VERSE" in the book of Exodus —the one which brings into sharpest focus what this book is most about: 3:7, 3:10, 6:6, 12:23, or 19:5-6.

3. What would you say is the main theme (or themes) in the book of Exodus?

4. SEARCH FOR THE SAVIOR—What words, images, or themes in Exodus have reminded you most of Jesus?

5. What to you personally is the strongest example in this book of someone doing what was right and good?

6. What to you personally is the strongest example in this book of someone doing what was wrong?

7. If Exodus were the only book in the Old Testament, in what ways would it still make a good introduction to the message of Jesus in the New Testament?

8. Based especially on your own experience, complete this statement in the way that's most meaningful for you: I believe it's important for Christians to read and explore the book of Exodus because...

Leviticus

OVERVIEW

(Discuss these OVERVIEW questions both at the beginning of your study of Leviticus, then again after you've studied all 27 chapters. Your answers may change significantly once you've looked more closely at the entire book.)

Startup: In the way we read and study the Bible, what kind of old mental habits or faulty assumptions or wrong first impressions can most easily block this book of Leviticus from coming alive in our minds and hearts?

SEEING WHAT'S THERE

1. Before launching into a closer look at Leviticus, how would you summarize what you already know about this book?

2. Find the phrase that reoccurs in the following verses—11:44, 11:45, 19:2, 20:26, and 21:8. How would you restate this phrase in your own words, and what clues does it offer about the central message of Leviticus?

3. Look also at the list of "Questions to Ask as You Begin Your Study of Each Book" on page 9.

CAPTURE THE ESSENCE

4. What would you say is the most helpful information in the book of Exodus for understanding the book of Leviticus?

FOR LIFE TODAY

5. Leviticus has been called "The Book of Atonement," "The Book of Holiness," "Provisions for Holy Living," and "The Book of Worship." With that reputation for this book, what kinds of answers and guidelines and solutions would you like to gain as you examine it more closely?

6. When you get to heaven, if you have a long talk with Moses (the author of this book) and he asks you, "What was most helpful to you in Leviticus?" how would you like to be able to answer him?

7. From what you see in God's words in 18:4-5, what would be a good personal prayer to offer to God as you study this book?

8. As you think first about *who God is*, and second about *what the Bible is*, how strongly would you rate your present desire to understand better the book of Leviticus? Use a scale of one to ten (one = "no desire at all," ten = "extremely intense desire") to help you decide.

FOR GOING DEEPER

Look at 1 Peter 1:13-21, and notice the phrase from Leviticus which is quoted here. How does this New Testament passage amplify the meaning of this Old Testament phrase?

LEVITICUS 1

SEEING WHAT'S THERE

1. Glance over chapters 1—7. What two or three words would you use to best summarize what these chapters seem to be most about?

2. If you were one of the priests who was to serve at the altar of the tabernacle, which details in chapter 1 would be of most interest to you?

3. As you read this chapter, what's the strongest impression or image it leaves in your mind?

4. What common requirement for the sacrificial animal do you see in verses 3 and 10?

5. How many times do you see *fire* mentioned in this chapter? And how many times do you see *blood* mentioned?

6. Look also on page 8 at the list of "Questions to Ask as You Study Each Chapter." You may want to look again at this list for each chapter in Leviticus.

FOR LIFE TODAY

7. Proverbs 2:1-5 tells about the sincere person who truly longs for wisdom and understanding, and who searches the Scriptures for it—as if it were buried treasure. That person, Solomon says, will come to understand the fear of the Lord, and discover the knowledge of God. As you begin exploring the book of Leviticus, what "buried treasure" would you like God to help you find here—to show you what God and His wisdom are really like? If you have this desire, how would you express it in your own words?

FOR GOING DEEPER

Was the offering of sacrifices something new for God's people at this time? Look in these verses to see *who* offered sacrifices to God hundreds of years earlier—Genesis 8:20, 22:13, 31:54, and 46:1.

LEVITICUS 2

SEEING WHAT'S THERE

1. Imagine again that you are one of the priests who is to serve at the altar of the tabernacle. Which details in this chapter would be of most interest to you?

2. How many times do you see *fire* mentioned in this chapter, and what is the context for each one?

LEVITICUS 3

SEEING WHAT'S THERE

1. Imagine again that you are one of the priests who is to serve at the altar of the tabernacle. Which details in this chapter would be of most interest to you?

2. What common requirement for the sacrificial animal do you see in verses 1 and 6?

3. How many times do you see *fire* mentioned in this chapter? And how many times do you see *blood* mentioned?

LEVITICUS 4

SEEING WHAT'S THERE

1. How many times do you see *fire* mentioned in this chapter? And how many times do you see *blood* mentioned?

2. What is the occasion and purpose for the offering described in this chapter, according to verse 2?

3. What common requirement for the sacrificial animal do you see in verses 3, 23, 28, and 32?

4. Imagine again that you are one of the priests who will serve at the altar of the tabernacle. Which details in this chapter would be of most interest to you?

CAPTURE THE ESSENCE

5. What does this chapter communicate about God's view of sin?

FOR GOING DEEPER

As you're learning about the sacrifices of the Old Testament, look ahead to the New—how does God want us to view the sacrifice of Christ? Look especially at Ephesians 5:1-2 to find an answer that's meant to change your life.

LEVITICUS 5

SEEING WHAT'S THERE

1. What is the occasion and purpose for the offering described in verses 14-19?

2. What common requirement for the sacrificial animal do you see in verses 15 and 18?

3. Suppose you were one of the Israelites who had come out of Egypt with Moses. You have heard Moses describing all the instructions from God (here in Leviticus 1—7) for offering sacrifices. Then you approached Moses and said, "These sacrifices are certainly going to be a lot of mess and bother; why do we really need to do this, anyway? What difference will it make in the end?" How do you think Moses would answer?

4. How many times do you see *fire* mentioned in this chapter? And how many times do you see *blood* mentioned?

5. What do you think are the most important lessons God wants us to learn from this chapter about sin and guilt?

LEVITICUS 6

SEEING WHAT'S THERE

1. What specific sins are mentioned in verses 1-3?

2. Imagine again that you are one of the priests who will serve at the altar of the tabernacle. Which details in this chapter would be of most interest to you?

3. How many times do you see *fire* mentioned in this chapter? And how many times do you see *blood* mentioned?

CAPTURE THE ESSENCE

4. In what ways, if any, have you seen God's *grace* in the system of sacrifices outlined here in Leviticus?

FOR LIFE TODAY

5. What do you think are the most important lessons God wants us to learn from this chapter about sin and guilt?

LEVITICUS 7

SEEING WHAT'S THERE

1. How many times do you see *fire* mentioned in this chapter? And how many times do you see *blood* mentioned?

2. Imagine once more that you are one of the priests who will serve at the altar of the tabernacle. Which details in this chapter would be of most interest to you?

3. EYE FOR DETAIL— *From what you recall seeing in chapters 1—7, try answering the following question without looking in your Bible:* As described in these chapters, what was the name of the only offering which did not involve the sacrifice of an animal? (See chapter 2.)

CAPTURE THE ESSENCE

4. From all that you've seen so far in Leviticus about the arrangements for the Hebrews to offer sacrifices to God, discuss how much you agree or disagree with

this statement: It is impossible to truly worship God without an understanding of His holy character.

FOR GOING DEEPER

If the animal sacrifices we've seen in Leviticus are no longer requested from us by God, what kind of sacrifices *does* He want? What answers do you see in these New Testament passages: Romans 12:1, Philippians 4:18, Hebrews 13:15-16, and 1 Peter 2:5?

LEVITICUS 8

Startup: What kind of pictures come to your mind when you think of the word *priest?*

SEEING WHAT'S THERE

1. Glance over chapters 8—10. What two or three words would you use to best summarize what these chapters seem to be most about?

2. How would you outline the different steps of the priestly ordination that takes place in chapter 8?

3. Review the instructions God gave Moses in Exodus 29 for the dedication of the priests. Here in Leviticus 8, how closely does Moses follow those directions?

4. How many times do you see *fire* mentioned in this chapter? And how many times do you see *blood* mentioned?

CAPTURE THE ESSENCE

5. What do you think were God's *reasons* for taking the priests through the actions described in this chapter?

LEVITICUS 9

SEEING WHAT'S THERE

1. How would you summarize the *action* that takes place in this chapter?

2. How many times do you see *fire* mentioned in this chapter? And how many times do you see *blood* mentioned?

CAPTURE THE ESSENCE

3. In what ways, if any, would you say that this chapter represents a major turning point or significant "hinge" in the history of God's people?

4. In verses 23-24, notice the concluding events of this day. How would you characterize the spiritual health of God's people at this time?

FOR LIFE TODAY

5. If God had written this chapter only for you, which words or phrases do you think He might have underlined, and why?

LEVITICUS 10

SEEING WHAT'S THERE

1. What did Nadab and Abihu do wrong?

2. Imagine yourself being present to witness everything that is described in verses 1-2. How do you think it would affect you?

3. How would you summarize the further action that takes place in this chapter?

4. How many times do you see *fire* mentioned in this chapter? And how many times do you see *blood* mentioned?

5. EYE FOR DETAIL— *From what you recall seeing in chapters 8—10, try answering the following question without looking in your Bible:* At the time when Aaron and his sons were ordained as priests, how many times did Moses sprinkle the anointing oil on the altar? (See 8:11.)

CAPTURE THE ESSENCE

6. Review again what God says and does in verses 1-3. How grievous do you think it was for God to administer this punishment to Nadab and Abihu?

7. How would you explain in your own words how God wants us to understand His words in verse 3?

8. From what you see in this chapter, how would you describe Aaron's character?

9. How does this chapter demonstrate both the power and the purpose of God?

10. After the death of his sons Nadab and Abihu, what do you think would be the greatest adjustments Aaron would have to make?

FOR LIFE TODAY

11. What do you think are the most important lessons God wants us to learn from this chapter?

12. Look at what God commands Aaron and his sons in verse 10. In what ways, if any, would you say that these words apply to us today? In what areas of our lives might these words offer us a helpful guideline?

FOR GOING DEEPER

Compare what happens to Nadab and Abihu in verses 1-3 with what happens to Ananias and Sapphira in Acts 5:1-11. What are the greatest similarities in these two passages, and what are the greatest differences?

LEVITICUS 11

Startup: What foods do you like least?

SEEING WHAT'S THERE

1. Glance over chapters 11—15. What two or three words would you use to best summarize what these chapters seem to be most about?

2. What *reason* for the commands in chapter 11 is given in verses 44-45?

3. How many times do you see *water* mentioned in this chapter? And what is the context for each one?

4. What in this chapter do you think might be most surprising to a new Christian reading it for the first time?

CAPTURE THE ESSENCE

5. What would you say is God's *intent* behind the laws in this chapter? What were the most important things He wanted these laws to accomplish?

6. From what you see in verses 44-45, how would you define the word *holiness?*

FOR LIFE TODAY

7. Choose one of these sentences, and complete it as fully and candidly as you would like: (a) What I see and understand in this chapter is important to my life because… OR: (b) What I see and understand in this chapter does NOT seem important to my life at this time, because…

8. In Isaiah 55:10-11, God reminds us that He sends rain and snow from the sky to water the earth and to nurture life. In the same way, God says that He sends His

words to accomplish specific purposes. From your study so far, what would you suggest as *God's* primary purposes for the book of Leviticus in the lives of Christians today?

FOR GOING DEEPER

Look again at verses 44-45. In what ways can you see the meaning of this passage carried through and intensified in the words of Jesus in Matthew 5:48, and in the words of the apostle Paul in Romans 12:1-2?

Look also at what the apostle Peter was told about unclean food in Acts 10:9-16. How might this passage influence your understanding of Leviticus 11?

LEVITICUS 12

CAPTURE THE ESSENCE

1. What would you say is God's *intent* behind the laws in this chapter? What were the most important things He wanted these laws to accomplish?

LEVITICUS 13

SEEING WHAT'S THERE

1. How many times do you see *fire* mentioned in this chapter, and what is the context for each one?

CAPTURE THE ESSENCE

2. What would you say is God's *intent* behind the laws in this chapter? What were the most important things He wanted these laws to accomplish?

LEVITICUS 14

SEEING WHAT'S THERE

1. How many times do you see *blood* mentioned in this chapter, and what is the context for each one?

2. How many times do you see *water* mentioned in this chapter?

CAPTURE THE ESSENCE

3. What would you say is God's *intent* behind the laws in this chapter? What were the most important things He wanted these laws to accomplish?

4. In Proverbs 13:13 we're told, "He who respects a command is rewarded," or in another translation, "He that feareth the commandment shall be rewarded." What would you say were the most likely *rewards* for the Israelites who respected and kept the commands in chapters 13 and 14?

5. Now that you're halfway through Leviticus, how would you summarize the most important teachings in this book?

LEVITICUS 15

SEEING WHAT'S THERE

1. In Romans 7:12, Paul says that God's commandments are "holy, righteous and good." What specific evidence for that assessment have you seen so far in this book?

2. How many times do you see *water* mentioned in this chapter?

3. EYE FOR DETAIL— *From what you recall seeing in chapters 11—15, try answering the following question without looking in your Bible:* As food for the Hebrew people, was the eagle considered clean or unclean? (See 11:13.)

CAPTURE THE ESSENCE

4. In chapters 11—15, how do you see God's concern for His people's physical health?

FOR LIFE TODAY

5. In Romans 15:4, Paul reminds us that the Old Testament Scriptures can give us patience and perseverance on one hand, as well as comfort and encouragement on the other. In your own life, how do you see this book of Leviticus living up to Paul's description? In what ways, if any, is it meeting your personal needs for both *perseverance* and *encouragement?*

LEVITICUS 16

Startup: At this point in your life, how strong is your appreciation for your salvation in Christ, compared with other times in the past? Use a scale of one to ten (one = "much weaker than ever," ten = "much stronger than ever") to help you decide.

SEEING WHAT'S THERE

1. Chapter 16 has been called the key to the book of Leviticus. What does this chapter include that could make it this significant?

2. After reading through this chapter, which words or phrases or sentences here would you most like to understand better?

3. Look at verses 11, 17, and 24, and tell what they have in common.

4. From what you see in verse 16, *why* is atonement needed? What is the reason for it?

5. How many times do you see the word *atonement* in this chapter? What would you say is the best definition for this word, in the way it's used in this chapter?

6. In verse 34, notice how often the atonement described in this chapter was to take place. Why do you think God chose this frequency, rather than more often or less often?

7. How many times do you see *fire* mentioned in this chapter? How many times do you see *blood* mentioned? And how many times do you see *water* mentioned?

8. EYE FOR DETAIL— *From what you recall seeing in chapter 16, try answering the following question without looking in your Bible:* What was the first thing Aaron was to do in carrying out the requirements of atonement? (See the last sentence in verse 4.)

CAPTURE THE ESSENCE

9. Describe in your own words what happens between Aaron and the goat in verses 20-22. How would you describe in your own words the significance of these actions?

10. In what ways does this chapter demonstrate God's hatred for sin?

11. What, if anything, does this chapter say about *forgiveness?* Does *atonement* accomplish forgiveness, and if so, how does it?

12. In how many ways do you see this chapter pointing toward Jesus the Savior?

13. Imagine yourself being present in the temple in Jerusalem as the twelve-year-old Jesus hears this chapter read and discussed by the rabbis there. In Luke 2:46 we read that He was listening to these teachers and asking them questions. What verses from this chapter do you think would most impress the boy Jesus, and what questions or comments do you suppose He might have spoken?

14. As this chapter closes, how do you think Aaron would answer this question: What are your deepest hurts these days, and what are your greatest joys?

FOR GOING DEEPER

How does the New Testament look back to the Day of Atonement described in Leviticus 16? In the following passages, explore how the Day of Atonement (and other elements in Leviticus) can deepen our understanding of what Christ did on the cross— Romans 3:21-26, and Hebrews 5:1-9, 7:26-28, 9:1-28, 10:1-14, and 10:24-29.

LEVITICUS 17

Startup: How squeamish do you get at the sight of blood?

SEEING WHAT'S THERE

1. Chapters 17—26 in Leviticus have been called the Holiness Code because of their focus on God's moral standards for His people. What moral standards are taught in chapter 17?

2. How many times do you see some form of the word *sacrifice* in this chapter? What definition would you give for this word—a definition that would be appropriate wherever it appears throughout Leviticus?

3. How many times do you see *blood* mentioned in this chapter, and what is the context for each one?

4. Summarize what God says in verse 11 about the significance of blood. How do you also see this significance expressed in Genesis 9:4-6 and in Deuteronomy 12:23-25?

5. What would you say is God's *intent* behind the laws in this chapter? What were the most important things He wanted these laws to accomplish?

FOR GOING DEEPER

Look again at verse 11. How is the meaning of this verse amplified in Hebrews 9:22?

The sacrificial shedding of blood has been called "the scarlet thread of redemption" that runs throughout the entire Bible. Look at the first hint of this thread in Genesis 4:4 (Abel's sacrificial offering), the end of it in Revelation 13:8, and these appearances in between—Isaiah 53:4-6, and John 10:15 and 10:17-18. From what you see in these passages, what are the most important truths for us to believe and understand about this theme?

LEVITICUS 18

SEEING WHAT'S THERE

1. How would you summarize the moral standards for God's people that are taught in this second chapter of the Holiness Code?

2. What do verses 24-30 reveal about God's attitude toward sin?

CAPTURE THE ESSENCE

3. Recall again Paul's statement in Romans 7:12 that God's commandments are "holy, righteous and good." What specific evidence for that assessment do you see in this chapter?

4. What would you say is God's *intent* behind the laws in this chapter? What were the most important things He wanted these laws to accomplish?

5. Discuss how much you agree or disagree with this statement: God designed His laws in Leviticus not as a *means* to salvation, but as a *reflection* or *demonstration* of salvation.

6. In Psalm 119:45, the psalmist says to God, "I will walk at liberty, for I seek Thy precepts." As you think about the "precepts" or commands given in this chapter, in what ways can you see it offering freedom to God's people? And how would *disobeying* these commands bring bondage?

FOR LIFE TODAY

7. Which commands in this chapter would you say are the most important for Christians today to remember and obey?

8. If God had written this chapter only for you, which words or phrases do you think He might have underlined, and why?

9. Jesus says in Matthew 5:17-18 that not the least portion of God's law will disappear until "all is accomplished" or "all be fulfilled." What do you think God's laws are meant to accomplish or fulfill? How much, if any, has already been done? How much, if any, is still unfinished?

LEVITICUS 19

SEEING WHAT'S THERE

1. How would you summarize the moral standards for God's people that are taught in this third chapter of the Holiness Code?

2. In the laws of this chapter, how many of the Ten Commandments can you see referred to either directly or indirectly? (You can refer back to the list of the commandments in Exodus 20.)

3. What do verses 20-22 reveal about God's attitude toward sin?

4. Which commands in this chapter indicate God's concern for the poor? Which commands indicate His concern for honesty and fairness? Which commands indicate His concern for faithfulness in our relationships? Which commands indicate His rejection of false religious practices and cults?

5. What in this chapter do you think might be most refreshing to someone who was learning about God for the first time?

6. What would you say is God's *intent* behind the laws in this chapter? What were the most important things He wanted these laws to accomplish?

7. In Proverbs 13:13 we're told, "He who respects a command is rewarded," or in another translation, "He that feareth the commandment shall be rewarded." As you look over the laws in this chapter, what would you say were the most likely *rewards* for the Israelites who respected and kept these laws?

8. From all that you've seen so far in Leviticus, summarize the most important teachings you see in this book about (a) sexual purity; (b) family relationships; and (c) relationships with neighbors.

9. Suppose that joining you here today was a Pharisee from the time of Jesus. You tell him you are studying Leviticus, and you ask his opinion about what is most important in this book. How do you think he might answer?

10. Suppose also that the apostle Paul was here with you today, and you asked him the same question you asked the Pharisee. How do you think Paul would answer?

FOR LIFE TODAY

11. Which commands in this chapter would you say are the most important for Christians today to remember and obey?

12. In light of how you're doing spiritually in your life today, which verse in this chapter do you think is the most important for you personally at this time—and why?

FOR GOING DEEPER

Look in the following passages at how a portion of verse 18 is quoted in the New Testament: Matthew 22:34-40, Luke 10:25-37, Romans 13:8-10, Galatians 5:13-15, and James 2:8-13. How do these passages amplify the meaning of this command in Leviticus?

LEVITICUS 20

SEEING WHAT'S THERE

1. How would you summarize the moral standards for God's people that are taught in this fourth chapter of the Holiness Code?

2. In verse 26, God tells Israel to be holy, and then gives two reasons. What are those reasons?

3. How many times do you see *fire* mentioned in this chapter? And how many times do you see *blood* mentioned?

CAPTURE THE ESSENCE

4. What would you say is God's *intent* behind the laws in this chapter? What were the most important things He wanted these laws to accomplish?

5. In Matthew 23:23, Jesus said the most important aspects of the law are "justice, mercy, and faithfulness." How do you see these important aspects reflected in the laws presented in Leviticus?

6. Look again at verse 2. Since God in Leviticus has set up a system of blood sacrifices, and since He will someday allow His own Son to be a flesh-and-blood sacrifice for sin, why do you think He is so opposed to the kind of human sacrifice mentioned here in this verse?

7. Suppose that at the end of this chapter, Moses added this line: "If you remember only one thing from this chapter, let it be this:…" How do you think he would complete that sentence?

LEVITICUS 21

SEEING WHAT'S THERE

1. Glance over chapters 21 and 22. What two or three words would you use to best summarize what these chapters seem to be most about?

2. In chapter 21, what requirement for the priesthood do you see emphasized most in verses 16-23?

3. If you were one of the priests who was to serve at the altar of the tabernacle, which details in this chapter would be of most interest to you?

4. How many times do you see *fire* mentioned in this chapter?

5. What would you say is God's *intent* behind the laws in this chapter? What were the most important things He wanted these laws to accomplish?

LEVITICUS 22

SEEING WHAT'S THERE

1. How many times do you see *fire* mentioned in this chapter?

2. Imagine again that you are one of the priests who is to serve at the altar of the tabernacle. Which details in this chapter would be of most interest to you?

3. What requirement for the sacrificial animals do you see emphasized in verses 17-25?

4. EYE FOR DETAIL— *From what you recall seeing in chapters 17—22, try answering the following question without looking in your Bible:* What was the prescribed penalty for cursing one's father or mother? (See 20:9.)

CAPTURE THE ESSENCE

5. What would you say is God's *intent* behind the laws in this chapter? What were the most important things He wanted these laws to accomplish?

LEVITICUS 23

Startup: Talk together about how you would define the word *worship*.

SEEING WHAT'S THERE

1. What common requirement for the sacrificial animal do you see in verses 12 and 18?

2. How many times do you see *fire* mentioned in this chapter?

3. What in this chapter do you think might be most interesting to someone who was reading the Bible for the first time?

4. From what you've seen in chapters 22 and 23, how would you describe the *beauty* of the of celebrations commanded in these chapters?

CAPTURE THE ESSENCE

5. Suppose you were one of the Israelites who had come out of Egypt with Moses. You have heard Moses describe all the instructions from God (here in Leviticus 23) for the ceremonial feasts and holidays. Then you approached Moses and said, "I'm sure these sacred days and seasons are a good idea; but in time they may well become empty, meaningless holidays. How can we keep that from happening?" How do you think Moses would answer?

LEVITICUS 24

SEEING WHAT'S THERE

1. As you read this chapter, what's the strongest impression or image which it leaves in your mind?

2. How would you summarize the moral standards for God's people that are taught in this chapter?

3. What emotions do you think God Himself may have been experiencing during the events of the last half of this chapter?

4. How many times do you see *fire* mentioned in this chapter?

CAPTURE THE ESSENCE

5. Once more, remember Paul's statement in Romans 7:12 that God's commandments are "holy, righteous and good." What specific evidence for that assessment do you see in this chapter?

6. How would you summarize what the people of Israel learn most about God's character and personality in this chapter?

FOR LIFE TODAY

7. What would you say are the most useful and important lessons to learn from the mistakes in this chapter?

LEVITICUS 25

SEEING WHAT'S THERE

1. How does this chapter indicate God's concern for the earth?

2. What specific promises does God make to Israel in verses 18-22?

3. EYE FOR DETAIL— *From what you recall seeing in chapters 23—25, try answering the following question without looking in your Bible:* What was the penalty for anyone who worked on the Day of Atonement? (See 23:28-31.)

CAPTURE THE ESSENCE

4. What would you say is God's *intent* behind the laws in this chapter? What were the most important things He wanted these laws to accomplish?

FOR LIFE TODAY

5. In what way, if any, would you say that the words of Jesus in John 14:15 and John 14:21 have a bearing on the laws of God which we see in the book of Leviticus?

LEVITICUS 26

Startup: What kind of pictures come to your mind when you think of the word *reward?*

SEEING WHAT'S THERE

1. What specific commands does God reiterate in verses 1-2?

2. Look over the promised blessings God describes in verses 3-13. Which, if any, do you think would be more meaningful than all the others?

3. In verses 14-39, notice the repeating pattern of God's discipline and correction, followed by the people's disobedience. How many times does this pattern appear in these verses?

4. Of the warnings listed in verses 14-39, which, if any, do you think would be more frightening than all the others?

5. In verses 40-45, what is the most important thing God wants His people to understand about His character and personality?

CAPTURE THE ESSENCE

6. What does this chapter reveal about God's attitude toward sin?

7. Recall how many of God's laws you have seen in this book, then discuss how much you agree or disagree with this statement: The most accurate definition for sin is that it is *a violation of God's laws.*

8. From what you see in this chapter, would you say God expects His people to be *obedient,* or *disobedient?*

FOR LIFE TODAY

9. From what you see in this chapter, discuss together how you would complete this sentence: What God really wants from me is…

10. In Jeremiah 23:29, God says that His Word is like fire, and like a hammer. He can use the Scriptures to burn away unclean thoughts and desires in our hearts. He can also use Scripture to hit hard like a hammer, with the power to crush our spiritual hardness. From your study in this book of Leviticus, how do you most want to see the "fire-and-hammer" power of God's Word at work in your own life?

LEVITICUS 27

SEEING WHAT'S THERE

1. Besides the detailing of God's various laws for His people, what are the most important *events* that have occurred in the book of Leviticus? (See especially chapters 8, 9, 10, and 24.)

2. EYE FOR DETAIL— *From what you recall seeing in chapters 26 and 27, try answering the following question without looking in your Bible:* In God's description of His rewards for Israel's obedience, how many of the people will chase a hundred of their enemies, and how many will chase ten thousand? (See 26:8.)

CAPTURE THE ESSENCE

3. From what you see in this chapter, what foundational principles did God want His people to understand about *redemption?*

4. Again, imagine yourself being present in the temple in Jerusalem as the twelve-year-old Jesus hears this chapter read and discussed by the Jewish teachers. What verses in this chapter do you think would most impress Him, and what questions or comments do you suppose He might have spoken?

5. Keeping in mind all that you've seen in Leviticus, imagine yourself asking Moses this question: *How is it possible for a holy God to have a relationship with sinful people, and to enjoy their true worship?* How do you think Moses would answer?

6. As this book concludes, what would you say are the greatest challenges or potential dangers facing the people of Israel at this time?

7. If you were responsible for giving Moses a job performance review (in his position as the leader of God's people), what comments would you make to him, based on what you have seen in Leviticus?

8. What is the best evidence you've seen in this book that Moses truly loves God?

9. What is the best evidence you've seen in this book that God truly loves His people?

FOR LIFE TODAY

10. Which verse in this chapter do you think God would like you to understand best?

11. If this was the last book of the Bible you read before you died, which verses from it would you most like to be lingering in your mind as you said goodbye to this earth?

12. If everyone in your church thoroughly understood this chapter, and they all had a passion for living out its truth in their lives, what kind of practical changes do you think would result?

13. What kind of questions or difficulties or doubts in a Christian's daily life do you think this book answers best?

LEVITICUS:
THE BIG PICTURE

(Discuss again the questions in the "Overview," plus the questions below.)

1. Look together at each of these passages, and discuss which one you believe is the best candidate for "KEY VERSE" in the book of Leviticus — the one which brings into sharpest focus what this book is most about: 17:11, 19:2, or 20:7-8.

2. What would you say is the main theme (or themes) in the book of Leviticus?

3. SEARCH FOR THE SAVIOR—What words, images, or themes in Leviticus have reminded you most of Jesus?

4. What would you say are the most important messages this book communicates about sin and death?

5. If Leviticus were the only book in the Old Testament, in what ways would it still make a good introduction to the message of Jesus in the New Testament?

6. Based especially on your own experience, complete this statement in the way that's most meaningful for you: I believe it's important for Christians to read and explore the book of Leviticus because…

Numbers

OVERVIEW

(Discuss these OVERVIEW questions both at the beginning of your study of Numbers, then again after you've studied together all 36 chapters. Your answers may change significantly once you've looked more closely at the entire book.)

Startup: Talk together about any times in your life when it was especially easy for you to complain or grumble. What was it that brought about this attitude?

SEEING WHAT'S THERE

1. Before launching into a closer look at Numbers, how would you summarize what you already know about this book?

2. What similar occurrence do you see in each of the following verses — 11:1, 14:2, 16:3, 16:41, 20:2, and 21:4-5? What clues does this offer about the central message of the book of Numbers?

3. To see how long is the time-span covered in this book, compare 1:1 with 33:38. How many years does this include?

4. A key passage in this book is 14:29-35. Look especially in verses 33-34 to see what the time period of the book of Numbers is generally referred to. From what you see throughout verses 29-35, what would be the general *flavor* of this time period for those who less than two years earlier had escaped from Egypt in the excitement of the Exodus?

5. Look also at the list of "Questions to Ask as You Begin Your Study of Each Book" on page 9.

CAPTURE THE ESSENCE

6. What would you say is the most helpful information in the book of Leviticus for understanding the book of Numbers?

FOR LIFE TODAY

7. Numbers has been called "The Book of Testing," "The Book of Pilgrimage," "The Wilderness Book," and "The Tragic Story of Israel's Unbelief." It has also been described as a book built around the theme of *worship*—in fact, a book whose very pulse is worship. With that reputation for this book, what kinds of answers and guidelines and solutions would you like to gain as you examine it more closely?

8. When you get to heaven, if you have a long talk with Moses (the author of this book) and he asks you, "What was most helpful to you in Numbers?" how would you like to be able to answer him?

9. From what you see in the words of blessing in 6:24-26, what would be a good personal prayer to offer to God as you study this book?

10. As you think first about *who God is,* and second about *what the Bible is,* how strongly would you rate your present desire to understand better the book of Numbers? Use a scale of one to ten (one = "no desire at all," ten = "extremely intense desire") to help you decide.

NUMBERS 1

Startup: In the way we read and study the Bible, what kind of old mental habits or faulty assumptions or wrong first impressions can most easily block this book of Numbers from coming alive in our minds and hearts?

SEEING WHAT'S THERE

1. What *repetitions* do you see in this chapter?

2. According to verses 47-53, why wasn't the tribe of Levi counted? What were the responsibilities of the Levites?

3. Look also on page 8 at the list of "Questions to Ask as You Study Each Chapter." You may want to look again at this list for each chapter in Numbers.

FOR LIFE TODAY

4. Proverbs 2:1-5 tells about the sincere person who truly longs for wisdom and understanding, and who searches the Scriptures for it—as if it were buried treasure. That person, Solomon says, will come to understand the fear of the Lord, and discover the knowledge of God. As you begin exploring the book of Numbers, what "buried treasure" would you like God to help you find here—to show you what God and His wisdom are really like? If you have this desire, how would you express it in your own words?

NUMBERS 2

SEEING WHAT'S THERE

CAPTURE THE ESSENCE

1. Why do you think God gave the Israelites specific instructions in how they arranged their camp?

2. What significance, if any, do you see in the particular *way* God told His people to arrange their camp?

NUMBERS 3

SEEING WHAT'S THERE

1. Glance over chapters 3 and 4. What two or three words would you use to best summarize what these chapters seem to be most about?

2. For helpful background to verses 2-4 here in chapter 3, review Leviticus 10:1-3. What does the incident communicate about the work of the priests?

CAPTURE THE ESSENCE

3. What reasons does God give in this chapter for setting apart the Levites?

FOR LIFE TODAY

4. Look again at what God says about the Levites in verse 9 and verses 12-13. Does God have the same ownership rights upon you that He had upon the Levites? Why or why not?

FOR GOING DEEPER

Look again at what the two sons of Aaron did wrong in verses 2-4. Then explore carefully the situation mentioned in 1 Samuel 2:12-36, 3:11-14, and 4:1-11. How would you compare the situation of Aaron's sons with that of Eli's sons? What are the greatest similarities, and what are the greatest differences?

NUMBERS 4

SEEING WHAT'S THERE

1. How would you summarize the work that was given to each of the three groups mentioned in this chapter—Kohathites, Gershonites, and Merarites?

NUMBERS 5

SEEING WHAT'S THERE

1. What specific laws and commands does God give in this chapter?

2. How many times do you see *water* mentioned in this chapter, and what is the context for each one?

CAPTURE THE ESSENCE

3. What would you say is God's *intent* behind the laws and commands given in this chapter? What does He want them to accomplish?

FOR LIFE TODAY

4. After thinking about this chapter, what conclusions would you make about the purity which God wants in your life? How is that purity achieved?

NUMBERS 6

SEEING WHAT'S THERE

1. As you read this chapter, what's the strongest impression or image which it leaves in your mind?

2. What exactly was to be different about a Nazirite, compared to other people in Israel?

3. In your own words, how would you describe the *beauty* of verses 24-26? What makes this blessing so appealing?

4. After reading through this chapter, which words or phrases or sentences here would you most like to understand better?

5. EYE FOR DETAIL— *From what you recall seeing in chapters 1—6, try answering the following question without looking in your Bible:* What was the total number of Israelite men counted in the census described in chapter 1? (See 1:46.)

CAPTURE THE ESSENCE

6. Since *worship* is considered a core theme in Numbers, what patterns and principles for worshiping God do you see in this chapter?

7. In what ways, if any, do you see verses 24-27 as a reflection of God's *desire* for His people? What does God want His people to experience in their relationship with Him?

FOR LIFE TODAY

8. In what practical ways can verses 24-26 help you as you pray for other Christians?

9. What do you think are the most likely obstacles that could keep you personally from seeking and learning all that God wants you to in this book of Numbers?

FOR GOING DEEPER

Think again about verse 25. What indication do you see that David may have had this blessing in mind in Psalm 4:6 and 31:16?

NUMBERS 7

Startup: Talk together about times in your life when you've especially enjoyed giving money for the Lord's work. What were the circumstances that brought this about?

SEEING WHAT'S THERE

1. From what you've seen so far in Numbers, what parts of this book do you think might be most surprising to a new Christian reading it for the first time?

2. How many silver bowls do you see in this chapter?

CAPTURE THE ESSENCE

3. Since *worship* is considered a core theme in Numbers, what patterns and principles for worshiping God do you see in this chapter?

FOR GOING DEEPER

Notice again the lengthy repetition present in the description of each tribe's offering for the tabernacle worship. In what ways, if any, do you see this chapter as a reflection of the worship principle stated in 1 Corinthians 14:40?

NUMBERS 8

CAPTURE THE ESSENCE

1. Since *worship* is considered a core theme in Numbers, what patterns and principles for worshiping God do you see in this chapter?

FOR LIFE TODAY

2. Think again about the purification requirements presented in this chapter for the Levites as they did their work for God in the tabernacle. In what practical and specific ways should we today be purified in order to do God's work?

NUMBERS 9

CAPTURE THE ESSENCE

1. Since *worship* is considered a core theme in Numbers, what patterns and principles for worshiping God do you see in this chapter?

FOR LIFE TODAY

2. From what you see in verses 15-23, what patterns and principles can you find for discovering and following God's will?

NUMBERS 10

SEEING WHAT'S THERE

1. What specific promise does God make to Israel in verses 8-9?

2. In verse 11, as the Israelites leave Sinai and begin their approach to the Promised Land, we come to a major division in the book of Numbers. In only a few sentences, how would you summarize the most important things that have happened so far in this book?

3. EYE FOR DETAIL— *From what you recall seeing in chapters 7—10, try answering the following question without looking in your Bible:* At what age were Levite men required to begin taking part in their work at the tabernacle? And at what age were they required to retire from this work? (See 8:24-26.)

CAPTURE THE ESSENCE

4. In verses 14-28, what significance, if any, do you see in the particular arrangement of the Israelites' marching order?

5. Look in verses 35-36 at the words Moses always spoke to mark the beginning and the end of each segment of Israel's journey. Why do you think he chose these particular words to speak. What was their significance to the people who heard these words?

FOR LIFE TODAY

6. What principles for encouraging others do you see in verses 29-32?

NUMBERS 11

Startup: Under what kind of circumstances are you most tempted to complain?

SEEING WHAT'S THERE

1. Which important details in this chapter do you think might be the easiest to overlook?

2. What are the most important decisions and choices that are made in this chapter, and how would you analyze each one?

3. Humanly speaking, what would you say is the best thing anybody does in this chapter? And what is the worst or most questionable thing anybody does in this chapter?

4. Take a "walk" together through the incidents that happen in this chapter: Using your imagination, talk about the kinds of sights, smells, sounds, and feelings you might experience.

5. From what you see in his prayer in verses 11-15, how would you describe the emotions and mental attitude of Moses at this time?

6. What promise does God make to Moses in verses 16-17?

CAPTURE THE ESSENCE

7. What would you conclude about the wisdom and character of Moses from what you see in verses 26-29?

8. How would you summarize what Moses and the people of Israel learn most about God in this chapter?

FOR LIFE TODAY

9. What would you say are the most useful and important lessons to learn from the mistakes in this chapter?

NUMBERS 12

SEEING WHAT'S THERE

1. As you read this chapter, what's the strongest impression or image it leaves in your mind?

2. Imagine yourself being present to witness what is described in verses 4-16. How do you think it would affect you?

3. EYE FOR DETAIL— *From what you recall seeing in chapters 11 and 12, try answering the following question without looking in your Bible:* What were the names of the two elders who stayed in the Hebrew camp and prophesied, while the other elders were with Moses in the tabernacle? (See 11:26-27.)

CAPTURE THE ESSENCE

4. Think about the observation in verse 3 about Moses' character. What's the strongest evidence you've seen for this conclusion, either here in Numbers or in other places in the Bible?

5. What would you do if you were in Moses' place in this chapter?

6. How would you summarize what Miriam and Aaron learn most about God in this chapter?

7. At the end of this chapter, how do you think Miriam would answer this question: How is your relationship with God right now?

FOR LIFE TODAY

8. If God had written this chapter only for you, which words or phrases do you think He might have underlined, and why?

NUMBERS 13

Startup: Talk about a time in your life when someone's confident word of encouragement helped you to accomplish something that you otherwise might not have.

SEEING WHAT'S THERE

1. To review, retrace your way through the last several chapters. What are the most important things that have happened since this book began?

2. Who are the most important people here in chapter 13, and what are the most important things that happen to them?

3. What are the most important decisions and choices that are made in this chapter, and how would you analyze each one?

4. Summarize the story of the exploration of Canaan and the people's response to it, keeping in mind that no historical account can include *every* detail of the events it describes. What are the most important details which *are* included here? And what kinds of details are left out, details which might otherwise be quite interesting to us? What does this selection process tell you about what God wants us to understand most from this story?

CAPTURE THE ESSENCE

5. Imagine that you are a the oldest son or daughter of Caleb. What things do you think Caleb might talk with you about upon his return from the exploration trip into Canaan? And what kinds of feelings do you think you might experience?

6. As this chapter concludes, how would you summarize the biggest problems or challenges that Moses is now facing ?

FOR LIFE TODAY

7. In verse 30, look again at Caleb's confident word of encouragement to the people. Suppose God sent someone into your life today to speak a confident word of encouragement. What task or goal do you think it would probably be about?

Numbers 14

SEEING WHAT'S THERE

1. Chapter 14 has been called the key to the book of Numbers. What does this chapter include that could make it this significant?

2. Which important details in this chapter do you think might be the easiest to overlook?

3. What are the most important decisions and choices that are made in this chapter, and how would you analyze each one?

4. What specific punishment does God announce in verses 21-23.

5. In verse 21, notice how God introduces this punishment. What do you think God most wanted Moses and Israel to understand from these words?

6. In verses 28-35, what does God tell Moses and Aaron that He will do?

CAPTURE THE ESSENCE

7. How much do you think it grieved God to have to administer this punishment to the people He delivered out of slavery in Egypt?

8. From what you see in verses 20-23, would you say that God wants to be considered *primarily* as the God of His people Israel, or as the God of the whole earth? Explain your answer.

9. Review verses 39-45. Was this true repentance on the part of the Israelites? If so, why did Moses respond as he did? And if it was *not* true repentance, what was missing? What *should* the people have done?

10. What would you say this chapter teaches us about God's forgiveness?

11. How would you summarize what the people of Israel learn most in this chapter about God's *love* for them?

12. In what ways, if any, would you say that this chapter represents a major turning point or significant "hinge" in the history of God's people?

FOR LIFE TODAY

13. Choose one of these sentences, and complete it as fully and candidly as you would like: (a) What I see and understand in this chapter is important to my life because… OR: (b) What I see and understand in this chapter does NOT seem important to my life at this time, because…

Numbers 15

SEEING WHAT'S THERE

1. After reading through this chapter, which words or phrases or sentences here would you most like to understand better?

2. How many times do you see *fire* mentioned in this chapter?

3. EYE FOR DETAIL— *From what you recall seeing in chapters 13—15, try answering the following question without looking in your Bible:* Joshua and Caleb were among the twelve men, one from each tribe, who were sent out to explore Canaan. Which tribe was Joshua from, and which tribe was Caleb from? (See 13:6 and 13:8.)

CAPTURE THE ESSENCE

4. In your own words, what would you say is revealed most about God's character and personality in verses 40-41?

5. Suppose that joining you here today was a Pharisee from the time of Jesus. You tell him you are studying the middle chapters in Numbers, and you ask his opinion about what is most important in these chapters. How do you think he might answer?

6. Suppose also that the apostle Paul was here with you today, and you asked him the same question you asked the Pharisee. How do you think Paul would answer?

FOR LIFE TODAY

7. In Isaiah 55:10-11, God reminds us that He sends rain and snow from the sky to water the earth and to nurture life. In the same way, God says that He sends His words to accomplish specific purposes. From your study so far, what would you suggest as *God's* primary purposes for the book of Numbers in the lives of Christians today?

NUMBERS 16

Startup: Besides the desire for money and possessions, what forms of greed do you think are the strongest temptations for people today?

SEEING WHAT'S THERE

1. Which important details in this chapter do you think might be the easiest to overlook?

2. Humanly speaking, what would you say is the best thing anybody does in this chapter? And what is the worst or most questionable thing anybody does in this chapter?

3. What specific commands does God give to Moses in this chapter?

4. How many times do you see *fire* mentioned in this chapter?

5. If this chapter was the only Scripture portion you had ever known, what would you conclude from it about God's holiness?

CAPTURE THE ESSENCE

6. If you could go back in time, and God brought you into the events of this chapter to act as a personal counselor to Korah, what kind of counsel would you give him, and how would you express it?

7. From what you see in this chapter, what conclusions would you make about the character of Moses?

8. Look at verse 46, then reflect on the events of the entire chapter. What does this chapter communicate about God's *wrath?*

9. How would you summarize what the people of Israel learn most about God in this chapter?

FOR LIFE TODAY

10. In light of how you're doing spiritually in your life today, which verse in this chapter do you think is the most important at this time—and why?

NUMBERS 17

SEEING WHAT'S THERE

1. How much of this chapter contains words spoken directly by God to Moses?

2. What has impressed you most about Moses in this book?

CAPTURE THE ESSENCE

3. Why do you think the people responded as they did in verses 12-13? What changes did this reflect in their thinking?

4. What would you say is the main point God is making by including this chapter in the Bible?

5. As this chapter concludes, what would you say are the biggest problems or challenges that Moses is now facing?

NUMBERS 18

SEEING WHAT'S THERE

1. Which verses in this chapter contain words spoken directly by God to Aaron? Which verses are His words to Moses? And which verses are His words to the Levites?

2. What would you conclude from this chapter about the right way for the Israelites to approach God?

3. EYE FOR DETAIL— *From what you recall seeing in chapters 16—18, try answering the following question without looking in your Bible:* When the people grumbled about the men who were destroyed in the rebellion of Korah, God sent a deadly plague upon them. How many people died from the plague? (See 16:49.)

CAPTURE THE ESSENCE

4. In what ways, if any, can you see God's *grace* in this chapter?

5. Since *worship* is considered a core theme in Numbers, what patterns and principles for worshiping God do you see in this chapter?

6. As you think about the overall story unfolding in the book of Numbers, what important step in that unfolding is played by this chapter? What strategic *purpose* does it serve in the larger picture?

7. Now that you're halfway through Numbers, how would you summarize the most important lessons to learn from this book?

FOR LIFE TODAY

8. If God were to write down a list of the ways in which you are currently serving Him, what do you think would be on that list?

NUMBERS 19

Startup: What kind of pictures come to your mind when you think of the word *purity?*

SEEING WHAT'S THERE

1. What would you conclude from this chapter about the right way for the Israelites to approach God?

2. How many times do you see *water* mentioned in this chapter?

CAPTURE THE ESSENCE

3. Since *worship* is considered a core theme in Numbers, what patterns and principles for worshiping God do you see in this chapter?

4. Imagine yourself being present in the temple in Jerusalem as the twelve-year-old Jesus hears this chapter read and discussed by the rabbis there. In Luke 2:46 we read that He was listening to these teachers and asking them questions. What verses from this chapter do you think would most impress the boy Jesus, and what questions or comments do you suppose He might have spoken?

FOR LIFE TODAY

5. What are the best ways in your life to "clean" your mind and heart for serving God?

NUMBERS 20

SEEING WHAT'S THERE

1. As you read this chapter, what's the strongest impression or image it leaves in your mind?

2. Once again, take a "walk" together through the incidents that happen in this chapter. Using your imagination, talk about the kinds of sights, smells, sounds, and feelings you might experience.

3. How many times do you see *water* mentioned in this chapter?

4. In verse 12, what exactly does God say that Moses and Aaron did wrong? How would you explain this in your own words?

CAPTURE THE ESSENCE

5. How accurate is it to say that God's words in verse 12 are a statement of His wrath? Explain your answer.

6. Looking again at verse 12, discuss how much you agree or disagree with this statement: Disobedience is always a result of not trusting God.

7. Review verses 22-29. Keeping in mind the lessons he may have learned, suppose Aaron was allowed to live his life over again. What, if anything, do you think he would most want to change, and how?

8. As this chapter closes, how do you think Moses would answer this question: How is your relationship with God right now?

FOR LIFE TODAY

9. In Jeremiah 23:29, God says that His Word is like fire, and like a hammer. He can use the Scriptures to burn away unclean thoughts and desires in our hearts. He can also use Scripture to hit hard like a hammer, with the power to crush our spiritual hardness. From your study in this book of Numbers, how do you most want to see the "fire-and-hammer" power of God's Word at work in your own life?

NUMBERS 21

SEEING WHAT'S THERE

1. In your own words, how would you explain all of God's actions in verses 4-9?

2. EYE FOR DETAIL.— *From what you recall seeing in chapters 19—21, try answering the following question without looking in your Bible:* Where did Aaron die? (See 20:23-28.)

CAPTURE THE ESSENCE

3. In the incident of the snakes in verses 4-9, what was the secret of healing power in the bronze snake on the pole?

4. Songs are often a way to express and release deep emotions. What emotions would you say are behind the song in verses 17-18?

5. Again, imagine yourself being present in the temple in Jerusalem as the twelve-year-old Jesus hears this chapter read and discussed by the Jewish teachers. What verses in this chapter do you think would most impress Him, and what questions or comments do you suppose He might have spoken?

FOR LIFE TODAY

6. In Romans 15:4, Paul reminds us that the Old Testament Scriptures can give us patience and perseverance on one hand, as well as comfort and encouragement on the other. In your own life, how do you see this book of Numbers living up to Paul's description? In what ways, if any, is it meeting your personal needs for both *perseverance* and *encouragement?*

FOR GOING DEEPER

With the incident of the bronze snake in mind (from verses 4-9), review the words of Jesus to Nicodemus in John 3:14-15. As teacher of Israel, Nicodemus would know well the story of the snakes here in Numbers 21. After hearing the words of Jesus, what questions or conclusions or further comparisons do you think might well have come to his mind?

NUMBERS 22

Startup: How long have you known about the story of Balaam and his talking donkey? What are some of the earliest impressions this story left with you?

SEEING WHAT'S THERE

1. To review, retrace your way through the last several chapters. What are the most important things that have happened since the twelve Hebrew spies returned from exploring Canaan?

2. Where are the people of Israel camped as this chapter begins?

3. What are the most important decisions and choices that are made in this chapter, and how would you analyze each one?

4. Are there any parts of this chapter which you think God may want us to smile at, or maybe even laugh over? If so, what are they, and why wouldn't God mind if we respond this way?

CAPTURE THE ESSENCE

5. If you knew Balaam while he was on earth, what do you think would most impress you about him?

6. Look again at what God told Balaam in verse 12, then at Balaam's words in verse 19. Then discuss how right or wrong it was for Balaam to go back to God and ask for further instructions.

FOR LIFE TODAY

7. What do you think are the most important lessons God wants us to learn from Balaam's example in this chapter?

FOR GOING DEEPER

Hundreds of years later in Israel's history, the leader Jephthah responded to a message from the enemy king of the Ammonites by reciting some of Israel's history recorded in the book of Numbers. Look at Jephthah's reply in Judges 11:15-27. In this passage, how many events and details can you recognize as being from Numbers?

NUMBERS 23

SEEING WHAT'S THERE

1. Look closely at the words Balaam speaks in this chapter. What are the most important things he understands about God's people?

CAPTURE THE ESSENCE

2. In how many ways do you see God's *grace* shining through in the words spoken by Balaam in this chapter?

3. In how many ways do you see God's *sovereign power* demonstrated in Balaam's words in this chapter?

4. How would you restate in your own words what is revealed about God's character and personality in verse 19?

5. How *honest* would you say Balaam is in this chapter?

FOR LIFE TODAY

6. Of all that Balaam says in this chapter about God's people, which statements are also true about you, and why? And which of these statements is most important to you?

NUMBERS 24

SEEING WHAT'S THERE

1. Summarize the story of Balaam presented in chapters 22—24, once again keeping in mind that no historical account can include *every* detail of the events it describes. What are the most important details which *are* included here? And what kinds of details are left out, details which might otherwise be quite interesting to us? What does this selection process tell you about what God wants us to understand most from this story?

2. What does the opening verse in chapter 24 communicate about God's love for Israel?

3. Notice how Balaam introduces his next words in verse 14. In the verses that follow, what are the most important things we learn about the future history of God's people?

4. In your own words, how would you describe the *beauty* in the words spoken by Balaam in this chapter? What is it that makes these passages so appealing?

5. Look back on the full story of Balaam in chapters 22—24. What are the most important indications in these chapters of God's continued *faithfulness* to His people Israel?

6. Look ahead to 31:7-8 to see what Scripture says next about Balaam.

CAPTURE THE ESSENCE

7. Once again, in how many ways do you see God's *grace* shining through in the words spoken by Balaam in this chapter?

8. And again, in how many ways do you see God's *sovereign power* demonstrated in Balaam's words in this chapter?

9. Look again at verses 17-19. As a prophetic passage about the coming Messiah, what does this Scripture teach us about the *character* and the *ministry* of Jesus Christ?

10. How do you think Moses and the Israelites might have responded when they first learned what Balaam had done here in chapters 22—24?

FOR LIFE TODAY

11. In light of how you're doing spiritually in your life today, which verse in this chapter do you think is the most important at this time—and why?

NUMBERS 25

SEEING WHAT'S THERE

1. Look ahead to 31:15-16. Who was the instigator of the Moabite seduction of Israel described in this chapter?

2. What were the action steps that took place in this seduction, according to what you see in verses 1-3?

3. What *risks* would you say Phinehas is taking by the action he pursues in verses 7-8?

4. What were the *results* of Phinehas' actions? (See especially verses 8 and 13.)

5. What specifically does God commend Phinehas for in verses 11-13?

6. EYE FOR DETAIL—*From what you recall seeing in chapters 22—25, try answer-*

ing the following question without looking in your Bible: What was the name of the city where Balaam lived? (See 22:5.)

CAPTURE THE ESSENCE

7. What does this chapter reveal about God's wrath?

8. What do you think were the most important factors that brought about the sinful behavior described in this chapter?

9. If you were responsible for giving Moses a job performance review, what comments would you make to him, based on what you see in this chapter?

FOR LIFE TODAY

10. In the patterns of your life, are there certain times when you are more vulnerable to temptation and sin than other times? If so, when are these times?

FOR GOING DEEPER

Reflect again upon the story of Phinehas in verses 6-13. In what ways would you say Phinehas is like the person described in Revelation 19:11-16?

NUMBERS 26

Startup: What is the most interesting thing you've read in the Bible in the past week?

SEEING WHAT'S THERE

1. From what you've seen so far in Numbers, what parts of this book do you think might be most interesting to someone who was reading the Bible for the first time?

2. The first census included in Numbers (in chapter 1) was of the first generation of Hebrews who left Egypt. The census here in chapter 26 is of the next generation. In each list, compare the total numbers for each of the twelve tribes. Which tribes increased in number, and which tribes decreased?

3. Scan the first 25 chapters of Numbers, which focus on the first generation of Hebrews to leave Egypt. How often in these chapters do you see reference made to someone dying?

4. Now scan over the rest of this book (chapters 26—36), where the focus is

on the second generation since the Exodus. How many times in these chapters do you see someone dying?

CAPTURE THE ESSENCE

5. In what ways, if any, would you say that this chapter represents a major turning point or significant "hinge" in the history of God's people?

NUMBERS 27

SEEING WHAT'S THERE

1. Who are the most important people in this chapter, and what are the most important things that happen to them?

2. Imagine that you are Joshua. As this chapter closes, how would you understand God's will for your life?

CAPTURE THE ESSENCE

3. What would you say are the biggest *risks* the daughters of Zelophehad are taking by their actions in this chapter?

NUMBERS 28

SEEING WHAT'S THERE

1. If you were one of the priests who was to serve at the altar of the tabernacle, which details in this chapter would be of most interest to you?

2. How many times in this chapter do you see the requirement for a sacrificial animal to be without defect?

CAPTURE THE ESSENCE

3. Since *worship* is considered a core theme in Numbers, what patterns and principles for worshiping God do you see in this chapter?

NUMBERS 29

SEEING WHAT'S THERE

1. Imagine again that you are one of the priests who is to serve at the altar of the tabernacle. Which details in this chapter would be of most interest to you?

2. How many times in this chapter do you see the requirement for a sacrificial animal to be without defect?

3. EYE FOR DETAIL— *From what you recall seeing in chapters 26—29, try answering the following question without looking in your Bible:* What was the total number of Israelite men counted in the census described in chapter 26? (See 26:51.)

CAPTURE THE ESSENCE

4. Since *worship* is considered a core theme in Numbers, what patterns and principles for worshiping God do you see in this chapter?

5. From what you've seen in chapters 28 and 29, discuss how much you agree or disagree with this statement: It is impossible to truly worship God without an understanding of His holy character.

FOR LIFE TODAY

6. Discuss how much you agree or disagree with this statement: The descriptions in Numbers of the offerings and feasts and holy days tells us that our worship of God should be both regular and special.

NUMBERS 30

Startup: If God asked you, "What are the three things you're most thankful for these days?"—how would you answer?

SEEING WHAT'S THERE

1. In Romans 7:12, Paul says that God's commandments are "holy, righteous and good." What specific evidence for that assessment have you seen so far in this book?

FOR LIFE TODAY

2. In what way, if any, would you say that the words of Jesus in John 14:15 and John 14:21 have a bearing on the laws of God which we see in the book of Numbers?

3. What practical principles for today could be drawn from this chapter about making and keeping commitments?

NUMBERS 31

SEEING WHAT'S THERE

1. What were God's reasons for sending the Israelites against the Midianites? (Refer back to chapter 25.)

2. What further indication of Balaam's activities and influence do you see in verses 15-16?

CAPTURE THE ESSENCE

3. From what you see in this chapter, what were God's guidelines for conducting a "holy war"?

FOR GOING DEEPER

Look again at verses 15-16. What is the biblical verdict about Balaam? Explore these verses to decide—Deuteronomy 23:3-5, Joshua 13:22 and 24:9-10, Nehemiah 13:1-3, 2 Peter 2:15-16, Jude 11, and Revelation 2:14. How many of these passages speak positively about Balaam, and how many speak negatively about him?

NUMBERS 32

SEEING WHAT'S THERE

1. What specific requests do the Reubenites and Gadites make in this chapter?

2. What specific commitment do the Reubenites and Gadites make?

3. What specific warning does Moses give to the Reubenites and Gadites?

FOR LIFE TODAY

4. Look at the last thing Moses says in verse 23. To what extent would you say that this is a universal principle, true in all situations and for all people?

NUMBERS 33

SEEING WHAT'S THERE

1. What commands does God give His people in verses 50-54?

2. What words of warning does God give His people in verses 55-56?

3. In verses 3-49, look over the list of the stages in Israel's journey. In which of these places can you recall some specific incidents that are recorded in Exodus, Leviticus, or Numbers?

FOR LIFE TODAY

4. In verse 53, notice again God's words to the Israelites about possessing the land. What exactly has God given you to possess?

NUMBERS 34

SEEING WHAT'S THERE

1. How much of this chapter contains words spoken directly by God to Moses?

NUMBERS 35

SEEING WHAT'S THERE

1. How would you explain the purpose of the cities of refuge in verses 6-28?

CAPTURE THE ESSENCE

2. How would you explain the meaning of verses 33-34? In what ways would murder be not only an offense against God and humanity, but also against the land?

NUMBERS 36

SEEING WHAT'S THERE

1. In review, scan chapters 26—36, where the focus of this book has shifted to the second generation of Hebrews since the Exodus from Egypt. In these final chapters, how often have you seen a reference made to any sin or wrongdoing by any of the Israelites?

2. According to verse 13, where are God's people camped as this book comes to a close?

3. EYE FOR DETAIL— *From what you recall seeing in chapters 30—36, try answering the following question without looking in your Bible:* According to God's instructions, how many witnesses were required before a Hebrew could be convicted of murder and sentenced to die? (See 35:30.)

CAPTURE THE ESSENCE

4. What do you see about God's character in the judgment He gave to Moses about the daughters of Zelophehad?

5. Recall again all the mistakes and misery experienced by the first generation of the Hebrews coming out of Egypt, as you witnessed in the first 25 chapters of Numbers. Then discuss how much you agree or disagree with this statement: Because of their human weakness and their heritage of failure from the parents, the second generation of Hebrews since the Exodus were essentially doomed to failure.

6. Keeping in mind all that you've seen in Numbers, imagine yourself asking Moses this question: *How is it possible for a holy God to have a relationship with sinful people, and to enjoy their true worship?* How do you think Moses would answer?

7. If you were responsible for giving Moses a job performance review (in his position as the leader of God's people), what comments would you make to him, based on what you have seen in Numbers?

8. What is the best evidence you've seen in this book that Moses truly loves God?

9. What is the best evidence you've seen in this book that God truly loves His people?

10. As this book concludes, what would you say are the greatest challenges or potential dangers facing the people of Israel at this time?

FOR LIFE TODAY

11. Think back on all that has happened to the people of Israel in the book of Numbers. If it's true that *the past is a lesson for the future,* then what would you say are the most important lessons for God's people today to learn from these events?

NUMBERS:
THE BIG PICTURE

(Discuss again the questions in the "Overview," plus the questions below.)

1. Imagine that you were helping to produce a film based on the book of Numbers. Describe the kinds of scenery, supporting characters, background music, lighting effects, etc., which you would use to help portray the central message of this book.

2. Look together at each of these passages, and discuss which one you believe is the best candidate for "KEY VERSE" in the book of Numbers —the one which brings into sharpest focus what this book is most about: 14:22-23, 20:12, or 33:1.

3. What would you say is the main theme (or themes) in the book of Numbers?

4. SEARCH FOR THE SAVIOR—What words, images, or themes in Numbers have reminded you most of Jesus?

5. What to you personally is the strongest example in this book of someone doing what was right and good?

6. What to you personally is the strongest example in this book of someone doing what was wrong?

7. If Numbers were the only book in the Old Testament, in what ways would it still make a good introduction to the message of Jesus in the New Testament?

8. Based especially on your own experience, complete this statement in the way that's most meaningful for you: I believe it's important for Christians to read and explore the book of Numbers because...

Deuteronomy

OVERVIEW

(Discuss these OVERVIEW questions both at the beginning of your study of Deuteronomy, then again after you've studied all 34 chapters. Your answers may change significantly once you've looked more closely at the entire book.)

Startup: Can you recall an occasion or circumstance when you made a commitment that you wanted to remember and keep for the rest of your life? How would you explain your reasons for wanting to maintain that commitment?

SEEING WHAT'S THERE

1. Before launching into a closer look at Deuteronomy, how would you summarize what you already know about this book?

2. Find the phrase that reoccurs in the following verses—4:40, 5:16, 5:29, 6:3, 6:18, 8:16, 12:25, 12:28, 19:13, and 22:7. How would you restate this phrase in your own words, and what clues does it offer about the central message of this book?

3. Find also the *gift* that you see mentioned in the following verses—1:8, 1:21, 8:10-11, and 12:1. From the evidence in these verses, what did God want His people to remember about this gift?

4. Now find the most prominent word that reoccurs in the following verses—5:15, 7:18, 8:2, 8:18, 9:7, 9:27, 15:15, 16:3, 16:12, 24:9, 24:18, 24:22, 25:17, and 32:7. What clues could this word offer about the central message of Deuteronomy?

5. Look also at the list of "Questions to Ask as You Begin Your Study of Each Book" on page 9.

CAPTURE THE ESSENCE

6. From what you see in 4:1 and 32:45-47, what would you say is God's overall purpose for the words which Moses recorded in this book?

7. What would you say is the most helpful information in the book of Numbers for understanding the book of Deuteronomy?

FOR LIFE TODAY

8. Deuteronomy has been called "The Book of Obedience," "The Book of Remembrance and Retrospect," and "The Book of Preparation for Possession." With that reputation for this book, what kinds of answers and guidelines and solutions would you like to gain as you examine it more closely?

9. When you get to heaven, if you have a long talk with Moses (the author of this book) and he asks you, "What was most helpful to you in Deuteronomy?" how would you like to be able to answer him?

10. From what you see in the words of promise in 4:29, what would be a good personal prayer to make to God as you study this book?

DEUTERONOMY 1

SEEING WHAT'S THERE

1. What do you learn in the first five verses about the setting for this book?

2. From what Moses says in this chapter, what does He most want the Israelites to understand about God's character?

3. Look also on page 8 at the list of "Questions to Ask as You Study Each Chapter." You may want to look again at this list for each chapter in Deuteronomy.

4. In what specific ways do you see God's grace in this first chapter?

5. How would you explain Moses' words in verse 37?

FOR LIFE TODAY

6. Look again at Israel's experiences in verses 41-45. In what ways, if any, does this remind you of any similar experiences in your life?

7. Proverbs 2:1-5 tells about the sincere person who truly longs for wisdom and understanding, and who searches the Scriptures for it—as if it were buried treasure. That person, Solomon says, will come to understand the fear of the Lord, and discover the knowledge of God. As you begin exploring the book of Deuteronomy, what "buried treasure" would you like God to help you find here—to show you what God and His wisdom are really like? If you have this desire, how would you express it in your own words?

FOR GOING DEEPER

For helpful background on the events mentioned in this chapter, look especially at chapters 13, 14, 20, and 27 in Numbers.

DEUTERONOMY 2

SEEING WHAT'S THERE

1. How would you summarize the history that Moses gives in this chapter?

2. What does verse 7 indicate about God's provision for the Israelites during their desert wanderings?

CAPTURE THE ESSENCE

3. In what specific ways do you see God's grace in this chapter?

DEUTERONOMY 3

SEEING WHAT'S THERE

1. How would you summarize the history that Moses gives in this chapter?

2. EYE FOR DETAIL— *From what you recall seeing in chapters 1—3, try answering the following question without looking in your Bible:* What was the name of the mountain Moses climbed to get a view of the Promised Land? (See 3:27.)

CAPTURE THE ESSENCE

3. In what specific ways do you see God's grace in this chapter?

4. From what you see in the prayer of Moses in verses 23-25, what are the most important things he understands about God's personality and character?

FOR LIFE TODAY

5. As you think first about *who God is,* and second about *what the Bible is,* how strongly would you rate your present desire to understand better the book of Deuteronomy? Use a scale of one to ten (one = "no desire at all," ten = "extremely intense desire") to help you decide.

DEUTERONOMY 4

Startup: Under what circumstances in life is it easiest for you to forget God? And under what circumstances is it easiest for you to remember Him?

SEEING WHAT'S THERE

1. What is the clear purpose of Deuteronomy, according to what you see in verses 1, 5-6, and 9-14?

2. What specific blessings for Israel does Moses describe in verses 7-8?

3. Restate in your own words what you believe are the most important truths revealed about God's character and personality in verses 23-24, verse 31, and verse 39.

4. From what you see in verses 32-34, what did God want the people of Israel to understand most about their uniqueness as a nation?

5. How many times do you see *fire* mentioned in this chapter, and what is the context for each one?

6. The book of Deuteronomy is often presented as containing three major "sermons" or "addresses" from Moses. The first of these closes with verse 40 in chapter 4. How would you summarize the most important things Moses has talked about in this first address?

7. What details of time and place do you see in verses 44-49?

8. Bible teachers often point out elements in Deuteronomy which are like a treaty or a legal contract. What evidence of this kind do you detect in the chapters you've studied so far?

CAPTURE THE ESSENCE

9. In what specific ways do you see God's grace in this chapter?

10. From what you see in this chapter, how would you summarize the *expectations* God has of His people?

11. Look again at the blessings for Israel which Moses describes in verses 7-8. Would you say that these are primarily a result of God's holy wrath, or His grace?

FOR LIFE TODAY

12. What would it mean for you personally to obey the command in verse 39? What practical significance do these words have for you?

13. Which verse in this chapter do you think God would like you to understand best?

14. Review the guidelines for our thought-life given in Philippians 4:8—"Whatever is true, whatever is noble, whatever is right, whatever is pure, whatever is lovely, whatever is admirable—if anything is excellent or praiseworthy—*think about such things.*" What food for thought can you find in this chapter that especially strikes you as being *true,* or *noble,* or *right,* or *pure,* or *lovely,* or *admirable,* or *excellent,* or *praiseworthy?*

DEUTERONOMY 5

SEEING WHAT'S THERE

1. In Romans 7:12, Paul says that God's commandments are "holy, righteous and good." What specific evidence for that assessment have you seen so far in this book?

2. How many times do you see *fire* mentioned in this chapter?

3. What important point is Moses making in verses 2-3?

4. Compare the wording of the fourth commandment in Exodus 20 with its wording here in verses 12-15 of Deuteronomy 5. What additional phrase is included in this later version (forty years after Mount Sinai), and why do you think it was added?

5. EYE FOR DETAIL—*From what you recall seeing in chapters 6—8, try answering the following question without looking in your Bible:* Which three commandments are the shortest? (See 5:17-19.)

CAPTURE THE ESSENCE

6. In your own words, what would you say is revealed most about God's character and personality in verses 6-10?

7. What do verses 28-29 communicate about God's heart for His people?

8. Which of these Ten Commandments would you say are the easiest for God's people to obey? And which would you say are the most difficult?

9. Which one of these statements would you say best describes the Ten Commandments: (a) the guidelines for Israel to follow in order to remain God's chosen people; (b) the eternal moral principles of the holy God; or (c) a Hebrew version of the law codes that were common throughout the ancient Middle East.

10. Compare the major teachings you remember from Jesus' "Sermon on the Mount" (Matthew 5—7) with what God teaches here in the Ten Commandments. Then decide which of the following statements is the most accurate: (a) The Sermon on the Mount *replaces* the Ten Commandments; (b) The Sermon

on the Mount *negates* the Ten Commandments; (c) The Sermon on the Mount *reflects and parallels* the Ten Commandments; (d) The Sermon on the Mount *deepens* the Ten Commandments.

FOR LIFE TODAY

11. If God wanted you to focus on only one of the Ten Commandments at this time in your life, which one do you think it would be?

12. To what extent would you say verses 32-33 apply to you today?

FOR GOING DEEPER

What happens when we break the Ten Commandments? Use the following references to help you decide—Exodus 32, Joshua 7:19-26, 1 Samuel 2:23-25, 2 Samuel 11-12, 1 Kings 11:1-11, 1 Kings 21:1-19, Jeremiah 14:14-16, Ezekiel 17:15-21, and Ezekiel 22:8-15. For each passage, tell *which* of the Ten Commandments was broken, and what the consequences were for the people involved.

DEUTERONOMY 6

Startup: What do you think is the best definition of *loving God?*

SEEING WHAT'S THERE

1. In your own words, how would you describe the *beauty* of this chapter? What is it that makes this passage so appealing?

2. From what you see in this chapter, how would you summarize the *expectations* God has of His people?

CAPTURE THE ESSENCE

3. What words or phrases in this chapter tell us the most about God's purpose and plan for His people?

4. Verses 4 and 5 have been called "the greatest doctrinal statement in the Old Testament." Why would you say these verses are so significant?

5. Immediately following these words that make up the "greatest doctrinal statement," what commands does God give (in verse 7)?

6. Review Matthew 22:34-40, where Jesus quotes verse 5. From the way Jesus views this verse, how should we understand it today?

7. Which of the Ten Commandments in chapter 5 would you say form the foundation for the teaching given here in chapter 6?

8. Imagine yourself being present in the temple in Jerusalem as the twelve-year-old Jesus hears this chapter read and discussed by the rabbis there. In Luke 2:46 we read that He was listening to these teachers and asking them questions. What verses from this chapter do you think would most impress the boy Jesus, and what questions or comments do you suppose He might have spoken?

FOR LIFE TODAY

9. Choose one of these sentences, and complete it as fully and candidly as you would like: (a) What I see and understand in this chapter is important to my life because… OR: (b) What I see and understand in this chapter does NOT seem important to my life at this time, because…

10. At this time in your life, how would you explain the practical meaning of each part of the command in verse 5? What does it mean in everyday life to love God in this way?

11. Look again at verses 6-7. How often are the words of Scripture heard spoken aloud in your home?

FOR GOING DEEPER

Look again at verses 13 and 16, and then review the circumstances in which Jesus quoted these passages in Matthew 4:7-10. In what ways does the context of each of these chapters—Matthew 4 and Deuteronomy 6—help us to better understand these verses that are included in both chapters?

DEUTERONOMY 7

SEEING WHAT'S THERE

1. From what you've seen so far in Deuteronomy, what parts of this book do you think might be most refreshing to someone who was learning about God for the first time?

2. From what you see in verses 7-10 here in chapter 7, what did God want the people of Israel to understand most about their uniqueness as a nation?

CAPTURE THE ESSENCE

3. Restate in your own words what you believe are the most important truths revealed about God's character and personality in this chapter.

4. In verses 12-26, what does God want us to understand most about His purpose and plan for His people?

5. How would you describe the *quality of life* which God wants His people to experience?

6. What would you say is the major point God is making by including this chapter in the Bible?

FOR LIFE TODAY

7. How well do you know and understand what the Israelites were told to know and understand in verses 10-11?

8. If this chapter were the only portion of Scripture you had access to, how could you use it to help answer this question: *What is the most powerful and effective way to improve my life?*

DEUTERONOMY 8

SEEING WHAT'S THERE

1. From what you see in this chapter, how would you summarize the *expectations* God has of His people?

2. EYE FOR DETAIL— *From what you recall seeing in chapters 6—8, try answering the following question without looking in your Bible:* At the beginning of chapter 7, the names of seven nations are mentioned as those which Israel will drive out of the land God promised to them.

How many of these seven can you name? (See 7:1.)

CAPTURE THE ESSENCE

3. Summarize in your own words what you believe are the most important truths revealed about God's character and personality in this chapter.

4. Look again at verses 10-18. In what ways would you say that wealth and prosperity are dangerous? And according to this passage, how can this danger be avoided?

FOR LIFE TODAY

5. Consider how strongly you desire to know God better, then ask yourself this question: *What are the truths revealed about Him in this chapter which He may want me to understand more deeply at this time in my life?*

6. What practical principle for enjoying life do you see in verse 10?

7. Look at the gift from God described in verse 18. Has this gift been given to you? If so, what is your proper response?

DEUTERONOMY 9

Startup: How would you define the word *righteousness?*

SEEING WHAT'S THERE

1. How many times do you see *fire* mentioned in this chapter?

2. What reminder does God give three times in verses 4-6?

3. How would you summarize the history that Moses gives in verses 7-29?

CAPTURE THE ESSENCE

4. What aspects of God's character and personality would you say He wants us to understand most from verse 3?

5. In the passage beginning in verse 7, Moses speaks of a black spot in Israel's past that he wants the people to never forget. If God had already forgiven them for this sin, why do you think He would want them to still remember it?

6. From what you've seen so far in Deuteronomy (and especially here in chapter 9), would you say that God wants to be considered *primarily* as the

God of His people Israel, or as the God of the whole earth? Explain your answer.

7. Look at verse 20. Why was God angry with Aaron? (See Exodus 32:1-6 and 32:21-25.)

FOR LIFE TODAY

8. If God had written this chapter only for you, which words or phrases do you think He might have underlined, and why?

DEUTERONOMY 10

SEEING WHAT'S THERE

1. What is the best evidence you've seen so far in Deuteronomy of God's faithful love for His people?

2. How would you summarize the history that Moses gives here in chapter 10?

3. What are the biggest promises which you see God making to His people in this chapter?

CAPTURE THE ESSENCE

4. State in your own words what you believe God wants us to understand most about Himself in verses 14-21.

5. In your own words, what would you say God wants us to understand most about Himself in verse 21?

FOR LIFE TODAY

6. Carefully review verses 12-21. Which words in this passage do you think God most wants you to better understand— and put into better practice—at this time in your life?

FOR GOING DEEPER

Look again at the *choice* God makes in verse 15. In the following passages, trace this theme through the entire Bible, and decide how God wants us to think about it— Psalm 33:12 and 135:3-4, Isaiah 41:8-10, John 15:16-19, and 1 Peter 2:9-10.

DEUTERONOMY 11

SEEING WHAT'S THERE

1. Glance over chapters 11—13. What two or three words would you use to best summarize what these chapters seem to be most about?

2. Here in chapter 11, what reason for obeying His commands does God give in verses 8-9?

3. In verses 10-12, how exactly does God describe the land He has promised to His people?

4. What promises does God make to His people in verses 13-15?

5. From what you see in this chapter, how would you summarize the *expectations* God has of His people?

6. EYE FOR DETAIL— *From what you recall seeing in chapters 9—11, try answering the following question without looking in your Bible:* What did Moses do for Aaron after the incident of the golden calf? (See 9:20.)

CAPTURE THE ESSENCE

7. What's the best evidence you see in this chapter of God's grace and God's love?

8. If you were one of the Hebrews listening to Moses give this address, in what way would the words of this chapter impress you? In light of your own personality, which verses here would be most meaningful to you?

FOR LIFE TODAY

9. If God asked you to write a sentence that contained what you believe to be your *duty* in life, how closely would it match the words of verse 1 in this chapter?

10. In Romans 15:4, Paul reminds us that the Old Testament Scriptures can give us patience and perseverance on one hand, as well as comfort and encouragement on the other. In your own life, how do you see this book of Deuteronomy living up to Paul's description? In what ways, if any, is it meeting your personal needs for both *perseverance* and *encouragement?*

DEUTERONOMY 12

Startup: What do you think is the best definition for the word *worship?*

SEEING WHAT'S THERE

1. How many times do you see *blood* mentioned in this chapter?

2. Notice how Israel's place of worship is descried in verses 5, 11, and 21. What conclusions can you make from these verses about God's *name?*

3. Summarize what God says in verses 23-25 about the significance of blood.

CAPTURE THE ESSENCE

4. What would you say is God's *intent* behind the laws in this chapter? What were the most important things He wanted these laws to accomplish?

5. From what you see in this chapter, how accurate is it to say that when the Bible refers to God's *name,* it's another way of saying God's *presence,* and God's *character?*

FOR LIFE TODAY

6. What principles can you learn from this chapter about how God desires to be worshiped?

7. How would you complete this sentence: I am convinced that the *right* way for me to worship God is…

FOR GOING DEEPER

Look again at what God says in verses 23-25 about the significance of blood. How do you see this significance expressed also in Genesis 9:4-6, Leviticus 17:11-12, and especially in Hebrews 9:22?

DEUTERONOMY 13

SEEING WHAT'S THERE

1. What was the prescribed penalty for those who encouraged worship of other gods, according to verses 6-10?

2. What reasons is stated for this penalty in verses 10-11?

CAPTURE THE ESSENCE

3. What is emphasized more in this chapter — God's holy wrath, or God's compassionate love? Or would you say both are equally emphasized? Explain your answer.

4. Which of the Ten Commandments in chapter 5 would you say form the foundation for the teaching given here in this chapter?

5. From what you've seen in chapters 12 and 13, discuss how much you agree or disagree with this statement: It is impossible to truly worship God without an understanding of His holy character.

6. What would you say is the major point God is making by including this chapter in the Bible?

DEUTERONOMY 14

SEEING WHAT'S THERE

1. If this chapter was the only Scripture portion you had ever known, what would you conclude from it about pleasing God?

CAPTURE THE ESSENCE

2. What would you say is God's *intent* behind the laws in this chapter? What were the most important things He wanted these laws to accomplish?

DEUTERONOMY 15

SEEING WHAT'S THERE

1. After reading through this chapter, which words or phrases or sentences here would you most like to understand better?

2. What promises from God do you see in verses 4-6?

3. EYE FOR DETAIL— *From what you recall seeing in chapters 12—15, try answering the following question without looking in your Bible:* What manner of death was prescribed for those who who encouraged the worship of other gods? (See 13:10.)

CAPTURE THE ESSENCE

4. What would you say is God's *intent* behind the laws in this chapter? What were the most important things He wanted these laws to accomplish?

5. In Matthew 23:23, Jesus said the most important aspects of the law are "justice, mercy, and faithfulness." How do you see these important aspects reflected in the laws presented in Deuteronomy?

FOR LIFE TODAY

6. Look again at verses 4-5. In what ways, if any, is it possible for this condition to be achieved today?

DEUTERONOMY 16

Startup: If God asked you, "What are the three things you're most thankful for these days?"—how would you answer?

SEEING WHAT'S THERE

1. What two or three words would you use to best summarize what this chapter is most about?

CAPTURE THE ESSENCE

2. Look at the promise from God in verse 15. What does it reveal about God's desire for His people?

3. What would you say is God's *intent* behind the laws in this chapter? What were the most important things He wanted these laws to accomplish?

4. Discuss how much you agree or disagree with this statement: God designed His laws in Deuteronomy not as a *means* to salvation, but as a *reflection* or *demonstration* of salvation.

DEUTERONOMY 17

SEEING WHAT'S THERE

1. Recall again Paul's statement in Romans 7:12 that God's commandments are "holy, righteous and good." What specific evidence for that assessment do you see in this chapter?

2. What specific means of giving guidance to His people does God set up in this chapter?

CAPTURE THE ESSENCE

3. What would you say is God's *intent* behind the laws in this chapter? What were the most important things He wanted these laws to accomplish?

4. Now that you're halfway through Deuteronomy, how would you summarize the most important teachings in this book?

DEUTERONOMY 18

SEEING WHAT'S THERE

1. What promise does God make in verse 18?

2. From what you see in verses 14-22, what is a suitable definition for the term *prophet?*

CAPTURE THE ESSENCE

3. What would you say is God's *intent* behind the laws in this chapter? What were the most important things He wanted these laws to accomplish?

4. Again, imagine yourself being present in the temple in Jerusalem as the twelve-year-old Jesus hears this chapter read and discussed by the Jewish teachers. What verses in this chapter do you think would most impress Him, and what questions or comments do you suppose He might have spoken?

FOR LIFE TODAY

5. What patterns or principles for government do you see in this chapter that have relevance for us today?

6. In Isaiah 55:10-11, God reminds us that He sends rain and snow from the sky to water the earth and to nurture life. In the same way, God says that He sends His words to accomplish specific purposes. From your study so far, what would you suggest as *God's* primary purposes for the book of Deuteronomy in the lives of Christians today?

FOR GOING DEEPER

Discuss together the prophetic fulfillment of verses 15-19 which you see in John 7:40. How else do you see this prophecy fulfilled in Christ?

DEUTERONOMY 19

SEEING WHAT'S THERE

1. For helpful background on the cities of refuge described in this chapter, what discoveries can you make in Numbers 35:6-34?

2. EYE FOR DETAIL— *From what you recall seeing in chapters 16—19, try answering the following question without looking in your Bible:* What was the prescribed penalty for a person who showed contempt toward one of Israel's judges or priests? (See 17:12.)

CAPTURE THE ESSENCE

3. From what you've seen so far in Deuteronomy, what parts of this book do you think might be most interesting to someone who was reading the Bible for the first time?

4. What would you say is God's *intent* behind the laws here in chapter 19? What were the most important things He wanted these laws to accomplish?

5. What does this chapter communicate to us about God's character?

DEUTERONOMY 20

Startup: What kind of pictures come to your mind when you think of the God as a *warrior*?

SEEING WHAT'S THERE

1. How would you summarize God's guidelines for waging war, as presented in this chapter?

2. How does this chapter demonstrate God's concern for our physical environment on earth?

CAPTURE THE ESSENCE

3. In your own words, what would you say is revealed most about God's character and personality in verse 4?

4. What would you say is God's *intent* behind the laws in this chapter? What were the most important things He wanted these laws to accomplish?

5. What would you say is the major point God is making by including this chapter in the Bible?

DEUTERONOMY 21

SEEING WHAT'S THERE

1. Once more, remember Paul's statement in Romans 7:12 that God's commandments are "holy, righteous and good." What specific evidence for that assessment do you see in this chapter?

CAPTURE THE ESSENCE

2. What would you say is God's *intent* behind the laws in this chapter? What were the most important things He wanted these laws to accomplish?

FOR LIFE TODAY

3. In the area of family relationships, what would you say are the best lessons to learn from this chapter?

DEUTERONOMY 22

CAPTURE THE ESSENCE

1. What would you say is God's *intent* behind the laws in this chapter? What were the most important things He wanted these laws to accomplish?

FOR LIFE TODAY

2. In what way, if any, would you say that the words of Jesus in John 14:15 and John 14:21 have a bearing on the laws of God which we see in the book of Leviticus?

DEUTERONOMY 23

SEEING WHAT'S THERE

1. What two or three words would you use to best summarize what this chapter is most about?

2. For helpful background on the people mentioned in verses 3-4, what can you discover in Genesis 19:36-38 and Numbers 23:7?

CAPTURE THE ESSENCE

3. In this chapter, how do you see God's concern for His people's physical health?

FOR LIFE TODAY

4. Which commands in this chapter would you say are the most important for Christians today to remember and obey?

DEUTERONOMY 24

SEEING WHAT'S THERE

1. In the laws in this chapter, what guidelines do you see for showing personal respect to others?

CAPTURE THE ESSENCE

2. What would you say is God's *intent* behind the laws in this chapter? What were the most important things He wanted these laws to accomplish?

3. Suppose that joining you here today was a Pharisee from the time of Jesus. You tell him you are studying the middle chapters in Deuteronomy, and you ask his opinion about what is most important in these chapters. How do you think he might answer?

4. Suppose also that the apostle Paul was here with you today, and you asked him the same question you asked the Pharisee. How do you think Paul would answer?

FOR LIFE TODAY

5. Which commands in this chapter would you say are the most important for Christians today to remember and obey?

DEUTERONOMY 25

CAPTURE THE ESSENCE

1. What would you say is God's *intent* behind the laws in this chapter? What were the most important things He wanted these laws to accomplish?

FOR LIFE TODAY

2. Which commands in this chapter would you say are the most important for Christians today to remember and obey?

DEUTERONOMY 26

SEEING WHAT'S THERE

1. From what you see in this chapter, how would you summarize the *expectations* God has of His people?

CAPTURE THE ESSENCE

2. Suppose you were a young Hebrew who has listened to Moses speak these words in Deuteronomy. Then you approached Moses and said, "I think you're overdoing it with all these rules and regulations. What difference will they make in the end, anyway? Won't we get along just as well if we just follow common sense and show basic respect for one another?" How do you think Moses would answer?

FOR LIFE TODAY

3. Jesus says in Matthew 5:17-18 that not the least portion of God's law will disappear until "all is accomplished" or "all be fulfilled." What do you think God's laws are meant to accomplish or fulfill? How much, if any, has already been done? How much, if any, is still unfinished?

4. In what ways do you think you should apply the principles in this chapter to your own financial giving to the Lord's work?

DEUTERONOMY 27

SEEING WHAT'S THERE

1. Glance over chapters 27 and 28. What two or three words would you use to best summarize what these chapters are most about?

2. What two mountains are mentioned in chapter 27, and what was to occur on top of each one?

3. EYE FOR DETAIL— *From what you recall seeing in chapters 20—27, try answering the following question without looking in your Bible:* When the tribes of Israel stood on the two mountains to pronounce blessings and curses, which six tribes were to repeat the blessings, and which six were to repeat the curses? (See 27:12-13.)

DEUTERONOMY 28

Startup: In the way we read and study the Bible, what kind of old mental habits or faulty assumptions can most easily block this book of Deuteronomy from coming alive in our minds and hearts?

SEEING WHAT'S THERE

1. If this chapter was the only Scripture portion you had ever known, what would you conclude from it about pleasing God?

2. Recall again that Bible teachers often point out elements in Deuteronomy which are like a treaty or a legal contract. What evidence of this kind do you detect in this chapter?

3. The book of Deuteronomy is often thought of as containing three major "sermons" or "addresses" from Moses. The second of these began in 4:44 and continued through the end of chapter 28. How would you summarize the most important things Moses has talked about in these chapters?

CAPTURE THE ESSENCE

4. Look at verse 1, then discuss how much you agree or disagree with this statement: Blessings *always* follow obedience.

5. If you were one of the Hebrews listening to Moses give this address, which of the promises listed in the first half of this chapter do you think would be the most significant to you? And which of the warnings in the last half of the chapter would be most significant?

6. Think about God's purpose behind the list of blessings and curses in this chapter. What response to this list do you think God most wanted to see in the minds and hearts of His people? Would you say He wanted them to be afraid, or confident, or both? Did He want them to be resolute, or yielding, or both?

FOR LIFE TODAY

7. If you wanted to reword verses 3-6 to indicate in a personal and relevant way God's promised blessings to you, what would this personal statement look like?

DEUTERONOMY 29

SEEING WHAT'S THERE

1. Chapter 29 has been called the key to the book of Deuteronomy. What does this chapter include that could make it this significant?

2. What predictions does Moses make in verses 22-28?

3. In your own words, what would you say is revealed most about God's character and personality in verse 29?

4. Think again of this book as a treaty or a legal contract. What evidence of this kind do you detect in this chapter?

DEUTERONOMY 30

SEEING WHAT'S THERE

1. What predictions does Moses make in this chapter?

2. How many times does God promise His people prosperity in this chapter, based upon their obedience?

3. From what you see in verses 1-6, what can you conclude about God's *mercy?*

4. How would you explain in your own words the action which God takes in verse 6? How does He accomplish this?

5. What are the biggest *promises* which you see God making to His people in this chapter?

6. Think once more of this book as a kind of treaty or legal contract. What evidence of this do you detect in this chapter?

CAPTURE THE ESSENCE

7. In what ways, if any, could you say that the gospel of Christ is foreshadowed in verses 6-10?

8. Review verses 11-14. What are the most significant truths this passage reveals about *God,* and what are the most significant truths it reveals about *us?*

9. Look at how the word *life* is used in verses 15 and 19. What do you think God most wants us to understand about this word? How does He want us to define it?

10. In verse 19, look again at the *choice* which Moses tells the people to make.

Do you think this is meant to be a one-time choice, or a continual choosing?

11. From what you see in this chapter, would you say that Moses already understood the truth about God's law which is stated in Romans 8:3? Why or why not?

12. From what you've seen so far in Deuteronomy, discuss how much you agree or disagree with this statement: God requires the total, absolute commitment of His people; nothing less is acceptable.

13. If you were responsible for giving Moses a job performance review (in his position as the leader of God's people), what comments would you make to him, based on what you have seen so far in Deuteronomy?

FOR LIFE TODAY

14. From what you see in verses 11-14, discuss how much you agree or disagree with this statement: It is always possible for us to obey what God commands.

15. Look again at verse 19. In what ways have you already made this choice? In what ways, if any, should you continue making it?

16. Look at the first sentence in verse 20. How accurate would it be to say these words are also God's personal plan and desire for *you?*

FOR GOING DEEPER

Compare verses 11-14 with the way Paul quotes this passage in Romans 10:6-10. What would you say are the important truths in this passage, as it relates to Christians today?

DEUTERONOMY 31

SEEING WHAT'S THERE

1. From what you see in this chapter, what things does Moses most want the Israelites to remember after he is dead?

2. How many things does Moses tell Joshua to do in this chapter?

3. What specific details about Israel's future does God tell Moses at this time?

4. EYE FOR DETAIL— *From what you recall seeing in chapters 28—31, try answering the following question without looking in your Bible:* How old was Moses at this time? (See 31:2.)

CAPTURE THE ESSENCE

5. In what ways, if any, would you say that this chapter represents a major turning point or significant "hinge" in the history of God's people?

FOR LIFE TODAY

6. In Jeremiah 23:29, God says that His Word is like fire, and like a hammer. He can use the Scriptures to burn away unclean thoughts and desires in our hearts. He can also use Scripture to hit hard like a hammer, with the power to crush our spiritual hardness. From your study in this book of Deuteronomy, how do you most want to see the "fire-and-hammer" power of God's Word at work in your own life?

DEUTERONOMY 32

Startup: What kind of pictures come to your mind when you think of the word *discipline?*

SEEING WHAT'S THERE

1. From what you see in verses 1-43, what are the most important things for the people of Israel at this point to understand about their past? And what are the most important things for them to know and understand about their future?

CAPTURE THE ESSENCE

2. What would you say God wants us to understand most about Himself in verses 3-4, and in verse 39?

3. Songs are often a way to express and release deep emotions. What emotions

would you say are behind the Song of Moses in this chapter?

FOR LIFE TODAY

4. Review again the guidelines for our thought-life given in Philippians 4:8— "Whatever is true, whatever is noble, whatever is right, whatever is pure, whatever is lovely, whatever is admirable—if anything is excellent or praiseworthy— *think about such things.*" What food for thought can you find in this chapter that especially strikes you as being *true,* or *noble,* or *right,* or *pure,* or *lovely,* or *admirable,* or *excellent,* or *praiseworthy?*

DEUTERONOMY 33

SEEING WHAT'S THERE

1. The book of Deuteronomy is often thought of as containing three major "sermons" or "addresses" from Moses. How would you summarize the most important things Moses has talked about since the third of these sermons began in chapter 29?

CAPTURE THE ESSENCE

2. Summarize in your own words what you believe are the most important truths revealed about God's character and personality in verses 1-5, and in verses 26-27.

3. From what you see in this chapter, what does God want life to be like for His people on earth?

4. In what ways would you say that verses 26-29 serve as a fitting climax to all that has happened in the Bible so far—from Genesis to Deuteronomy?

FOR LIFE TODAY

5. From all that you've seen so far in Deuteronomy, what kind of questions or difficulties or doubts in a Christian's daily life do you think this book answers best?

DEUTERONOMY 34

SEEING WHAT'S THERE

1. From what you see in verses 1-5, what do you think may have been the last thing Moses saw before he died?

2. How is Joshua described in verse 9?

3. EYE FOR DETAIL—*From what you recall seeing in chapters 32—34, try answering the following question without looking in your Bible:* How long was the people's time of mourning for Moses? (See 34:8.)

CAPTURE THE ESSENCE

4. Moses is described as a "prophet" in verse 10, and also in 18:18. In what specific ways was he a prophet?

5. Keeping in mind all that you've seen in Deuteronomy, imagine yourself asking Moses this question: *How is it possible for a holy God to have a relationship with sinful people, and to enjoy their true worship?* How do you think Moses would answer?

6. Keeping in mind the lessons he may have learned, suppose Moses was allowed to live his life over again. What, if anything, do you think he would most want to change, and how?

7. Discuss how much you agree or disagree with this statement: In terms of service to God, no one in the Bible except Jesus Himself is greater than Moses.

8. What is the best evidence you've seen in this book that Moses truly loved God?

9. What is the best evidence you've seen in this book that God truly loves His people?

FOR LIFE TODAY

10. Notice how Moses' knowledge of God is described at the end of verse 10. In what ways can we also know God "face to face"? Look at 2 Corinthians 4:6 to help you answer.

11. Think back on all that has happened to the people of Israel in the book of Deuteronomy. If it's true that *the past is a lesson for the future,* then what would you say are the most important lessons for God's people today to learn from these events?

12. If everyone in your church thoroughly understood this book, and they all had a passion for living out its truth in their lives, what kind of practical changes do you think would result?

FOR GOING DEEPER

Look together at the psalm of Moses, Psalm 90. What are the major teachings of that psalm, and how do they match up with what Moses has spoken about in Deuteronomy?

DEUTERONOMY:
THE BIG PICTURE

(Discuss again the questions in the "Overview," plus the questions below.)

1. Imagine that you were helping to produce a film based on the book of Deuteronomy. Describe the kinds of scenery, supporting characters, background music, lighting effects, etc., which you would use to help portray the central message of this book.

2. Look together at each of these passages, and discuss which one you believe is the best candidate for "KEY VERSE" in the book of Deuteronomy —the one which brings into sharpest focus what this book is most about: 6:5, 7:9, 10:12-13, or 30:19-20.

3. What would you say is the main theme (or themes) in the book of Deuteronomy?

4. SEARCH FOR THE SAVIOR—What words, images, or themes in Deuteronomy have reminded you most of Jesus?

5. What do you think is the strongest example in this book of someone doing what was right and good?

6. What do you think is the strongest example in this book of someone doing what was wrong?

7. If this were the only book in the Old Testament, in what ways would it still make a good introduction to the message of Jesus in the New Testament?

8. Based especially on your own experience, complete this statement in the way that's most meaningful for you: I believe it's

important for Christians to read and explore the book of Deuteronomy because...

Joshua

OVERVIEW

(Discuss these OVERVIEW questions both at the beginning of your study of Joshua, then again after you've studied all 24 chapters. Your answers may change significantly once you've looked more closely at the entire book.)

Startup: Talk about the people you've known whom you consider to be outstanding leaders. What were their strongest leadership qualities?

SEEING WHAT'S THERE

1. Look together at these passages to discover more about the man Joshua: Exodus 17:9-14, 24:13-14, and 33:11; Numbers 14:6-9 and 14:38; Deuteronomy 1:37-38, 31:1-8, 31:23, and 34:9.

2. The events recorded in this book are sometimes considered the high point of Israel's spiritual strength and obedience as the people of God. What would be the strongest evidence for this?

3. How would you compare Israel's physical situation at the beginning of the book with her situation at the end of it? (See especially 21:43-45.)

4. How would you compare Israel's *spiritual* situation at the beginning of the book with her situation at the end of it? (See especially 1:16-18 and 24:16-24.)

5. Look also at the list of "Questions to Ask as You Begin Your Study of Each Book" on page 9.

CAPTURE THE ESSENCE

6. What would you consider to be the high points of Joshua's exciting life?

7. How does this book show that the whole world belongs to God?

8. How does this book show God's commitment to His people?

FOR LIFE TODAY

9. God led His people into battle to take back the land of Canaan. As you think about this, discuss how much you agree or disagree with this statement: Only God has the right to decide when a war is truly a just war.

10. In what ways is it easy for you to consider Joshua a personal hero? In what ways is it difficult?

11. From what you see in the Lord's words to Joshua in 1:8, what would be a good personal prayer to offer to God as you study this book?

12. The book of Joshua has been titled "The Book of Conflict and Conquest" and "The Book of Triumph and Victory." With that reputation for this book, what kinds of answers and guidelines and solutions would you like to gain as you examine it more closely?

13. As you think first about *who God is,* and second about *what the Bible is,* how strongly would you rate your present desire to understand better the book of Joshua? Use a scale of one to ten (one = "no desire at all," ten = "extremely intense desire") to help you decide.

FOR GOING DEEPER

How do you think the message of this book compares with what we read in Revelation 19:11-16?

JOSHUA 1

Startup: If you can, describe a time in the past when you knew a certain stage in your life was over, and you needed to press fully ahead into the next stage.

SEEING WHAT'S THERE

1. What reason does God give Joshua and Israel for being strong and courageous? What would be the "secret" of their strength?

2. Think about all that has happened to Israel in the forty years prior to this chapter. What kind of emotions can you imagine the people experiencing when the officers gave them the instructions in verses 10-11?

3. What lessons do you think Israel has learned in the prior forty years in the wilderness?

4. For background information on verses 12-15, what do you see in Numbers 32:1-27?

5. Look also on page 8 at the list of "Questions to Ask as You Study Each Chapter." You may want to look again at this list for each chapter in Joshua.

6. EYE FOR DETAIL—*From what you recall seeing in chapter 1, try answering the following question without looking in your Bible:* Who was the father of Joshua? (See verse 1.)

CAPTURE THE ESSENCE

7. Both God and the people of Israel told Joshua to be strong and brave. Discuss your thoughts on the following question: Do true leaders really need this kind of reminder?

8. From what you see in this chapter, how would you define good leadership?

9. How does God's Word provide strength to His people?

10. Discuss why you agree or disagree with this statement: A Christian must *meditate* on God's Word in order to fully experience true prosperity and success.

FOR LIFE TODAY

11. How would you define true courage? And how would you describe the source of true courage?

12. What do you need most in life: a calling or cause to give yourself to, or the courage to give yourself to a calling or cause that you've already received?

13. In what areas of life do you have a leadership role? As a leader, what needs for encouragement do you have?

14. Practically speaking, how does a person find strength and courage in God?

15. Proverbs 2:1-5 tells about the sincere person who truly longs for wisdom and understanding, and who searches the Scriptures for it—as if it were buried treasure. That person, Solomon says, will come to understand the fear of the Lord, and discover the knowledge of God. As you begin exploring the book of Joshua, what "buried treasure" would you like God to help you find here—to show you what God and His wisdom are really like? If you have this desire, how would you express it in your own words?

FOR GOING DEEPER

The name *Jesus* is the Greek form of the name *Joshua*. In what ways in this chapter do you see that Joshua was like Jesus Christ?

JOSHUA 2

Startup: Has there ever been a time when you felt you had to do something you would normally consider wrong, in order to avoid doing something even worse? If so, tell about it.

SEEING WHAT'S THERE

1. What do you learn about Rahab from Hebrews 11:31 and James 2:25?

2. From the evidence you see here, how would you describe Rahab's character and personality?

3. Summarize in your own words where the two spies went and what happened to them before they returned to Joshua.

4. Look again at verse 24. Compare the report given by the spies here with the report given by the earlier generation of spies (including Joshua and Caleb) in Numbers 13:26-33 and 14:6-9. Discuss what thoughts and emotions Joshua

might have had in each of the two situations.

5. EYE FOR DETAIL— *From what you recall seeing in chapter 2, try answering the following question without looking in your Bible:* After Rahab sent them away from her house, where exactly did the men of Jericho go in search of the two Hebrew spies? (See verse 7.)

CAPTURE THE ESSENCE

6. Discuss why you agree or disagree with this statement: It was wrong for Rahab to lie to the officials of Jericho's king when she said that the two spies from Israel had left.

7. Do you agree with the way the spies handled the situation with Rahab, or do you think you might have responded differently?

8. What do you think is most important about Rahab's understanding of God, as revealed in this chapter?

FOR LIFE TODAY

9. In what ways do you think Rahab's example is a worthy model for us? In what ways, if any, do you think it is not?

FOR GOING DEEPER

Compare Rahab's words about God (in verse 11) with statements made by these other Gentiles: Melchizedek (Genesis 14:18-19), Naaman (2 Kings 5:15), Nebuchadnezzar (Daniel 4:34-37), and Darius (Daniel 6:25-27).

JOSHUA 3

Startup: What do you look for in a leader?

SEEING WHAT'S THERE

1. In what ways was Joshua well trained for his present position of leadership?

2. Describe in your own words the way in which the people of Israel crossed the Jordan River—and why it was important for them to do it that way.

3. EYE FOR DETAIL— *From what you recall seeing in chapter 3, try answering the following question without looking in your Bible:* What was the name of the town where the waters of the Jordan River piled up? (See verse 16.)

CAPTURE THE ESSENCE

4. Why do you think God wanted to "exalt" Joshua? (verse 7) What does this tell you about God's perspective regarding human leaders?

5. How do you think the events of this chapter helped to "exalt" Joshua in the eyes of the people of Israel?

FOR LIFE TODAY

6. How can you "consecrate" yourself (verse 5) for the work God has for you in the immediate future?

FOR GOING DEEPER

In what ways is the message of this book an illustration of the principle found in 2 Corinthians 5:17?

JOSHUA 4

Startup: What are your most important keepsakes—the things you treasure and hold onto because of their "memory value"?

SEEING WHAT'S THERE

1. What do you think is the significance of the way in which the memorial pile of stones was gathered and put together? (verses 1-9, and 20-24)

2. EYE FOR DETAIL— *From what you recall seeing in chapter 4, try answering the following question without looking in your Bible:* Where did the people of Israel camp first after leaving the Jordan River? (See verse 19.)

CAPTURE THE ESSENCE

3. In what ways do you think the events of chapters 3 and 4 were an important part of Israel's preparation for the future?

FOR LIFE TODAY

4. Look again at verse 14. Does God do this with leaders today?

5. We don't always know the reasons behind what God is doing in our lives, but God gave His reasons to Israel in verses 23-24. How do you think the reasons presented there compare to the reasons

God might have for the things He is doing in *your* life right now?

6. What insights do you find in chapters 3—4 regarding the right way to approach God in worship?

7. What insights do you find in chapters 3—4 regarding the sense of mission and unity in a church?

FOR GOING DEEPER

In light of what you see happening in the book of Joshua, what deeper significance do you find in the promises to Abraham found in Genesis 12:1-3, 15:12-16, and 17:7-8?

JOSHUA 5

Startup: In general, do you consider yourself more of a leader or a follower?

SEEING WHAT'S THERE

1. What can you tell about the significance of both circumcision (verses 2-3) and the Passover (verses 10-11) in the history of God's people?

2. What can you tell about the significance of manna (verse 12) in the history of God's people?

3. How do verses 13-15 compare with the experience Moses had in Exodus 3:1-6?

4. EYE FOR DETAIL— *From what you recall seeing in chapter 5, try answering the following question without looking in your Bible:* What happened on the day after the Israelites celebrated the Passover? (See verse 11.)

CAPTURE THE ESSENCE

5. In the first five chapters of Joshua, how have the people of Israel been demonstrating their faith?

6. Summarize how the people of Israel are now prepared—spiritually, militarily, mentally, and physically—for their conquest of Canaan.

7. What do you think was the personal significance for Joshua of his encounter with the commander of the Lord's army in verses 13-15?

FOR LIFE TODAY

8. How well do you feel your church is prepared—spiritually, physically, mentally,

and emotionally—for living out God's will for your church at this time? In what area do you think more preparation might be needed?

9. How well do you feel you're prepared personally—spiritually, physically, mentally, emotionally—for living out God's will for you at this time? In what area do you think more preparation might be needed?

FOR GOING DEEPER

From what you've seen so far in Joshua, how is this book an illustration of the principle found in Philippians 3:12-14.

JOSHUA 6

Startup: Can you describe a time in the past when you learned—perhaps the hard way—the importance of following directions?

SEEING WHAT'S THERE

1. In your own words, what exactly did the Lord command Joshua to do in verses 2-5?

2. Look ahead to 1 Kings 16:34 to see how Joshua's words in Joshua 6:26 were fulfilled. What does this tell you about Joshua?

3. Imagine yourself being a part of the processions described in verses 8-15. In light of your own personality, what thoughts and emotions do you think you would have?

4. For helpful information on Israel's destruction of Jericho in verse 21, what do you discover in Leviticus 27:28-29, and Deuteronomy 13:12-18 and 20:16-18?

5. EYE FOR DETAIL— *From what you recall seeing in chapter 6, try answering the following question without looking in your Bible:* In the people's march around the walls of Jericho, how many priests carried trumpets? (See verse 4.)

CAPTURE THE ESSENCE

6. In verse 2, why do you think the Lord used the past tense in saying He had given Jericho into Israel's hands, instead of saying "I *will* give Jericho into your hands"?

7. Why do you think priests with the ark were told to lead the procession around Jericho's walls, instead of Israel's soldiers?

8. How would you describe God's "military strategy" for His people as they engage in battle to conquer the Promised Land?

9. What do you think are the most important lessons for Israel to learn from their victory over Jericho?

10. How was the battle of Jericho a testing from God for Joshua and Israel?

11. What general principles does this chapter give you regarding God's way of doing things?

FOR LIFE TODAY

12. In what ways do you think of yourself as being in a battle? And what do you think is God's "military strategy" for you?

FOR GOING DEEPER

In what ways is the message of this book an illustration of the principle found in 2 Corinthians 2:14 and Romans 8:37-39?

JOSHUA 7

Startup: In your own life and or in the lives of others you know, how have you seen the continuing tragic consequences of a single sinful act?

SEEING WHAT'S THERE

1. In what ways is this chapter about a test of Joshua's leadership?

2. Discuss any evidence you may have seen in this book that Joshua's fame made him fall into pride.

3. How many negative consequences of Achan's sin can you identify in this chapter?

4. EYE FOR DETAIL— *From what you recall seeing in chapter 7, try answering the following question without looking in your Bible:* What exactly did Achan keep for himself from the plunder at Jericho? (See verse 21.)

CAPTURE THE ESSENCE

5. What reasons would you give in justifying God's anger in verse 1?

6. Imagine yourself as being a part of the group of leaders mentioned in verse 6. In light of your own personality, what thoughts and emotions would you have?

7. What insight does the prayer in verses 6-9 offer into Joshua's heart and character?

8. What insight does God's response in verses 11-15 offer into God's heart and character?

9. Why do you think God required *everyone* to go through the purification or "consecration" mentioned in verse 13? (Compare this verse with the situation in 3:5.)

10. What wrong understanding did Achan have about possessions?

11. How would you explain the correctness of the punishment which God required in verse 15, and which Israel carried out against Achan and his family in verses 24-26?

12. Does this chapter reflect any failure on Joshua's part? Give reasons for your answer.

13. What are the most important lessons for Joshua and Israel to learn from the incidents in this chapter?

FOR LIFE TODAY

14. What kinds of things in our lives can sometimes correspond to the things Achan took and hid?

15. What principles for dealing with sin can you glean from this chapter?

FOR GOING DEEPER

Discuss how this chapter relates to the following passages, each of which includes the execution of someone by stoning: Leviticus 24:10-23, Numbers 15:32-36, and Acts 7:54-60.

JOSHUA 8

Startup: Discuss why you agree or disagree with this statement: I could get along better in life if I received more specific guidance from God.

SEEING WHAT'S THERE

1. How would you compare the "tone" of God's words in verses 1-2 with that of His words in 7:10-15?

2. So far in the book of Joshua, in what different ways have you seen God providing specific guidance for Joshua and Israel?

3. In your own words, describe the strategy Israel followed to win the battle of Ai.

4. How would you summarize what Joshua and Israel have accomplished militarily so far? (It will be helpful to use a Bible atlas as you examine the military campaign described in this book.)

5. For helpful information on verses 30-35, what do you discover in the instructions of Moses in Deuteronomy 11:29-32 and 27:1-8?

6. EYE FOR DETAIL— *From what you recall seeing in chapter 8, try answering the following question without looking in your Bible:* How many people of Ai died in their battle with the Israelites? (See verse 25.)

CAPTURE THE ESSENCE

7. What insight does this chapter offer us for how to deal with past failures and sin?

8. Look at verses 30-35, and also review 4:10-14. In what ways does the success of Joshua and Israel point to the wisdom and successful leadership of Moses?

FOR LIFE TODAY

9. What insights do you find in this chapter about receiving a "second chance" from God after failing at something the first time?

10. What insights do you find in verses 30-35 regarding the right way to approach God in worship?

JOSHUA 9

Startup: Have you ever believed and trusted someone when it would have been wiser not to do so? What lessons have you learned in life about when to trust others, and when not to?

SEEING WHAT'S THERE

1. So far in this book, how have you seen Joshua's leadership develop? What has he been learning?

2. What does this chapter tell us about the values and standards and priorities of Joshua and the leaders of Israel?

3. For helpful information to this chapter, what do you find in Exodus 23:31-33 and 34:11-12, Numbers 33:55, and Deuteronomy 20:16-18?

4. EYE FOR DETAIL— *From what you recall seeing in chapter 9, try answering the following question without looking in your Bible:* After the Gibeonites made a deceptive treaty with Joshua, how many days did it take for the Israelites learned the truth about them? (See verse 16.)

CAPTURE THE ESSENCE

5. Discuss why you agree or disagree with this statement: The incident with Gibeon described in Joshua 9 represents failure on the part of Joshua and Israel.

FOR LIFE TODAY

6. What insight does this chapter offer us about making commitments based on wrong information—and about how to respond when you discover you've made such an unwise commitment?

7. In Jeremiah 23:29, God says that His Word is like fire, and like a hammer. He can use the Scriptures to burn away unclean thoughts and desires in our hearts. He can also use Scripture to hit hard like a hammer, with the power to crush our spiritual hardness. From your study in this book of Joshua, how do you most want to see the "fire-and-hammer" power of God's Word at work in your own life?

Look at the guidelines which Moses taught
the people of Israel in Deuteronomy 4:5-6.
How does that passage relate to Joshua 9?

Look at the guidelines which Moses taught the people of Israel in Deuteronomy 4:5-6. How does that passage relate to Joshua 9?

JOSHUA 10

Startup: Have you ever prayed a prayer that might easily seem ridiculous or foolish to others…and yet God answered it in just the way you requested? If so, tell about the experience.

SEEING WHAT'S THERE

1. At this point in the book, how would you describe Joshua's relationship with God?

2. How would you summarize what Joshua and Israel have accomplished militarily so far?

3. How would you explain the meaning of verse 14?

4. EYE FOR DETAIL— *From what you recall seeing in chapter 10, try answering the following question without looking in your Bible:* How many kings did Joshua defeat on the day the sun stood still? (See verses 16-26.)

CAPTURE THE ESSENCE

5. Why do you think God is continuing to intervene miraculously on behalf of His people, rather than letting them win battles in the "usual" way?

6. Imagine yourself standing within hearing distance of Joshua when he spoke the prayer in verse 12. In light of your own personality, what thoughts would have come to your mind as you heard Joshua pray?

7. What do you think were Joshua's reasons for the public execution of the five enemy kings in verses 22-26?

FOR LIFE TODAY

8. Look again at verses 30, 32, and 42. What has the Lord accomplished in *your* life? What battles has He won for you? What battles is He fighting for you now?

FOR GOING DEEPER

Review the commands given to the people of Israel in Deuteronomy 7:1-6 and 12:1-7.

What are the true reasons for what God is having His people do under Joshua now in the land of Canaan?

JOSHUA 11

Startup (for chapters 11-12): For your own life, how do you define *success?* How would you define it when you think in terms of other people?

SEEING WHAT'S THERE

1. How does this chapter continue patterns of God's guidance and Israel's response which you have seen earlier in this book?

2. How would you summarize what Joshua and Israel have accomplished militarily so far?

3. EYE FOR DETAIL— *From what you recall seeing in chapter 11, try answering the following question without looking in your Bible:* What were the only three cities where the Anakites survived the conquest by the Israelites? (See verse 22.)

CAPTURE THE ESSENCE

4. At this point in this book, how would you evaluate Joshua's leadership? What have been his strong points? Where might he have improved?

FOR LIFE TODAY

5. What appropriate standards or values for your own daily life can you draw from Joshua's example in verse 15?

FOR GOING DEEPER

Compare verses 19-20 to the story of Pharaoh in the time of Moses, especially in Exodus 7:1-4 and 14:8. How were the situations of Pharaoh and the Canaanite kings the same, and how were they different?

JOSHUA 12

CAPTURE THE ESSENCE

1. How does this chapter bring together the work of Moses and Joshua?

FOR LIFE TODAY

2. Look again at the list of defeated kings in verses 9-24, and imagine them as a list of the "enemies" which God has overcome in your life—bad habits, temptations, and other spiritual dangers. What specific things would be on the list?

3. In Romans 15:4, Paul reminds us that the Old Testament Scriptures can give us patience and perseverance on one hand, as well as comfort and encouragement on the other. In your own life, how do you see this book of Joshua living up to Paul's description? In what ways, if any, is it meeting your personal needs for both *perseverance* and *encouragement*?

FOR GOING DEEPER

In light of what has happened so far in the book of Joshua, look back at the promises God made to Moses in Exodus 3:7-8 and 33:1-2.

JOSHUA 13

Startup: Which is harder for you: to take on a new, very challenging task, or to keep going in an old task that has dragged on much longer than you anticipated?

CAPTURE THE ESSENCE

1. What do verses 1-7 indicate about the work still remaining for Joshua and Israel to do?

2. What do you think is the significance of verse 13? (Look ahead also to 15:63, 16:10, and 17:12-13.)

3. With chapter 13, we come to a major division in the book of Joshua. In only a few sentences, how would you summarize the most important things that have happened so far in this book?

FOR LIFE TODAY

4. What further spiritual victories still need to be won in your life? What "unconquered lands" need to be conquered?

5. In Isaiah 55:10-11, God reminds us that He sends rain and snow from the sky to water the earth and to nurture life. In the same way, God says that He sends His words to accomplish specific purposes. From your study so far, what would you suggest as *God's* primary purposes for the book of Joshua in the lives of Christians today?

FOR GOING DEEPER

How have you seen this book of Joshua living up to the description of Old Testament Scriptures in Romans 15:4?

JOSHUA 14

Startup (for chapters 14-19): What older people do you know who impress you with their vigor? What do you think are the keys to remaining strong—mentally, physically, emotionally, and spiritually—in old age?

SEEING WHAT'S THERE

1. Review together Caleb's story in Numbers 13—14. What personality traits do you see in Caleb both there and in Joshua 14?

2. EYE FOR DETAIL—*From what you recall seeing in chapter 14, try answering the following question without looking in your Bible:* How old was Caleb when Joshua gave him the city of Hebron? (See verse 10.)

CAPTURE THE ESSENCE

3. What impresses you about Caleb?

FOR LIFE TODAY

4. In practical terms, what do you think it really means for us to follow the Lord "fully" or "wholeheartedly," as Caleb did (verse 14)?

JOSHUA 15

SEEING WHAT'S THERE

1. What else do you find out about Caleb in this chapter?

CAPTURE THE ESSENCE

2. Why do you think God gave the tribes of Israel such specific details regarding the boundaries of their territory?

FOR GOING DEEPER

What else do you learn about Othniel (mentioned in verse 17) in Judges 3:7-11?

JOSHUA 16

SEEING WHAT'S THERE

1. For helpful information on the tribes of Ephraim and Manasseh, what can you find out about these two men in Genesis 48:1-20?

JOSHUA 17

SEEING WHAT'S THERE

1. For helpful information on verses 3-6, what do you see in Numbers 27:1-11?

CAPTURE THE ESSENCE

2. From what you see of the man Joshua in this chapter, how would you describe the style and the effectiveness of his leadership?

JOSHUA 18

SEEING WHAT'S THERE

1. What do you learn about Joshua's leadership in the first half of this chapter?

CAPTURE THE ESSENCE

2. Look at verse 6, and compare it with Joshua 14:1-2. What do these verses together say about *how* God controlled the allotment of the land to Israel's tribes?

FOR GOING DEEPER

Listen to David's prayer of contentment in Psalm 16:5-6. How do David's words relate to (a) what is happening to Israel in the book of Joshua, and (b) what is happening in your life today?

JOSHUA 19

SEEING WHAT'S THERE

1. EYE FOR DETAIL— *From what you recall seeing in chapter 19, try answering the following question without looking in your Bible:* What town was Joshua given? (See verse 50.)

CAPTURE THE ESSENCE

2. The last three verses in this chapter close out the description of the allotment of the land, a description that began with chapter 14. Notice in chapter 14 whose allotment is mentioned *first,* and at the end of chapter 19, whose allotment is mentioned *last.* What did these two men have in common?

3. At the end of verse 50, notice the work which Joshua now did. How do you think he might have felt about this work, after all that he had done in leading Israel?

FOR GOING DEEPER

Look ahead to the place mentioned in Joshua 24:29-30. During Joshua's lifetime, and after he had settled here, what kind of emotions do you think he would have had toward this place?

JOSHUA 20

Startup (for chapters 20-22): What does the word *refuge* mean to you?

SEEING WHAT'S THERE

1. For the reference in verse 2 regarding God's instructions to Moses, look at Numbers 35:6-34.

CAPTURE THE ESSENCE

2. From what you see in this chapter, discuss how much (and *why*) you agree or disagree with this statement: God cares more about mercy than He does about justice.

FOR LIFE TODAY

3. What principles can you draw from this chapter which you believe relate well to the legal system in our society today?

From God's point of view and from Israel's point of view, what is the significance of the "cities of refuge"? Compare what you see about them in this chapter with what you see in the following passages—Exodus 21:12-14; Numbers 35:6-34; and Deuteronomy 4:41-43 and 19:1-13.

JOSHUA 21

SEEING WHAT'S THERE

1. Verses 43-45 are the climax of the book of Joshua. Summarize this passage in your own words.

CAPTURE THE ESSENCE

2. What do verses 43-45 tell us about God's character?

3. From what you see in verses 43-45, how would you explain the further work required in Joshua 23:4-5?

FOR LIFE TODAY

4. From what you see in this chapter, what *expectations* can we rightly have of God?

FOR GOING DEEPER

Look again at verse 44, and discuss it in light of Hebrews 4:8-11.

JOSHUA 22

SEEING WHAT'S THERE

1. What is the basic misunderstanding presented in this chapter?

2. EYE FOR DETAIL—*From what you recall seeing in chapter 22, try answering the following question without looking in your Bible:* Who was the priest who led the Israelite delegation in a meeting with the tribes from the west side of the Jordan? (See verse 13.)

FOR LIFE TODAY

3. What principles for right relationships can you see represented in verses 30-34?

FOR GOING DEEPER

From what you see in verses 30-32, how would you describe the character of Phinehas? For more information on this man, look at Numbers 25:10-13 and 31:6, Judges 20:27-28, and Psalm 106:28-31.

JOSHUA 23

Startup: In the way we read and study the Bible, what kind of old mental habits or faulty assumptions can most easily block this book of Joshua from coming alive in our minds and hearts?

SEEING WHAT'S THERE

1. At this point in this book, how would you evaluate Joshua's leadership? What have been his strong points? Where might he have improved?

2. How would you describe Joshua's relationship with God?

CAPTURE THE ESSENCE

3. In Joshua's thinking, what are the most important lessons for Israel to learn from the experiences described in this book?

4. Imagine yourself as one of the leaders of Israel gathered together to hear this farewell speech from Joshua. In light of your own personality, what words spoken by Joshua stand out most to you?

FOR LIFE TODAY

5. Choose one of these sentences, and complete it as fully and candidly as you would like: (a) What I see and understand in this chapter is important to my life because… OR: (b) What I see and understand in this chapter does NOT seem important to my life at this time, because…

6. Look again at verses 9-11. In what ways are you convinced that God is "fighting" for you? In what areas do you need more confidence of His involvement?

FOR GOING DEEPER

Evaluate verse 11 in light of these New Testament verses: Mark 12:30, John 14:23, and 1 John 4:20.

JOSHUA 24

Startup: Discuss why you agree or disagree with this statement: All true happiness and fulfillment in my life is a result of the choices I make.

SEEING WHAT'S THERE

1. What did Joshua and the people of Israel gain by following the Lord? And what did it cost them?

2. At this point in their history, how prepared are the people of Israel for facing the future with confidence? Do you think anything necessary has been left out of their preparation?

3. EYE FOR DETAIL— *From what you recall seeing in chapter 24, try answering the following question without looking in your Bible:* What was the name of the place where the events of this chapter took place? (See verse 1.)

CAPTURE THE ESSENCE

4. From what you see in the final chapters of this book, what conditions must Israel meet in order to continue enjoying God's blessing in the Promised Land?

5. The final verses of the book, 24:28-33, may have been written by someone such as Phinehas, the high priest mentioned in the last line. Joshua is called "the servant of the Lord" in verse 29. Together, compare this verse to Deuteronomy 34:5, Genesis 26:24, 2 Samuel 7:5, and Romans 1:1. What do you think qualifies a person to be called "God's servant"?

6. What significance do you find in the mention of the burial places for Joshua, Joseph, and Eleazar (verses 30-33)?

7. Look ahead to the summary of the book of Joshua in Judges 2:6-7. How does that passage reflect the most important themes in Joshua?

FOR LIFE TODAY

8. God may be asking you to make some important decisions in your life at this time—if not now, then perhaps soon. What helpful guidelines for making correct decisions do you see in this chapter, or earlier in Joshua?

9. What are the most practical ways in which you can pattern your life and leadership after the example of Joshua?

FOR GOING DEEPER

Look again at verses 14-15, and evaluate them in light of these New Testament verses: Matthew 6:24, John 7:17, James 4:4, and 1 Peter 4:3.

JOSHUA:
THE BIG PICTURE

(Discuss again the questions in the "Overview," plus the questions below.)

1. For getting the most from the book of Joshua, one of the best guidelines is found in 2 Timothy 3:16-17, words which Paul wrote with the Old Testament first in view. He said that *all* Scripture is of great benefit to (a) teach us, (b) rebuke us, (c) correct us, and (d) train us in righteousness. Paul added that these Scriptures completely equip the person of God "for every good work." As you think seriously about those guidelines, in which of these areas do you especially see the usefulness of Joshua?

2. Imagine that you were helping produce a film based on the book of Joshua. Describe the kinds of scenery, supporting characters, background music, lighting effects, etc., which you would use to help portray the central message of this book.

3. Look together at each of these passages, and discuss which one you believe is the best candidate for "KEY VERSE" in the book of Joshua—the one which brings into sharpest focus what this book is most about—1:9, 1:11, 4:24, 11:15, or 21:45.

4. What four-to-eight-word title would you give to this book, to best summarize its content and significance?

5. What would you say are the most important ways in which this book is *unique* in all the Bible?

6. What to you personally is the strongest example in this book of someone doing what was right and good?

7. What to you personally is the strongest example in this book of someone doing what was wrong?

8. From the teaching and the examples you've seen in this book, what *expectations* would you say God has of Christian leaders?

9. If everyone in your church thoroughly understood the book of Joshua, and you all had a passion for living out its truth in their lives, what kind of practical changes do you think would result?

10. From what you've seen in this book, what are the most important ways in which Joshua and Jesus are alike?

11. SEARCH FOR THE SAVIOR—What words, images, or themes in Joshua have reminded you most of Jesus?

12. If Joshua were the only book in the Old Testament, in what ways would it still make a good introduction to the message of Jesus in the New Testament?

13. Based especially on your experience in studying Joshua, complete this statement in the way that's most meaningful to you: I believe it is important for Christians to study the Old Testament because...

Judges

❖

OVERVIEW

(Discuss these OVERVIEW questions both at the beginning of your study of Judges, then again after you've studied all 21 chapters. Your answers may change significantly once you've looked more closely at the entire book.)

Startup: Talk together about times in your life when you've especially learned that there are always consequences for our wrongdoing. What were the circumstances that taught you this lesson?

SEEING WHAT'S THERE

1. Before launching into a closer look at Judges, how would you summarize what you already know about this book?

2. What phrase is repeated as a description of God's people in 3:7, 3:12, 4:1, 6:1, 10:6, and 13:1? What clues does it offer about the central message of Judges?

3. Find the phrase that reoccurs in the following verses—17:6, 18:1, 19:1, and 21:25. What clues does this phrase offer about the central message of this book?

4. Look also at the list of "Questions to Ask as You Begin Your Study of Each Book" on page 9.

FOR LIFE TODAY

5. The book of Judges has been called "A Book of Heroes," "A Book about Sin and Its Consequences," "The Monotony and Misery of Sin," "The Folly of Forsaking God," and "The Book of Decline and Apostasy." With that reputation for this book, what kinds of answers and guidelines and solutions would you like to gain as you examine it more closely?

6. From what you see in the example of the Israelites in 2:10-13, what would be a good personal prayer to offer to God as you study this book?

7. As you think first about *who God is,* and second about *what the Bible is,* how strongly would you rate your present desire to understand better the book of Judges? Use a scale of one to ten (one = "no desire at all," ten = "extremely intense desire") to help you decide.

JUDGES 1

SEEING WHAT'S THERE

1. What question do the Israelites ask God as this book opens, and how does God answer them?

2. What indications do you see in this chapter of God's direct involvement with His people?

3. What "danger signals" do you see in this chapter that all may not go well for Israel in the book of Judges?

4. Look also on page 8 at the list of "Questions to Ask as You Study Each Chapter." You may want to look again at this list for each chapter in Judges.

5. EYE FOR DETAIL—*From what you recall seeing in chapter 1, try answering the following question without looking in your Bible:* Who was Othniel's father-in-law? (See verses 12-13.)

CAPTURE THE ESSENCE

6. What would you say is the main point being made in verses 27-36?

7. Discuss how much you agree or disagree with this statement: From God's perspective, incomplete obedience on our part is no better than total disobedience.

FOR LIFE TODAY

8. Think again about the example of the tribes of Israel in the last part of this chapter. In your life, are there any major

tasks facing you right now that you consider incomplete? If so, what are they?

9. Proverbs 2:1-5 tells about the sincere person who truly longs for wisdom and understanding, and who searches the Scriptures for it—as if it were buried treasure. That person, Solomon says, will come to understand the fear of the Lord, and discover the knowledge of God. As you begin exploring the book of Judges, what "buried treasure" would you like God to help you find here—to show you what God and His wisdom are really like? If you have this desire, how would you express it in your own words?

FOR GOING DEEPER

Look together at Deuteronomy 7:1-2 and 20:16-18. What commands there relate directly to what you see happening in the book of Judges?

JUDGES 2

SEEING WHAT'S THERE

1. Chapter 2 has been called the key to the book of Judges. What does this chapter include that could make it this significant?

2. What important message does the angel of the Lord tell the Israelites in verses 1-3, and how do they respond?

3. Verses 11-19 outline a pattern that is repeated throughout this book. Look carefully at this passage, and summarize step-by-step what happens in this pattern.

4. What specific judgment does God speak upon Israel in verses 20-22, and what reasons does He give for it?

5. EYE FOR DETAIL—*From what you recall seeing in chapter 2, try answering the following question without looking in your Bible:* What was the name of the place where the angel of the Lord gave his message to the Israelites? (See verses 1 and 5.)

CAPTURE THE ESSENCE

6. What do you think is the correct answer to the question the angel asks at the end of verse 2?

7. Would you say the people's tears in verse 4 were genuine, or false? Explain your answer.

8. Summarize in your own words what you believe are the most important truths revealed about God's character and personality in this chapter.

9. In what ways, if any, would you say that this chapter represents a major turning point or significant "hinge" in the history of God's people?

10. Imagine yourself being present in the temple in Jerusalem as the twelve-year-old Jesus hears this chapter read and discussed by the rabbis there. In Luke 2:46 we read that He was listening to these teachers and asking them questions. What verses from this chapter do you think would most impress the boy Jesus, and what questions or comments do you suppose He might have spoken?

FOR LIFE TODAY

11. Look again at verses 1-3. Which word or phrase in this passage do you think God would like you to understand best?

12. Discuss how much you agree or disagree with this statement: Whenever we aren't enjoying God's blessings, our disobedience to Him is always the cause.

JUDGES 3

SEEING WHAT'S THERE

1. Beginning with verse 7, we come to a major division in the book of Judges. In only a few sentences, how would you summarize the most important things that have happened so far in this book?

2. A recurring pattern in Judges is (a) Israel sins, (b) Israel is oppressed by an enemy, and (c) Israel is delivered through a leader chosen by God. Where in chapter 3 do you see elements of that pattern?

3. In verses 1-4, what does God do, and what are His reasons for doing it?

4. What repeated action by the people of Israel do you see in verses 9 and 15?

5. What specific action does God's Spirit accomplish in verse 10?

6. In verses 16-29, how would you summarize Ehud's strategy for defeating the king of Eglon?

7. EYE FOR DETAIL— *From what you recall seeing in chapter 3, try answering the following question without looking in your Bible:* After Othniel's victory over the king of Aram, for how many years did Israel enjoy peace? (See verse 11.)

CAPTURE THE ESSENCE

8. In verse 8, what verb is used to depict God's actions? (Notice also how it is used in 2:14, 4:2, and 10:7.) Why do you think this particular word is used? What does it call to mind?

FOR GOING DEEPER

Examine these verses to see how they show God's Spirit at work in the time of the Judges—3:10, 6:34, 11:29, 13:25, 14:6, 14:19, and 15:14.

JUDGES 4

Startup: When you get to heaven, and you meet Deborah, what's the first question you'd like to ask her?

SEEING WHAT'S THERE

1. What are the most important decisions and choices that are made in this chapter, and how would you analyze each one?

2. Recall again the recurring pattern in Judges: (a) Israel sins, (b) Israel is oppressed by an enemy, and (c) Israel is delivered through a leader chosen by God. Where in chapter 4 do you see elements of that pattern?

3. What do God's people do in verse 3?

4. Summarize the story of Deborah, keeping in mind that no historical account can include every detail of the events it describes. What are the most important details which *are* included here? And what kinds of details are left out, details which might otherwise be quite interesting to us? What does this selection process tell you about what God wants us to understand most from this story?

5. EYE FOR DETAIL— *From what you recall seeing in chapter 4, try answering the following question without looking in your Bible:* How many chariots did Jabin king of Canaan have? (See verse 3.)

CAPTURE THE ESSENCE

6. If you could go back in time, and God brought you into the events of this chapter to act as a personal counselor to Barak, what kind of counsel would you give him, and how would you express it?

FOR LIFE TODAY

7. What would you say are the most useful and important lessons to learn from Deborah's example in this chapter?

JUDGES 5

SEEING WHAT'S THERE

1. In what ways does the song in this chapter make mention of God? What does it say about Him?

2. EYE FOR DETAIL— *From what you recall seeing in chapter 5, try answering the following question without looking in your Bible:* What color are the donkeys mentioned in the song of Deborah and Barak? (See verse 10.)

CAPTURE THE ESSENCE

3. Songs are often a way to express and release deep emotions. What emotions do you think were behind the song that Deborah and Barak sing in this chapter?

4. From what you see in this chapter, would you say that God wants to be considered *primarily* as the God of His people Israel, or as the God of the whole earth? Explain your answer.

FOR LIFE TODAY

5. In Jeremiah 23:29, God says that His Word is like fire, and like a hammer. He can use the Scriptures to burn away unclean thoughts and desires in our hearts. He can also use Scripture to hit hard like a hammer, with the power to crush our spiritual hardness. From your study in this book of Judges, how do you most want to see the "fire-and-hammer" power of God's Word at work in your own life?

JUDGES 6

Startup: When you get to heaven, and you meet Gideon, what's the first question you'd like to ask him?

SEEING WHAT'S THERE

1. Imagine that you live in Israel but are a spy for the Midianites. You send back regular reports to your leaders about your observations. What would you tell them about the events recorded in this chapter?

2. Remember again the pattern in Judges: (a) Israel sins, (b) Israel is oppressed by an enemy, and (c) Israel is delivered through a leader chosen by God. Where in chapter 6 do you see elements of this pattern?

3. What do God's people do in verses 6-7?

4. Look at what God's prophet said to the Israelites in verses 7-10. Would you say it's best to categorize these words as a warning, a reminder, a promise, or a rebuke?

5. What specific commands did the Lord give to Gideon in this chapter, and how does Gideon respond to each one?

6. What specific action does God's Spirit accomplish in verse 34?

7. EYE FOR DETAIL— *From what you recall seeing in chapter 6, try answering the following question without looking in your Bible:* What did Gideon call the altar he built? (See verse 24.)

CAPTURE THE ESSENCE

8. How would you summarize what Gideon learns most about God in this chapter?

FOR LIFE TODAY

9. Look again at the words of God's prophet in verses 7-10. Then discuss together how you would complete this sentence: What God really wants from me is...

10. Look also at the angel's words to Gideon in verse 12. To what extent would you say that this statement is also God's statement to you?

11. What can you learn about faith from Gideon's example in this chapter?

JUDGES 7

SEEING WHAT'S THERE

1. How would you summarize God's strategy for defeating the Midianites? And by what methods and stages did he reveal that strategy to Gideon?

2. What specific commands does God give to Gideon in this chapter?

3. Summarize the story of Gideon in this book, once again keeping in mind that no historical account can include every detail of the events it describes. What are the most important details which *are* included here? And what kinds of details are left out, details which might otherwise be quite interesting to us? What does this selection process tell you about what God wants us to understand most from this story?

4. EYE FOR DETAIL— *From what you recall seeing in chapter 7, try answering the following question without looking in your Bible:* What was the dream that the man told his fellow Midianite? (See verse 13.)

CAPTURE THE ESSENCE

5. If you were giving Gideon a job performance review (in his positions as a servant of God and leader of God's people), what comments would you make to him, based on what you see in this chapter?

6. How would you summarize what Gideon learns most about God in this chapter?

FOR LIFE TODAY

7. Choose one of these sentences, and complete it as fully and candidly as you would like: (a) What I see and understand in this chapter is important to my life because... OR: (b) What I see and understand in this chapter does NOT seem important to my life at this time, because...

JUDGES 8

SEEING WHAT'S THERE

1. Imagine again that you live in Israel, but as a spy for her enemies. You send back regular reports to your leaders about your observations. What would you tell them about the events recorded in this chapter?

2. How would you summarize the actions which Gideon takes in this chapter as the leader of God's people?

3. In verses 22-24, what request do the people make of Gideon, and how does he respond?

4. How is Israel's spiritual condition described at the end of this chapter?

5. EYE FOR DETAIL— *From what you recall seeing in chapter 8, try answering the following question without looking in your Bible:* How many sons did Gideon have? (See verse 30.)

CAPTURE THE ESSENCE

6. Look at the last sentence in Gideon's statement in verse 23. How well do you think these words capture the main point of why God included this book of Judges in the Bible? Explain your answer.

7. In Matthew 6:33, Jesus tells us to "seek first the kingdom of God and His righteousness." What can you learn about God's kingdom in this book of Judges?

8. Review verses 28-33. Keeping in mind the possible lessons he had learned, suppose Gideon was allowed to live his life over again. What, if anything, do you think he would most want to change, and how?

FOR LIFE TODAY

9. In Romans 15:4, Paul reminds us that the Old Testament Scriptures can give us patience and perseverance on one hand, as well as comfort and encouragement on the other. In your own life, how do you see this book of Judges living up to Paul's description? In what ways, if any, is it meeting your personal needs for both *perseverance* and *encouragement?*

JUDGES 9

Startup: In the way we read and study the Bible, what kind of old mental habits or faulty assumptions can most easily block this book of Judges from coming alive in our minds and hearts?

SEEING WHAT'S THERE

1. To review, retrace your way through the last few chapters. What are the most important things that have happened since Gideon first appeared on the scene?

2. What human actions in this chapter do you think were most pleasing to God? And which do you think were most displeasing?

3. In verses 56-57, how would you summarize God's perspective on the events of this chapter?

CAPTURE THE ESSENCE

4. What conclusions would you make from this chapter about the character of Abimelech? How would you compare him with his father, Gideon?

5. If you could go back in time, and God brought you into the events of this chapter to act as a personal counselor to Abimelech, what kind of counsel would you give him, and how would you express it?

6. As you think about the overall story unfolding in the book of Judges, what important step in that unfolding is played by the story of Abimelech? Do you see a strategic *purpose* which this account serves in the larger picture?

FOR LIFE TODAY

7. What would you say are the most useful and important lessons to learn from the mistakes in this chapter?

JUDGES 10

SEEING WHAT'S THERE

1. Remember once more the pattern of (a) Israel sins, (b) Israel is oppressed by an enemy, and (c) Israel is delivered through a leader chosen by God. Where in chapter 10 do you see elements of this pattern?

2. What do God's people do in verse 10?

3. Look at God's words in verses 11-14. Would you say it's best to categorize these words as a warning, a reminder, a promise, or a rebuke?

FOR LIFE TODAY

4. Look again at God's words in verses 11-14. Then discuss together how you would complete this sentence: What God really wants from me is…

5. In Isaiah 55:10-11, God reminds us that He sends rain and snow from the sky to water the earth and to nurture life. In the same way, God says that He sends His words to accomplish specific purposes. From your study so far, what would you suggest as *God's* primary purposes for the book of Judges in the lives of Christians today?

JUDGES 11

SEEING WHAT'S THERE

1. Reflect again on this book's pattern of (a) Israel sins, (b) Israel is oppressed by an enemy, and (c) Israel is delivered through a leader chosen by God. Where in chapter 11 do you see elements of this pattern?

2. What are the major points in Israel's history that Jephthah recounts in verses 14-27?

3. What specific action does God's Spirit accomplish in verse 29?

CAPTURE THE ESSENCE

4. What would you say is the major point God is making by including in the Bible the incident about Jephthah's daughter in verses 34-40?

5. Now that you're halfway through Judges, how would you summarize the most im-portant lessons for us to learn in this book?

FOR LIFE TODAY

6. What would you say are the most useful and important lessons to learn from the example of Jephthah in this chapter?

JUDGES 12

SEEING WHAT'S THERE

1. Where in chapter 12 do you see elements of this pattern: (a) Israel sins, (b) Israel is oppressed by an enemy, and (c) Israel is delivered through a leader chosen by God?

2. EYE FOR DETAIL— *From what you recall seeing in chapter 13, try answering the following question without looking in your Bible:* What was the "password" which the Gileadites asked for at the ford of the Jordan? (See verse 6.)

CAPTURE THE ESSENCE

3. Review verse 7. Keeping in mind the possible lessons he had learned, suppose Jephthah was allowed to live his life over again. What, if anything, do you think he would most want to change, and how?

JUDGES 13

Startup: How long have you known about the story of Samson? What are some of the earliest impressions this story left with you?

SEEING WHAT'S THERE

1. Where in chapter 13 do you see this pattern: (a) Israel sins, (b) Israel is oppressed by an enemy, and (c) Israel is delivered through a leader chosen by God?

2. What specific action does God's Spirit accomplish in the last verse of this chapter?

3. EYE FOR DETAIL— *From what you recall seeing in chapter 13, try answering the following question without looking in your Bible:* What tribe was Samson's family from? (See verse 2.)

4. What impresses you most about Manoah and his wife?

JUDGES 14

SEEING WHAT'S THERE

1. Who is the most important person in this chapter, and what are the most important things that happen to him?

2. What specific action does God's Spirit accomplish in verses 6 and 19?

3. EYE FOR DETAIL— *From what you recall seeing in chapter 14, try answering the following question without looking in your Bible:* What gift did Samson promise his companions if they guessed his riddle in seven days? (See verse 12.)

CAPTURE THE ESSENCE

4. If you could go back in time, and God brought you into the events of this chapter to act as a personal counselor to Samson, what kind of counsel would you give him, and how would you express it?

JUDGES 15

SEEING WHAT'S THERE

1. What do the events of this chapter reveal about Samson's character and personality?

2. What specific action does God's Spirit accomplish in verse 14?

3. EYE FOR DETAIL— *From what you recall seeing in chapter 15, try answering the following question without looking in your Bible:* How many foxes did Samson send into the fields of the Philistines? (See verse 4.)

CAPTURE THE ESSENCE

4. From what you see in Samson's prayer in verse 18, what are the most important things he understands about God's personality and character?

FOR GOING DEEPER

Look again at verse 14, and recall also other passages in Judges where you've seen the Holy Spirit at work. How does the Spirit's work in these Old Testament times compare to what He did in New Testament times? What similarities and differences do you see in the following passages—Acts 1:8, 2:2-4, 10:38, 10:44-46, 11:28, 13:9-11, and 19:6, and Romans 1:4 and 15:18-19?

JUDGES 16

SEEING WHAT'S THERE

1. What are the most important decisions and choices that are made in this chapter, and how would you analyze each one?

2. Summarize the story of Samson in this book, once again keeping in mind that no historical account can include every detail of the events it describes. What are the most important details which *are* included here? And what kinds of details are left out, details which might otherwise be quite interesting to us? What does this selection process tell you about what God wants us to understand most from this story?

3. EYE FOR DETAIL— *From what you recall seeing in chapter 16, try answering the following question without looking in your Bible:* How many braids were in Samson's hair? (See verse 13.)

CAPTURE THE ESSENCE

4. Look again at verses 30-31. Keeping in mind the possible lessons he had learned, suppose Samson was allowed to live his life over again. What, if anything, do you think he would most want to change, and how?

5. From what you see in Samson's prayer in verses 28 and 30, what are the most important things he understands about God's personality and character?

JUDGES 17

Startup: In recent years, have there been any changes in your understanding of what is *right* and what is *wrong?* If so, what brought about these changes?

SEEING WHAT'S THERE

1. With chapter 17, we begin a major new division in the book of Judges. In only a few sentences, how would you summarize the most important things that have happened so far in this book?

2. What things in this chapter do you see Micah doing wrong?

JUDGES 18

SEEING WHAT'S THERE

1. How would you summarize what the tribe of Dan does in this chapter?

2. What do the Israelites ask God in verse 18, and how does God answer? (Compare this account with the way the book of Judges begins, in 1:1-2.)

3. EYE FOR DETAIL— *From what you recall seeing in chapter 18, try answering the following question without looking in your Bible:* How many warriors from the tribe of Dan are mentioned as going from Dan to Ephraim? (See verse 11.)

CAPTURE THE ESSENCE

4. How would you describe the spiritual condition of the people mentioned in this chapter?

JUDGES 19

Startup: What is the most interesting thing you've read in the Bible in the past week?

SEEING WHAT'S THERE

1. What are the most important decisions and choices that are made in this chapter, and how would you analyze each one?

FOR LIFE TODAY

2. What would you say are the most useful and important lessons to learn from the mistakes in this chapter?

JUDGES 20

SEEING WHAT'S THERE

1. Humanly speaking, what would you say is the best thing anybody does in this chapter? And what is the worst or most questionable thing anybody does in this chapter?

2. EYE FOR DETAIL— *From what you recall seeing in chapter 20, try answering the following question without looking in your Bible:* How many Israelite soldiers assembled at Mizpah? (See verse 2.)

CAPTURE THE ESSENCE

3. What emotions do you think God Himself may have been experiencing during the events of this chapter?

JUDGES 21

SEEING WHAT'S THERE

1. What do the events of this chapter say about the spiritual and moral conditions of Israel at this time?

2. What would you say is the main point God is making by including this last chapter of Judges in the Bible?

FOR LIFE TODAY

3. Think back on all that has happened to the people of Israel in the book of Judges. If it's true that *the past is a lesson for the future,* then what would you say are the most important lessons for God's people today to learn from these events?

FOR GOING DEEPER

How many people from the book of Judges do you see listed by name in Hebrews 11:32? And which comments in the rest of that chapter (11:33-40) would you say are especially fitting for the people from Judges who are named?

JUDGES:

THE BIG PICTURE

(Discuss again the questions in "Judges: An Overview," plus the questions below.)

1. Who would you say are the most important individuals whose stories are told in the book of Judges? And in what order would you rank them, according to their importance to this book?

2. How would you summarize the most important lessons this book teaches about sin and disobedience?

3. For getting the most from the book of Judges, one of the best guidelines is found in 2 Timothy 3:16-17, words which Paul wrote with the Old Testament first in view. He said that *all* Scripture is of great benefit to (a) teach us, (b) rebuke us, (c) correct us, and (d) train us in righteousness. Paul added that these Scriptures completely equip the person of God "for every good work." As you think seriously about those guidelines, in which of these areas do you especially see the usefulness of Judges?

4. Imagine that you were helping to produce a film based on the book of Judges. Describe the kinds of scenery, supporting characters, background music, lighting effects, etc., which you would use to help portray the central message of this book.

5. Look together at each of these passages, and discuss which one you believe is the best candidate for "KEY VERSE" in the book of Judges—the one which brings into sharpest focus what this book is most about: 2:20-21, 8:23, 17:6, or 21:25.

6. What would you say is the main theme (or themes) in the book of Judges?

7. SEARCH FOR THE SAVIOR—What words, images, or themes in Judges have reminded you most of Jesus?

8. Based especially on your own experience, complete this statement in the way that's most meaningful to you: I believe it's important for Christians to read and explore the book of Judges because...

9. What to you personally is the strongest example in this book of someone doing what was right and good?

10. What to you personally is the strongest example in this book of someone doing what was wrong?

11. If Judges were the only book in the Old Testament, in what ways would it still make a good introduction to the message of Jesus in the New Testament?

Ruth

OVERVIEW

(Discuss these OVERVIEW questions both at the beginning of your study of Ruth, then again after you've studied all four chapters. Your answers may change significantly once you've looked more closely at the entire book.)

Startup: Talk together about people you've known who especially impressed you as being loyal.

SEEING WHAT'S THERE

1. Before launching into a closer look at Ruth, how would you summarize what you already know about this book?

2. How many times do you see the words *kinsman* or *relative* in this short book? And how many times do you see some form of the word *redeem* in this book? What clues could these words offer about the central message of Ruth?

3. Look also at the list of "Questions to Ask as You Begin Your Study of Each Book" on page 9.

FOR LIFE TODAY

4. The book of Ruth has been called "The Rendezvous of Romance and Redemption," "The Story of God's Grace in Difficult Circumstances," "The Book of Love and Loyalty" and "The Virtuous Woman." With that reputation for this book, what kinds of answers and guidelines and solutions would you like to gain as you examine it more closely?

5. When you get to heaven, if you have a long talk with Ruth and she asks you, "What was most helpful to you in the book about me?" how would you like to be able to answer her?

6. As you think first about *who God is,* and second about *what the Bible is,* how strongly would you rate your present desire to understand better the book of Ruth? Use a scale of one to ten (one = "no desire at all," ten = "extremely intense desire") to help you decide.

RUTH 1

SEEING WHAT'S THERE

1. For helpful background on the Moabite nation mentioned in this chapter, what can you discover in Genesis 19:36-38, Numbers 22:1-6, and Deuteronomy 23:3-6?

2. Summarize the events presented in chapter 1, keeping in mind that no historical account can include every detail of the events it describes. What are the most important details which *are* included here? And what kinds of details are left out, details which might otherwise be quite interesting to us? What does this selection process tell you about what God wants us to understand most from this story?

3. Look also on page 8 at the list of "Questions to Ask as You Study Each Chapter." You may want to look again at this list for each chapter in Ruth.

4. EYE FOR DETAIL— *From what you recall seeing in chapter 1, try answering the following question without looking in your Bible:* By the time her husband and sons had died, how many years had Naomi lived in Moab? (See verse 4.)

CAPTURE THE ESSENCE

5. How would you describe both the character of Ruth and the character of Naomi, as you see them in this chapter?

6. If you could go back in time, and God brought you into the events of this chapter to act as a personal counselor to Naomi, what kind of counsel would you give her, and how would you express it?

7. As this chapter closes, how do you think Naomi would answer this question: What are your deepest hurts these days, and what are your greatest joys?

FOR LIFE TODAY

8. What do you think are the most important lessons God wants us to learn from this chapter about love and loyalty?

9. Proverbs 2:1-5 tells about the sincere person who truly longs for wisdom and understanding, and who searches the Scriptures for it—as if it were buried treasure. That person, Solomon says, will come to understand the fear of the Lord, and discover the knowledge of God. As you begin exploring the book of Ruth, what "buried treasure" would you like God to help you find here—to show you what God and His wisdom are really like? If you have this desire, how would you express it in your own words?

RUTH 2

SEEING WHAT'S THERE

1. What specific steps of action do Naomi and Ruth take in this chapter?

2. Notice especially what Boaz says in verse 12. What would you say this verse indicates about Boaz's spiritual condition?

3. EYE FOR DETAIL—*From what you recall seeing in chapter 2, try answering the following question without looking in your Bible:* How did Boaz and his harvesters greet one another? (See verse 4.)

CAPTURE THE ESSENCE

4. Imagine yourself being present in the temple in Jerusalem as the twelve-year-old Jesus hears this book read and discussed by the rabbis there. In Luke 2:46 we read that He was listening to these teachers and asking them questions. What passages in this book do you think would most impress the boy Jesus, and what questions or comments do you suppose He might have spoken?

FOR LIFE TODAY

5. Notice in verse 11 what Boaz tells Ruth about her reputation. What are the most important things people have told you about *your* reputation?

6. Look again at the words of blessing which Boaz speaks to Ruth in verse 12. To what degree, if any, do these words reflect your own past, present, and future?

7. In Romans 15:4, Paul reminds us that the Old Testament Scriptures can give us patience and perseverance on one hand, as well as comfort and encouragement on the other. In your own life, how do you see this book of Ruth living up to Paul's description? In what ways, if any, is it meeting your personal needs for both *perseverance* and *encouragement*?

FOR GOING DEEPER

The books of Ruth and Judges both take place in the same period of Israel's history. From what you know of both books, how do they differ in tone and teaching?

RUTH 3

Startup: When you get to heaven, and you meet Ruth and Boaz, what's the first question you'd like to ask them?

SEEING WHAT'S THERE

1. What are the most important decisions and choices that are made in this chapter, and how would you analyze each one?

2. What impresses you most about Boaz in this chapter?

3. EYE FOR DETAIL—*From what you recall seeing in chapter 3, try answering the following question without looking in your Bible:* How much grain did Boaz give Ruth to take home with her? (See verse 15.)

FOR LIFE TODAY

4. If God had written this chapter only for you, which words or phrases do you think He might have underlined, and why?

5. In Isaiah 55:10-11, God reminds us that He sends rain and snow from the sky to water the earth and to nurture life. In the same way, God says that He sends His words to accomplish specific purposes.

From your study so far, what would you suggest as *God's* primary purposes for the book of Ruth in the lives of Christians today?

FOR GOING DEEPER

In what specific ways do you see Naomi, Ruth, and Boaz living out the moral standard which God presents in Leviticus 19:18?

RUTH 4

SEEING WHAT'S THERE

1. Summarize the events that have taken place since chapter 1, once again keeping in mind that no historical account can include every detail of the events it describes. What are the most important details which *are* included here? And what kinds of details are left out, details which might otherwise be quite interesting to us? What does this selection process tell you about what God wants us to understand most from this story?

2. How often have you seen *kindness* expressed in either word or deed in the book of Ruth?

3. What are the most important changes you see in Naomi's life since this book began?

4. What is the best evidence you see in this book of God's sovereign control over circumstances?

5. Would you call the book of Ruth a love story? How many times have you seen the word *love* in this book?

6. EYE FOR DETAIL— *From what you recall seeing in chapter 4, try answering the following question without looking in your Bible:* What other women besides Ruth and Naomi are mentioned by name in this chapter? (See verses 11-12.)

CAPTURE THE ESSENCE

7. Looking back over the entire book, what would you say is the *turning point* in Ruth's story?

8. If you were asked to give a character reference for each of the three major people in this story—Ruth, Naomi, and Boaz —what would you say about each one?

9. In verse 17, the man David is mentioned for the first time in the Bible. Through all the rest of the Old Testament, David and his family and descendants will be on center-stage—and through the entire New Testament as well, because of David's descendant Jesus. Why do you think God chose the story of Ruth to be the introduction to David's story?

10. In what ways do you see the ministry of Jesus Christ foreshadowed in what Boaz did for Ruth?

11. From what you've seen in this book, would you say that God wants to be considered *primarily* as the God of His people Israel, or as the God of the whole earth? Explain your answer.

FOR LIFE TODAY

12. In your life, what are the most important relationships in which you feel you should emulate the examples of love and loyalty seen in this book?

13. Think again about the growth in character you've witnessed in Naomi's life in this book. In what one or two areas do you most want to see character growth in your own life in the next few years?

14. Review the guidelines for our thought-life given in Philippians 4:8— "Whatever is true, whatever is noble, whatever is right, whatever is pure, whatever is lovely, whatever is admirable—if anything is excellent or praiseworthy— *think about such things."* What food for thought can you find in the story of Ruth that especially strikes you as being *true*, or *noble*, or *right*, or *pure*, or *lovely*, or *admirable*, or *excellent*, or *praiseworthy*?

FOR GOING DEEPER

Notice the mention made of Ruth in the genealogy of Jesus in Matthew 1. (Ruth's name is in verse 5.) What other women are mentioned in this genealogy?

RUTH:

THE BIG PICTURE

(Discuss again the questions in the "Overview," plus the questions below.)

1. In your own words, how would you describe the *beauty* of the book of Ruth? What makes this book so appealing?

2. For getting the most from the book of Ruth, one of the best guidelines is found in 2 Timothy 3:16-17, words which Paul wrote with the Old Testament first in view. He said that *all* Scripture is of great benefit to (a) teach us, (b) rebuke us, (c) correct us, and (d) train us in righteousness. Paul added that these Scriptures completely equip the person of God "for every good work." As you think seriously about those guidelines, in which of these areas do you especially see the usefulness of Ruth?

3. Look together at each of these passages, and discuss which one you believe is the best candidate for "KEY VERSE" in the book of Ruth—the one which brings into sharpest focus what this book is most about: 1:16, 3:11, or 4:14.

4. What would you say is the main theme (or themes) in the book of Ruth?

5. SEARCH FOR THE SAVIOR—What words, images, or themes in Ruth have reminded you most of Jesus?

6. Imagine that you were helping to produce a film based on the book of Ruth. Describe the kinds of scenery, supporting characters, background music, lighting effects, etc., which you would use to help portray the central message of this book.

7. If Ruth were the only book in the Old Testament, in what ways would it still make a good introduction to the message of Jesus in the New Testament?

8. Based especially on your own experience, complete this statement in the way that's most meaningful to you: I believe it's important for Christians to read and explore the book of Ruth because...

1 Samuel

OVERVIEW

(Discuss these OVERVIEW questions both at the beginning of your study of First Samuel, then again after you've studied all 31 chapters. Your answers may change significantly once you've looked more closely at the entire book.)

Startup: Talk together about people you've known who especially impressed you as being good leaders.

SEEING WHAT'S THERE

1. Before launching into a closer look at First Samuel, how would you summarize what you already know about this book?

2. Find the word that reoccurs in the following verses—2:17, 2:25, 7:6, 12:10, 12:19, and 15:24. What clues could this word offer about the central message of First Samuel?

3. Look also at the list of "Questions to Ask as You Begin Your Study of Each Book" on page 9.

FOR LIFE TODAY

4. The book of First Samuel has been called "The Book of the People's King," "The Organization of the Kingdom," and "A Book of Great Beginnings and Tragic Endings." With that reputation for this book, what kinds of answers and guidelines and solutions would you like to gain as you examine it more closely?

5. From what you see in Samuel's words in 12:23-24, what would be a good personal prayer to offer to God as you study this book?

6. As you think first about *who God is,* and second about *what the Bible is,* how strongly would you rate your present desire to understand better the book of First Samuel? Use a scale of one to ten (one = "no desire at all," ten = "extremely intense desire") to help you decide.

1 SAMUEL 1

Startup: When you get to heaven, and you meet Hannah, what's the first question you'd like to ask her?

SEEING WHAT'S THERE

1. What vow did Hannah make to God?

2. What observations about the character of Hannah and the character of her husband can you make from this chapter?

3. How does Hannah reply to Eli's rebuke, and what effect does it have on him?

4. In verse 19, what action by God is mentioned?

5. Look also on page 8 at the list of "Questions to Ask as You Study Each Chapter." You may want to look again at this list for each chapter in First Samuel.

6. EYE FOR DETAIL—*From what you recall seeing in chapter 1, try answering the following question without looking in your Bible:* What was the name of Samuel's father, and what tribe in Israel was he from? (See verse 1.)

CAPTURE THE ESSENCE

7. In your own words, how would you describe the *beauty* of this chapter? What makes it so appealing?

8. *Why* is Hannah's longing for a son so intense? How many possible reasons can you discover in this chapter?

9. Look again at verse 11, then discuss which of these statements you agree with most: (a) Hannah's vow was essentially a bargain with God. (b) Hannah's vow was an expression of thanksgiving—in advance—for the blessing she asked for from God. (c) Hannah's vow was a way for her to test her own faith.

10. The book of 1 Samuel will focus on Israel's first two kings—Saul and David—

but the book doesn't mention the birth of either one. Instead it begins with the story of the birth of Samuel the prophet. What significance do you see in this? What conclusions could you make about how God wanted the kingship of Israel to be viewed?

11. Imagine yourself being present in the temple in Jerusalem as the twelve-year-old Jesus hears this chapter read and discussed by the rabbis there. In Luke 2:46 we read that He was listening to these teachers and asking them questions. What verses from this chapter do you think would most impress the boy Jesus, and what questions or comments do you suppose He might have spoken?

FOR LIFE TODAY

12. What do you think are the most important lessons God wants us to learn from this chapter about faith and prayer?

13. Notice again in this chapter the intensity of Hannah's longing for a son. What do you most long for from God at this time in your life?

14. Proverbs 2:1-5 tells about the sincere person who truly longs for wisdom and understanding, and who searches the Scriptures for it—as if it were buried treasure. That person, Solomon says, will come to understand the fear of the Lord, and discover the knowledge of God. As you begin exploring the book of First Samuel, what "buried treasure" would you like God to help you find here—to show you what God and His wisdom are really like? If you have this desire, how would you express it in your own words?

FOR GOING DEEPER

Notice again the action by God mentioned in verse 19. In what ways would you say God's "remembering" of Hannah was similar to His "remembering" of Noah in Genesis 8:1, and his "remembering" of Abraham and his family in Exodus 2:24? In what ways was it most different? Look also at God's promise to "remember" something in Genesis 9:15, and His "remembering" someone in Genesis 30:22. From what you see in these passages, what is the best biblical definition for this word?

1 SAMUEL 2

SEEING WHAT'S THERE

1. From what you see in verses 1-10, what are the most important things that Hannah understands about God's personality and character?

2. From what you see in verses 8-10, would you say that God wants to be considered *primarily* as the God of His people Israel, or as the God of the whole earth? Explain your answer.

3. How are Eli's sons described in verse 12? In contrast, how is Samuel described in verse 18?

4. What are the major points made in the prophecy given to Eli by the man of God in verses 27-36?

5. What do you think are the correct answers to the questions asked by the man of God in verse 29?

6. EYE FOR DETAIL— *From what you recall seeing in chapter 2, try answering the following question without looking in your Bible:* How many other children did Hannah have after she gave Samuel to the Lord's service? (See verse 21.)

CAPTURE THE ESSENCE

7. How many contrasts do you see between Eli and Samuel in this chapter?

8. Again, imagine yourself being present in the temple in Jerusalem as the twelve-year-old Jesus hears this chapter read and discussed by the Jewish teachers. What verses in this chapter do you think would most impress Him, and what questions or comments do you suppose He might have spoken?

FOR LIFE TODAY

9. In light of how you're doing spiritually in your life today, which elements of Hannah's prayer in this chapter do you think should be incorporated in your own prayers to God?

FOR GOING DEEPER

What similarities do you find between Hannah's song (in verses 1-10) and the song of Mary in Luke 1:46-55?

Look also at the similarity between 1 Samuel 2:26 and Luke 2:52. How do these passages serve as a model for the proper growth of children?

1 SAMUEL 3

SEEING WHAT'S THERE

1. What did God tell the boy Samuel, and how does His message compare with the message given to Eli in chapter 2?

2. What does this chapter reveal about the boy Samuel's character?

3. In your own words, what do you think God wants us to understand most from the final three verses of this chapter?

4. EYE FOR DETAIL— *From what you recall seeing in chapter 3, try answering the following question without looking in your Bible:* How many times did the Lord call to Samuel in this chapter? (See verses 8 and 10.)

CAPTURE THE ESSENCE

5. What further contrasts do you see between Eli and Samuel in this chapter?

6. If you could go back in time, and God brought you into the events of this chapter to act as a personal counselor to Eli, what kind of counsel would you give him, and how would you express it?

7. How would you summarize what Samuel learns most about God in this chapter?

8. From all that you've seen so far in this book, what would you say are the most important ways that God has laid a foundation for Samuel's future ministry?

FOR LIFE TODAY

9. What are the most important ways that God has laid a foundation for *your* future ministry?

10. What can you learn about listening to God from Samuel's example in this chapter?

1 SAMUEL 4

Startup: What memorable example can you give in your life of a short-term defeat that contributed to a long-term victory?

SEEING WHAT'S THERE

1. How would you summarize the military developments in this chapter?

2. What would you say is the correct answer to the question asked by the elders of Israel in verse 3?

3. EYE FOR DETAIL— *From what you recall seeing in chapter 4, try answering the following question without looking in your Bible:* How many soldiers of Israel are lost in battle in this chapter? (See verses 2 and 10.)

CAPTURE THE ESSENCE

4. Look again at verse 18. Keeping in mind the lessons he may have learned, suppose Eli was allowed to live his life over again. What, if anything, do you think he would most want to change, and how?

1 SAMUEL 5

SEEING WHAT'S THERE

1. What three Philistine cities was the ark taken to in this chapter, and what happened in each city?

1 SAMUEL 6

SEEING WHAT'S THERE

1. What was the Philistine strategy for returning the ark, and what were the reasons for that strategy?

2. EYE FOR DETAIL— *From what you recall seeing in chapter 6, try answering the following question without looking in your Bible:* How long was the ark in Philistine territory? (See verse 1.)

1 SAMUEL 7

SEEING WHAT'S THERE

1. How would you summarize the military developments in this chapter?

2. How would you summarize what Samuel does for Israel in this chapter?

3. What are the most important conclusions this chapter makes about Samuel's life and ministry?

4. EYE FOR DETAIL— *From what you recall seeing in chapter 7, try answering the following question without looking in your Bible:* After the Philistines were defeated at Mizpah, what did Samuel call the memorial stone he set up? (See verse 12.)

FOR LIFE TODAY

5. In verse 3, notice Samuel's words about wholeheartedly serving God. If God were to write down a list of the ways in which you wholeheartedly served Him in the past week, what do you think would be on that list?

1 SAMUEL 8

Startup: In the way we read and study the Bible, what kind of old mental habits or faulty assumptions can most easily block this book of First Samuel from coming alive in our minds and hearts?

SEEING WHAT'S THERE

1. With chapter 8, we begin a major new division in the book of First Samuel. In only a few sentences, how would you summarize the most important things that have happened so far in this book?

2. Chapter 8 has been called the key to the book of First Samuel. What does this chapter include that could make it this significant?

3. What does the Lord tell Samuel in this chapter?

4. As Samuel tells the people what having a king will be like, what would you say are the most important points he makes?

5. EYE FOR DETAIL— *From what you recall seeing in chapter 8, try answering the following question without looking in your*

Bible: What were the names of Samuel's two sons? (See verse 2.)

CAPTURE THE ESSENCE

6. What would you say verse 20 reveals about the spiritual condition of Israel at this time?

1 SAMUEL 9

SEEING WHAT'S THERE

1. What does verse 6 reveal about Samuel's reputation in Israel?

2. What does the Lord tell Samuel in this chapter?

3. EYE FOR DETAIL— *From what you recall seeing in chapter 9, try answering the following question without looking in your Bible:* How much money was Saul's servant carrying with him? (See verse 8.)

CAPTURE THE ESSENCE

4. What does this chapter reveal about Saul's character?

1 SAMUEL 10

SEEING WHAT'S THERE

1. What specific prophecies does Samuel make about Saul?

2. At the end of verse 7, what command does Samuel give Saul?

3. What further commands does Samuel add in verse 8?

4. What specific action does God's Spirit accomplish in verse 10?

5. As Samuel speaks to the people in verses 17-19, what important points does he remind them of?

6. What does verses 26-27 indicate about Saul's leadership?

CAPTURE THE ESSENCE

7. How would you summarize what Saul learns most about God in this chapter?

8. What does verse 6 indicate about God's commitment to Saul and to his kingship?

9. From what you've seen so far in this book, how would you summarize God's design for the kingship of Israel? What

are the most important things He wants His people to understand about it?

10. Look again at what Samuel says to Saul at the end of verse 7. To what extent do you think these are also God's words to you, at this time in your life?

1 SAMUEL 11

SEEING WHAT'S THERE

1. How would you summarize the military developments in this chapter?

2. What specific action does God's Spirit accomplish in verse 6?

3. EYE FOR DETAIL— *From what you recall seeing in chapter 11, try answering the following question without looking in your Bible:* How many soldiers of Israel assembled at Bezek to fight against the Ammonites? (See verse 8.)

CAPTURE THE ESSENCE

4. How does Saul demonstrate his leadership capabilities in this chapter?

5. How is Saul's character portrayed in this chapter?

6. Look at Samuel's words in verse 14. Would you say the "kingship" or "kingdom" he is referring to is the kingship of Saul, or the kingship of God? What evidence can you give for your answer?

1 SAMUEL 12

Startup: When you get to heaven and meet Samuel, what's the first question you'd like to ask him?

SEEING WHAT'S THERE

1. In his farewell speech to the people in this chapter, what specific *reminders* does Samuel offer the people, what specific *commands* does he give, and what specific *warnings* does he pronounce?

2. In verses 17-18, what action on God's part confirms the words of Samuel?

3. How would you explain the people's response in verse 19?

4. What commitments does Samuel make to the people?

5. What final warning closes this chapter?

CAPTURE THE ESSENCE

6. How is Samuel's character most revealed in this chapter?

7. From what you see in this chapter, how would you summarize God's design for the kingship of Israel? What are the most important things He wants His people to understand about it?

FOR LIFE TODAY

8. Think about all that Samuel says in this chapter about serving God wholeheartedly, especially in verse 24. In practical terms, what do you think serving God wholeheartedly means most for you at this time in your life?

9. If God were to write down a list of the ways in which you truly served Him in the past week, what do you think would be on that list?

FOR GOING DEEPER

Look again at the requirement and the warning Samuel gives the people in verses 14-15. What can you discover about the history and fuller meaning of this requirement in the following passages—Exodus 19:5-6, Deuteronomy 8:19, 11:13-15, and 11:22-28, and Joshua 24:20?

1 SAMUEL 13

SEEING WHAT'S THERE

1. How would you summarize the military developments in this chapter?

2. In your own words, how would you summarize what Saul does wrong in this chapter?

3. In Samuel's response to Saul, what specific rebuke do you see, and what specific prophecy?

4. EYE FOR DETAIL— *From what you recall seeing in chapter 13, try answering the following question without looking in your Bible:* How many chariots and charioteers did the Philistines assemble against Israel at Micmash? (See verse 5.)

CAPTURE THE ESSENCE

5. Look again at verse 13, then discuss how much you agree or disagree with this

statement, and why: With such an important destiny at stake — the establishment of Israel's royal family — God should have given Saul another chance to prove himself.

FOR LIFE TODAY

6. In what kinds of circumstances is it hardest for you to be patient and to wait on God's timing and leading?

7. What do you think are the most important lessons God wants us to learn from this chapter about sin and disobedience?

1 SAMUEL 14

SEEING WHAT'S THERE

1. How would you summarize the military developments in this chapter?

2. Look at God's response to Saul's questions in verse 37. Why do you think God responded this way?

3. EYE FOR DETAIL— *From what you recall seeing in chapter 14, try answering the following question without looking in your Bible:* What children of Saul are named in this chapter? (See verse 49.)

CAPTURE THE ESSENCE

4. What do you learn about Jonathan's character in this chapter?

5. What more do you learn about Saul's character in this chapter?

6. What more do you learn about Saul's leadership capabilities?

7. What comparisons would you make between Saul the king and Jonathan his son? How are they most alike? How are they most different?

1 SAMUEL 15

SEEING WHAT'S THERE

1. In verses 2-3, what specific commands does the Lord give Saul through the prophet Samuel? And what is God's stated reason for this command?

2. In rejecting Saul as king, what specific reason does God give Samuel, in verse 11?

3. How does Samuel respond to this news from God?

4. EYE FOR DETAIL— *From what you recall seeing in chapter 15, try answering the following question without looking in your Bible:* What was the name of the king of the Amalekites? (See verse 8.)

CAPTURE THE ESSENCE

5. What more do you learn about Saul's character in this chapter?

6. What more do you learn about Samuel's character?

7. Restate in your own words what you believe are the most important truths revealed about God's character and personality in verses 22 and 29.

8. Again, imagine yourself being present in the temple in Jerusalem as the twelve-year-old Jesus hears this chapter read and discussed by the Jewish teachers. What verses in this chapter do you think would most impress Him, and what questions or comments do you suppose He might have spoken?

FOR LIFE TODAY

9. What would you say are the most useful and important lessons to learn from the examples of both Saul and Samuel in this chapter?

FOR GOING DEEPER

Restate in your own words the principle Samuel talked about in verses 22-23. How does it compare with the words Jesus spoke in Matthew 9:13 and 12:7?

1 SAMUEL 16

Startup: What experiences can you recall that helped you learn to look beyond outward appearances?

SEEING WHAT'S THERE

1. How many specific commands does God give Samuel in this chapter?

2. What specific action does God's Spirit accomplish in verse 13?

3. How many descriptions of David do you see in this chapter?

4. EYE FOR DETAIL— *From what you recall seeing in chapter 16, try answering the*

following question without looking in your Bible: How many brothers of David are named in this chapter, and what are their names? (See verses 6-9.)

5. From verse 7, what conclusions can you make about God's *character*, and about God's *judgment* upon human beings?

6. Look at verse 12. From your own imagination, what details could you add to this physical description of David? What do you think he might have looked like?

7. Once more, imagine yourself being present in the temple in Jerusalem as the twelve-year-old Jesus hears this chapter read and discussed by the Jewish teachers. What verses in this chapter do you think would most impress Him, and what questions or comments do you suppose He might have spoken?

FOR LIFE TODAY

8. Look again at verse 7. How can we see people and situations from God's perspective, instead of from a human perspective? What are the most important ways we can learn to do this?

1 SAMUEL 17

SEEING WHAT'S THERE

1. To review, retrace your way through the last several chapters. What are the most important things that have happened since Saul was chosen king?

2. How long have you known about the story of David and Goliath? What are some of the earliest impressions this story left with you?

3. How would you summarize the military developments in this chapter?

4. What are the most important decisions and choices that are made in this chapter, and how would you analyze each one?

5. EYE FOR DETAIL— *From what you recall seeing in chapter 17, try answering the following question without looking in your Bible:* What specific weapons and pieces of armor did Goliath carry? (See verses 5-7.)

CAPTURE THE ESSENCE

6. How much can you learn about David's character in this chapter?

7. What more can you learn about Saul's character in this chapter?

8. How do you see God's power and purpose displayed in this chapter?

FOR LIFE TODAY

9. Choose one of these sentences, and complete it as fully and candidly as you would like: (a) What I see and understand in this chapter is important to my life because... OR: (b) What I see and understand in this chapter does NOT seem important to my life at this time, because...

1 SAMUEL 18

Startup: Describe one of the most memorable acts of friendship that you can recall someone doing for you.

SEEING WHAT'S THERE

1. How would you summarize the most important events of this chapter?

2. How would you evaluate Saul's spiritual condition in this chapter?

3. EYE FOR DETAIL— *From what you recall seeing in chapter 18, try answering the following question without looking in your Bible:* How many Philistine foreskins did David bring to Saul? (See verse 27.)

CAPTURE THE ESSENCE

4. What more can you learn in this chapter about the character of Saul, the character of Jonathan, and the character of David?

5. If you could go back in time, and God brought you into the events of this chapter to act as a royal adviser to King Saul, what kind of counsel would you give him, and how would you express it?

6. Look again at verse 18, then discuss how much you agree or disagree with this statement: Fearing other people's success is always a sign of insecurity.

FOR LIFE TODAY

7. In Isaiah 55:10-11, God reminds us that He sends rain and snow from the sky to water the earth and to nurture life. In the

same way, God says that He sends His words to accomplish specific purposes. From your study so far, what would you suggest are *God's* primary purposes for the book of First Samuel in the lives of Christians today?

1 SAMUEL 19

SEEING WHAT'S THERE

1. How would you summarize the most important developments in this chapter?

2. For a glimpse of what was going on in David's heart during the events described in this chapter, what can you discover in Psalm 59?

CAPTURE THE ESSENCE

3. In your own words, how would you explain what happens in verse 24? In what ways would you say this is the climax of all that has happened so far in Saul's relationships to Samuel and David?

4. Once again, what is revealed most in this chapter about the characters of Saul, Jonathan, and David?

FOR LIFE TODAY

5. In Romans 15:4, Paul reminds us that the Old Testament Scriptures can give us patience and perseverance on one hand, as well as comfort and encouragement on the other. In your own life, how do you see this book of First Samuel living up to Paul's description? In what ways, if any, is it meeting your personal needs for both *perseverance* and *encouragement?*

1 SAMUEL 20

Startup: When you get to heaven, and you meet Jonathan, what's the first question you'd like to ask him?

SEEING WHAT'S THERE

1. How would you summarize the communication between David and Jonathan in this chapter?

2. EYE FOR DETAIL— *From what you recall seeing in chapter 20, try answering the following question without looking in your Bible:* How many times did David bow before Jonathan? (See verse 41.)

CAPTURE THE ESSENCE

3. What would you say were the strongest features in David's relationship with Jonathan? What foundation was their friendship built upon?

FOR LIFE TODAY

4. What useful principles can you find in this chapter for relationships in your own life?

1 SAMUEL 21

SEEING WHAT'S THERE

1. How would you summarize the most important developments in this chapter?

2. For a glimpse of what was going on in David's heart during the time described in verses 10-15, what can you discover in Psalms 34 and 56?

3. EYE FOR DETAIL— *From what you recall seeing in chapter 21, try answering the following question without looking in your Bible:* Doeg was the servant of Saul who was at Nob when David came there. What kind of work did Doeg do for Saul? (See verse 7.)

1 SAMUEL 22

SEEING WHAT'S THERE

1. How would you summarize the most important developments in this chapter?

2. For a glimpse of what was going on in David's heart during the events described in this chapter, what can you discover in Psalms 52 and 142?

3. EYE FOR DETAIL— *From what you recall seeing in chapter 22, try answering the following question without looking in your Bible:* How many priests at Nob did Doeg kill at Saul's command? (See verse 18.)

1 SAMUEL 23

Startup: At this point in your life, how strong is your ability to sense God's guidance, compared with other times in the past? Use a scale of one to ten (one = "much weaker than ever," ten = "much stronger than ever") to help you decide.

SEEING WHAT'S THERE

1. What are the most important things that happen to David in this chapter?

2. For a glimpse of what was going in David's heart during the events described in verses 15-29, what can you discover in Psalm 54?

3. EYE FOR DETAIL— *From what you recall seeing in chapter 23, try answering the following question without looking in your Bible:* Where is David when this chapter concludes? (See verse 29.)

CAPTURE THE ESSENCE

4. How would you describe David's daily relationship with God, from what you see in this chapter?

5. From what you see in verses 16-18, what further conclusions can you make about the friendship of Jonathan and David?

1 SAMUEL 24

SEEING WHAT'S THERE

1. In your own words, how would you describe the *power* of this chapter? What makes this incident so interesting?

2. For a glimpse of what was going on in David's heart during the events described in this chapter, what can you discover in Psalm 57?

3. In verses 16-21, how does Saul respond to David's words to him? What request does Saul make of David?

4. EYE FOR DETAIL— *From what you recall seeing in chapter 24, try answering the following question without looking in your Bible:* How many men did Saul have with him at this time? (See verse 2.)

CAPTURE THE ESSENCE

5. As this chapter closes, why do you think David did not return with Saul?

1 SAMUEL 25

SEEING WHAT'S THERE

1. What are the most important decisions and choices that are made in this chapter, and how would you analyze each one?

2. Look at the descriptions of Abigail and Nabal in verse 3. Using your imagination, give a fuller description in today's language of their appearances and personalities.

3. EYE FOR DETAIL— *From what you recall seeing in chapter 25, try answering the following question without looking in your Bible:* How many loaves of bread did Abigail include in her gifts for David and his men? (See verse 18.)

CAPTURE THE ESSENCE

4. Notice how this chapter begins. Keeping in mind the lessons Samuel may have learned, suppose he was allowed to live his life over again. What, if anything, do you think he would most want to change, and how?

5. What impresses you most about Abigail?

6. How would you summarize what David learns most about God in this chapter?

7. What do you think is the main point God is making by including the story of Nabal and David in this book?

FOR LIFE TODAY

8. What would you say are the most useful and important lessons to learn from the mistakes and near-mistakes in this chapter?

1 SAMUEL 26

Startup: What is the most interesting thing you've read in the Bible in the past week?

SEEING WHAT'S THERE

1. What are the most important decisions and choices that are made in this chapter, and how would you analyze each one?

2. EYE FOR DETAIL— *From what you recall seeing in chapter 26, try answering the following question without looking in your Bible:* Who accompanied David when

he went by night into Saul's camp? (See verses 6-7.)

CAPTURE THE ESSENCE

3. What further insight does this chapter give about the character of Saul and the character of David?

FOR LIFE TODAY

4. In Jeremiah 23:29, God says that His Word is like fire, and like a hammer. He can use the Scriptures to burn away unclean thoughts and desires in our hearts. He can also use Scripture to hit hard like a hammer, with the power to crush our spiritual hardness. From your study in this book of First Samuel, how do you most want to see the "fire-and-hammer" power of God's Word at work in your own life?

1 SAMUEL 27

SEEING WHAT'S THERE

1. To review, retrace your way through the last several chapters. What are the most important things that have happened since David killed Goliath?

2. In your own words, how would you explain David's thinking in verse 1?

3. EYE FOR DETAIL—*From what you recall seeing in chapter 27, try answering the following question without looking in your Bible:* What was the name of the Philistine king at Gath? (See verse 2.)

1 SAMUEL 28

SEEING WHAT'S THERE

1. What does this chapter reveal about Saul's character, and his spiritual condition at this time?

2. What words of prophesy does Saul hear in verses 16-19?

3. EYE FOR DETAIL—*From what you recall seeing in chapter 28, try answering the following question without looking in your Bible:* What position did King Achish offer to David? (See verse 2.)

1 SAMUEL 29

Startup: What three things are you most thankful for these days?

SEEING WHAT'S THERE

1. How would you summarize the most important developments in this chapter?

2. EYE FOR DETAIL—*From what you recall seeing in chapter 29, try answering the following question without looking in your Bible:* How long has David been living among the Philistines? (See verse 3.)

1 SAMUEL 30

SEEING WHAT'S THERE

1. How would you summarize the crisis David faces in this chapter? What is most needed from him at this time?

2. EYE FOR DETAIL—*From what you recall seeing in chapter 30, try answering the following question without looking in your Bible:* How many men followed David in his attack upon the Amalekites? (See verses 9-10.)

CAPTURE THE ESSENCE

3. If you were giving David a job performance review (in his position as a leader of men), what comments would you make to him, based on what you've seen so far in this book?

4. Why was David the right man to become Israel's king?

FOR LIFE TODAY

5. What principles for living by faith do you see in David's example in this book?

1 SAMUEL 31

SEEING WHAT'S THERE

1. How would you summarize the military developments in this chapter?

2. EYE FOR DETAIL—*From what you recall seeing in chapter 31, try answering the following question without looking in your Bible:* How many of Saul's sons were killed in this chapter? (See verse 2.)

3. Keeping in mind the lessons each of them may have learned, suppose that both Jonathan and Saul were allowed to live their lives over again. What, if anything, do you think each one would most want to change, and how?

FOR LIFE TODAY

4. Think back on all that has happened to the people of Israel in the book of First Samuel. If it's true that *the past is a lesson for the future,* then what would you say are the most important lessons for God's people today to learn from these events?

1 SAMUEL:
THE BIG PICTURE

(Discuss again the questions in the "Overview," plus the questions below.)

1. Who would you say are the most important individuals whose stories are told in the book of 1 Samuel? And in what order would you rank them, according to their importance to this book?

2. For getting the most from the book of First Samuel, one of the best guidelines is found in 2 Timothy 3:16-17, words which Paul wrote with the Old Testament first in view. He said that *all* Scripture is of great benefit to (a) teach us, (b) rebuke us, (c) correct us, and (d) train us in righteousness. Paul added that these Scriptures completely equip the person of God "for every good work." As you think seriously about those guidelines, in which of these areas do you especially see the usefulness of First Samuel?

3. Look together at each of these passages, and discuss which one you believe is the best candidate for "KEY VERSE" in the book of First Samuel—the one which brings into sharpest focus what this book is most about: 8:7-9, 10:25, 13:14, or 15:22.

4. What would you say is the main theme (or themes) in the book of First Samuel?

5. SEARCH FOR THE SAVIOR—What words, images, or themes in First Samuel have reminded you most of Jesus?

6. Based especially on your own experience, complete this statement in the way that's most meaningful to you: I believe it's important for Christians to read and explore the book of First Samuel because...

7. What to you personally is the strongest example in this book of someone doing what was right and good?

8. What to you personally is the strongest example in this book of someone doing what was wrong?

9. If First Samuel were the only book in the Old Testament, in what ways would it still make a good introduction to the message of Jesus in the New Testament?

2 Samuel

OVERVIEW

(Discuss these OVERVIEW questions both at the beginning of your study of Second Samuel, then again after you've studied all 24 chapters. Your answers may change significantly once you've looked more closely at the entire book.)

Startup: King David was born halfway between the time of Abraham and the time of Jesus. Talk together about how you would compare David to both Abraham and Jesus. How was he most like them? How was he especially different from them?

SEEING WHAT'S THERE

1. Before launching into a closer look at Second Samuel, how would you summarize what you already know about this book?

2. Find the short phrase that reoccurs in the following verses—3:28, 5:3, 6:5, 6:14, 6:16, 6:17, 6:21, 7:18, 21:9, and 23:16. What clues does this phrase offer about the central message of Second Samuel?

3. Look also at the list of "Questions to Ask as You Begin Your Study of Each Book" on page 9.

FOR LIFE TODAY

4. The book of Second Samuel has been called "The Book of God's King" and "Israel Comes of Age." With that reputation for this book, what kinds of answers and guidelines and solutions would you like to gain as you examine it more closely?

5. From what you see in David's words to God in 7:28, what would be a good personal prayer to offer to God as you study this book?

6. As you think first about *who God is,* and second about *what the Bible is,* how strongly would you rate your present desire to understand better the book of Second Samuel? Use a scale of one to ten (one = "no desire at all," ten = "extremely intense desire") to help you decide.

2 SAMUEL 1

SEEING WHAT'S THERE

1. Review first the content in 1 Samuel. What are the most important developments in that book in the lives of Samuel, Saul, Jonathan, and David? What is revealed most about the character of each of these four men? And what is revealed most about God's design for the kingship of Israel? What are the most important things He wants His people to understand about it?

2. In verses 19-27, what praise does David offer to Saul and Jonathan's memory?

3. EYE FOR DETAIL— *From what you recall seeing in chapter 1, try answering the following question without looking in your Bible:* Where was Saul killed? (See verses 6 and 21.)

CAPTURE THE ESSENCE

4. Look again at verses 15-16. Legally speaking, was it right or wrong for David to kill the Amalekite who confessed to killing Saul? Was it right or wrong *morally?* Was it right or wrong *politically?* How would you explain your answers?

5. What does this chapter reveal most about David's character?

FOR LIFE TODAY

6. Proverbs 2:1-5 tells about the sincere person who truly longs for wisdom and understanding, and who searches the Scriptures for it—as if it were buried treasure. That person, Solomon says, will come to understand the fear of the Lord, and discover the knowledge of God. As

you begin exploring the book of Second Samuel, what "buried treasure" would you like God to help you find here—to show you what God and His wisdom are really like? If you have this desire, how would you express it in your own words?

2 SAMUEL 2

SEEING WHAT'S THERE

1. What are the most important decisions and choices that are made in this chapter, and how would you analyze each one?

2. EYE FOR DETAIL—*From what you recall seeing in chapter 2, try answering the following question without looking in your Bible:* Who was the commander of Saul's army? (See verse 8.)

2 SAMUEL 3

SEEING WHAT'S THERE

1. How would you describe David's leadership skills, as you see them displayed in this chapter?

2. EYE FOR DETAIL—*From what you recall seeing in chapter 3, try answering the following question without looking in your Bible:* How many sons were born to David while he was in Hebron? (See verses 2-5.)

CAPTURE THE ESSENCE

3. What does this chapter reveal most about David's character?

2 SAMUEL 4

SEEING WHAT'S THERE

1. What human actions in this chapter do you think were most pleasing to God? And which do you think were most displeasing?

2. EYE FOR DETAIL—*From what you recall seeing in chapter 4, try answering the following question without looking in your Bible:* How old was Jonathan's son Mephibosheth when he was accidentally crippled? (See verse 4.)

2 SAMUEL 5

Startup: What accomplishments in your life have meant the most to you?

SEEING WHAT'S THERE

1. Chapter 5 has been called the key to the book of Second Samuel. What does this chapter include that could make it this significant?

2. How would you summarize the most important developments in this chapter?

3. How would you evaluate David's leadership skills, as you see them on display in this chapter?

4. How would you summarize the military developments in this chapter?

5. EYE FOR DETAIL—*From what you recall seeing in chapter 5, try answering the following question without looking in your Bible:* How old was David when he became king? (See verse 4.)

FOR LIFE TODAY

6. From what you've seen so far in this book, what can you learn from David's example about dependence upon God?

2 SAMUEL 6

SEEING WHAT'S THERE

1. Take a "walk" together through the incidents that happen in this chapter. Using your imagination, talk about the kinds of sights, smells, sounds, and feelings you might experience.

2. EYE FOR DETAIL—*From what you recall seeing in chapter 6, try answering the following question without looking in your Bible:* What was the name of the man whom the Lord struck down in this chapter? (See verse 8.)

CAPTURE THE ESSENCE

3. What does this chapter reveal most about David's character?

4. How would you summarize what David learns most about God in this chapter?

FOR LIFE TODAY

5. If it's true that *the past is a lesson for the future,* then what would you say are the

most important lessons for God's people today to learn from this chapter?

2 SAMUEL 7

SEEING WHAT'S THERE

1. Look carefully at God's words for David in this chapter. What *reminders* are included in this message? And what specific *promises* are included?

2. What does God mean by the word *house* in verse 11?

3. In this chapter, what does God reveal about His character to David? What does He most want David to understand about this?

4. In David's prayer in verses 18-29, what does David specifically ask God to do?

5. What different names does David use to address God?

6. What specific points of praise does David include in his prayer?

7. Look at how God describes the future temple in verse 13. What does He mean by the word *name* here?

CAPTURE THE ESSENCE

8. What does this chapter reveal most about David's character?

9. From what you see in this chapter, would you say that God wants to be considered *primarily* as the God of His people Israel, or as the God of the whole earth? Explain your answer.

10. Imagine yourself being present in the temple in Jerusalem as the twelve-year-old Jesus hears this chapter read and discussed by the rabbis there. In Luke 2:46 we read that He was listening to these teachers and asking them questions. What verses from this chapter do you think would most impress the boy Jesus, and what questions or comments do you suppose He might have spoken?

FOR LIFE TODAY

11. In light of how you're doing spiritually in your life today, which elements of David's prayer in this chapter do you think should be incorporated in your own prayers to God?

12. In verse 27, look at David's expressed reason for finding courage to bring this prayer to God. What most encourages you to go to God in prayer?

13. What do you believe are God's greatest promises to you?

14. Review the guidelines for our thought-life given in Philippians 4:8—"Whatever is true, whatever is noble, whatever is right, whatever is pure, whatever is lovely, whatever is admirable—if anything is excellent or praiseworthy—*think about such things.*" What food for thought can you find in this chapter that especially strikes you as being *true,* or *noble,* or *right,* or *pure,* or *lovely,* or *admirable,* or *excellent,* or *praiseworthy?*

FOR GOING DEEPER

Look again at how the Lord describes the future temple in verse 13. What else can you discover about God's *name* in Exodus 3:13-15, Deuteronomy 12:5, Psalm 52:9, and Proverbs 18:10?

Review also God's promise to David in verses 11-12. What deeper meaning do you see in this promise in the following passages— Isaiah 9:6-7 and 11:1-16, Jeremiah 23:5-6 and 33:14-18, and Ezekiel 34:23-24 and 37:24-28?

2 SAMUEL 8

Startup: When you get to heaven, and you meet David, what's the first question you'd like to ask him?

SEEING WHAT'S THERE

1. How would you summarize the military developments in this chapter?

2. From the evidence in this chapter, how would you evaluate David's leadership skills?

3. EYE FOR DETAIL— *From what you recall seeing in chapter 8, try answering the following question without looking in your Bible:* How many of the nations David defeated in this chapter can you list?

2 SAMUEL 9

SEEING WHAT'S THERE

1. What exactly does David do for Mephibosheth, and why?

2. EYE FOR DETAIL— *From what you recall seeing in chapter 9, try answering the following question without looking in your Bible:* What was the name of Saul's household servant whom David spoke to in this chapter? (See verse 2.)

CAPTURE THE ESSENCE

3. What does this chapter reveal most about David's character?

2 SAMUEL 10

SEEING WHAT'S THERE

1. How would you summarize the political and military developments in this chapter?

2. How would you evaluate David's leadership skills, as you see them in this chapter?

3. EYE FOR DETAIL— *From what you recall seeing in chapter 10, try answering the following question without looking in your Bible:* What exactly did the Ammonites do to David's officials? (See verse 4.)

FOR LIFE TODAY

4. In Romans 15:4, Paul reminds us that the Old Testament Scriptures can give us patience and perseverance on one hand, as well as comfort and encouragement on the other. In your own life, how do you see this book of Second Samuel living up to Paul's description? In what ways, if any, is it meeting your personal needs for both *perseverance* and *encouragement?*

2 SAMUEL 11

Startup: At this point in your life, how strong is your ability to resist temptation, compared with other times in the past? Use a scale of one to ten (one = "much weaker than ever," ten = "much stronger than ever") to help you decide.

SEEING WHAT'S THERE

1. With chapter 11, we begin a major new division in the book of Second Samuel. In only a few sentences, how would you summarize the most important things that have happened so far in this book?

2. Here in chapter 11, what are the most important decisions and choices that are made, and how would you analyze each one?

3. EYE FOR DETAIL— *From what you recall seeing in chapter 11, try answering the following question without looking in your Bible:* What was the name of the city where the Israelites were fighting in this chapter? (See verse 1.)

CAPTURE THE ESSENCE

4. What does this chapter reveal most about David's character?

5. If you could go back in time, and God brought you into the events of this chapter to act as a royal adviser to King David, what kind of counsel would you give him, and how would you express it?

FOR LIFE TODAY

6. Choose one of these sentences, and complete it as fully and candidly as you would like: (a) What I see and understand in this chapter is important to my life because… OR: (b) What I see and understand in this chapter does NOT seem important to my life at this time, because…

2 SAMUEL 12

SEEING WHAT'S THERE

1. In your own words, how would you describe the *power* of this chapter? What makes this passage so gripping?

2. For a glimpse of what was going on in David's heart during the events described in this chapter, what do you discover in Psalm 51?

3. How would you summarize the story Nathan tells in verses 1-4?

4. What specific punishment did David announce in verses 5-6?

5. What reminders does God give to David in verses 7-8?

6. What specific sins does God accuse David of in verses 9-10?

7. What specific punishment does God announce in verse 10?

8. After Nathan confronted David with his sin, what action did God take in verse 15? And how did David respond to this action?

9. In your own words, how would you explain David's response to the child's death in verses 20-23?

10. What are the most important things David does in this chapter after he stopped mourning for his dead son?

11. EYE FOR DETAIL—*From what you recall seeing in chapter 12, try answering the following question without looking in your Bible:* After being struck ill by the Lord's hand, how long did David and Bathsheba's baby live? (See verse 18.)

CAPTURE THE ESSENCE

12. What's the best evidence you see in this chapter of God's grace?

13. What impresses you most in this chapter about the prophet Nathan?

14. Look carefully at the words David spoke in verse 13. How much of each of these character traits do you think is reflected in David's words—courage, fear, humility, boldness, pragmatism, wisdom, and faithfulness?

15. How would you summarize what David learns most about God in this chapter?

16. In what ways would you say this chapter represents a major turning point in the story of David?

17. Again, imagine yourself being present in the temple in Jerusalem as the twelve-year-old Jesus hears this chapter read and discussed by the Jewish teachers. What verses in this chapter do you think would most impress Him, and what questions or comments do you suppose He might have spoken?

FOR LIFE TODAY

18. What are the most significant times in life in which you have needed to speak the words David spoke in verse 13?

19. Look again at God's words of commitment to David in this chapter, especially at the end of verse 8. Do you think God is equally committed to you?

20. Look again at the specific accusation at the beginning of verse 9. In what ways are we sometimes guilty of this today?

21. Discuss your answers to this question: Why do we still sin, even after gratefully receiving all that God has given us?

2 SAMUEL 13

Startup: What would you say are the most important principles for keeping good relationships among family members?

SEEING WHAT'S THERE

1. What are the most important decisions and choices that are made in this chapter, and how would you analyze each one?

2. How would you evaluate David's leadership performance in this chapter?

3. From what you see in verse 21, how did David respond when he heard of Amnon's actions?

4. EYE FOR DETAIL—*From what you recall seeing in chapter 13, try answering the following question without looking in your Bible:* Where did Absalom flee to, and how long did he stay there? (See verse 38.)

5. Again, if you could go back in time, and God brought you into the events of this chapter to act as a royal adviser to King David, what kind of counsel would you give him, and how would you express it?

FOR LIFE TODAY

6. What would you say are the most useful and important lessons to learn from the mistakes in this chapter?

7. In Isaiah 55:10-11, God reminds us that He sends rain and snow from the sky to water the earth and to nurture life. In the same way, God says that He sends His words to accomplish specific purposes. From your study so far, what would you suggest are *God's* primary purposes for the book of Second Samuel in the lives of Christians today?

2 SAMUEL 14

SEEING WHAT'S THERE

1. Again, what are the most important decisions and choices that are made in this chapter, and how would you analyze each one?

2. Imagine that you live in Israel but are a spy for Israel's enemies. You send back regular reports to your leaders about your observations. What would you tell them about the events recorded in this chapter?

3. Look at the last line in verse 25. From your own imagination, what details could you add to this physical description of Absalom? What do you think he might have looked like?

4. EYE FOR DETAIL— *From what you recall seeing in chapter 14, try answering the following question without looking in your Bible:* How many children were born to Absalom? (See verse 27.)

CAPTURE THE ESSENCE

5. Once more, if you could go back in time, and God brought you into the events of this chapter to act as a royal adviser to King David, what kind of counsel would you give him, and how would you express it?

2 SAMUEL 15

Startup: Can you recall a time in life when you felt you had to "run away" from a difficult situation? If so, what were the circumstances?

SEEING WHAT'S THERE

1. What human actions in this chapter do you think were most pleasing to God? And which do you think were most displeasing?

2. How would you summarize the crisis David faces in this chapter? What is most needed from him at this time? And how well is David responding to the need?

3. For a glimpse of what was going on in David's heart during the time described in chapters 15—17, what do you discover in Psalms 3 and 63?

4. What do verses 25 and 26 reveal about David's relationship with God during the events of this chapter?

5. What plan does David set into motion in verses 32-37?

6. EYE FOR DETAIL— *From what you recall seeing in chapter 15, try answering the following question without looking in your Bible:* What were the names of the two priests who took the ark back to Jerusalem upon David's instructions? (See verses 27-29.)

CAPTURE THE ESSENCE

7. What does this chapter reveal most about David's character?

2 SAMUEL 16

SEEING WHAT'S THERE

1. Again, what are the most important decisions and choices that are made in this chapter, and how would you analyze each one?

2. How would you further evaluate David's leadership skills, as seen in this chapter?

3. EYE FOR DETAIL— *From what you recall seeing in chapter 16, try answering the following question without looking in your Bible:* What was the name of the man

who cursed David and threw stones at him? (See verse 5.)

CAPTURE THE ESSENCE

4. What does this chapter reveal most about David's character?

2 SAMUEL 17

SEEING WHAT'S THERE

1. What are the most important events occurring in this chapter?

2. What direct involvement by God is revealed in verse 14?

3. EYE FOR DETAIL— *From what you recall seeing in chapter 17, try answering the following question without looking in your Bible:* What did Ahithophel do after Absalom refused to take his advice? (See verse 23.)

2 SAMUEL 18

Startup: What do you feel are the three most valuable character traits a father can have?

SEEING WHAT'S THERE

1. How would you summarize the military developments in this chapter?

2. What was David's part in the military actions taking place in this chapter?

3. EYE FOR DETAIL— *From what you recall seeing in chapter 18, try answering the following question without looking in your Bible:* How many casualties were there in the fight between David's men and Absalom's men? (See verse 7.)

2 SAMUEL 19

SEEING WHAT'S THERE

1. What are the most important decisions and choices that are made in this chapter, and how would you analyze each one?

2. How would you evaluate David's leadership performance in this chapter?

3. As this chapter closes, what additional major challenges are facing David?

CAPTURE THE ESSENCE

4. What does this chapter reveal most about David's character?

FOR LIFE TODAY

5. In Jeremiah 23:29, God says that His Word is like fire, and like a hammer. He can use the Scriptures to burn away unclean thoughts and desires in our hearts. He can also use Scripture to hit hard like a hammer, with the power to crush our spiritual hardness. From your study in this book of Second Samuel, how do you most want to see the "fire-and-hammer" power of God's Word at work in your own life?

2 SAMUEL 20

SEEING WHAT'S THERE

1. To review, retrace your way through the last several chapters. What are the most important things that have happened since David's sin with Bathsheba?

2. What human actions in this chapter do you think were most pleasing to God? And which do you think were most displeasing?

3. How would you summarize the crisis David faces in this chapter? What is most needed from him at this time? And how well is David responding to the need?

FOR LIFE TODAY

4. What would you say are the most useful and important lessons to learn from the mistakes you see in this chapter?

2 SAMUEL 21

Startup: What is the most interesting thing you've read in the Bible in the past week?

SEEING WHAT'S THERE

1. How would you summarize the military developments in this chapter?

2. EYE FOR DETAIL—*From what you recall seeing in chapter 21, try answering the following question without looking in your Bible:* How long did the famine in this chapter last? (See verse 1.)

2 SAMUEL 22

SEEING WHAT'S THERE

1. This chapter is recorded also in Scripture as Psalm 18. How does the message and tone of this song fit well with what you know of David's character and personality?

2. In David's song, how would you summarize all the *action* that has taken place, beginning in verse 5?

CAPTURE THE ESSENCE

3. From what you see in this chapter, what are the most important things that David understands about God's personality and character?

4. What do you think is the "righteousness" that David speaks of in verses 21 and 25? How does a person get this righteousness?

5. Songs are often a way to express and release deep emotions. What emotions do you think were behind the song David sings in this chapter?

6. In what ways would you say this psalm sums up David's personal story in Scripture?

FOR LIFE TODAY

7. If this was the last Bible chapter you read before you died, which verses from it would you most like to have lingering in your mind as you said goodbye to this earth?

8. Are the words in verse 29 true for you as well? If so, in what ways has God done this for you?

9. Consider how strongly you desire to know God better, then ask yourself this question: *What are the truths revealed about Him in this chapter which He may want me to understand more deeply at this time in my life?*

2 SAMUEL 23

Startup: If you learned you were going to die tonight, what would you want your last words to be?

SEEING WHAT'S THERE

1. In verses 1-7, how would you summarize what was on David's mind and heart as his life came to a close?

2. EYE FOR DETAIL—*From what you recall seeing in chapter 23, try answering the following question without looking in your Bible:* What was the name of David's mighty man who killed a lion on a snowy day? (See verse 20.)

FOR LIFE TODAY

3. If you died tonight, would you be able to express the same confidence that David does in verse 5?

2 SAMUEL 24

SEEING WHAT'S THERE

1. What are the most important decisions and choices that are made in this chapter, and how would you analyze each one?

2. How would you summarize the crisis David faces in this chapter? What is most needed from him at this time? And how well is David responding to the need?

3. How would you summarize what David learns most about God in this chapter?

4. How would you compare David's life in the first part of this book with his life in the second part (beginning with his relationship with Bathsheba in chapter 11)?

5. EYE FOR DETAIL—*From what you recall seeing in chapter 24, try answering the following question without looking in your Bible:* How many people died in the plague in this chapter? (See verse 15.)

6. What does this last chapter in 2 Samuel reveal most about David's character?

7. Once more, imagine yourself being present in the temple in Jerusalem as the twelve-year-old Jesus hears this chapter read and discussed by the Jewish teachers. What verses in this chapter do you think would most impress Him, and what questions or comments do you suppose He might have spoken?

2 SAMUEL:

THE BIG PICTURE

(Discuss again the questions in the "Overview," plus the questions below.)

1. For getting the most from the book of Second Samuel, one of the best guidelines is found in 2 Timothy 3:16-17, words which Paul wrote with the Old Testament first in view. He said that *all* Scripture is of great benefit to (a) teach us, (b) rebuke us, (c) correct us, and (d) train us in righteousness. Paul added that these Scriptures completely equip the person of God "for every good work." As you think seriously about those guidelines, in which of these areas do you especially see the usefulness of Second Samuel?

2. Look together at each of these passages, and discuss which one you believe is the best candidate for "KEY VERSE" in the book of Second Samuel—the one which brings into sharpest focus what this book is most about: 5:12, 7:12-13, or 22:21.

3. What would you say is the main theme (or themes) in the book of Second Samuel?

4. SEARCH FOR THE SAVIOR—What words, images, or themes in Second Samuel have reminded you most of Jesus?

5. Based especially on your own experience, complete this statement in the way that's most meaningful to you: I believe it's important for Christians to read and explore the book of Second Samuel because...

6. What to you personally is the strongest example in this book of someone doing what was right and good?

7. What to you personally is the strongest example in this book of someone doing what was wrong?

8. If Second Samuel were the only book in the Old Testament, in what ways would it still make a good introduction to the message of Jesus in the New Testament?

1 Kings

OVERVIEW

(Discuss these OVERVIEW questions both at the beginning of your study of First Kings, then again after you've studied all 22 chapters. Your answers may change significantly once you've looked more closely at the entire book.)

Startup: Talk together about what you consider to be the most important qualifications for a king.

SEEING WHAT'S THERE

1. Before launching into a closer look at First Kings, how would you summarize what you already know about this book?

2. Find the theme or thought that reoccurs in the following verses—2:4, 8:23, 8:48, 11:4, 14:8, 15:3, and 15:14. What clues does this offer about the central message of First Kings?

3. Look also at the list of "Questions to Ask as You Begin Your Study of Each Book" on page 9.

FOR LIFE TODAY

4. The book of First Kings has been called "From Splendor to Decay" and "The Book of the Kingdom's Division." With that reputation for this book, what kinds of answers and guidelines and solutions would you like to gain as you examine it more closely?

5. From what you see in David's words to Solomon in 2:2-3, what would be a good personal prayer to offer to God as you study this book?

6. As you think first about *who God is,* and second about *what the Bible is,* how strongly would you rate your present desire to understand better the book of First Kings? Use a scale of one to ten (one = "no desire at all," ten = "extremely intense desire") to help you decide.

1 KINGS 1

SEEING WHAT'S THERE

1. How would you summarize the crisis David faces in this chapter? What is most needed from him at this time?

2. From what you see in this chapter, who were the most influential people who wanted Adonijah to be king after David, and who were the most influential people who sided with Solomon?

3. What was the plan devised by Nathan and Bathsheba, and how well would you say it worked?

4. Look also on page 8 at the list of "Questions to Ask as You Study Each Chapter." You may want to look again at this list for each chapter in First Kings.

5. EYE FOR DETAIL—*From what you recall seeing in chapter 1, try answering the following question without looking in your Bible:* On the day he was made king, what animal did Solomon ride? (See verse 38.)

CAPTURE THE ESSENCE

6. What are the most important decisions and choices that are made in this chapter, and how would you analyze each one?

7. From what you see in this chapter, how would you evaluate David's leadership skills at this time in his life?

8. If you could go back in time, and God brought you into the events of this chapter to act as a royal adviser to King David, what kind of counsel would you give him, and how would you express it?

FOR LIFE TODAY

9. Proverbs 2:1-5 tells about the sincere person who truly longs for wisdom and understanding, and who searches the

Scriptures for it—as if it were buried treasure. That person, Solomon says, will come to understand the fear of the Lord, and discover the knowledge of God. As you begin exploring the book of First Kings, what "buried treasure" would you like God to help you find here—to show you what God and His wisdom are really like? If you have this desire, how would you express it in your own words?

1 KINGS 2

SEEING WHAT'S THERE

1. In verses 2-4, what specific commands are included in David's charge to Solomon?

2. In verses 5-9, notice the three men whom David gives Solomon instructions about. What do you know about their background in the book of 2 Samuel? (See especially 2 Samuel 3:22-32, 16:5-13, 19:31-39, and 20:7-10.)

3. What specific actions does Solomon take in this chapter to make his kingship secure, and how would you evaluate each one?

4. How does Solomon demonstrate justice in verses 31-33?

5. EYE FOR DETAIL—*From what you recall seeing in chapter 2, try answering the following question without looking in your Bible:* Who did Solomon put in Joab's place as commander of the army? (See verse 35.)

CAPTURE THE ESSENCE

6. From what you see in David's charge to Solomon, what conclusions can you make about how David would define the role and responsibilities of Israel's king?

7. Look again at verses 10-11. Keeping in mind the lessons he may have learned, suppose David was allowed to live his life over again. What, if anything, do you think he would most want to change, and how?

FOR LIFE TODAY

8. In a typical day, how often would the commands in verses 2 and 3 offer useful and timely guidelines for your immediate situation?

1 KINGS 3

Startup: If God invited you to ask Him for anything you wanted, what would you ask for?

SEEING WHAT'S THERE

1. What conclusion about Solomon's spiritual life is made in verse 3?

2. What question does God ask Solomon in verse 5? How does Solomon answer, and what specific reasons does he give for his answer? (See verses 6-9.)

3. In verses 10-14, what specific promises does God make after hearing Solomon's answer?

4. What exactly did Solomon do after he woke up from his dream-encounter with God? (See verse 15.)

5. In verse 28, what important truth did the people recognize about Solomon?

6. EYE FOR DETAIL—*From what you recall seeing in chapter 3, try answering the following question without looking in your Bible:* Where was Solomon when the Lord appeared to him in a dream? (See verses 4-5.)

CAPTURE THE ESSENCE

7. If this chapter was the only portion of Scripture you had access to, what conclusions would you make from it about God's character and personality?

8. Imagine yourself being present in the temple in Jerusalem as the twelve-year-old Jesus hears this chapter read and discussed by the rabbis there. In Luke 2:46 we read that He was listening to these teachers and asking them questions. What verses from this chapter do you think would most impress the boy Jesus, and what questions or comments do you suppose He might have spoken?

FOR LIFE TODAY

9. What gifts from God are you most thankful for today?

1 KINGS 4

SEEING WHAT'S THERE

1. What impresses you most in the way Solomon's wisdom is described in verses 29-34?

2. EYE FOR DETAIL— *From what you recall seeing in chapter 4, try answering the following question without looking in your Bible:* How much meat was consumed each day by Solomon and those with him? (See verses 22-23.)

CAPTURE THE ESSENCE

3. Notice especially verse 25, and the picture presented in the last phrase of this verse. What does that picture communicate to you?

1 KINGS 5

SEEING WHAT'S THERE

1. What were the specifics of the agreement made in this chapter between Solomon and King Hiram of Tyre?

2. What is the total number of workers mentioned in verses 13-16?

3. EYE FOR DETAIL— *From what you recall seeing in chapter 5, try answering the following question without looking in your Bible:* How were the logs for Solomon's construction projects transported from Hiram's land to Israel? (See verse 9.)

1 KINGS 6

SEEING WHAT'S THERE

1. In verse 16, what name is given to the innermost room in the tabernacle? What separates this room from the rest of the tabernacle, and is included inside this room?

2. In verses 23-28, how is this inner room furnished?

3. Look ahead also to 8:6-9—what will be placed inside this inner room?

4. How many years did it take Solomon to build the temple? (See verse 38.)

5. EYE FOR DETAIL— *From what you recall seeing in chapter 6, try answering the following question without looking in your*

Bible: When Solomon began building the temple, how many years had it been since the Israelites came out of Egypt? (See verse 1.)

CAPTURE THE ESSENCE

6. It's often said that a person's home is a reflection of his personality. From what you see in this chapter, how would the temple be a reflection of God's personality?

FOR GOING DEEPER

Look again in verses 16 and 23-28 at the description of the innermost room in the temple. Explore together at how this same inner room was configured and furnished in the tabernacle built by Moses — in Exodus 26:33-34—and in the temple which Ezekiel saw in his vision from God—in Ezekiel 41:3-4 and 41:21-23. For both the tabernacle and Ezekiel's temple, tell what differences you see from the description of the inner room here in Solomon's temple.

This inner room was also included in the temple which Herod built in Jerusalem, and which was there at the time of Jesus' ministry. Look at Matthew 27:50-51 to see what happened to the curtain that separated the Most Holy Place in this temple.

Finally, review Hebrews 9:3-9 and 10:19-22 to see how God's people today are to view this innermost room in God's dwelling place.

In the Old Testament setup of this room in both the tabernacle and the temple, would you say it was meant more to represent God's *nearness* to His people, or God's *holy distance* from them? Explain your answer.

1 KINGS 7

SEEING WHAT'S THERE

1. If you were a visitor to Jerusalem in Solomon's day, and he showed you all the things in the temple which are described in chapters 6 and 7, which of them do you think would impress you most?

2. Once the temple work was complete, what else did Solomon put inside it, according to the last verse of this chapter?

3. EYE FOR DETAIL—*From what you recall seeing in chapter 7, try answering the following question without looking in your Bible:* How many years did it take Solomon to build his palace? (See verse 1.)

1 KINGS 8

Startup: Talk together about times in your life when you've especially enjoyed worshiping God. What were the circumstances?

SEEING WHAT'S THERE

1. How does God show His presence in the temple in verses 10-11?

2. In Solomon's words to the assembly of Israel (verses 15-21) and in the prayer that follows, how many times does Solomon speak of his father, King David? In these passages, what conclusions can you make about Solomon's understanding of the role and responsibilities of Israel's king?

3. What specific points of praise to God does Solomon speak in this chapter?

4. What specific requests does Solomon make to God, beginning in verse 25?

5. What important observation about all human beings does Solomon make in verse 46?

6. Study carefully verses 33-40 and 46-51. Notice Solomon's repeated request for God's future forgiveness for His people. According to Solomon's words in these passages, what would be the reason for that forgiveness? On what basis would God choose to forgive them?

7. EYE FOR DETAIL—*From what you recall seeing in chapter 8, try answering the*

following question without looking in your Bible: What physical position was Solomon in as he prayed the long prayer in this chapter? (See verse 54.)

CAPTURE THE ESSENCE

8. From what you see in this chapter, what are the most important things Solomon understands about God's personality and character? What evidence do you see that Solomon especially understands (a) God's *love and faithfulness,* (b) God's *holiness and justice,* and (c) God's *power?*

9. From what you see in Solomon's dedication prayer in verses 22-61, would you say that God wants to be considered *primarily* as the God of His people Israel, or as the God of the whole earth? Explain your answer.

10. In what ways would you say this chapter represents a major turning point in the history of God's people?

FOR LIFE TODAY

11. In light of how you're doing spiritually in your life today, which elements of Solomon's prayer in verses 23-53 do you think should be incorporated in your own prayers to God?

FOR GOING DEEPER

Solomon had a message for the entire world! Look again at what he says in verse 60. How consistent is Solomon's statement with what these other men say in Scripture—Joshua (Joshua 4:23-24); David (Psalm 86:8-10); Hezekiah (Isaiah 37:18-20); and Isaiah (Isaiah 52:10)?

1 KINGS 9

SEEING WHAT'S THERE

1. Chapter 9 has been called the key to the book of First Kings. What does this chapter include that could make it this significant?

2. What *promises* does God make in His words to Solomon in verses 3-9? What *conditions* are mentioned in connection with these promises? And what *warnings* does the Lord give Solomon?

3. Look over the list of Solomon's achievements and activities in verses 10-28.

Which of these do you think were most pleasing to God, and why?

4. EYE FOR DETAIL— *From what you recall seeing in chapter 9, try answering the following question without looking in your Bible:* What gifts did Solomon and Hiram exchange? (See verses 10-14.)

CAPTURE THE ESSENCE

5. How would you summarize what Solomon learns most about God in this chapter?

6. From what you see in His words to Solomon, what conclusions can you make about how God views the role and responsibilities of Israel's king?

7. Again, imagine yourself being present in the temple in Jerusalem as the twelve-year-old Jesus hears this chapter read and discussed by the Jewish teachers. What verses in this chapter do you think would most impress Him, and what questions or comments do you suppose He might have spoken?

1 KINGS 10

SEEING WHAT'S THERE

1. Compare Solomon's actions in verse 26 with the law for Israel's kings in Deuteronomy 17:16. Was he guilty, or not?

2. EYE FOR DETAIL— *From what you recall seeing in chapter 10, try answering the following question without looking in your Bible:* If you stood before the throne of Solomon, how many lions would you see? (See verses 19-20.)

CAPTURE THE ESSENCE

3. What do you think God wants us to understand most from this chapter?

FOR GOING DEEPER

Compare what you see in this chapter with what Jesus says in Matthew 6:28-30. How did Jesus view the wealth and splendor of Solomon?

1 KINGS 11

SEEING WHAT'S THERE

1. What monumental failure by Solomon is spelled out in verses 1-8?

2. What specific reason is stated for God's anger against Solomon in verses 9-10?

3. What specific punishment did the Lord announce against Solomon in verse 11? And what limitations on this punishment are added in verses 12-13?

4. In verses 29-39, study carefully what the Lord said to Jeroboam through the prophet Ahijah. What specific action does God say He will take, and for what reasons?

5. EYE FOR DETAIL— *From what you recall seeing in chapter 11, try answering the following question without looking in your Bible:* How long did Solomon rule Israel? (See verse 42.)

CAPTURE THE ESSENCE

6. Look again at verses 29-39. In these words spoken through the prophet Ahijah, what further conclusions can you make about God's view of the role and responsibilities of a king in Israel?

7. If you could go back in time, and God brought you into the events of this chapter to act as a royal adviser to King Solomon, what kind of counsel would you give him, and how would you express it?

8. Look again at how this chapter ends. Keeping in mind the lessons he may have learned, suppose Solomon was allowed to live his life over again. What, if anything, do you think he would most want to change, and how?

9. Now that you're halfway through First Kings, how would you summarize the most important lessons to learn from this book?

FOR LIFE TODAY

10. What would you say are the most useful and important lessons to learn from Solomon's mistakes in this chapter?

11. Choose one of these sentences, and complete it as fully and candidly as you would like: (a) What I see and under-

stand in this chapter is important to my life because… OR: (b) What I see and understand in this chapter does NOT seem important to my life at this time, because…

1 KINGS 12

Startup: In the way we read and study the Bible, what kind of old mental habits or faulty assumptions can most easily block this book of First Kings from coming alive in our minds and hearts?

SEEING WHAT'S THERE

1. What are the most important decisions and choices that are made in this chapter, and how would you analyze each one?

2. With chapter 12, we begin a major new division in the book of First Kings. In only a few sentences, how would you summarize the most important things that have happened so far in this book?

3. EYE FOR DETAIL— *From what you recall seeing in chapter 12, try answering the following question without looking in your Bible:* Where was Jeroboam when Rehoboam became king after Solomon? (See verse 2.)

FOR LIFE TODAY

4. What do you think are the most important lessons God wants us to learn from this chapter about sin and disobedience?

1 KINGS 13

SEEING WHAT'S THERE

1. In this chapter, what did the man of God do right, and what did he do wrong?

2. What does this chapter reveal about the character of Jeroboam, and how would you compare this with what you've seen earlier in this book?

3. EYE FOR DETAIL— *From what you recall seeing in chapter 13, try answering the following question without looking in your Bible:* What two animals are mentioned in this chapter? (See verses 13 and 24.)

FOR LIFE TODAY

4. What do you think are the most important lessons God wants us to learn from this chapter?

1 KINGS 14

SEEING WHAT'S THERE

1. Through the words of the prophet Ahijah in verses 7-11, what specific punishment does God pronounce against Jeroboam, and for what specific reasons?

2. What prophecy concerning Israel's future does Ahijah speak about in verses 14-16?

3. From what you see in verses 21-31, how would you summarize the spiritual condition of Judah during the reign of Rehoboam?

4. EYE FOR DETAIL— *From what you recall seeing in chapter 14, try answering the following question without looking in your Bible:* What did Jeroboam's wife take with her when she went in disguise to see the prophet Ahijah? (See verse 3.)

1 KINGS 15

SEEING WHAT'S THERE

1. What's the best compliment spoken about any king in this chapter, and what is the worst criticism?

2. How would you summarize the military developments in this chapter?

3. EYE FOR DETAIL— *From what you recall seeing in chapter 15, try answering the following question without looking in your Bible:* Which king in this chapter had the longest reign? (See verse 10.)

1 KINGS 16

SEEING WHAT'S THERE

1. Humanly speaking, what would you say is the best thing anybody does in this chapter? And what is the worst or most questionable thing anybody does in this chapter?

2. EYE FOR DETAIL—*From what you recall seeing in chapter 16, try answering the following question without looking in your Bible:* Which king in this chapter commits suicide? (See verse 18.)

CAPTURE THE ESSENCE

3. If you could go back in time, and God brought you into the events of this chapter to act as a royal adviser to King Ahab, what kind of counsel would you give him, and how would you express it?

FOR LIFE TODAY

4. In Isaiah 55:10-11, God reminds us that He sends rain and snow from the sky to water the earth and to nurture life. In the same way, God says that He sends His words to accomplish specific purposes. From your study so far, what would you suggest are *God's* primary purposes for the book of First Kings in the lives of Christians today?

1 KINGS 17

Startup: How "tough" are you these days? At this point in your life, how strong is your ability to endure hardship, compared with other times in the past? Use a scale of one to ten (one = "much weaker than ever," ten = "much stronger than ever") to help you decide.

SEEING WHAT'S THERE

1. What miracles do you see in this chapter?

2. Look at the similarity between what Elijah says in verse 1 and what the widow of Zarephath says in verse 12. What did they both understand about God?

3. What specific actions does God tell Elijah to take in verses 2-4 and 8-9?

4. In verse 14, what specific word from the Lord does Elijah give to the widow?

5. In verse 18, what conclusions did the widow come to after her son died? And in verse 24, what conclusions did she immediately come to after her dead son was brought back to life?

6. What would you give as the correct answer to the question Elijah asked God in verse 20?

FOR LIFE TODAY

7. What principles for living by faith do you see in this chapter?

1 KINGS 18

SEEING WHAT'S THERE

1. What phrase do you see on the lips of both the prophet Obadiah (in verse 10) and the prophet Elijah (verse 15)? Do you think this was a significant thing for them to say, or only a casual expression? (Notice also how the prophet Micaiah uses this phrase in 22:14, and how the prophet Elisha uses it in 2 Kings 5:16.)

2. How long have you known about the story of Elijah and the prophets of Baal on Mount Carmel? What are some of the earliest impressions this story left with you?

3. What was the people's first response when they saw God send down fire on Elijah's sacrifice? (See verse 39.)

4. EYE FOR DETAIL—*From what you recall seeing in chapter 18, try answering the following question without looking in your Bible:* What did Ahab call Elijah when they met? (See verse 17.)

CAPTURE THE ESSENCE

5. From what you see in this chapter, what are the most important things Elijah understands about God's personality and character?

FOR LIFE TODAY

6. Consider how strongly you desire to know God better, then ask yourself this question: *What are the truths revealed about Him in this chapter which He may want me to understand more deeply at this time in my life?*

1 KINGS 19

Startup: When you get to heaven, and you meet Elijah, what's the first question you'd like to ask him?

SEEING WHAT'S THERE

1. How would you describe Elijah's situation in the opening verses of this chapter?

2. How consistent is Elijah's action in verse 3 with what you have seen of him earlier? How would you explain what Elijah does here?

3. What did Elijah ask God to do in verse 4? And how did God respond to that request, in verses 5-7?

4. In verse 8, why do you think Elijah then traveled to Horeb, the mountain of God located in Sinai? Notice what God asks Elijah in verse 9.

5. In verses 9-14, what question does God ask Elijah twice, and what answer does Elijah give both times?

6. What did God command Elijah to do in verse 11? After giving this command, notice God's further communication to Elijah in verses 11-12. What was more important here in verse 12—*what* God said, or *how* He said it?

7. What specific commands does the Lord give Elijah in verses 15-16, and what words of prophecy does He add in verse 17?

8. What concluding information does Elijah receive from God in verse 18?

9. How does Elijah begin acting upon God's commands in verses 19-21?

CAPTURE THE ESSENCE

10. How would you summarize what Elijah learns most about God in this chapter?

FOR LIFE TODAY

11. In this chapter, what can you learn about following God's guidance from the examples of both Elijah and Elisha?

12. Review the guidelines for our thought-life given in Philippians 4:8—"Whatever is true, whatever is noble, whatever is right, whatever is pure, whatever is lovely, whatever is admirable—if anything is excellent or praiseworthy—*think about such things.*" What food for thought can you find in this chapter that especially strikes you as being *true,* or *noble,* or *right,* or *pure,* or *lovely,* or *admirable,* or *excellent,* or *praiseworthy?*

1 KINGS 20

SEEING WHAT'S THERE

1. What human actions in this chapter do you think were most pleasing to God? And which do you think were most displeasing?

2. How would you summarize the military developments in this chapter?

3. EYE FOR DETAIL—*From what you recall seeing in chapter 20, try answering the following question without looking in your Bible:* What were the officials of King Ben-Hadad wearing when they approached King Ahab to ask for mercy? (See verses 31-32.)

FOR LIFE TODAY

4. What do you think are the most important lessons God wants us to learn from this chapter about sin and disobedience?

5. In Romans 15:4, Paul reminds us that the Old Testament Scriptures can give us patience and perseverance on one hand, as well as comfort and encouragement on the other. In your own life, how do you see this book of First Kings living up to Paul's description? In what ways, if any, is it meeting your personal needs for both *perseverance* and *encouragement?*

1 KINGS 21

Startup: What is the most interesting thing you've read in the Bible in the past week?

SEEING WHAT'S THERE

1. How would you summarize what this chapter reveals about the character of Ahab and the character of Jezebel?

2. What specific events in the future does God prophesy to Ahab in this chapter, through the prophet Elijah? And how does Ahab respond to these words?

3. How would you summarize what Ahab learns most about God in this chapter?

FOR LIFE TODAY

4. What would you say are the most useful and important lessons to learn from the personal mistakes you see in this chapter?

5. In Jeremiah 23:29, God says that His Word is like fire, and like a hammer. He can use the Scriptures to burn away unclean thoughts and desires in our hearts. He can also use Scripture to hit hard like a hammer, with the power to crush our spiritual hardness. From your study in this book of First Kings, how do you most want to see the "fire-and-hammer" power of God's Word at work in your own life?

1 KINGS 22

SEEING WHAT'S THERE

1. In your own words, how would you describe the *power* of the story of Micaiah and the two kings? What is it that makes this passage so gripping?

2. What's the best compliment spoken about any king in this chapter, and what is the worst criticism?

3. How would you summarize the military developments in this chapter?

FOR LIFE TODAY

4. Reflect back on all that has happened to the people of Israel in the book of First Kings. If it's true that *the past is a lesson for the future,* then what would you say are the most important lessons for God's people today to learn from these events?

1 KINGS:
THE BIG PICTURE

(Discuss again the questions in the "Overview," plus the questions below.)

1. Who would you say are the most important individuals whose stories are told in the book of 1 Kings? And in what order would you rank them, according to their importance to this book?

2. For getting the most from the book of First Kings, one of the best guidelines is found in 2 Timothy 3:16-17, words which Paul wrote with the Old Testament first in view. He said that *all* Scripture is of great benefit to (a) teach us, (b) rebuke us, (c) correct us, and (d) train us in righteousness. Paul added that these Scriptures completely equip the person of God "for every good work." As you think seriously about those guidelines, in which of these areas do you especially see the usefulness of First Kings?

3. Look together at each of these passages, and discuss which one you believe is the best candidate for "KEY VERSE" in the book of First Kings—the one which brings into sharpest focus what this book is most about: 9:4-5, 11:11, or 11:13.

4. What would you say is the main theme (or themes) in the book of First Kings?

5. SEARCH FOR THE SAVIOR—What words, images, or themes in First Kings have reminded you most of Jesus?

6. Based especially on your own experience, complete this statement in the way that's most meaningful to you: I believe it's important for Christians to read and explore the book of First Kings because…

7. What to you personally is the strongest example in this book of someone doing what was right and good?

8. What to you personally is the strongest example in this book of someone doing what was wrong?

9. If First Kings were the only book in the Old Testament, in what ways would it still make a good introduction to the message of Jesus in the New Testament?

2 Kings

OVERVIEW

(Discuss these OVERVIEW questions both at the beginning of your study of Second Kings, then again after you've studied all 25 chapters. Your answers may change significantly once you've looked more closely at the entire book.)

Startup: Talk together about people you've known who especially impressed you as being persevering and courageous in the face of stiff opposition.

SEEING WHAT'S THERE

1. Before launching into a closer look at Second Kings, how would you summarize what you already know about this book?

2. Scan the 22 chapters of this book to see how many times you can find the phrase "evil in the sight of the Lord" or "evil in the eyes of the Lord." From the ways in which you find this phrase used in Second Kings, what clues does it offer about the book's central message?

3. Look also at the list of "Questions to Ask as You Begin Your Study of Each Book" on page 9.

FOR LIFE TODAY

4. The book of Second Kings has been called "Israel Faces the Sunset" and "The Book of Two Captivities." With that reputation for this book, what kinds of answers and guidelines and solutions would you like to gain as you examine it more closely?

5. From what you see of Hezekiah's example in 18:5-7, what would be a good personal prayer to offer to God as you study this book?

6. As you think first about *who God is,* and second about *what the Bible is,* how strongly would you rate your present desire to understand better the book of Second Kings? Use a scale of one to ten (one = "no desire at all," ten = "extremely intense desire") to help you decide.

2 KINGS 1

SEEING WHAT'S THERE

1. Review first the content in 1 Kings. What are the most important developments in that book in the history of Israel? What are the most important developments in the life and ministry of Elijah? And what is revealed most about God's plan and purpose for His people Israel?

2. What specific judgment from God does the prophet Elijah announce against King Ahaziah in this chapter, and for what expressed reason?

3. EYE FOR DETAIL—*From what you recall seeing in chapter 1, try answering the following question without looking in your Bible:* What was Elijah wearing in this chapter? (See verse 8.)

FOR LIFE TODAY

4. What do you find in this chapter that can most easily be translated into a principle or guideline for God's people today to live by?

5. Proverbs 2:1-5 tells about the sincere person who truly longs for wisdom and understanding, and who searches the Scriptures for it—as if it were buried treasure. That person, Solomon says, will come to understand the fear of the Lord, and discover the knowledge of God. As you begin exploring the book of Second Kings, what "buried treasure" would you like God to help you find here—to show you what God and His wisdom are really like? If you have this desire, how would you express it in your own words?

2 KINGS 2

SEEING WHAT'S THERE

1. In what specific ways in this chapter does God show his approval of the ministries of both Elijah and Elisha?

2. Look again at verses 23-25. What do you think is the main point God is making by including this incident in the Bible?

3. EYE FOR DETAIL— *From what you recall seeing in chapter 2, try answering the following question without looking in your Bible:* What question is Elisha asked twice in this chapter? (See verses 3 and 5.)

CAPTURE THE ESSENCE

4. Look again at what Elijah says about Elisha's choice in verses 9-10. How would you explain Elijah's response?

5. Keeping in mind the lessons he may have learned, suppose Elijah was allowed to live over again his life on earth. What, if anything, do you think he would most want to change, and how?

6. How would you summarize what Elisha learns most about God in this chapter?

7. Imagine yourself being present in the temple in Jerusalem as the twelve-year-old Jesus hears this chapter read and discussed by the rabbis there. In Luke 2:46 we read that He was listening to these teachers and asking them questions. What verses from this chapter do you think would most impress the boy Jesus, and what questions or comments do you suppose He might have spoken?

FOR LIFE TODAY

8. In what specific ways do you sense God's approval at this time in your life?

2 KINGS 3

Startup: What three things are you most thankful for these days?

SEEING WHAT'S THERE

1. How would you summarize the military developments in this chapter, both from man's viewpoint and from God's?

2. How would you explain Elisha's response in verse 14?

3. EYE FOR DETAIL— *From what you recall seeing in chapter 3, try answering the following question without looking in your Bible:* How many lambs and how much wool was the king of Moab required to pay as tribute to King Ahab? (See verse 4.)

2 KINGS 4

SEEING WHAT'S THERE

1. Which of the miracles in this chapter are most impressive to you, and why?

2. EYE FOR DETAIL— *From what you've seen in chapter 4, try answering the following question without looking in your Bible:* Where did the Shunammite woman find Elisha? (See verse 25.)

CAPTURE THE ESSENCE

3. How would you summarize what the woman from Shunem learns most about God in this chapter?

4. Again, imagine yourself being present in the temple in Jerusalem as the twelve-year-old Jesus hears this chapter read and discussed by the Jewish teachers. What verses in this chapter do you think would most impress Him, and what questions or comments do you suppose He might have spoken?

2 KINGS 5

Startup: When you get to heaven, and you meet Elisha, what's the first question you'd like to ask him?

SEEING WHAT'S THERE

1. When Naaman was healed, what knowledge did that engrave in his mind? (See verse 15.)

2. What would you say is revealed most about Elisha's character and values in verse 26?

3. How many things did Elisha's servant Gehazi do wrong in this chapter?

4. EYE FOR DETAIL— *From what you recall seeing in chapter 5, try answering the following question without looking in your*

Bible: How many times did Naaman dip himself in the Jordan River? (See verse 14.)

CAPTURE THE ESSENCE

5. How would you summarize what Naaman learns most about God in this chapter?

FOR LIFE TODAY

6. Choose one of these sentences, and complete it as fully and candidly as you would like: (a) What I see and understand in this chapter is important to my life because... OR: (b) What I see and understand in this chapter does NOT seem important to my life at this time, because...

7. What would you say are the most useful and important lessons to learn from the mistakes of Gehazi in this chapter?

2 KINGS 6

SEEING WHAT'S THERE

1. What do you see as the *purpose* behind each of the miracles in this chapter?

2. How would you answer the question that ends this chapter?

3. EYE FOR DETAIL— *From what you recall seeing in chapter 6, try answering the following question without looking in your Bible:* As the famine intensified, what was the going price for a donkey's head? (See verse 25.)

CAPTURE THE ESSENCE

4. From what you see in this chapter, what are the most important things that Elisha understands about God's personality and character?

2 KINGS 7

SEEING WHAT'S THERE

1. What do you think God wants us to understand most from this chapter?

2. EYE FOR DETAIL— *From what you recall seeing in chapter 7, try answering the following question without looking in your Bible:* At what time of day did the four lepers go out to the camp of the Aramean army? (See verses 5-7.)

FOR LIFE TODAY

3. In Romans 15:4, Paul reminds us that the Old Testament Scriptures can give us patience and perseverance on one hand, as well as comfort and encouragement on the other. In your own life, how do you see this book of Second Kings living up to Paul's description? In what ways, if any, is it meeting your personal needs for both *perseverance* and *encouragement?*

2 KINGS 8

Startup: In the recent past, what is the most memorable way you have recognized God's loving and sovereign control over circumstances in your life?

SEEING WHAT'S THERE

1. What human actions in this chapter do you think were most pleasing to God? And which do you think were most displeasing?

2. For helpful background on the events of verses 7-15, what do you discover in 1 Kings 19:15?

3. What promise from God are we reminded of in verse 19? (Look back at the promise spoken earlier in 1 Kings 11:29-39.) What does this promise communicate about God's plans for His people?

4. EYE FOR DETAIL— *From what you recall seeing in chapter 8, try answering the following question without looking in your Bible:* How did Hazael kill his master, the king of Aram? (See verse 15.)

2 KINGS 9

SEEING WHAT'S THERE

1. How would you summarize the events of this chapter in two or three sentences?

2. For helpful background on the events of this chapter, what do you discover in 1 Kings 19:16-17?

FOR LIFE TODAY

3. In Isaiah 55:10-11, God reminds us that He sends rain and snow from the sky to water the earth and to nurture life. In the

same way, God says that He sends His words to accomplish specific purposes. From your study so far, what would you suggest as *God's* primary purposes for the book of Second Kings in the lives of Christians today?

2 KINGS 10

SEEING WHAT'S THERE

1. What are the most important decisions and choices that are made in this chapter, and how would you analyze each one?

2. EYE FOR DETAIL— *From what you recall seeing in chapter 10, try answering the following question without looking in your Bible:* How many soldiers did Jehu post around the temple of Baal to help him kill the priests of Baal? (See verse 24.)

2 KINGS 11

SEEING WHAT'S THERE

1. How would you summarize Jehoiada's plan for dealing with Athaliah, and how would you evaluate its success?

2. EYE FOR DETAIL— *From what you recall seeing in chapter 11, try answering the following question without looking in your Bible:* How old was Joash when he became king of Judah? (See verse 21.)

2 KINGS 12

Startup: What's the most recent "repair" work you've needed to do? In what way have you helped to rebuild or restore or heal?

SEEING WHAT'S THERE

1. From what you see in this chapter, how would you summarize the most important accomplishments of King Joash?

2. EYE FOR DETAIL— *From what you recall seeing in chapter 12, try answering the following question without looking in your Bible:* How long did Joash serve as king in Jerusalem? (See verse 1.)

2 KINGS 13

SEEING WHAT'S THERE

1. How would you summarize all that happened in the meeting between the dying Elisha and King Jehoash of Israel? If you had been present in this meeting, how do you think it would have affected you?

2. What do you think God wants us to understand most from the incident in verse 21?

CAPTURE THE ESSENCE

3. Review again verses 14-20. Keeping in mind the lessons he may have learned, suppose Elisha was allowed to live his life over again. What, if anything, do you think he would most want to change, and how?

4. Now that you're halfway through Second Kings, how would you summarize the most important lessons to learn from this book?

FOR LIFE TODAY

5. Look again at verses 18-19. At this point in your life, how strongly would you rate your *enthusiasm* for serving God, compared with other times in the past? Use a scale of one to ten (one = "much weaker than ever," ten = "much stronger than ever") to help you decide.

2 KINGS 14

SEEING WHAT'S THERE

1. What's the best compliment spoken about any king in this chapter, and what is the worst criticism?

2. EYE FOR DETAIL— *From what you recall seeing in chapter 14, try answering the following question without looking in your Bible:* How many Edomites did King Amaziah's forces kill in the Valley of Salt? (See verse 7.)

2 KINGS 15

SEEING WHAT'S THERE

1. What's the best compliment spoken about any king in this chapter, and what is the worst criticism?

2. EYE FOR DETAIL—*From what you re-call seeing in chapter 15, try answering the following question without looking in your Bible:* Which king in this chapter had the shortest reign? (See verse 13.)

CAPTURE THE ESSENCE

3. How would you evaluate Israel's political stability at this time? And how would you evaluate Israel's spiritual condition?

2 KINGS 16

SEEING WHAT'S THERE

1. In this chapter, how many things do you see King Ahaz doing wrong?

2 KINGS 17

SEEING WHAT'S THERE

1. Chapter 17 has been called the key to the book of Second Kings. What does this chapter include that could make it this significant?

2. What specific sins and failures on Israel's part are mentioned in this chapter?

3. What specific action on God's part do you see in verse 25?

4. From what you see in this chapter, what are God's *expectations* of His people?

CAPTURE THE ESSENCE

5. What indications do you see of God's love in verses 7-23?

FOR LIFE TODAY

6. Think again about the conclusions made in verses 7-23. Then discuss how you would complete this sentence: What God really wants from me is…

2 KINGS 18

Startup: What is the most interesting thing you've read in the Bible in the past week?

SEEING WHAT'S THERE

1. With chapter 18, we begin a major new division in the book of Second Kings. In only a few sentences, how would you summarize the most important things that have happened so far in this book?

2. How is Hezekiah described in verses 6-8?

3. As this chapter closes, how would you summarize the crisis Hezekiah faces? What is most needed from him at this time?

4. EYE FOR DETAIL—*From what you re-call seeing in chapter 18, try answering the following question without looking in your Bible:* What did Hezekiah send as tribute to King Sennacherib of Assyria? (See verses 15-16.)

2 KINGS 19

SEEING WHAT'S THERE

1. In verses 2-4, look closely at the words of Hezekiah's message to Isaiah. What was Hezekiah's hope at this time?

2. Through Isaiah's words in verses 6-7, what specific promises did the Lord give to Hezekiah?

3. From the words of his message to Heze-kiah in verses 9-13, how would you summarize Sennacherib's view of God?

4. What specific requests does Hezekiah make to God in verses 15-19?

5. In the words of Isaiah in verses 20-34, look carefully at how God answers Hezekiah. What specific *facts*—past, present, and future—does God want Hezekiah to understand?

CAPTURE THE ESSENCE

6. From what you see in Hezekiah's prayer in verses 15-19, what are the most important things he understands about God's personality and character?

7. How would you summarize what the people of Israel learn most about God in this chapter?

FOR LIFE TODAY

8. In light of how you're doing spiritually in your life today, which elements of Heze-kiah's prayer in verses 15-19 do you think should be incorporated in your own prayers to God?

9. Consider how strongly you desire to know God better, then ask yourself this question: *What are the truths revealed about Him in this chapter which He may*

want me to understand more deeply at this time in my life?

10. Review the guidelines for our thought-life given in Philippians 4:8—"Whatever is true, whatever is noble, whatever is right, whatever is pure, whatever is lovely, whatever is admirable—if anything is excellent or praiseworthy—*think about such things."* What food for thought can you find in this chapter that especially strikes you as being *true,* or *noble,* or *right,* or *pure,* or *lovely,* or *admirable,* or *excellent,* or *praiseworthy?*

2 KINGS 20

SEEING WHAT'S THERE

1. Which important details in this chapter do you think might be the easiest to overlook?

2. EYE FOR DETAIL—*From what you recall seeing in chapter 20, try answering the following question without looking in your Bible:* How many years did the Lord add to Hezekiah's life? (See verse 6.)

CAPTURE THE ESSENCE

3. How would you summarize what Hezekiah learned most about God in this chapter?

2 KINGS 21

Startup: From God's point of view, what would you say is the most harmful thing anyone could do in your church at this time?

SEEING WHAT'S THERE

1. What is the main message in the words from God which are recalled in verse 4 and in verses 7-8?

2. According to verse 9, why did people not listen to this message from God?

3. Look carefully at God's words in verses 10-15. What specific punishment does God promise to bring, and for what stated reasons?

4. What further failure on Manasseh's part is mentioned in verse 16?

FOR LIFE TODAY

5. In Jeremiah 23:29, God says that His Word is like fire, and like a hammer. He can use the Scriptures to burn away unclean thoughts and desires in our hearts. He can also use Scripture to hit hard like a hammer, with the power to crush our spiritual hardness. From your study in this book of Second Kings, how do you most want to see the "fire-and-hammer" power of God's Word at work in your own life?

2 KINGS 22

SEEING WHAT'S THERE

1. What are the most important decisions and choices that are made in this chapter, and how would you analyze each one?

2. In verses 16-20, what specific prophecies are given to Josiah through the prophetess Huldah?

3. EYE FOR DETAIL—*From what you recall seeing in chapter 22, try answering the following question without looking in your Bible:* What did Josiah do when he first heard the words of the Scriptures that were found in the temple? (See verse 11.)

2 KINGS 23

SEEING WHAT'S THERE

1. As you analyze the revival taking place in chapters 22 and 23 under King Josiah, how would you analyze its *reasons* and its *results?*

2. What's the best compliment spoken about any king in this chapter, and what is the worst criticism?

3. EYE FOR DETAIL—*From what you recall seeing in chapter 23, try answering the following question without looking in your Bible:* In what year of Josiah's reign did the Israelites renew their celebration of the Passover? (See verse 23.)

2 KINGS 24

SEEING WHAT'S THERE

1. What are the most important political and military developments in this chapter?

2. Look carefully at verses 1-4. What specific action and intention on God's part is mentioned in verse 2? And what reason and purpose for this action is given in verses 3-4?

3. What additional reason is mentioned in verse 20?

2 KINGS 25

SEEING WHAT'S THERE

1. What are the most important decisions and choices that are made in this chapter, and how would you analyze each one?

2. EYE FOR DETAIL— *From what you recall seeing in chapter 25, try answering the following question without looking in your Bible:* For how long was Jerusalem under siege from Nebuchadnezzar and his army? (See verses 1-2.)

CAPTURE THE ESSENCE

3. What is the best evidence you've seen in this book of God's love for His people?

FOR LIFE TODAY

4. Think back on all that has happened to the people of Israel in the book of Second Kings. If it's true that *the past is a lesson for the future,* then what would you say are the most important lessons for God's people today to learn from these events?

2 KINGS:

THE BIG PICTURE

(Discuss again the questions in the "Overview," plus the questions below.)

1. Who would you say are the most important individuals whose stories are told in the book of Second Kings? And in what order would you rank them, according to their importance to this book?

2. For getting the most from the book of Second Kings, one of the best guidelines is found in 2 Timothy 3:16-17, words which Paul wrote with the Old Testament first in view. He said that *all* Scripture is of great benefit to (a) teach us, (b) rebuke us, (c) correct us, and (d) train us in righteousness. Paul added that these Scriptures completely equip the person of God "for every good work." As you think seriously about those guidelines, in which of these areas do you especially see the usefulness of Second Kings?

3. Look together at each of these passages, and discuss which one you believe is the best candidate for "KEY VERSE" in the book of Second Kings—the one which brings into sharpest focus what this book is most about: 10:10, 17:13-14, 17:22-23, or 23:27.

4. What would you say is the main theme (or themes) in the book of Second Kings?

5. SEARCH FOR THE SAVIOR—What words, images, or themes in Second Kings have reminded you most of Jesus?

6. Based especially on your own experience, complete this statement in the way that's most meaningful to you: I believe it's important for Christians to read and explore the book of Second Kings because...

7. What to you personally is the strongest example in this book of someone doing what was right and good?

8. What to you personally is the strongest example in this book of someone doing what was wrong?

9. If Second Kings were the only book in the Old Testament, in what ways would it still make a good introduction to the message of Jesus in the New Testament?

1 Chronicles

OVERVIEW

(Discuss these OVERVIEW questions both at the beginning of your study of First Chronicles, then after you've studied all 29 chapters. Your answers may change significantly once you've looked more closely at the entire book.)

Startup: Talk together about what you've enjoyed most about family reunions.

SEEING WHAT'S THERE

1. Before launching into a closer look at First Chronicles, how would you summarize what you already know about this book?

2. Find the theme or thought that reoccurs in the following verses—17:4, 17:10, 17:12, and 17:25; 22:5 and 22:11; and 28:2-3. What clues do you think this offers about the central message of First Chronicles?

3. Look also at the list of "Questions to Ask as You Begin Your Study of Each Book" on page 9.

FOR LIFE TODAY

4. The book of First Chronicles has been called "The Book of Godly Heritage" and "The Godly Reign of David." With that reputation for this book, what kinds of answers and guidelines and solutions would you like to gain as you examine it more closely?

5. From what you see in the words of David's song in 16:11, what would be a good personal prayer to offer to God as you study this book?

1 CHRONICLES 1

SEEING WHAT'S THERE

1. How many names in this chapter do you recognize from other parts of Scripture?

1 CHRONICLES 2

SEEING WHAT'S THERE

1. In presenting the genealogy of the twelve tribes of Israel, why do you think the extended list for Judah is presented first (beginning in verse 3), even though he had three older brothers?

1 CHRONICLES 3

SEEING WHAT'S THERE

1. How many children of David are listed in verses 1-9?

1 CHRONICLES 4

SEEING WHAT'S THERE

1. In verse 40, how is the land described where the tribe of Simeon lived?

CAPTURE THE ESSENCE

2. From what you see in the prayer of Jabez in verse 10, what are the most important things he understands about God's personality and character?

1 CHRONICLES 5

SEEING WHAT'S THERE

1. In beginning the genealogical record of Reuben's tribe, what comments about he and his brother Judah are included?

2. What action by God is indicated in verse 20?

3. What fact about God is mentioned in verse 22?

4. How are the men of Manasseh described in verse 24? What failure of theirs is mentioned in verse 25? In verse 26, how does God respond to their failure?

1 CHRONICLES 6

SEEING WHAT'S THERE

1. What duties of the Levites are described in this chapter?

1 CHRONICLES 7

SEEING WHAT'S THERE

1 How many remaining tribes are presented in this chapter?

2. What would you say is the main point being made by including in this chapter the incident in verses 21-24?

1 CHRONICLES 8

SEEING WHAT'S THERE

1. Where does Saul appear in this record of the tribe of Benjamin?

1 CHRONICLES 9

SEEING WHAT'S THERE

1. What do verses 1-2 indicate about the people named in the lists that follow?

2. In verse 3, which of the twelve tribes are shown as having descendants returning to Jerusalem after the Babylonian captivity? Which additional tribe is mentioned in verse 14?

3. In verses 35-44, why do you think Saul's family record is repeated here from the previous chapter?

CAPTURE THE ESSENCE

4. The resettling of Jerusalem after the Babylonian captivity does not take place until long after the other events recorded in both First and Second Chronicles. Why then do you think the author of the Chronicles placed this information here in this book, instead of at the end of Second Chronicles?

1 CHRONICLES 10

Startup: In the way we read and study the Bible, what kind of old mental habits or faulty assumptions can most easily block this book of First Chronicles from coming alive in our minds and hearts?

SEEING WHAT'S THERE

1. With chapter 10, we begin a major new division in the book of First Chronicles. In only a few sentences, how would you summarize the most important things that have happened so far in this book?

2. How would you summarize the events surrounding Saul's death, as presented here in chapter 10? What important details in this account might be easily overlooked?

3. What reason for Saul's death is given in verses 13-14?

4. What's the best evidence in this chapter that God is the Lord of history and the cause of its events?

5. As you continue studying First Chronicles, remember to look also on page 8 at the list of "Questions to Ask as You Study Each Chapter."

FOR LIFE TODAY

6. Proverbs 2:1-5 tells about the sincere person who truly longs for wisdom and understanding, and who searches the Scriptures for it—as if it were buried treasure. That person, Solomon says, will come to understand the fear of the Lord, and discover the knowledge of God. As you begin exploring the book of First Chronicles, what "buried treasure" would you like God to help you find here—to show you what God and His wisdom are really like? If you have this desire, how would you express it in your own words?

1 CHRONICLES 11

SEEING WHAT'S THERE

1. In verses 1-2, what do the people of Israel acknowledge about David?

2. In verse 3, who exactly is it who anoints David as king over Israel?

3. How would you summarize the way in which David and the Israelites conquered Jerusalem in verses 4-9?

4. What impresses you most in the accounts of David's mighty men in verses 10-25?

FOR LIFE TODAY

5. In Philippians 4:8 we're given this command: "Whatever is true, whatever is noble, whatever is right, whatever is pure, whatever is lovely, whatever is admirable—if anything is excellent or praiseworthy—*think about such things.*" What food for thought can you find in this chapter that especially strikes you as being *true,* or *noble,* or *right,* or *pure,* or *lovely,* or *admirable,* or *excellent,* or *praiseworthy?*

1 CHRONICLES 12

SEEING WHAT'S THERE

1. What conclusions can you make from this chapter about David's leadership, and about the loyalty and skill of the men he led?

2. What action on the part of God's Spirit do you see in verse 18, and what does this passage tell you about how the Spirit works?

3. EYE FOR DETAIL—*From what you recall seeing in chapter 12, try answering the following question without looking in your Bible:* In the listing of men who came to David at Hebron, how many tribes are mentioned? (See verses 23-37.)

FOR LIFE TODAY

4. What lessons for leadership do you see in this chapter?

5. What lessons for spiritual warfare do you see in this chapter?

6. In Isaiah 55:10-11, God reminds us that He sends rain and snow from the sky to water the earth and to nurture life. In the same way, God says that He sends His words to accomplish specific purposes. From your study so far, what would you suggest as *God's* primary purposes for the book of First Chronicles in the lives of Christians today?

1 CHRONICLES 13

Startup: At this point in your life, how much do you enjoy worshiping God, compared with other times in the past? Use a scale of one to ten (one = "much less than ever," ten = "much more than ever") to help you decide.

SEEING WHAT'S THERE

1. What do you discover about David's heart and character in this chapter?

2. What would you say is the major point God is making by including this chapter in the Bible?

1 CHRONICLES 14

SEEING WHAT'S THERE

1. Chapter 14 has been called the key to the book of First Chronicles. What does this chapter include that could make it this significant?

2. What action on God's part is revealed in verses 2 and 17?

3. EYE FOR DETAIL—*From what you recall seeing in chapter 14, try answering the following question without looking in your Bible:* How many children were born to David in Jerusalem? (See verses 3-6.)

CAPTURE THE ESSENCE

4. From what you see in this chapter, how would you describe David's relationship with God?

1 CHRONICLES 15

SEEING WHAT'S THERE

1. How would you summarize David's preparations for keeping the ark in Jerusalem?

2. What confession or acknowledgment does David make in verse 13?

3. What command does David give the Levites in verse 16?

4. What reason for offering a sacrifice is mentioned in verse 26?

5. EYE FOR DETAIL—*From what you recall seeing in chapter 15, try answering the following question without looking in your Bible:* What did David wear while he

joined the procession that carried the ark? (See verse 27.)

CAPTURE THE ESSENCE

6. Now that you're halfway through First Chronicles, how would you summarize the most important lessons to learn from this book?

1 CHRONICLES 16

SEEING WHAT'S THERE

1. What specifically does David exhort God's people to do in verses 8-13?

2. In verses 14-22, what does David emphasize about God's character?

3. In verses 23-30, who does David address, what specific commands does he give them, and what reasons does he give for these commands?

4. What specific prophecy does David foretell in verse 33?

5. What exhortations does David add in verses 34-35?

6. What specific prayer does David tell the people to offer in verse 35, and for what purpose?

CAPTURE THE ESSENCE

7. From what you see in David's psalm in verses 7-36, what are the most important things that David understands about God's personality and character?

FOR LIFE TODAY

8. Look again at David's exhortations to God's people in verses 8-13 and 34-35. In light of how you're doing spiritually in your life today, which of these commands do you think God most wants you to pay attention to at this time?

9. Consider how strongly you desire to know God better, then ask yourself this question: *What are the truths revealed about Him in this chapter which He may want me to understand more deeply at this time in my life?*

10. Consider again the command in Philippians 4:8—"Whatever is true, whatever is noble, whatever is right, whatever is pure, whatever is lovely, whatever is admirable—if anything is excellent or praiseworthy—*think about such things.*" What food for thought can you find in this chapter that especially strikes you as being *true,* or *noble,* or *right,* or *pure,* or *lovely,* or *admirable,* or *excellent,* or *praiseworthy?*

1 CHRONICLES 17

Startup: What are you looking forward to most in your earthly future? What are your dreams? What is your vision?

SEEING WHAT'S THERE

1. What brief sentence would you use to best summarize what this chapter is most about?

2. How would you explain in your own words the promise in verse 14?

CAPTURE THE ESSENCE

3. How would you summarize what David learns most about God in this chapter?

4. Imagine yourself being present in the temple in Jerusalem as the twelve-year-old Jesus hears this chapter read and discussed by the rabbis there. In Luke 2:46 we read that He was listening to these teachers and asking them questions. What verses from this chapter do you think would most impress the boy Jesus, and what questions or comments do you suppose He might have spoken?

1 CHRONICLES 18

SEEING WHAT'S THERE

1. From what you see in this chapter, how would you evaluate David's leadership?

1 CHRONICLES 19

SEEING WHAT'S THERE

1. How would you summarize the political and military developments in this chapter? And how does David respond to them?

1 Chronicles 20

SEEING WHAT'S THERE

1. Again, how would you summarize the military developments in this chapter?

FOR GOING DEEPER

Look again at verses 1-3, and compare this to what you know from 2 Samuel 11—12 about a tragic incident occurring at this time in David's life. In telling David's story, the writer of 1 Chronicles has omitted much of what is included in 1 and 2 Samuel. Scan the following passages to discover the content of these omissions: chapter 15—31 in 1 Samuel, and chapters 1—4 and 11—21 in 2 Samuel. The author of the Chronicles and the author of the books of Samuel obviously have different purposes in their portrayals of David. How would you describe these different purposes?

1 Chronicles 21

SEEING WHAT'S THERE

1. What would you say is the major point God is making by including this chapter in the Bible?

2. What does God's angel do in this chapter?

CAPTURE THE ESSENCE

3. How would you summarize what David learns most about God in this chapter?

FOR LIFE TODAY

4. Choose one of these sentences, and complete it as fully and candidly as you would like: (a) What I see and understand in this chapter is important to my life because… OR: (b) What I see and understand in this chapter does NOT seem important to my life at this time, because…

1 Chronicles 22

Startup: What is the most interesting thing you've read in the Bible in the past week?

SEEING WHAT'S THERE

1. In verse 8, look closely at the reason God gives for not allowing David to build the temple. How would you explain this in your own words?

2. What promises for David and for Israel did God give in verses 9-10?

3. What command does David give to Israel's leaders in verse 17?

4. What additional requests does David add in verse 19? And what reasons for these requests does he give in verse 18?

5. EYE FOR DETAIL— *From what you recall seeing in chapter 22, try answering the following question without looking in your Bible:* What were nails used for in the construction of the temple, and what were they made of? (See verse 3.)

CAPTURE THE ESSENCE

6. What conclusions could you make from verse 7 about what Scripture means when it refers to God's *name?* (Look also at 1 Chronicles 29:16 and 2 Chronicles 12:13.)

FOR LIFE TODAY

7. Think again about David's exhortation at the beginning of verse 19. What are the most important ways for you to heed these words at this time in your life?

8. In Jeremiah 23:29, God says that His Word is like fire, and like a hammer. He can use the Scriptures to burn away unclean thoughts and desires in our hearts. He can also use Scripture to hit hard like a hammer, with the power to crush our spiritual hardness. From your study in this book of First Chronicles, how do you most want to see the "fire-and-hammer" power of God's Word at work in your own life?

1 Chronicles 23

SEEING WHAT'S THERE

1. What two or three words would you use to best summarize what this chapter is most about?

2. How would you summarize the duties of the Levites?

3. What gift of God does David emphasize in verse 25?

4. EYE FOR DETAIL—*From what you re-call seeing in chapter 23, try answering the following question without looking in your Bible:* What was the total number of Levites above age 30? (See verse 3.)

1 CHRONICLES 24

SEEING WHAT'S THERE

1. For helpful background on verse 2, what do you discover in Leviticus 10:1-3?

2. EYE FOR DETAIL—*From what you re-call seeing in chapter 24, try answering the following question without looking in your Bible:* Of the two surviving sons of Aaron—Eleazar and Ithamar—one had twice the number of descendants among the leaders of the priests in David's day as the other son did. Which son had the most? (See verse 4.)

1 CHRONICLES 25

SEEING WHAT'S THERE

1. What three families did David set apart for the ministry of music in Israel's wor-ship? What do verses 6-8 indicate about their training and organization?

2. EYE FOR DETAIL—*From what you re-call seeing in chapter 25, try answering the following question without looking in your Bible:* Who assisted David in setting apart these families for the ministry of music? (See verse 1.)

1 CHRONICLES 26

SEEING WHAT'S THERE

1. What two or three words would you use to best summarize what this chapter is most about?

2. What do verses 16-18 indicate about how the gatekeepers were arranged in their work?

1 CHRONICLES 27

SEEING WHAT'S THERE

1. What brief sentence would you use to best summarize what this chapter is most about?

2. Look carefully at verses 23-24. How might this passage shed light on Joab's reaction to David's census in 1 Chroni-cles 21:1-3 and 2 Samuel 24:1-3?

1 CHRONICLES 28

Startup: What three things are you most thankful for these days?

SEEING WHAT'S THERE

1. What specific charge does David give to the people in this chapter?

2. What specific charge does David give to Solomon in this chapter?

3. What action on the part of God's Spirit do you see in verse 12, and what does this passage tell you about how the Holy Spirit works?

CAPTURE THE ESSENCE

4. If this book was the only portion of Scripture you had access to, how would you use it to help you define the proper worship of God?

5. How does David describe his kingdom in verse 5? (See also verse 23 in chapter 29.)

FOR LIFE TODAY

6. Think about all that David tells Sol-omon in verse 9 about serving God wholeheartedly. In practical terms, what do you think serving God wholehearted-ly means most for you at this time in your life?

7. Look also at David's words in verse 10. What unfinished work do you believe God has chosen *you* for?

FOR GOING DEEPER

Study carefully David's God-given instruc-tions for the temple in verses 11-19, then compare these with the Lord's instructions for building the tabernacle in Exodus 25— 30. What are the biggest similarities you see?

1 CHRONICLES 29

1. How many times do you see the words *heart* or *wholehearted* in this chapter?

2. What specific points of praise does David offer God in verses 10-13.

3. What does David tell the people to do in verse 20, and how do they respond?

4. What does God do in verse 25?

5. EYE FOR DETAIL— *From what you recall seeing in chapter 29, try answering the following question without looking in your Bible:* Who was anointed as high priest at the same time Solomon was anointed king? (See verse 22.)

CAPTURE THE ESSENCE

6. From what you see in verses 10-19, what are the most important things that David understands about God's personality and character?

7. Once more, imagine yourself being present in the temple in Jerusalem as the twelve-year-old Jesus hears this chapter read and discussed by the Jewish teachers. What verses in this chapter do you think would most impress Him, and what questions or comments do you suppose He might have spoken?

FOR LIFE TODAY

8. Look again at the ways in which David praised God in verses 10-13. How would you express this same praise in your own words?

9. Review once more the guidelines for our thought-life given in Philippians 4:8— "Whatever is true, whatever is noble, whatever is right, whatever is pure, whatever is lovely, whatever is admirable—if anything is excellent or praiseworthy— *think about such things.*" What food for thought can you find in this chapter that especially strikes you as being *true,* or *noble,* or *right,* or *pure,* or *lovely,* or *admirable,* or *excellent,* or *praiseworthy?*

FOR GOING DEEPER

Notice again in verses 6-9 how the people gave freely and generously for the building of the temple. Then compare this to how their ancestors gave for the building of the tabernacle in Exodus 35:20-29. What are the biggest similarities you see in these two accounts, and what principles can you draw from them about our giving to the Lord's work today?

1 CHRONICLES:
THE BIG PICTURE

(Discuss again the questions in the "Overview," plus the questions below.)

1. Look together at each of these passages, and discuss which one you believe is the best candidate for "KEY VERSE" in the book of First Chronicles— the one which brings into sharpest focus what this book is most about: 14:2, 15:2, 17:11-14, or 29:11.

2. What would you say is the main theme (or themes) in the book of First Chronicles?

3. SEARCH FOR THE SAVIOR—What words, images, or themes in First Chronicles have reminded you most of Jesus?

4. Based especially on your own experience, complete this statement in the way that's most meaningful to you: I believe it's important for Christians to read and explore the book of First Chronicles because...

5. What to you personally is the strongest example in this book of someone doing what was right and good?

6. What to you personally is the strongest example in this book of someone doing what was wrong?

7. If First Chronicles were the only book in the Old Testament, in what ways would it still make a good introduction to the message of Jesus in the New Testament?

2 Chronicles

OVERVIEW

(Discuss these OVERVIEW questions both at the beginning of your study of Second Chronicles, then again after you've studied all 36 chapters. Your answers may change significantly once you've looked more closely at the entire book.)

Startup: Talk together about what you feel are the most powerful *idols* in our society today.

SEEING WHAT'S THERE

1. Before launching into a closer look at Second Chronicles, how would you summarize what you already know about this book?

2. The word *temple* occurs more often in Second Chronicles than in any other book of the Bible. As you examine the following passages, decide what God wants us to understand most from this book about the temple—2:5-6, 5:13-14, 6:18-21, 7:1-3, 7:12, 7:16, 7:20-22, 29:3-8, and 33:7-9.

3. Look also at the list of "Questions to Ask as You Begin Your Study of Each Book" on page 9.

FOR LIFE TODAY

4. The book of Second Chronicles has been called "The Book of Israel's Final Apostasy" and "The Road to Captivity." With that reputation for this book, what kinds of answers and guidelines and solutions would you like to gain as you examine it more closely?

5. From what you see in Hezekiah's example in 31:20-21, what would be a good personal prayer to offer to God as you study this book?

6. As you think first about *who God is,* and second about *what the Bible is,* how strongly would you rate your present desire to understand better the book of Second Chronicles? Use a scale of one to ten (one = "no desire at all," ten = "extremely intense desire") to help you decide.

2 CHRONICLES 1

SEEING WHAT'S THERE

1. Review first the content in 1 Chronicles. What are the most important developments in that book in the life of David? What is revealed most about David's character? And what is revealed most about God's plan and purpose for His people Israel?

2. What individuals from Israel's history are mentioned in verses 1-5?

3. What does this chapter communicate most about Solomon's character?

4. From what you see in this chapter and elsewhere, how well did God do in fulfilling His promises to Solomon in verse 12?

5. EYE FOR DETAIL—*From what you recall seeing in chapter 1, try answering the following question without looking in your Bible:* Where were Solomon's horses imported from? (See verse 16.)

CAPTURE THE ESSENCE

6. How would you summarize what Solomon learns most about God in this chapter?

FOR LIFE TODAY

7. If God asked you the same question He asked Solomon in verse 7, how would you answer?

8. Proverbs 2:1-5 tells about the sincere person who truly longs for wisdom and understanding, and who searches the Scriptures for it — as if it were buried treasure. That person, Solomon says, will

come to understand the fear of the Lord, and discover the knowledge of God. As you begin exploring the book of Second Chronicles, what "buried treasure" would you like God to help you find here—to show you what God and His wisdom are really like? If you have this desire, how would you express it in your own words?

2 CHRONICLES 2

SEEING WHAT'S THERE

1. What observation does King Hiram—a foreigner—make about God's people in verse 11? How do you think Hiram came to this conclusion?

2. EYE FOR DETAIL— *From what you recall seeing in chapter 2, try answering the following question without looking in your Bible:* In the census which Solomon took in this chapter, how many aliens were found in Israel? (See verse 17.)

CAPTURE THE ESSENCE

3. From what you see in Solomon's prayer in verses 5-6, what are the most important things he understands about God's personality and character?

2 CHRONICLES 3

SEEING WHAT'S THERE

1. In verse 1, where in Jerusalem did Solomon build the temple? What can you discover about this place in Genesis 22:1-18?

2. How does this account of the temple's construction compare with the parallel passage in 1 Kings 6? What details have been added by the writer of Chronicles, and what information has he left out or abridged?

2 CHRONICLES 4

SEEING WHAT'S THERE

1. Compare this chapter with 1 Kings 7. Which account includes more details about the temple furnishings?

2. EYE FOR DETAIL— *From what you recall seeing in chapter 4, try answering the following question without looking in your Bible:* How many tables were made for the temple? (See verse 8.)

CAPTURE THE ESSENCE

3. It's often said that a person's home is a reflection of his personality. From what you see in chapters 3 and 4, how would the temple be a reflection of God's personality?

2 CHRONICLES 5

SEEING WHAT'S THERE

1. Compare this chapter with 1 Kings 8. What differences, if any, do you see in these two accounts of the ark being brought to the temple?

2. EYE FOR DETAIL— *From what you recall seeing in chapter 5, try answering the following question without looking in your Bible:* What three Levite musicians are mentioned by name as taking part in the ceremonies in this chapter? (See verse 12.)

2 CHRONICLES 6

Startup: At this point in your life, how often do you sense God's daily presence, compared with other times in the past? Use a scale of one to ten (one = "much less than ever," ten = "much more than ever") to help you decide.

SEEING WHAT'S THERE

1. How many times do you see the word *heart* in this chapter?

2. What does Solomon say about God's love and faithfulness in verses 14-15?

3. In verses 32-33, what was Solomon's understanding of God's desire to save the world, and Israel's part in that salvation?

4. EYE FOR DETAIL— *From what you recall seeing in chapter 6, try answering the following question without looking in your Bible:* What did Solomon make for himself to stand on while he dedicated the altar? (See verse 13.)

CAPTURE THE ESSENCE

5. From what you see in this chapter, what are the most important things that Solomon understands about God's personality and character?

6. Imagine yourself being present in the temple in Jerusalem as the twelve-year-old Jesus hears this chapter read and discussed by the rabbis there. In Luke 2:46 we read that He was listening to these teachers and asking them questions. What verses from this chapter do you think would most impress the boy Jesus, and what questions or comments do you suppose He might have spoken?

FOR LIFE TODAY

7. Look again at Solomon's words of praise for God's love and faithfulness in verse 14-15. How often in your prayers to God do you openly affirm in this way God's personal love and faithfulness toward *you?*

2 CHRONICLES 7

SEEING WHAT'S THERE

1. Chapter 7 has been called the key to the book of Second Chronicles. What does this chapter include that could make it this significant?

CAPTURE THE ESSENCE

2. God's words in verses 14-15 have been called "The Greatest Prescription for Revival." From what you see in this passage, how much do you agree with that assessment, and why?

3. From what you see in this chapter, what are the most important truths God wants us to understand about His presence with His people?

4. How would you summarize what Solomon learns most about God in this chapter?

5. If this book was the only portion of Scripture you had access to, how would you use it to help you define the proper worship of God?

FOR LIFE TODAY

6. If everyone in your church thoroughly understood verse 14, and they all had a passion for living out its truth in their lives, what kind of practical changes do you think would result?

FOR GOING DEEPER

Look again at what God did in verses 1-3, then compare it with what He did in Exodus 40:34-35 and Leviticus 9:23-24. What are the biggest similarities in these incidents, and what do you think God wants us to understand most about them?

2 CHRONICLES 8

SEEING WHAT'S THERE

1. How would you summarize Solomon's dealings with other nations, as indicated in verses 1-8?

2. On what three occasions each year did Solomon sacrifice burnt offerings to the Lord, according to verses 12-13?

3. What foreign trade endeavors do you see mentioned in verses 17-18?

4. EYE FOR DETAIL— *From what you recall seeing in chapter 8, try answering the following question without looking in your Bible:* What is the name of the city Solomon built up in the desert (or wilderness)? (See verse 4.)

2 CHRONICLES 9

SEEING WHAT'S THERE

1. How do the accounts in this chapter compare to what you see in 1 Kings 10 and 11?

2. What observation does the queen of Sheba—a foreigner—make about God's people in verse 8? How do you think she came to this conclusion?

CAPTURE THE ESSENCE

3. If you could go back in time, and God brought you into the events of this chap-

ter to act as a royal adviser to King Solomon, what kind of counsel would you give him, and how would you express it?

FOR GOING DEEPER

In telling Solomon's story, the writer of 2 Chronicles has omitted much of what is included in 1 Kings. Scan the following passages to discover the content of these omissions: 1 Kings 1:1-27, 2:13-46, and 11:1-40. The author of the Chronicles and the author of 1 Kings appear to have different purposes in their portrayals of Solomon. How would you describe these different purposes?

2 CHRONICLES 10

Startup: Can you recall a time when you experienced difficulty because you failed to follow someone's advice? What were the circumstances?

SEEING WHAT'S THERE

1. With chapter 10, we begin a major new division in the book of Second Chronicles. In only a few sentences, how would you summarize the most important things that have happened so far in this book?

2. From what you see in this chapter, who was most to blame for the breakup of the kingdom after Solomon's death?

3. What does verse 15 reveal about God's power and God's character?

2 CHRONICLES 11

SEEING WHAT'S THERE

1. In verses 5-23, how would you summarize the most important achievements of Rehoboam during his reign?

2. Look closely at verses 16-17. What exactly did these people do, and why did they do it?

3. EYE FOR DETAIL—*From what you recall seeing in chapter 11, try answering the following question without looking in your Bible:* What weapons did Rehoboam distribute throughout his kingdom? (See verse 12.)

CAPTURE THE ESSENCE

4. Again, if you could go back in time to act as a royal adviser—this time to King Rehoboam—what kind of counsel would you give him, and how would you express it?

2 CHRONICLES 12

SEEING WHAT'S THERE

1. As you explore the events of this chapter, discuss how much you agree or disagree with this statement: In God's perspective, the responsibility for His people's obedience rested mainly on the shoulders of the king.

2. According to verse 14, *why* did King Rehoboam do evil?

FOR LIFE TODAY

3. In Isaiah 55:10-11, God reminds us that He sends rain and snow from the sky to water the earth and to nurture life. In the same way, God says that He sends His words to accomplish specific purposes. From your study so far, what would you suggest are *God's* primary purposes for the book of Second Chronicles in the lives of Christians today?

2 CHRONICLES 13

SEEING WHAT'S THERE

1. How would you summarize this chapter's military developments in the fighting between the men of Israel and the men of Judah? And what reason for the outcome is given in verse 18?

2. What are the main points Abijah makes in his message to the king and people of the northern kingdom in verses 4-12?

3. How would you summarize the leadership abilities of King Abijah as seen in this chapter?

CAPTURE THE ESSENCE

4. How significant would you say is King Ahijah's statement in verse 5?

5. What's the best evidence in this chapter that God is the Lord of history and the cause of its events?

6. Look at the confident words which Abijah spoke at the beginning of verse 10 and the beginning of verse 12. Could *you* speak those same words with the same confidence today? Why or why not?

2 CHRONICLES 14

Startup: What kind of thoughts and images come to mind when you think of someone who *seeks God?*

SEEING WHAT'S THERE

1. What commands did King Asa give his people in verse 4?

2. What gift from God is highlighted at the end of verse 6?

3. What does verse 7 indicate about Asa's plans and his motives for those plans?

4. Look at Asa's prayer in verse 11. What is his *praise,* what is his *confession,* and what is his *request?*

5. With what specific actions did God answer Asa's prayer?

6. EYE FOR DETAIL— *From what you recall seeing in chapter 14, try answering the following question without looking in your Bible:* How large was Asa's army? (See verse 8.)

FOR LIFE TODAY

7. Look again at the gift God gives at the end of verse 6. What are the most significant ways in which God has given this gift to you?

2 CHRONICLES 15

SEEING WHAT'S THERE

1. How many times do you see the words *heart* or *wholehearted* in this chapter?

2. What additional evidence do you see in this chapter that God is the Lord of history and the cause of its events?

3. What action on the part of God's Spirit do you see beginning in verse 1, and what does this tell you about how the Spirit works?

4. What command does God give to King Asa in verse 7?

5. What specific commitment do the people make in verse 12?

6. EYE FOR DETAIL— *From what you recall seeing in chapter 15, try answering the following question without looking in your Bible:* At the great assembly in Jerusalem mentioned in this chapter, how many animals were sacrificed? (See verse 11.)

CAPTURE THE ESSENCE

7. What principles does God express in verse 2, and how would you evaluate their importance?

FOR LIFE TODAY

8. In practical terms, how do the principles stated in verse 2 apply to you today?

9. Look also at the command from God in verse 7. In what ways, if any, is God speaking these words to you today?

10. How easily could you make the same commitment today which God's people make in verse 12? What do you feel would be the biggest obstacles to overcome before personally making this commitment?

2 CHRONICLES 16

SEEING WHAT'S THERE

1. What judgment of God on King Asa is revealed through the prophet Hanani in verses 7-8, and what reason for that judgment?

2. What does the first half of verse 9 reveal about God's actions? How would you explain this statement in your own words?

3. In the last half of verse 9, what judgment does God announce upon King Asa?

4. What more is revealed about Asa in verse 12?

CAPTURE THE ESSENCE

5. In your own words, what would you say is revealed most about God's character and personality in verse 9?

6. Think again about the statement in the first half of verse 9. In practical and personal terms, what meaning do these words have for you today?

7. Look again at the statement in verse 12, then discuss how much you agree or disagree with this statement: When Christians have physical ailments, it is wrong for them to rely on the help of medical doctors if they have not also sought God's help.

8. In Romans 15:4, Paul reminds us that the Old Testament Scriptures can give us patience and perseverance on one hand, as well as comfort and encouragement on the other. In your own life, how do you see this book of Second Chronicles living up to Paul's description? In what ways, if any, is it meeting your personal needs for both *perseverance* and *encouragement?*

2 CHRONICLES 17

Startup: What do you see as the most important decision you'll be making in the next year? Next month? Next week?

SEEING WHAT'S THERE

1. What activity on God's part is described in verse 5?

2. How is Jehoshaphat's spiritual condition described in verse 6?

3. What activity on the part of Jehoshaphat and his officials and priests is described in verses 7-9? How important do you think this was at that time in Israel's history?

4. What immediate result from Jehoshaphat's leadership is seen in verses 10-12?

2 CHRONICLES 18

SEEING WHAT'S THERE

1. How is Jehoshaphat described in verse 1?

2. How would you evaluate the responsibility of Jehoshaphat in the joint defeat which Israel and Judah experienced in this chapter?

3. What does verse 31 indicate about Jehoshaphat's dependence on God?

FOR LIFE TODAY

4. Now that you're halfway through 2 Chronicles, how would you summarize the most important lessons to learn in this book?

2 CHRONICLES 19

SEEING WHAT'S THERE

1. How would you summarize Jehoshaphat's actions in this chapter?

2. What was the "good news" and the "bad news" in the words spoken to Jehoshaphat by the prophet Jehu in verses 2 and 3?

3. How many times do you see the words *heart* or *wholehearted* in this chapter?

2 CHRONICLES 20

SEEING WHAT'S THERE

1. How would you summarize the crisis Jehoshaphat faces in this chapter? What is most needed from him at this time?

2. Look closely at Jehoshaphat's prayer in verses 6-12. What points of praise does it include? What does Jehoshaphat "remind" God of? What confessions does he make? And what specifically does he ask God to do?

3. Now consider God's answer to Jehoshaphat in verses 15-17. What commands does God give? What facts does God state? And what promises does He make?

4. What specific action does God accomplish in verse 22?

5. What critical results of the incidents in this chapter do you see in verses 29-30?

6. How does God reveal Himself to Jehoshaphat in verses 35-37?

7. EYE FOR DETAIL— *From what you recall seeing in chapter 20, try answering the following question without looking in your Bible:* What was the name of the prophet who spoke to Jehoshaphat and the people in this chapter? (See verse 14.)

CAPTURE THE ESSENCE

8. Again, if you could go back in time to act as a royal adviser—this time to King Jehoshaphat—what kind of counsel would you give him, and how would you express it?

9. How would you summarize what Jehoshaphat learns most about God in this chapter?

FOR LIFE TODAY

10. Choose one of these sentences, and complete it as fully and candidly as you would like: (a) What I see and understand in this chapter is important to my life because… OR: (b) What I see and understand in this chapter does NOT seem important to my life at this time, because…

11. In light of how you're doing spiritually in your life today, which elements of Jehoshaphat's prayer in verses 6-12 do you think should be incorporated in your own prayers to God?

12. In practical terms, how do you see Jehoshaphat's words in verse 20 applying also to you?

2 CHRONICLES 21

SEEING WHAT'S THERE

1. Humanly speaking, what would you say is the best thing anybody does in this chapter? And what is the worst or most questionable thing anybody does in this chapter?

2. Read again the letter from Elijah in verses 12-15. What did God say King Jehoram was guilty of? And what punishment did God promise to bring upon him?

3. EYE FOR DETAIL— *From what you recall seeing in chapter 21, try answering the following question without looking in your*

Bible: How did Jehoram die, and how old was he? (See verses 19-20.)

FOR LIFE TODAY

4. In verse 20, notice the response to Jehoram's death. What would you say is the best way for you to prevent the same kind of response to *your* death?

2 CHRONICLES 22

SEEING WHAT'S THERE

1. What human actions in this chapter do you think were most pleasing to God? And which do you think were most displeasing?

2. How would you summarize the events surrounding the death of Ahaziah, and the political developments that followed?

2 CHRONICLES 23

Startup: What two or three problems, if solved, would make the most difference in your life (in your marriage, in your family, in your home, in your church) today?

SEEING WHAT'S THERE

1. How would you summarize the events that brought young Joash to the throne?

2. How would you evaluate the leadership capabilities of the priest Jehoiada?

2 CHRONICLES 24

SEEING WHAT'S THERE

1. What are the most important decisions and choices that are made in this chapter, and how would you analyze each one?

2. What action on the part of God's Spirit do you see beginning in verse 20?

3. What would you say is the correct answer to the question asked by Zechariah the prophet in verse 20?

CAPTURE THE ESSENCE

4. Again, if you could go back in time to be a royal adviser—this time to King Joash—what kind of counsel would you give him, and how would you express it?

5. What would you say are the most useful and important lessons to learn from the life of Joash?

2 Chronicles 25

SEEING WHAT'S THERE

1. What are the most important decisions and choices that Amaziah made in this chapter, and how would you analyze each one?

2. EYE FOR DETAIL—*From what you recall seeing in chapter 25, try answering the following question without looking in your Bible:* How big was Amaziah's army? (See verses 5-6.)

FOR LIFE TODAY

3. What would you say are the most useful and important lessons to learn from the life of Amaziah?

2 Chronicles 26

SEEING WHAT'S THERE

1. How would you analyze the strengths and weaknesses of Uzziah, as you see him in this chapter?

2. Look carefully at verses 16-21. What punishment was inflicted upon Uzziah, and for what specific reason?

CAPTURE THE ESSENCE

3. Again, if you could go back in time to be a royal adviser—this time to King Uzziah—what kind of counsel would you give him, and how would you express it?

4. How would you summarize what Uzziah learns most about God in this chapter?

FOR LIFE TODAY

5. In Jeremiah 23:29, God says that His Word is like fire, and like a hammer. He can use the Scriptures to burn away unclean thoughts and desires in our hearts. He can also use Scripture to hit hard like a hammer, with the power to crush our spiritual hardness. From your study in this book of Second Chronicles, how do you most want to see the "fire-and-hammer" power of God's Word at work in your own life?

2 Chronicles 27

SEEING WHAT'S THERE

1. What do we learn in verse 6 about the reason for Jotham's success?

2 Chronicles 28

SEEING WHAT'S THERE

1. How many favorable things can you find mentioned about Ahaz in this chapter?

2 Chronicles 29

Startup: When you get to heaven, and you meet Hezekiah, what's the first question you'd like to ask him?

SEEING WHAT'S THERE

1. How would you summarize Hezekiah's actions in this chapter?

2. What reason for these actions does Hezekiah give in verse 10?

3. How many times do you see the word *heart* in this chapter?

4. Once the work in this chapter was accomplished, how did Hezekiah and the people view it, according to verse 36?

5. EYE FOR DETAIL—*From what you recall seeing in chapter 29, try answering the following question without looking in your Bible:* After the Levites purified the temple, how many animals did Hezekiah and the leaders of Jerusalem offer as a sin offering for the people? (See verse 21.)

FOR LIFE TODAY

6. In verse 11, look carefully at Hezekiah's words about what God had chosen the priests and Levites for. As fully as you can explain it, what has God chosen *you* for?

7. Look again at verse 36. What accomplishments by God can the people of your church find to rejoice about today?

2 Chronicles 30

SEEING WHAT'S THERE

1. What special arrangements did Hezekiah have to make in connection with the celebration of Passover in this chapter?

2. According to verse 1, who was invited to this Passover feast?

3. In verses 6-9, what specific exhortations would God's people read in the king's letter?

4. What various responses to Hezekiah's invitation are mentioned in verses 10-12?

5. What specific requests does Hezekiah make to God in his prayer in verses 18-19, and how does God respond in verse 20?

6. EYE FOR DETAIL— *From what you recall seeing in chapter 30 try answering the following question without looking in your Bible:* How long did this Passover celebration last? (See verses 22-23.)

FOR LIFE TODAY

7. In verse 8, look at Hezekiah's words about serving God. If God were to write down a list of the ways in which you truly served Him in the past week, what do you think would be on that list?

2 Chronicles 31

SEEING WHAT'S THERE

1. How would you describe the spiritual health of God's people, as indicated in this chapter?

2. What order does Hezekiah give in verse 4, and why is it significant?

3. What does verse 21 reveal about Hezekiah's heart?

2 Chronicles 32

SEEING WHAT'S THERE

1. In what ways does this chapter make clear that God is the Lord of history and the cause of its events?

2. For helpful background on verse 24, what do you discover in 2 Kings 20:1-11?

3. In your own words, how would you describe the stages of Hezekiah's relationship with God in verses 25-26?

CAPTURE THE ESSENCE

4. Once again, if you could go back in time to be a royal adviser—this time to King Hezekiah—what kind of counsel would you give him, and how would you express it?

5. How would you summarize what Hezekiah learns most about God in this chapter?

2 Chronicles 33

SEEING WHAT'S THERE

1. What specific punishment does God bring upon Manasseh in verse 11?

2. In verse 12, how does King Manasseh respond to his punishment from God? And what does God do in return in verse 13?

2 Chronicles 34

Startup: What is the most interesting thing you've read in the Bible in the past week?

SEEING WHAT'S THERE

1. Look at Josiah's commitment at the beginning of verse 3. How do you see this commitment reflected in the further events of this chapter and the next?

FOR LIFE TODAY

2. Review the guidelines for our thought-life given in Philippians 4:8—"Whatever is true, whatever is noble, whatever is right, whatever is pure, whatever is lovely, whatever is admirable—if anything is excellent or praiseworthy— *think about such things."* What food for thought can you find in this chapter that especially strikes you as being *true,* or *noble,* or *right,* or *pure,* or *lovely,* or *admirable,* or *excellent,* or *praiseworthy?*

2 CHRONICLES 35

SEEING WHAT'S THERE

1. How does verse 22 show God's sovereign control over the events of history?

CAPTURE THE ESSENCE

2. Once more, if you could go back in time to be a royal adviser—this time to King Josiah—what kind of counsel would you give him, and how would you express it?

2 CHRONICLES 36

SEEING WHAT'S THERE

1. Which important details in this chapter do you think might be the easiest to overlook?

2. Look at the statement at the end of verse 21. What does this reveal about God's power and God's character?

3. How do you also see God's sovereign control in verses 22-23?

2 CHRONICLES:
THE BIG PICTURE

(Discuss again the questions in the "Overview," plus the questions below.)

1. Although the two books of Chronicles cover much of the history found also in First and Second Kings, what major differences do you see in the themes and messages of these two sets of books?

2. For getting the most from the book of Second Chronicles, one of the best guidelines is found in 2 Timothy 3:16-17, words which Paul wrote with the Old Testament first in view. He said that *all* Scripture is of great benefit to (a) teach us, (b) rebuke us, (c) correct us, and (d) train us in righteousness. Paul added that these Scriptures completely equip the person of God "for every good work." As you think seriously about those guidelines, in which of these areas do you especially see the usefulness of Second Chronicles?

3. Look together at each of these passages, and discuss which one you believe is the best candidate for "KEY VERSE" in the book of Second Chronicles—the one which brings into sharpest focus what this book is most about: 7:14, 15:2, 16:9, or 20:20.

4. What would you say is the main theme (or themes) in the book of Second Chronicles?

5. SEARCH FOR THE SAVIOR—What words, images, or themes in Second Chronicles have reminded you most of Jesus?

6. Based especially on your own experience, complete this statement in the way that's most meaningful to you: I believe it's important for Christians to read and explore the book of Second Chronicles because...

7. What to you personally is the strongest example in this book of someone doing what was right and good?

8. What to you personally is the strongest example in this book of someone doing what was wrong?

9. If Second Chronicles were the only book in the Old Testament, in what ways would it still make a good introduction to the message of Jesus in the New Testament?

Ezra

OVERVIEW

(Discuss these OVERVIEW questions both at the beginning of your study of Ezra, then again after you've studied all ten chapters. Your answers may change significantly once you've looked more closely at the entire book.)

Startup: Talk together about any impressive experiences you've had going back to some place which you once knew well, but then were away from for a long time.

SEEING WHAT'S THERE

1. Before launching into a closer look at Ezra, how would you summarize what you already know about this book?

2. Find the most prominent theme that re-occurs in the following verses—1:2-3, 1:5, 4:3, 5:11, and 6:14. What clues would you say this offers about the central message of Ezra?

3. For helpful background to the events in the book of Ezra, look over 2 Kings 25 and 2 Chronicles 36:5-23. How would you summarize these background events?

4. In the following passages, notice the different Persian kings referred to in this book, and describe how God used them to serve His own purposes for His people —1:1-8; 4:5-7, 6:1-15, and 7:11-28.

5. Imagine that you were helping to produce a film based on the book of Ezra. Describe the kinds of scenery, supporting characters, Seeing What's There music, lighting effects, etc., which you would use to help portray the central message of this book.

6. Look also at the list of "Questions to Ask as You Begin Your Study of Each Book" on page 9.

FOR LIFE TODAY

7. The book of Ezra has been called "Return from Captivity" and "The Book of the Returning Remnant." With that reputation for this book, what kinds of answers and guidelines and solutions would you like to gain as you examine it more closely?

8. When you get to heaven, if you have a long talk with Ezra and he asks you, "What was most helpful to you in my book?" how would you like to be able to answer him?

9. From what you see in Ezra's example in 7:10, what would be a good personal prayer to offer to God as you study this book?

10. As you think first about *who God is,* and second about *what the Bible is,* how strongly would you rate your present desire to understand better the book of Ezra? Use a scale of one to ten (one = "no desire at all," ten = "extremely intense desire") to help you decide.

EZRA 1

SEEING WHAT'S THERE

1. What is the best evidence you see in this chapter of God's sovereign control over all circumstances?

2. How would you summarize the events of this chapter?

3. Look also on page 8 at the list of "Questions to Ask as You Study Each Chapter." You may want to look again at this list for each chapter in Ezra.

FOR LIFE TODAY

4. Proverbs 2:1-5 tells about the sincere person who truly longs for wisdom and understanding, and who searches the

Scriptures for it—as if it were buried treasure. That person, Solomon says, will come to understand the fear of the Lord, and discover the knowledge of God. As you begin exploring the book of Ezra, what "buried treasure" would you like God to help you find here—to show you what God and His wisdom are really like? If you have this desire, how would you express it in your own words?

EZRA 2

SEEING WHAT'S THERE

1. What evidence of teamwork and leadership do you see in this chapter?

EZRA 3

SEEING WHAT'S THERE

1. How would you summarize what happens in this chapter?

2. Songs are often a way to express and release deep emotions. What emotions are behind the song in verse 11?

3. In verses 10-13, what conclusions can you draw about the people's attitudes toward God at this time?

CAPTURE THE ESSENCE

4. Imagine yourself being present in the temple in Jerusalem as the twelve-year-old Jesus hears this book read and discussed by the rabbis there. In Luke 2:46 we read that He was listening to these teachers and asking them questions. What passages from this book do you think would most impress the boy Jesus, and what questions or comments do you suppose He might have spoken?

EZRA 4

Startup: What is the most interesting thing you've read in the Bible in the past week?

SEEING WHAT'S THERE

1. In this chapter, how many different people or groups of people can you find who are opposed to the rebuilding which the Jews are attempting?

CAPTURE THE ESSENCE

2. Discuss how much you agree or disagree with this statement: Doing God's work will always bring worldly opposition.

EZRA 5

SEEING WHAT'S THERE

1. How would you summarize the contents of this chapter?

CAPTURE THE ESSENCE

2. Now that you're halfway through Ezra, how would you summarize the most important lessons to learn from this book?

EZRA 6

SEEING WHAT'S THERE

1. Chapter 6 has been called the key to the book of Ezra. What does this chapter include that could make it this significant?

2. How many clues do you see in verses 13-15 for *why* the Jews were successful in rebuilding the temple?

FOR LIFE TODAY

3. In Romans 15:4, Paul reminds us that the Old Testament Scriptures can give us patience and perseverance on one hand, as well as comfort and encouragement on the other. In your own life, how do you see this book of Ezra living up to Paul's description? In what ways, if any, is it meeting your personal needs for both *perseverance* and *encouragement*?

EZRA 7

Startup: What do you expect to be your greatest opportunities in the coming year? And how do you think you can best prepare yourself for those opportunities?

SEEING WHAT'S THERE

1. In verses 6 and 12, what do we learn about Ezra's vocation?

2. From verse 10 and verses 27-28, what conclusions can you make about Ezra's character, motives, and personality?

3. With chapter 7 we begin a major new division in the book of Ezra. In only a few sentences, how would you summarize the most important things that have happened so far in this book?

FOR LIFE TODAY

4. Look again at Ezra's devotion to studying and obeying the Scriptures in verse 10. How strongly would you say this verse reflects your own devotion to the Scriptures at this time in your life? To help you decide, use a scale of one to ten (one = "no heart commitment to the Scriptures at all," ten = "a heart commitment equivalent to Ezra's").

EZRA 8

SEEING WHAT'S THERE

1. From what you see in verses 15-30, what conclusions can you make about Ezra's leadership abilities?

FOR LIFE TODAY

2. In Isaiah 55:10-11, God reminds us that He sends rain and snow from the sky to water the earth and to nurture life. In the same way, God says that He sends His words to accomplish specific purposes. From your study so far, what would you suggest are *God's* primary purposes for the book of Ezra in the lives of Christians today?

EZRA 9

Startup: When you get to heaven, and you meet Ezra, what's the first question you'd like to ask him?

SEEING WHAT'S THERE

1. From Ezra's response in verses 3-5, and from the words of his prayer in verses 6-15, what conclusions can you make about Ezra's character and his spiritual condition?

CAPTURE THE ESSENCE

2. From what you see in this chapter, what are the most important things that Ezra understands about God's personality and character?

FOR LIFE TODAY

3. In light of how you're doing spiritually in your life today, which elements of Ezra's prayer in this chapter do you think should be incorporated in your own prayers to God?

4. In Jeremiah 23:29, God says that His Word is like fire, and like a hammer. He can use the Scriptures to burn away unclean thoughts and desires in our hearts. He can also use Scripture to hit hard like a hammer, with the power to crush our spiritual hardness. From your study in this book of Ezra, how do you most want to see the "fire-and-hammer" power of God's Word at work in your own life?

EZRA 10

SEEING WHAT'S THERE

1. What are the most important developments in this chapter?

2. What do we learn in verse 6 about Ezra's character and spiritual condition, and how does this fit with what you've seen earlier in this book?

FOR LIFE TODAY

3. Think back on all that has happened to the people of Israel in the book of Ezra. If it's true that *the past is a lesson for the future,* then what would you say are the most important lessons for God's people today to learn from these events?

4. Choose one of these sentences, and complete it as fully and candidly as you would like: (a) What I see and understand in the book of Ezra is important to my life because... OR: (b) What I see and understand in this book does NOT seem important to my life at this time, because...

Ezra:
The Big Picture

(Discuss again the questions in the "Overview," plus the questions below.)

1. For getting the most from the book of Ezra, one of the best guidelines is found in 2 Timothy 3:16-17, words which Paul wrote with the Old Testament first in view. He said that *all* Scripture is of great benefit to (a) teach us, (b) rebuke us, (c) correct us, and (d) train us in righteousness. Paul added that these Scriptures completely equip the person of God "for every good work." As you think seriously about those guidelines, in which of these areas do you especially see the usefulness of Ezra?

2. Look together at each of these passages, and discuss which one you believe is the best candidate for "KEY VERSE" in the book of Ezra—the one which brings into sharpest focus what this book is most about: 1:3, 1:5, 6:21-22, or 7:10.

3. What would you say is the main theme (or themes) in the book of Ezra?

4. SEARCH FOR THE SAVIOR—What words, images, or themes in Ezra have reminded you most of Jesus?

5. If Ezra were the only book in the Old Testament, in what ways would it still make a good introduction to the message of Jesus in the New Testament?

6. Based especially on your own experience, complete this statement in the way that's most meaningful to you: I believe it's important for Christians to read and explore the book of Ezra because...

Nehemiah

OVERVIEW

(Discuss these OVERVIEW questions both at the beginning of your study of Nehemiah, then again after you've studied all thirteen chapters. Your answers may change significantly once you've looked more closely at the entire book.)

Startup: Talk together about this question: In general, what do you enjoy most— making something new, or repairing something old?

SEEING WHAT'S THERE

1. Before launching into a closer look at Nehemiah, how would you summarize what you already know about this book?

2. Find the word that reoccurs in the following verses—1:8, 4:14, 5:19, 6:14, 9:17, 13:14, 13:22, 13:29, and 13:31. What clues could this word offer about the central message of Nehemiah?

3. For helpful background to the events in the book of Nehemiah, look over the following passages, then summarize the events they tell about—2 Chronicles 36:15-23, and Ezra 1:5-8, 3:1-13, 4:1-5, 6:1-18, and 7:1-10.

4. Look also at the list of "Questions to Ask as You Begin Your Study of Each Book" on page 9.

FOR LIFE TODAY

5. The book of Nehemiah has been called "The Book of Rebuilding," "The Book of Consolidation and Conclusion," and "The Story of God's Man in Action." With that reputation for this book, what kinds of answers and guidelines and solutions would you like to gain as you examine it more closely?

6. When you get to heaven, if you have a long talk with Nehemiah and he asks you, "What was most helpful to you in my book?" how would you like to be able to answer him?

7. From what you see in the example of Ezra and the Israelites in 8:5-6, what would be a good personal prayer to offer to God as you study this book?

8. As you think first about *who God is,* and second about *what the Bible is,* how strongly would you rate your present desire to understand better the book of Nehemiah? Use a scale of one to ten (one = "no desire at all," ten = "extremely intense desire") to help you decide.

NEHEMIAH 1

SEEING WHAT'S THERE

1. What specific requests does Nehemiah make in his prayer in this chapter?

2. Look also on page 8 at the list of "Questions to Ask as You Study Each Chapter." You may want to look again at this list for each chapter in Nehemiah.

3. EYE FOR DETAIL—*From what you recall seeing in chapter 1, try answering the following question without looking in your Bible:* What was the name of Nehemiah's brother who brought him news from Judah? (See verse 2.)

CAPTURE THE ESSENCE

4. From what you see in this chapter, what are the most important things that Nehemiah understands about God's personality and character?

FOR LIFE TODAY

5. What can you learn from Nehemiah's example in this chapter about discovering God's will in your life?

6. Proverbs 2:1-5 tells about the sincere person who truly longs for wisdom and understanding, and who searches the

Scriptures for it—as if it were buried treasure. That person, Solomon says, will come to understand the fear of the Lord, and discover the knowledge of God. As you begin exploring the book of Nehemiah, what "buried treasure" would you like God to help you find here—to show you what God and His wisdom are really like? If you have this desire, how would you express it in your own words?

NEHEMIAH 2

SEEING WHAT'S THERE

1. For helpful background on the king mentioned in verse 1, what can you discover in Ezra 4:7, 6:14, and 7:1-28?

2. Compare Ezra 7:7-8 with Nehemiah 2:1. How many years after Ezra went to Jerusalem did Nehemiah decide to return?

3. What specific requests does Nehemiah make of the king in this chapter?

4. In verses 11-20, what would you say are the most important things Nehemiah does after his arrival in Jerusalem?

5. What evidence do you see in this chapter that Nehemiah knew he was following God's will?

CAPTURE THE ESSENCE

6. From the limited information you see in this chapter, how would you describe the relationship between Nehemiah and the king?

7. Nehemiah has been called a *man of responsibility* and a *man of vision*. What evidence for these conclusions have you seen so far in this book?

8. From what you see in the last half of this chapter, how would you describe Nehemiah's leadership abilities?

9. Look again in verse 20 at Nehemiah's reply to his enemies. Why do you think Nehemiah was so confident that God would help the Israelites rebuild the wall?

10. As this chapter closes, how do you think Nehemiah would answer this question: What important challenges do you think you're going to face in the near future?

11. What would you say this chapter teaches most about *faith in God?*

FOR LIFE TODAY

12. What important challenges do you think *you* will face in the near future?

13. Again, what can you learn from Nehemiah's example in this chapter about discovering God's will in your life?

14. Look again at verse 12. What are the most important tasks which God has put into *your* heart?

15. In Romans 15:4, Paul reminds us that the Old Testament Scriptures can give us patience and perseverance on one hand, as well as comfort and encouragement on the other. In your own life, how do you see this book of Nehemiah living up to Paul's description? In what ways, if any, is it meeting your personal needs for both *perseverance* and *encouragement?*

FOR GOING DEEPER

Look at Nehemiah's prayers in 4:4-5, 5:19, 6:9, 6:14, 13:14, 13:22, 13:29, and 13:31. What do they tell us about Nehemiah's expectations of God, and his personal relationship with God?

NEHEMIAH 3

Startup: What do you see as the most important decision you'll be making in the next year? Next month? next week?

SEEING WHAT'S THERE

1. What specific evidence for Nehemiah's leadership abilities do you see in this chapter?

2. EYE FOR DETAIL— *From what you recall seeing in chapter 3, try answering the following question without looking in your Bible:* What was the name of the builder who had help from his daughters? (See verse 12.)

Nehemiah 4

SEEING WHAT'S THERE

1. What are the most important events occurring in this chapter?

2. What further evidence for Nehemiah's leadership abilities do you see in this chapter?

3. What specific requests does Nehemiah make to God in this chapter?

4. What specific words does Nehemiah speak to his fellow builders in this chapter?

5. EYE FOR DETAIL— *From what you recall seeing in chapter 4, try answering the following question without looking in your Bible:* What weapons and pieces of armor are mentioned in this chapter? (See verses 13, 16, and 18.)

CAPTURE THE ESSENCE

6. From what you see in this chapter, what are the most important things that Nehemiah understands about God's personality and character?

FOR LIFE TODAY

7. Choose one of these sentences, and complete it as fully and candidly as you would like: (a) What I see and understand in this chapter is important to my life because… OR: (b) What I see and understand in this chapter does NOT seem important to my life at this time, because…

Nehemiah 5

Startup: What things produce the most stress in your personal life? In your home? In your family? In your work?

SEEING WHAT'S THERE

1. What further evidence for Nehemiah's leadership abilities do you see in this chapter?

2. What evidence do you see in this chapter of Nehemiah's compassion?

3. What specific commands does Nehemiah give the people in this chapter?

4. EYE FOR DETAIL— *From what you recall seeing in chapter 5, try answering the following question without looking in your Bible:* How many Jewish officials ate at Nehemiah's table? (See verse 17.)

CAPTURE THE ESSENCE

5. From what you've seen so far in this book, how would you summarize in your own words Nehemiah's *motives* for the work he was doing in Jerusalem? What rewards was Nehemiah looking for?

FOR LIFE TODAY

6. What would you say are the most useful and important lessons to learn from Nehemiah's example in this chapter?

7. In Isaiah 55:10-11, God reminds us that He sends rain and snow from the sky to water the earth and to nurture life. In the same way, God says that He sends His words to accomplish specific purposes. From your study so far, what would you suggest are *God's* primary purposes for the book of Nehemiah in the lives of Christians today?

Nehemiah 6

SEEING WHAT'S THERE

1. Chapter 6 has been called the key to the book of Nehemiah. What does this chapter include that could make it this significant?

2. What most impresses you about Nehemiah in this chapter?

3. What further evidence for Nehemiah's leadership abilities do you see in this chapter?

4. How many different responses does Nehemiah give to his enemies in this chapter? And how would you summarize what he says each time?

5. EYE FOR DETAIL— *From what you recall seeing in chapter 6, try answering the following question without looking in your Bible:* How many days did it take for the wall to be completed? (See verse 15.)

CAPTURE THE ESSENCE

6. From what you see in this chapter, what are the most important things that Nehemiah understands about God's personality and character?

NEHEMIAH 7

Startup: What is the most fulfilling accomplishment you can recall having completed?

SEEING WHAT'S THERE

1. What further evidence for Nehemiah's leadership abilities do you see in this chapter?

2. EYE FOR DETAIL—*From what you recall seeing in chapter 7, try answering the following question without looking in your Bible:* Who did Nehemiah place in charge of Jerusalem? (See verse 2.)

CAPTURE THE ESSENCE

3. Now that you're halfway through Nehemiah, how would you summarize the most important lessons Nehemiah has learned in this book?

4. Imagine yourself being present in the temple in Jerusalem as the twelve-year-old Jesus hears this book read and discussed by the rabbis there. In Luke 2:46 we read that He was listening to these teachers and asking them questions. What passages from this book do you think would most impress the boy Jesus, and what questions or comments do you suppose He might have spoken?

NEHEMIAH 8

SEEING WHAT'S THERE

1. With chapter 8, we begin a major new division in the book of Nehemiah. In only a few sentences, how would you summarize the most important things that have happened so far in this book?

2. What specific message does Nehemiah give to the people here in chapter 8?

3. EYE FOR DETAIL—*From what you recall seeing in chapter 8, try answering the following question without looking in your Bible:* For how many days in this chapter did Israel celebrate a feast? (See verse 18.)

CAPTURE THE ESSENCE

4. What insights do you find in this chapter regarding the right way to approach God in worship?

FOR LIFE TODAY

5. Look again at verse 10. What to you is the most practical and relevant meaning of the truth that the joy of the Lord is your strength?

6. Review the guidelines for our thought-life given in Philippians 4:8—"Whatever is true, whatever is noble, whatever is right, whatever is pure, whatever is lovely, whatever is admirable—if anything is excellent or praiseworthy—*think about such things.*" What food for thought can you find in this chapter that especially strikes you as being *true,* or *noble,* or *right,* or *pure,* or *lovely,* or *admirable,* or *excellent,* or *praiseworthy?*

NEHEMIAH 9

Startup: At this point in your life, how sensitive is your heart and conscience to God's laws, compared with other times in the past? Use a scale of one to ten (one = "much weaker than ever," ten = "much stronger than ever") to help you decide.

SEEING WHAT'S THERE

1. What would you say are the strongest points of praise to God in the long prayer in this chapter?

2. How would you summarize the events of Israel's history which are included in this prayer?

3. What specific request is made to God in verse 32?

4. What conclusion is expressed at the end of the prayer?

5. EYE FOR DETAIL—*From what you recall seeing in chapter 9, try answering the following question without looking in your Bible:* What specific individuals from Israel's history are mentioned in the prayer in this chapter? (See verses 7 and 14.)

CAPTURE THE ESSENCE

6. From what you see in the prayer in verses 5-37, what are the most important things that the Israelites understand about God's personality and character?

FOR LIFE TODAY

7. In light of how you're doing spiritually in your life today, which elements of the

long prayer in this chapter do you think should be incorporated in your own prayers to God?

NEHEMIAH 10

SEEING WHAT'S THERE

1. What specific commitments are made by the people in this chapter?

2. EYE FOR DETAIL— *From what you recall seeing in chapter 10, try answering the following question without looking in your Bible:* Which men from Israel's history are mentioned in the statement of commitment which the people make in this chapter? (See verses 29 and 38.)

FOR LIFE TODAY

3. Which of the commitments expressed in this chapter are the most relevant to your own life?

NEHEMIAH 11

Startup: When you get to heaven, and you meet Nehemiah, what's the first question you'd like to ask him?

SEEING WHAT'S THERE

1. How many of the twelve Hebrew tribes are mentioned in this chapter?

2. EYE FOR DETAIL— *From what you recall seeing in chapter 11, try answering the following question without looking in your Bible:* What percentage of people living in other towns were chosen to live in Jerusalem? (See verse 1.)

NEHEMIAH 12

SEEING WHAT'S THERE

1. How would you summarize the details of the dedication ceremony for the new wall?

2. EYE FOR DETAIL— *From what you recall seeing in chapter 12, try answering the following question without looking in your Bible:* At the dedication of Jerusalem's new wall, what did the priests and Levites do first before purifying the people, the gates, and the wall? (See verse 30.)

NEHEMIAH 13

SEEING WHAT'S THERE

1. What further evidence for Nehemiah's leadership abilities do you see in this chapter?

2. Compare verse 6 of this chapter with the first verse in chapter 2. How much time elapsed between the events of these two chapters?

3. Review verses 23-28, then compare this situation with the one described in Ezra 9—10. What differences and what similarities do you see in the way Ezra and Nehemiah responded to the same problem? (For example, compare Ezra 9:3 with Nehemiah 13:25.)

4. From what you've seen in this book, and especially in the last two chapters, would you describe Nehemiah's writing style as simple and straightforward, or more elaborate and delicate? What does his writing style tell us about Nehemiah as a man?

5. EYE FOR DETAIL— *From what you recall seeing in chapter 13, try answering the following question without looking in your Bible:* What was the name of the priest who provided a room in the temple for Tobiah? (See verse 4.)

CAPTURE THE ESSENCE

6. From what you've seen throughout this book, how would you summarize in your own words Nehemiah's *motives* for the work he was doing in Jerusalem? What rewards was Nehemiah looking for?

7. From what you see in this chapter, what are the most important things that Nehemiah understands about God's personality and character?

FOR LIFE TODAY

8. Think back on all that has happened to the people of Israel in the book of Nehemiah. If it's true that *the past is a lesson for the future,* then what would you say are the most important lessons for God's people today to learn from these events?

9. In Jeremiah 23:29, God says that His Word is like fire, and like a hammer. He can use the Scriptures to burn away un-

clean thoughts and desires in our hearts. He can also use Scripture to hit hard like a hammer, with the power to crush our spiritual hardness. From your study in this book of Nehemiah, how do you most want to see the "fire-and-hammer" power of God's Word at work in your own life?

NEHEMIAH:
THE BIG PICTURE

(Discuss again the questions in the "Overview," plus the questions below.)

1. For getting the most from the book of Nehemiah, one of the best guidelines is found in 2 Timothy 3:16-17, words which Paul wrote with the Old Testament first in view. He said that *all* Scripture is of great benefit to (a) teach us, (b) rebuke us, (c) correct us, and (d) train us in righteousness. Paul added that these Scriptures completely equip the person of God "for every good work." As you think seriously about those guidelines, in which of these areas do you especially see the usefulness of Nehemiah?

2. Imagine that you were helping to produce a film based on the book of Nehemiah. Describe the kinds of scenery, supporting characters, background music, lighting effects, etc., which you would use to help portray the central message of this book.

3. Look together at each of these passages, and discuss which one you believe is the best candidate for "KEY VERSE" in the book of Nehemiah—the one which brings into sharpest focus what this book is most about: 1:8-9, 6:15-16, or 8:8.

4. What would you say is the main theme (or themes) in the book of Nehemiah?

5. SEARCH FOR THE SAVIOR—What words, images, or themes in Nehemiah have reminded you most of Jesus?

6. If Nehemiah were the only book in the Old Testament, in what ways would it still make a good introduction to the message of Jesus in the New Testament?

7. Based especially on your own experience, complete this statement in the way that's most meaningful to you: I believe it's important for Christians to read and explore the book of Nehemiah because...

Esther

OVERVIEW

(Discuss these OVERVIEW questions both at the beginning of your study of Esther, then again after you've studied all ten chapters. Your answers may change significantly once you've looked more closely at the entire book.)

Startup: Talk together about some of the most unforgettable situations in which you have witnessed God's control over circumstances.

SEEING WHAT'S THERE

1. Before launching into a closer look at Esther, how would you summarize what you already know about this book?

2. Scan the 10 chapters of Esther to see how many banquets or times of feasting you find mention of. What appears to be the significance of each one?

3. Bible scholars and teachers date the events in Esther as occurring between chapters 6 and 7 of the book of Ezra. Review these chapters to learn more of the historical background for Esther.

4. Look also at the list of "Questions to Ask as You Begin Your Study of Each Book" on page 9.

FOR LIFE TODAY

5. The book of Esther has been called "The Book of Divine Providence," "The Story of a Woman's Courage," and "A Brave Woman Saves Her People." With that reputation for this book, what kinds of answers and guidelines and solutions would you like to gain as you examine it more closely?

6. When you get to heaven, if you have a long talk with Esther and she asks you, "What was most helpful to you in the book about me?" how would you like to be able to answer her?

ESTHER 1

SEEING WHAT'S THERE

1. For background information on the king mentioned in verse 1, what can you discover in Ezra 4:6 and Daniel 9:1?

2. Look also on page 8 at the list of "Questions to Ask as You Study Each Chapter." You may want to look again at this list for each chapter in Esther.

3. EYE FOR DETAIL— *From what you recall seeing in chapter 1, try answering the following question without looking in your Bible:* As this book opens, how long had Xerxes (called Ahasuerus in some versions) reigned as king? (See verse 3.)

FOR LIFE TODAY

4. Proverbs 2:1-5 tells about the sincere person who truly longs for wisdom and understanding, and who searches the Scriptures for it—as if it were buried treasure. That person, Solomon says, will come to understand the fear of the Lord, and discover the knowledge of God. As you begin exploring the book of Esther, what "buried treasure" would you like God to help you find here—to show you what God and His wisdom are really like? If you have this desire, how would you express it in your own words?

ESTHER 2

SEEING WHAT'S THERE

1. How would you summarize the events of this chapter?

2. EYE FOR DETAIL— *From what you recall seeing in chapter 2, try answering the following question without looking in your Bible:* From what tribe of Israel was Mordecai descended? (See verse 5.)

ESTHER 3

Startup: Look ahead to 6:1 to see what King Xerxes (Ahasuerus) did when he couldn't sleep. What do *you* most often do when you can't sleep?

SEEING WHAT'S THERE

1. What are the most important decisions and choices that are made in this chapter, and how would you analyze each one?

CAPTURE THE ESSENCE

2. What would you say are the dominant emotions in Haman's life at this time?

ESTHER 4

SEEING WHAT'S THERE

1. What are the most important decisions and choices that are made in this chapter, and how would you analyze each one?

2. What evidence do you see in this chapter of Esther and Mordecai's faith in God?

3. EYE FOR DETAIL— *From what you recall seeing in chapter 4, try answering the following question without looking in your Bible:* For how long did Esther ask the Jews to fast? (See verse 16.)

ESTHER 5

SEEING WHAT'S THERE

1. What are the most important decisions and choices that are made in this chapter, and how would you analyze each one?

2. EYE FOR DETAIL— *From what you recall seeing in chapter 5, try answering the following question without looking in your Bible:* What was the name of Haman's wife? (See verse 10.)

CAPTURE THE ESSENCE

3. Now that you're halfway through Esther, how would you summarize the most important lessons to learn from this book?

ESTHER 6

SEEING WHAT'S THERE

1. Chapter 6 has been called the key to the book of Esther. What does this chapter include that could make it this significant?

2. How would you summarize the crisis Esther faces as this chapter opens? What is most needed from her at this time?

3. Which important details in this chapter do you think might be the easiest to overlook?

FOR LIFE TODAY

4. In Romans 15:4, Paul reminds us that the Old Testament Scriptures can give us patience and perseverance on one hand, as well as comfort and encouragement on the other. In your own life, how do you see this book of Esther living up to Paul's description? In what ways, if any, is it meeting your personal needs for both *perseverance* and *encouragement?*

ESTHER 7

SEEING WHAT'S THERE

1. God's name isn't mentioned in the book of Esther. But in each of the following passages, notice that He is either referred to indirectly, or else shown to be at work "behind the scenes"— 2:17, 2:21-23, 4:14, 4:16, 6:1-2, and 7:9-10.

FOR LIFE TODAY

2. In Isaiah 55:10-11, God reminds us that He sends rain and snow from the sky to water the earth and to nurture life. In the same way, God says that He sends His words to accomplish specific purposes. From your study so far, what would you suggest are *God's* primary purposes for the book of Esther in the lives of Christians today?

ESTHER 8

Startup: When you get to heaven, and you meet Esther, what's the first question you'd like to ask her?

SEEING WHAT'S THERE

1. What are the most important things that happen in this chapter, and why are they important?

ESTHER 9

SEEING WHAT'S THERE

1. How would you summarize the developments in this chapter?

2. EYE FOR DETAIL— *From what you recall seeing in chapter 9, try answering the following question without looking in your Bible:* How many people did the Jews kill on the day appointed by the king's edict for their destruction? (See verses 15-16.)

ESTHER 10

SEEING WHAT'S THERE

1. What status did Mordecai achieve in the Persian kingdom and among his fellow Jews?

CAPTURE THE ESSENCE

2. Review Romans 8:28. In the book of Esther, how fully do you see this New Testament truth demonstrated?

FOR LIFE TODAY

3. Choose one of these sentences, and complete it as fully and candidly as you would like: (a) What I see and understand in the book of Esther is important to my life because... OR: (b) What I see and understand in this book does NOT seem important to my life at this time, because...

ESTHER:
THE BIG PICTURE

(Discuss again the questions in the "Overview," plus the questions below.)

1. Looking back over the entire book, what would you say is the *turning point* in Esther's story?

2. Give a brief character description for each of the four major people in this story: Esther, Mordecai, Haman, and Xerxes (Ahasuerus).

3. Imagine that you were helping to produce a film based on the book of Esther. Describe the kinds of scenery, supporting characters, background music, lighting effects, etc., which you would use to help portray the central message of this book.

4. Look together at each of these passages, and discuss which one you believe is the best candidate for "KEY VERSE" in the book of Esther—the one which brings into sharpest focus what this book is most about: 4:14, 8:17, or 9:27-28.

5. What would you say is the main theme (or themes) in the book of Esther?

6. SEARCH FOR THE SAVIOR—What words, images, or themes in Esther have reminded you most of Jesus?

7. If Esther were the only book in the Old Testament, in what ways would it still make a good introduction to the message of Jesus in the New Testament?

8. Based especially on your own experience, complete this statement in the way that's most meaningful to you: I believe it's important for Christians to read and explore the book of Esther because...

Job

OVERVIEW

(Discuss these OVERVIEW questions both at the beginning of your study of Job, then again after you've studied all 42 chapters. Your answers may change significantly once you've looked more closely at the entire book.)

Startup: Talk together about times in your life when you felt especially that you were being tested. What caused you to feel this way?

SEEING WHAT'S THERE

1. Before launching into a closer look at Job, how would you summarize what you already know about this book?

2. Scan the following verses to see what impressions you gain of the intensity of Job's pain—2:13, 6:2, 7:4-5, 16:6, 17:1, 17:7, 19:20, 30:16-17, and 30:27-30. As the book continues, does it appear that Job's physical pain lessens, deepens, or stays the same?

3. Find the theme that reoccurs in 7:17-18, 23:10, and 34:36. What clues would you say this offers about the central message of Job?

4. Look also at the list of "Questions to Ask as You Begin Your Study of Each Book" on page 9.

FOR LIFE TODAY

5. The book of Job has been called "The Problem of Pain," "A Good Man Suffers," and "Meditations on the Ways of God." With that reputation for this book, what kinds of answers and guidelines and solutions would you like to gain as you examine it more closely?

6. When you get to heaven, if you have a long talk with Job and he asks you, "What was most helpful to you in the book about me?" how would you like to be able to answer him?

7. As you think first about *who God is,* and second about *what the Bible is,* how strongly would you rate your present desire to understand better the book of Job? Use a scale of one to ten (one = "no desire at all," ten = "extremely intense desire") to help you decide.

8. From what you see in Job's words in 23:10-12, what would be a good personal prayer to offer to God as you study this book?

JOB 1

SEEING WHAT'S THERE

1. From what you see in chapter 1, how fully can you describe Job's character, lifestyle, and family relationships?

2. What does God say about Job, in opening the conversation with Satan?

3. How does Satan respond to God's words? And what does God allow Satan to do?

4. What are the immediate results in Job's world?

5. How does Job respond to these dramatic losses?

CAPTURE THE ESSENCE

6. What would you say are Satan's objectives in the action that has taken place so far? And what are God's objectives?

FOR LIFE TODAY

7. Proverbs 2:1-5 tells about the sincere person who truly longs for wisdom and understanding, and who searches the Scriptures for it—as if it were buried treasure. That person, Solomon says, will come to understand the fear of the Lord, and discover the knowledge of God. As you begin exploring the book of Job, what "buried treasure" would you like

God to help you find here—to show you what God and His wisdom are really like? If you have this desire, how would you express it in your own words?

JOB 2

SEEING WHAT'S THERE

1. What is God's conversation with Satan in chapter 2? What does God now allow Satan to do?

2. What does Satan do to Job?

3. What is the response from Job, from his wife, and from Job's three friends?

CAPTURE THE ESSENCE

4. Imagine yourself being present in the temple in Jerusalem as the twelve-year-old Jesus hears this book read and discussed by the rabbis there. In Luke 2:46 we read that He was listening to these teachers and asking them questions. What verses from the first two chapters in Job do you think would most impress the boy Jesus, and what questions or comments do you suppose He might have spoken?

FOR LIFE TODAY

5. In verses 11-13, what can you learn from the example of Job's three friends about offering comfort to others who are in great pain?

JOB 3

SEEING WHAT'S THERE

1. When Job finally speaks, what does he say he wishes for? And what questions does he ask?

CAPTURE THE ESSENCE

2. As you think about Job's feelings and thoughts as expressed in this chapter, how typical do you think they are of the thoughts and feelings of Christians today who experience great loss and pain?

FOR LIFE TODAY

3. Review again 2:11-13. Job broke this long silence with his words here in chapter 3. If you were present in this situa-tion, how would you most likely respond to what Job says in this chapter?

JOB 4

SEEING WHAT'S THERE

1. What opinions does Eliphaz express, and what questions does he ask Job?

JOB 5

SEEING WHAT'S THERE

1. What observations does Eliphaz recall from the past? What does he say he would do if he were Job? And what does he say about God?

JOB 6

SEEING WHAT'S THERE

1. What does Job say God is doing to him? What does Job want God to do? How does Job view himself at this time? How does he view his friends? What does he ask from them?

JOB 7

SEEING WHAT'S THERE

1. How does Job describe the destiny of man? And how does he describe his own suffering? What are his future expecta-tions? What does he pray to God?

JOB 8

SEEING WHAT'S THERE

1. What questions does Bildad ask Job, and what suggestion does he give him? How does he say God will respond, and on what basis?

CAPTURE THE ESSENCE

2. How accurate would you say is Bildad's understanding of God, as we see it ex-pressed in this chapter? And how accu-rate would you say is his understanding of Job?

JOB 9

1. What questions does Job ask Bildad? What does Job say now about God? What various thoughts does Job have about his own guilt or innocence?

CAPTURE THE ESSENCE

2. How accurate would you say is Job's understanding of God, as we see it expressed in verses 3-13?

JOB 10

SEEING WHAT'S THERE

1. What does Job say now about himself? What questions does he have for God? What does he acknowledge that God has done for him? What does Job long for?

JOB 11

SEEING WHAT'S THERE

1. How does Zophar interpret Job's comments? What does Zophar say about God, and about God's view of evil? What does Zophar suggest that Job do, and what does he say will be the results?

2. How would you summarize what Job's friends have told him so far?

CAPTURE THE ESSENCE

3. How accurate would you say is Zophar's understanding of God, especially as we see it expressed in verses 7-11? And how accurate would you say is his understanding of Job?

JOB 12

SEEING WHAT'S THERE

1. How does Job defend himself? What more does Job say about God?

CAPTURE THE ESSENCE

2. How accurate would you say are Job's comments here on God's personality and character?

JOB 13

SEEING WHAT'S THERE

1. What does Job accuse his friends of doing? What does he want them to do? What does Job ask for from God?

JOB 14

SEEING WHAT'S THERE

1. How does Job view man's fate? What does he say he wants God to do for him?

JOB 15

SEEING WHAT'S THERE

1. What evaluation does Eliphaz make of Job's words? How does Eliphaz depict the fate of godless men?

CAPTURE THE ESSENCE

2. How accurate would you say is Eliphaz's understanding of God, as we see it expressed in this chapter? And how accurate would you say is his understanding of Job?

JOB 16

SEEING WHAT'S THERE

1. How does Job assess what he has heard so far from his friends? What does he say God is doing to him? What does he say other men are doing to him? What does he say now about his own guilt or innocence? What are Job's emotions at this time?

JOB 17

SEEING WHAT'S THERE

1. How does Job view his future? How does he view his friends? How does he view his reputation? What thoughts and questions does he express about his future hope?

JOB 18

SEEING WHAT'S THERE

1. How does Bildad evaluate Job's remarks and his treatment of his friends? How does he picture Job's condition? What conclusion does he make about Job's moral state?

JOB 19

SEEING WHAT'S THERE

1. How does Job defend himself? What does he object to in his relationship with God? How does he view his own situation? What does he ask for from his friend? How does he affirm his faith in God? What warning does he give to his friends?

CAPTURE THE ESSENCE

2. Again, imagine yourself being present in the temple in Jerusalem as the twelve-year-old Jesus hears this chapter read and discussed by the Jewish teachers. What verses in this chapter do you think would most impress Him, and what questions or comments do you suppose He might have spoken?

JOB 20

SEEING WHAT'S THERE

1. How has Zophar taken Job's remarks? Why does he now speak up? What does he object to in Job's recent words? What does he say about the fate of the wicked? What does he say about God's judgment of the wicked?

JOB 21

SEEING WHAT'S THERE

1. How does Job justify his impatience? How does Job's view of the wicked differ from Zophar's? How does he refute Zophar?

JOB 22

SEEING WHAT'S THERE

1. How does Eliphaz describe Job? What does he accuse Job of? What does Eliphaz object to in Job's remarks? What does he counsel Job to do? What does he say will be the result?

JOB 23

SEEING WHAT'S THERE

1. What does Job long for most? What is he confident of regarding God's view of him? Why is Job afraid?

CAPTURE THE ESSENCE

2. From what you see in this chapter, what are the most important things that Job understands about God's personality and character?

3. Look again at Job's confident statement in verses 10-12. What would you say is the reason for this confidence?

FOR LIFE TODAY

4. How accurately would you say verses 10-12 describe your own life?

JOB 24

SEEING WHAT'S THERE

1. What further questions does Job have of God? How does he depict the injury caused by the wicked—and the ignoring of it by God? How does Job comment upon man's encounter with death?

JOB 25

SEEING WHAT'S THERE

1. What fundamental question does Bildad raise?

CAPTURE THE ESSENCE

2. How accurate would you say is Bildad's understanding of God, as expressed in this chapter?

JOB 26

SEEING WHAT'S THERE

1. How does Job cut off Bildad's remarks? What more does Job say about death? How does Job describe the sovereignty of God?

CAPTURE THE ESSENCE

2. How accurate would you say is Job's understanding of God, as expressed in this chapter?

JOB 27

SEEING WHAT'S THERE

1. How strongly does Job now defend his innocence? What more does he say about the destiny of the wicked before God?

FOR LIFE TODAY

2. In Isaiah 55:10-11, God reminds us that He sends rain and snow from the sky to water the earth and to nurture life. In the same way, God says that He sends His words to accomplish specific purposes. From your study so far, what would you suggest are *God's* primary purposes for the book of Job in the lives of Christians today?

JOB 28

SEEING WHAT'S THERE

1. How does Job depict the elusiveness of wisdom? What does he say is wisdom's true source?

CAPTURE THE ESSENCE

2. From what you see in this chapter, how would Job define true wisdom?

FOR LIFE TODAY

3. In Romans 15:4, Paul reminds us that the Old Testament Scriptures can give us patience and perseverance on one hand, as well as comfort and encouragement on the other. In your own life, how do you see this book of Job living up to Paul's description? In what ways, if any, is it meeting your personal needs for both *perseverance* and *encouragement*?

JOB 29

SEEING WHAT'S THERE

1. What does Job now long for? How does Job defend his righteousness and justice? How does he recall his past prominence and personality?

JOB 30

SEEING WHAT'S THERE

1. How does Job describe his present dishonor and suffering? How does he describe his search for God's answers? How does he view his future?

JOB 31

SEEING WHAT'S THERE

1. How does Job defend his purity, justice, and integrity? How does he express his desire again for dialogue with God?

JOB 32

SEEING WHAT'S THERE

1. Why was Elihu angry with Job, as well as with his three friends? Why does he now speak up?

CAPTURE THE ESSENCE

2. From what you see in this chapter, what are the most important things that Elihu understands about God's personality and character?

JOB 33

SEEING WHAT'S THERE

1. How does Elihu summarize Job's statements? What conclusion does Elihu object to, and on what basis? What does Elihu say about God's involvement with men?

CAPTURE THE ESSENCE

2. From what you see in this chapter, what are the most important things that Elihu understands about God's personality and character?

JOB 34

SEEING WHAT'S THERE

1. What more does Elihu object to in Job's remarks? What does Elihu say about God's character and actions? What does Elihu conclude about Job's character?

CAPTURE THE ESSENCE

2. From what you have seen so far in the words of Elihu, how accurate is his understanding of Job?

JOB 35

SEEING WHAT'S THERE

1. What more does Elihu say about God's nature? What reason does he give for Job's unanswered prayers?

CAPTURE THE ESSENCE

2. From what you see in this chapter, what are the most important things that Elihu understands about God's personality and character?

JOB 36

SEEING WHAT'S THERE

1. How does Elihu describe himself? How does he describe God? How does he describe the godless?

CAPTURE THE ESSENCE

2. How accurate would you say is Elihu's understanding of God, as expressed in this chapter?

JOB 37

SEEING WHAT'S THERE

1. What does Elihu say about God's power? What does he ask Job to do? What concluding remarks does he make about God?

2. How would you summarize what Elihu has told Job in chapters 32—37?

CAPTURE THE ESSENCE

3. Once again, how accurate would you say is Elihu's understanding of God, as expressed in this chapter?

JOB 38

SEEING WHAT'S THERE

1. Chapter 38 has been called the key to the book of Job. What does this chapter include that could make it this significant?

2. How does God begin His message to Job? What is the main point of all the questions God asks? Does God say anything about Job's suffering? Does He say anything about Job's guilt or innocence? Does He shed any light on the issues Job and his friends had been wrestling with regarding God's treatment of the wicked?

CAPTURE THE ESSENCE

3. From what you see in this chapter, what is it that God most wants Job to understand about Himself?

JOB 39

SEEING WHAT'S THERE

1. What is the theme of God's questions and comments to Job in this chapter?

CAPTURE THE ESSENCE

2. Once again, from what you see in this chapter, what is it that God most wants Job to understand about Himself?

JOB 40

SEEING WHAT'S THERE

1. As God continues speaking, what questions does He ask concerning His own nature, for Job's benefit? What further observations does He make about His power and wisdom displayed in creation?

CAPTURE THE ESSENCE

2. How would you summarize what Job learns most about God in this chapter?

FOR LIFE TODAY

3. Suppose the voice of God sounded out to you in a thunderstorm, and began saying to the same things God tells Job in chapters 38-41. How do you think it would affect you? What thoughts would go through your mind?

JOB 41

SEEING WHAT'S THERE

1. What does God communicate about His power and sovereignty?

2. How would you summarize what God has revealed to Job in chapters 38—41?

CAPTURE THE ESSENCE

3. Considering both what God *says* and what He does *not* say in chapters 38—41, what would you say is His primary purpose in these words to Job?

4. In what ways, if any, do you sense God's love for Job in these words?

FOR LIFE TODAY

5. Consider how strongly you desire to know God better, and think also about what God revealed about Himself to Job in chapters 38-41. Then ask yourself this question: *What are the truths in these chapters which God may want me to understand more deeply at this time in my life?*

6. Which of these statements would you say is the best conclusion to draw from what we see in chapters 38—41: (a) God always knows exactly what He is doing, and He is not bound in any way to give us His reasons for our suffering, no matter how loudly we cry out for an explanation. (b) God is all-powerful, and God loves us; and that should be enough for us. (c) If our spiritual eyes are open wide, seeing the majesty and power of God's creation all around should be enough to convince us of His power and love.

JOB 42

SEEING WHAT'S THERE

1. What has Job learned? How does he respond to God's words? What words does God speak to Job's three friends? What did God do next for Job?

CAPTURE THE ESSENCE

2. Once more, imagine yourself being present in the temple in Jerusalem as the twelve-year-old Jesus hears this chapter read and discussed by the Jewish teachers. What verses in this chapter do you think would most impress Him, and what questions or comments do you suppose He might have spoken?

JOB:

THE BIG PICTURE

(Discuss again the questions in the "Overview," plus the questions below.)

1. For getting the most from the book of Job, one of the best guidelines is found in 2 Timothy 3:16-17, words which Paul wrote with the Old Testament first in view. He said that *all* Scripture is of great benefit to (a) teach us, (b) rebuke us, (c) correct us, and (d) train us in righteousness. Paul added that these Scriptures completely equip the person of God "for every good work." As you think seriously about those guidelines, in which of these areas do you especially see the usefulness of Job?

2. Imagine that you were helping to produce a film based on the book of Job. Describe the kinds of scenery, supporting characters, background music, lighting effects, etc., which you would use to help portray the central message of this book.

3. Look together at each of these passages, and discuss which one you believe is the best candidate for "KEY VERSE" in the book of Job—the one which brings into sharpest focus what this book is most about: 2:3, 13:15, 23:10, or 37:23-24.

4. SEARCH FOR THE SAVIOR—What words, images, or themes in Job have reminded you most of Jesus?

5. If Job were the only book in the Old Testament, in what ways would it still make a good introduction to the message of Jesus in the New Testament?

6. Based especially on your own experience, complete this statement in the way that's most meaningful to you: I believe it's important for Christians to read and explore the book of Job because…

Psalms

OVERVIEW

(Discuss these OVERVIEW questions both at the beginning of your study of this book, then again after you've studied all 150 Psalms. Your answers may change significantly once you've looked more closely at the entire book.)

Startup: Talk together about what it means to be honest and transparent before God. In your experience, what obstacles must be overcome before we can be this way with God?

SEEING WHAT'S THERE

1. Scan the opening lines (verses 1 and 2) in each of these psalms—5, 17, 28, 57, 61, 88, 102, 116, 130, and 142. Decide what theme is repeated in each one, and what this reveals about the nature of this book.

2. Find the most prominent word that reoccurs in the first verse of each of these psalms—1, 32, 41, 112, 119, and 128. In your own words, how fully can you define this key term in the book of Psalms?

3. As this book came together thousands of years ago, the Psalms were divided into five portions (which we call Book One through Book Five). Each of these five "books" ends with a statement of praise. Look carefully at each of these five praise statements (in 41:13, 72:18-19, 89:52, 106:48, and 150:6). From what you see in these passages, what are the most important things God wants us to understand about praising Him?

4. Look also at the list of "Questions to Ask as You Begin Your Study of Each Book" on page 9.

CAPTURE THE ESSENCE

5. What key aspects of God's perfect character are repeated in these verses— 86:15, 103:8, 111:4, 116:5, and 145:8. Which of these attributes would you say is the most important for us to understand better today, and why?

FOR LIFE TODAY

6. The book of Psalms has been called "The Way to Pray," "The Songbook of Israel," "The Book of Devotion and Praise," and "Being Honest with God." The Psalms have also been called "God's prescription for a complacent church." With that reputation for this book, what kinds of answers and guidelines and solutions would you like to gain as you examine it more closely?

7. As you think first about *who God is,* and second about *what the Bible is,* how strongly would you rate your present desire to understand better the book of Psalms? Use a scale of one to ten (one = "no desire at all," ten = "extremely intense desire") to help you decide.

8. From what you see in David's words in 86:11, what would be a good personal prayer to offer to God as you study this book?

PSALM 1

Startup: What kind of pictures come to your mind when you think of the word *blessed?*

SEEING WHAT'S THERE

1. In verses 1-2, what specific things does the blessed man *do,* and what specific things does he *not* do? How would you explain these in your own words?

2. From what you see in the last line of verse 3, discuss how much you agree or disagree with this statement: The prosperity of life promised here is something higher and richer than prosperity of bank accounts.

3. In your own words, how would you restate the warning in verses 4-6?

4. What would you say is the *key word, key phrase,* or *key sentence* in each stanza of this psalm? (In most Bible versions, the stanza breaks are marked by extra space between verses.)

CAPTURE THE ESSENCE

5. What would you say God most wants us to understand from this psalm about what is *right* and what is *wrong?*

6. If the word *blessed* means "happy," then how would you summarize what this psalm says about the best way to happiness?

FOR LIFE TODAY

7. Notice how the relationship between the Lord and the righteous person is stated at the beginning of verse 6. Describe as fully as you can what this statement means personally to you.

8. Review the guidelines for our thought-life given in Philippians 4:8—"Whatever is true, whatever is noble, whatever is right, whatever is pure, whatever is lovely, whatever is admirable—if anything is excellent or praiseworthy—*think about such things."* What food for thought can you find in Psalm 1 that especially strikes you as being *true,* or *noble,* or *right,* or *pure,* or *lovely,* or *admirable,* or *excellent,* or *praiseworthy?*

9. Proverbs 2:1-5 tells about the sincere person who truly longs for wisdom and understanding, and who searches the Scriptures for it—as if it were buried treasure. That person, Solomon says, will come to understand the fear of the Lord, and discover the knowledge of God. As you begin exploring the Psalms, what "buried treasure" would you like God to help you find in this book—to show you what God and His wisdom are really like? If you have this desire, how would you express it in your own words?

PSALM 2

SEEING WHAT'S THERE

1. What situation is described in verses 1-2? And is that situation still true today?

2. What aspects of God's character are revealed in verses 4-6?

3. Who is the king mentioned in verse 6?

4. Who is the speaker in verses 7-8?

5. What promises does God make in verses 8 and 9?

6. What commands are given to earthly rulers in verses 10-12?

7. Select a *key word, key phrase,* or *key sentence* in each stanza of this psalm.

CAPTURE THE ESSENCE

8. In Matthew 6:33, Jesus tells us to "seek first the kingdom of God and His righteousness." What would you say this psalm teaches most about God's kingdom?

9. Imagine yourself being present in the temple in Jerusalem as the twelve-year-old Jesus hears this psalm read and discussed by the rabbis there. In Luke 2:46 we read that He was listening to these teachers and asking them questions. What verses from this psalm do you think would most impress the boy Jesus, and what questions or comments do you suppose He might have spoken?

FOR LIFE TODAY

10. In verse 11, look again at the command given to the rulers of the earth. If God addressed these same words to you, what do you think He would mean by them, in practical terms? What does it mean for you to approach God in this way?

To explore how the life and ministry of Jesus the Messiah was foretold in the Psalms, compare verse 7 with Hebrews 1:5-6, and verse 9 with Revelation 12:5 and 19:15..

PSALM 3

SEEING WHAT'S THERE

1. For useful background to this psalm, review together the events of David's life recorded in 2 Samuel 15—17.

2. What fears and concerns does David reveal in this psalm?

3. How would you summarize what David asks God for?

4. Select a *key phrase* or *key sentence* in each stanza of this psalm.

CAPTURE THE ESSENCE

5. What is the reason for David's confident security in verses 5-6?

6. David is described in the Bible as "a man after God's own heart" (see Acts 13:22 and 1 Samuel 13:14).What are the most significant things this psalm reveals about David's heart? What are his desires, his longings, his commitments?

7. Are you convinced that David's words in this psalm represent his *heart*-knowledge, and not just *head*-knowledge? If so, what convinces you?

PSALM 4

SEEING WHAT'S THERE

1. How would you summarize what David asks God for in this psalm?

2. What is the reason for David's confident security in verse 8?

3. Choose a *key word, key phrase,* or *key sentence* in each stanza of this psalm.

CAPTURE THE ESSENCE

4. What patterns and principles does this psalm offer for teaching us how to pray when we're in serious trouble?

FOR LIFE TODAY

5. If this psalm was the last Bible chapter you read before you died, which words from it would you most like to be lingering in your mind as you said goodbye to this earth?

PSALM 5

SEEING WHAT'S THERE

1. How would you summarize what David asks God for in this psalm?

2. What commitment does David make in this psalm?

3. Identify a *key word, key phrase,* or *key sentence* in each stanza of this psalm.

CAPTURE THE ESSENCE

4. Restate in your own words what you believe are the most important truths revealed about God's character and personality in verses 4-6.

5. What patterns and principles does this psalm offer for teaching us how to pray when we're in serious trouble?

6. After studying Psalms 1—5, what title would you give to each of them? (Use this exercise to help you focus on what you believe is the essential message in each psalm.)

7. What is the best evidence you see in Psalms 1—5 that total honesty and openness in our prayers are important to God?

FOR LIFE TODAY

8. What would you say are the most important lessons a new Christian could learn from this psalm about meeting with God each day?

9. Scan Psalms 1—5, and find the verse or passage which most closely reflects your own spiritual and emotional feelings at this time.

PSALM 6

Startup: What comes to your mind when you think of the word *mercy?*

SEEING WHAT'S THERE

1. What exactly does David ask God for in this psalm?

2. Select a *key word, key phrase,* or *key sentence* in each stanza of this psalm.

CAPTURE THE ESSENCE

3. What are the most important reasons for David's confident prediction in verse 10?

4. From the evidence you see in this psalm, how would you describe David's relationship with God?

5. From what you see in verse 5, tell how much you agree or disagree with this statement: From God's point of view, to truly *remember* Him is to *praise* Him; if we aren't praising Him, then we've essentially forgotten Him.

FOR LIFE TODAY

6. Recall the promise in 1 John 1:9—that *if we confess our sins,* God will forgive us and cleanse us from unrighteousness. What parts of this psalm can serve as a model and inspiration for the way you confess your personal sins?

7. If you were to rephrase some or all of this psalm as an expression of your own heart to God at this time, how would you begin it? What would be "verse 1" in your own personal "Psalm 6"?

PSALM 7

SEEING WHAT'S THERE

1. What are David's fears in this psalm?

2. What do you know about David's life that helps you understand his feelings expressed in this psalm?

3. In Matthew 6:33, Jesus tells us to "seek first the kingdom of God and His righteousness." What would you say this psalm teaches most about God's righteousness?

4. What specific requests does David make in this psalm?

5. What commitment does David make at the end of this psalm?

6. Choose a *key word, key phrase,* or *key sentence* in each stanza of this psalm.

CAPTURE THE ESSENCE

7. From the evidence you see in this psalm, how would you describe in your own words David's understanding of God's personality and character?

8. Consider how strongly you desire to know God better, then ask yourself this question: What are the truths revealed about Him in this psalm which He may want me to understand more deeply at this time in my life?

PSALM 8

SEEING WHAT'S THERE

1. In this psalm, what acts of God does David acknowledge? What does he say God has already done?

2. What does David ask God in verse 4?

3. Notice the word of praise that both begins and ends this psalm. How would you restate this in your own words?

4. Identify a *key word, key phrase,* or *key sentence* in each stanza of this psalm.

CAPTURE THE ESSENCE

5. What meaning do you think David has in mind for the word *name* in verses 1 and 9?

6. What words or phrases in this psalm tell us the most about God's *purpose* and *plan* for His people?

7. What words or phrases in this psalm tell us the most about God's *character?*

8. What would you say God wants us to understand most from this psalm about the earth and our environment?

9. What would you say God wants us to understand most from this psalm about who we are as human beings?

10. Discuss how much you agree or disagree with this statement: It is impossible to understand truly what man is until you first understand what God is.

11. From what you see in this psalm, how would you complete this statement: "I

know God is a God of love because He…"

12. Again, imagine yourself being present in the temple in Jerusalem as the twelve-year-old Jesus hears this psalm read and discussed by the Jewish teachers. What verses in this psalm do you think would most impress Him, and what questions or comments do you suppose He might have spoken?

13. From what you see in this psalm, answer these two questions: Who is God? And who am I?

PSALM 9

1. Select a *key word, key phrase,* or *key sentence* in each stanza of this psalm.

2. What specific commitments does David make in the first two verses of this psalm?

3. Jesus tells us to "seek first the kingdom of God and His righteousness" (Matthew 6:33). What would you say this psalm teaches most about God's kingdom and His righteousness?

4. Imagine yourself with David as he is writing this psalm. How do you think he would answer if you interrupted him to quietly ask, "David, what are you most thankful to God for today?"

5. What would you say God wants us to understand most about Himself in verses 7-9?

6. What are the reasons for David's confident words in verse 18?

7. To what extent would you say that the commitments David makes in verses 1 and 2 are also your commitments?

PSALM 10

1. Choose a *key word, key phrase,* or *key sentence* in each stanza of this psalm.

2. What would you say God most wants us to understand from this psalm about what is *right* and what is *wrong?*

3. What are the reasons for the wicked man's confidence in verses 2-11?

4. What prophecy is made in verse 16?

5. Jesus tells us to "seek first the kingdom of God and His righteousness" (Matthew 6:33). What would you say verses 16-18 teach us most about God's kingdom?

6. After studying Psalms 6—10, what title would you give to each of them?

7. What is the best evidence you see in Psalms 6—10 of total honesty and openness while praying to God?

8. As you scan Psalms 6—10, which verse or passage most closely reflects your own spiritual and emotional feelings at this time?

PSALM 11

Startup: What memorable experience can you recall from your past in which you felt extreme danger?

1. What is David's prophecy in verse 6? And what reasons does David give for it in the rest of the psalm?

2. Identify a *key word, key phrase,* or *key sentence* in each stanza of this psalm.

3. From what you see in this psalm, what are the most important things David understands about God's personality and character?

4. From this psalm, how would you answer the question, Where is God?

5. Look again at the advice given to David at the end of verse 1 (and the reasons for that advice in verses 2 and 3). Would

you say this advice in verse 1 was good or poor? Explain your answer.

FOR LIFE TODAY

6. What promise do you see at the end of verse 7? How exactly does it apply to you?

7. Suppose a Christian friend in difficult and uncontrollable circumstances said to you, "I feel so discouraged and defeated by what's going on. What should I do?" How could you use this psalm to help you give a meaningful response?

PSALM 12

SEEING WHAT'S THERE

1. What exactly does David ask God for in this psalm?

2. What promises does God make in verse 5?

3. Select a *key word, key phrase,* or *key sentence* in each stanza of this psalm.

CAPTURE THE ESSENCE

4. What are the reasons for David's confident statement in verse 7?

5. What are the most important truths revealed about God's character and personality in this psalm?

PSALM 13

SEEING WHAT'S THERE

1. What questions does David ask God in verses 1-2?

2. How would you summarize David's fears?

3. What commitment does David make in verse 6?

4. Choose a *key word, key phrase,* or *key sentence* in each stanza of this psalm.

CAPTURE THE ESSENCE

5. From the evidence you see in this psalm, how would you describe David's relationship with God?

FOR LIFE TODAY

6. If you were to rephrase some or all of this psalm as an expression of your own heart to God at this time, how would

you begin it? What would be "verse 1" in your own personal "Psalm 13"?

FOR GOING DEEPER

In what ways have you most experienced the same fears David expresses in the opening verses of this psalm?

PSALM 14

SEEING WHAT'S THERE

1. What question does David ask in this psalm?

2. Select a *key word, key phrase,* or *key sentence* in each stanza of this psalm.

CAPTURE THE ESSENCE

3. From what you see in verse 2, what conclusions can you make about God's character and personality?

4. What does David understand about God's plan and purpose for His people?

5. How has God responded to David's longing in verse 7?

FOR GOING DEEPER

Notice in Romans 3:9-23 how Paul uses a portion of this psalm to help him make a major point about our salvation. What other parts of this psalm lend support to Paul's teaching?

PSALM 15

SEEING WHAT'S THERE

1. The first sentence of this psalm seems to relate to worshiping God, while the last sentence seems to apply more to the way we live life. How would you describe the right relationship between worship and everyday living?

2. Look at the descriptions of blameless living in verses 2-5. Are these mostly *inward* things, *outward* things, or an even blend of both?

CAPTURE THE ESSENCE

3. Look at David's bold statement in the last line of this psalm. How would you explain what David means by this, and on what basis does he come to this conclusion?

4. Consider again the guidelines for blameless living in verses 2-5. For each guideline, what kind of pressure do we sometimes receive to act in just the opposite way?

5. Which of the guidelines in verses 2-5 are the toughest for you to live by?

6. What do you think it means in day-to-day life to be the kind of person described in the last sentence of this psalm?

7. It's been said that "the human heart resists nothing more than change." What truths in this psalm—truths that could require some changes in your life—cause some degree of hesitation and resistance inside you?

PSALM 16

SEEING WHAT'S THERE

1. How would you summarize what David asks God for in this psalm?

2. What commitments does David make in this psalm?

3. What verses in this psalm seem to you to especially reflect the heart of Jesus Christ?

4. Identify a *key word, key phrase,* or *key sentence* in each stanza of this psalm.

CAPTURE THE ESSENCE

5. From what you see in Psalm 16, what impresses you most about David's relationship with God?

6. In practical terms, how do you think David accomplishes what he speaks about in the first line of verse 8—setting the Lord before him?

7. What do you think David means by the expression "path of life" in verse 11?

8. If verse 11 was the only Scripture portion you had access to, what would you conclude from it about heaven?

9. Are you convinced that David's words in this psalm represent his *heart*-knowledge, and not just *head*-knowledge? If so, what convinces you?

10. Again, imagine yourself being present in the temple in Jerusalem as the twelve-year-old Jesus hears this psalm read and discussed by the Jewish teachers. What verses in this psalm do you think would most impress Him, and what questions or comments do you suppose He might have spoken?

11. After studying Psalms 11—16, what title would you give to each of them?

12. What is the best evidence you see in Psalms 11—16 of total honesty and openness while praying to God?

FOR LIFE TODAY

13. How often do you pray the kind of prayer that David expresses in verse 1?

14. Review the guidelines for our thought-life given in Philippians 4:8—"Whatever is true, whatever is noble, whatever is right, whatever is pure, whatever is lovely, whatever is admirable—if anything is excellent or praiseworthy—*think about such things.*" What food for thought can you find in Psalm 16 that especially strikes you as being *true,* or *noble,* or *right,* or *pure,* or *lovely,* or *admirable,* or *excellent,* or *praiseworthy?*

15. As you scan Psalms 11—16, which verse or passage most closely reflects your own spiritual and emotional feelings at this time?

FOR GOING DEEPER

Review verse 10. Then look together in Acts 13:32-37 at how Paul pointed out the prophetic fulfillment of this verse in Christ. What would have happened if this prophecy had been broken—if Christ's body had indeed decayed in the grave?

PSALM 17

Startup: What people have you known whom you would describe as being *righteous?*

SEEING WHAT'S THERE

1. How would you summarize what David asks God for in this psalm?

2. Choose a *key word, key phrase,* or *key sentence* in each stanza of this psalm.

CAPTURE THE ESSENCE

3. Look at David's bold statement in verse 3. What are his reasons for making this claim?

4. Look also at his words in the last verse of the psalm. How does David come to this conclusion?

5. Recall again the description of David (in Acts 13:22 and 1 Samuel 13:14) as "a man after God's own heart." What are the most significant things this psalm reveals about David's heart? What are his desires, his longings, his commitments?

FOR LIFE TODAY

6. Which verse in this psalm do you think God would like you to understand best?

PSALM 18

SEEING WHAT'S THERE

1. This psalm is recorded also in 2 Samuel 22, near the end of the account of David's life. Review together all you can remember of the main events surrounding Saul's conflict with David.

2. Select a *key word, key phrase,* or *key sentence* in each stanza of this psalm.

3. In your own words, how would you summarize the *action* that has taken place in this psalm, beginning in verse 4?

4. From what you see in this psalm, what does God think of David?

5. What commitment does David make at the end of this psalm?

CAPTURE THE ESSENCE

6. What do you think is the "righteousness" that David speaks of in verses 20 and 24? How does a person get this righteousness?

7. How exactly does God "show" Himself in the four ways mentioned in verses 25-26?

8. Using only this psalm as evidence for your answer, which would you say is more important to David: God's *character,* or what God does to help David? Explain your answer.

9. From the evidence you see in this psalm, what would you say David considered to be the most important things in life?

10. Again, imagine yourself being present in the temple in Jerusalem as the twelve-year-old Jesus hears this psalm read and discussed by the Jewish teachers. What verses in this psalm do you think would most impress Him, and what questions or comments do you suppose He might have spoken?

11. After studying Psalms 17 and 18, what title would you give to each of them?

12. What is the best evidence you see in Psalms 17 and 18 of total honesty and openness while praying to God?

FOR LIFE TODAY

13. Are the words in verse 28 true for you as well? If so, in what ways has God done this for you?

14. In Romans 15:4, Paul reminds us that the Old Testament Scriptures can give us patience and perseverance on one hand, as well as comfort and encouragement on the other. In your own life, how do you see the Psalms living up to Paul's description? In what ways, if any, are they meeting your personal needs for both *perseverance* and *encouragement?*

15. As you scan Psalms 17 and 18, which verse or passage most closely reflects your own spiritual and emotional feelings at this time?

PSALM 19

Startup: What were the first thoughts or questions about heaven that you can remember having as a child?

SEEING WHAT'S THERE

1. From what you see in the opening verses of this psalm, what is the *message* the sky is giving us, and what is God's *reason* for giving us this message?

2. In verses 7-9, what different phrases are used to describe God's Word?

3. From what you see in verse 13, what goal or desire is prominent in David's heart?

4. In how many ways does God speak to us, according to what we see in this psalm?

5. Identify a *key word, key phrase,* or *key sentence* in each stanza of this psalm.

CAPTURE THE ESSENCE

6. Think again about the description of David (in Acts 13:22 and 1 Samuel 13:14) as "a man after God's own heart." What are the most significant things this psalm reveals about David's heart? What are his desires, his longings, and his commitments?

7. In the midst of a list of the benefits of God's Word, we find in verse 9 a phrase describing the fear of the Lord. Why is that phrase here?

8. Look again at verse 1. How would you define "the glory of God"? And why does God want us to know what this means?

FOR LIFE TODAY

9. In verses 7-11, look again at the listed benefits from God's Word. Which of these benefits is most personally meaningful to you?

10. From what you see in this psalm, how would you summarize the *response* which God wants you to continually experience from reading His Word?

FOR GOING DEEPER

Compare verse 10 with 1 Peter 2:2, and discuss what these verses say together about our *appetite* for the Scriptures.

Keep verse 14 in mind as you look also at Ephesians 4:29 and 5:4, Colossians 3:8, and Matthew 12:36-37. From what you see in these passages, and what you know of other Scriptures, discuss how much you agree or disagree with this statement: God's guidelines and requirements for our speech—our outward expressions—also apply fully to our thoughts—our inward expressions.

PSALM 20

SEEING WHAT'S THERE

1. Choose a *key word, key phrase,* or *key sentence* in each stanza of this psalm.

CAPTURE THE ESSENCE

2. Notice the second half of verse 1. How does God's name offer protection?

3. What is the reason for the joy in verse 5?

4. How does David know what he says he knows in verse 6?

5. Again, what verses in this psalm do you think would most impress the boy Jesus as He heard them read and discussed in the Temple in Jerusalem, and what questions or comments do you suppose He might have spoken to the teachers there?

FOR LIFE TODAY

6. If God had written this psalm only for you, which words or phrases do you think He might have underlined, and why?

PSALM 21

SEEING WHAT'S THERE

1. Select a *key word, key phrase,* or *key sentence* in each stanza of this psalm.

2. What is David most thankful for, from what you see in this psalm?

3. What words of prophecy does David give in verses 8-12?

CAPTURE THE ESSENCE

4. From the evidence you see in this psalm, how would you describe David's relationship with God?

5. Based on your own experience, to what extent can you repeat all that David says to God in verse 2?

PSALM 22

SEEING WHAT'S THERE

1. Identify a *key word, key phrase,* or *key sentence* in each stanza of this psalm.

2. What specific requests are made to God in this psalm?

3. What commitment is stated in verse 22?

4. What words of prophecy are given in verses 26-31? When will these prophecies be fulfilled?

CAPTURE THE ESSENCE

5. As a prophetic passage about the coming Messiah, what does this psalm teach us about both the *character* and the *ministry* of Jesus Christ?

6. From what you see in verses 3-4, what are the most important things David understands about God's personality and character?

7. Jesus tells us to "seek first the kingdom of God and His righteousness" (Matthew 6:33). From what you see in verses 25-31, what would you say this psalm teaches most about God's kingdom? And what does it teach most about God's righteousness?

8. After studying Psalms 19—22, what title would you give to each of them?

9. What is the best evidence you see in Psalms 19—22 of total honesty and openness while praying to God?

FOR LIFE TODAY

10. As you scan Psalms 19—22, which verse or passage most closely reflects your own spiritual and emotional feelings at this time?

11. Which verse in this psalm do you think God would like you to understand best?

FOR GOING DEEPER

In the New Testament, this psalm is quoted more frequently than any other. Spend time looking together at Matthew 27:27-46, and find as much as you can there which is in

prophetic fulfillment of something in Psalm 22. Do the same with John 19:23-30, and Hebrews 2:11-12.

PSALM 23

Startup: How long have you been familiar with Psalm 23? What are some of the earliest impressions these words left with you?

SEEING WHAT'S THERE

1. Because this psalm is so familiar to most people, try restating it in completely different language, without using any words from the original (except those that are three letters or less). You may want to go around the group and have each person paraphrase one line from the psalm.

2. From what David says in this psalm, what specific things does God do for him?

3. Which of these would you say was most in David's mind as he wrote this psalm —God's protection, God's guidance, or God's comfort? Explain your answer.

4. Choose a *key word, key phrase,* or *key sentence* in each stanza of this psalm.

CAPTURE THE ESSENCE

5. How does David know the things he says in verse 4?

6. On what basis does David arrive at the conclusion he states in verse 6?

7. How would you describe David's basic *mindset* or *attitude* in life?

8. From what you see in this psalm, what would David consider to be the most important benefits of God's shepherding care?

9. From what you see in this psalm, how would you complete this statement: "I know God is a God of love because He..."

FOR LIFE TODAY

10. Discuss which of the following people you think this psalm would be the greatest help to, and why: (a) someone who felt like a failure; (b) someone who struggled with excessive pride and self-cen-

teredness; (c) someone who longed for deeper intimacy with God.

11. If this psalm was the only Scripture you had access to, how could you use it to teacher a new Christian (a) how to live, and (b) how to die?

12. If God had written this psalm only for you, which words or phrases do you think He might have underlined, and why?

13. Read again through the psalm and summarize what David is most confident about in his relationship with God. How confident are you about these same things?

FOR GOING DEEPER

Look at how Jesus is presented as our Shepherd in John 10:11-18, and in Revelation 7:17. How would you expand on the meaning of those passages by using the concepts and images given in Psalm 23?

Explore also these other passages to see how they expand the picture of God as our shepherd—Psalm 74:1-2 and 77:20, and Isaiah 40:10-11.

PSALM 24

SEEING WHAT'S THERE

1. Select a *key word, key phrase,* or *key sentence* in each stanza of this psalm.

2. What questions does David ask in this psalm?

3. Jesus tells us to "seek first the kingdom of God and His righteousness" (Matthew 6:33). What would you say this psalm teaches most about God's kingdom?

4. In what ways can you see verses 7-10 as a depiction of Christ?

CAPTURE THE ESSENCE

5. From what you see in this psalm, what are the most important things David understands about God's personality and character?

6. What would you say God wants us to understand most from verses 1-2 about the earth and our environment?

7. Practically speaking, how would you define what David means in the first line in verse 4?

8. What are the qualifications for receiving the promised blessings mentioned in verse 5, according to what you see in the verses around it?

9. Once more, what verses in this psalm do you think would most impress the 12-year-old Jesus as He heard them read and discussed in the Temple in Jerusalem, and what questions or comments do you suppose He might have spoken to the teachers there?

10. Look again at verse 1, and discuss how much you agree or disagree with this statement: It is impossible to have a completely correct view of the earth without recognizing God's ownership of it.

FOR LIFE TODAY

11. Notice again the questions David asks in verse 3 and the answers that follow. From what you see in this passage, how should you prepare yourself to be in God's presence?

FOR GOING DEEPER

Compare verses 3-6 with Psalm 15. How do these passages support each other?

PSALM 25

SEEING WHAT'S THERE

1. What specific requests does David make to God in this psalm?

2. In verses 12-14, what promises are made to the person who fears God?

3. Identify a *key word, key phrase,* or *key sentence* in each stanza of this psalm.

CAPTURE THE ESSENCE

4. What exactly is the basis for David's confident claims in verses 3 and 15?

5. From the evidence you see in this psalm, how would you describe David's relationship with God?

FOR LIFE TODAY

6. In light of how you're doing spiritually in your life today, which verse in this psalm

do you think is the most important at this time—and why?

7. Review the guidelines for our thought-life given in Philippians 4:8—"Whatever is true, whatever is noble, whatever is right, whatever is pure, whatever is lovely, whatever is admirable—if anything is excellent or praiseworthy—*think about such things.*" What food for thought can you find in Psalm 25 that especially strikes you as being *true,* or *noble,* or *right,* or *pure,* or *lovely,* or *admirable,* or *excellent,* or *praiseworthy?*

PSALM 26

SEEING WHAT'S THERE

1. How would you summarize what David asks God for in this psalm?

2. Look at David's confident words about himself in verses 1-8. Are these words of pride, or words of humility? Explain your answer.

3. What commitment does David make at the end of this psalm?

4. Choose a *key word, key phrase,* or *key sentence* in each stanza of this psalm.

CAPTURE THE ESSENCE

5. Remember again the description of David as "a man after God's own heart." What are the most significant things this psalm reveals about David's heart? What are his desires, his longings, and his commitments?

FOR LIFE TODAY

6. Review again the statements David makes about himself in verses 1-8. Which of these statements can you make about yourself?

PSALM 27

SEEING WHAT'S THERE

1. What exactly does David ask God for in this psalm? What is he longing for, and praying for?

2. What three personal descriptions does David give for God in verse 1?

3. What prophecy is made in verse 5?

4. Select a *key word, key phrase,* or *key sentence* in each stanza of this psalm.

CAPTURE THE ESSENCE

5. What do you think David means when he says in verse 1 that the Lord is his *light?*

6. From the evidence you see in this psalm, how would you describe David's relationship with God?

7. What would you say is the reason for the confidence David expresses in verse 13?

8. In verse 14, look at the strength we are told to have. What is this particular strength? How would you describe someone who is strong in this way?

9. What kind of *waiting* is David speaking of in verse 14?

10. After studying Psalms 23—27, what title would you give to each of them?

11. What is the best evidence you see in Psalms 23—27 of total honesty and openness while praying to God?

FOR LIFE TODAY

12. Look again at verses 1-3. What are your greatest fears at this time in life?

13. Think again about David's reminder in verse 14 to *wait on God.* What are the most important areas in life for you to be waiting on Him at this time?

14. What are the most important things you are asking from God now, and expecting from Him in the future?

15. As you scan Psalms 23—27, which verse or passage most closely reflects your own spiritual and emotional feelings at this time?

PSALM 28

Startup: What are the biggest lessons you've learned in life about answered prayer?

SEEING WHAT'S THERE

1. Choose a *key word, key phrase,* or *key sentence* in each stanza of this psalm.

2. What are David's concerns in verse 1?

3. What commitment does David express in this psalm?

4. Look at the place David mentions at the end of verse 2. What do we learn about this place in Exodus 26:33-34?

CAPTURE THE ESSENCE

5. What patterns and principles does this psalm offer for teaching us how to pray when we're in serious trouble?

FOR LIFE TODAY

6. How strongly does verse 7 reflect your own experience of God at this time in your life, compared with times in your past? Use a scale of one to ten (one = "much less than ever," ten = "much more than ever") to help you decide.

FOR GOING DEEPER

Look again at the place David mentions in verse 2. What else do you learn about this place in 1 Kings 6:16 and 8:6-9, 2 Chronicles 3:8-14, Ezekiel 41:3-4, and especially in Hebrews 9:3-9 and 10:19-22?

PSALM 29

SEEING WHAT'S THERE

1. What two gifts from God are mentioned in the concluding verse of this psalm?

2. What commands to the "mighty" are given in verses 1-2? And who do you think these "mighty" ones are?

3. Jesus tells us to "seek first the kingdom of God and His righteousness" (Matthew 6:33). What would you say this psalm teaches most about God's kingdom?

4. Identify a *key word, key phrase,* or *key sentence* in each stanza of this psalm.

FOR LIFE TODAY

5. Look again at verse 11. As you think about what *has* happened or *is* happening in your family or church, or in your personal life, what convinces you most of the truth of this verse? How are you seeing the gift of God's strength and the gift of God's peace?

CAPTURE THE ESSENCE

6. What are the most important things this psalm communicates about God's character and personality?

PSALM 30

SEEING WHAT'S THERE

1. Choose a *key word, key phrase,* or *key sentence* in each stanza of this psalm.

2. What commitments does David make at the beginning and the end of this psalm? And how fully can you explain the reasons for this commitment?

3. What did David ask God in verses 8-10?

CAPTURE THE ESSENCE

4. Imagine yourself with David as he is writing this psalm. How do you think he would answer if you interrupted him to quietly ask, "David, what are you most thankful to God for today?"

5. From what you see in verse 5, what conclusions can you make about God's character and personality?

6. Are you convinced that David's words in this psalm represent his *heart*-knowledge, and not just *head*-knowledge? If so, what convinces you?

FOR LIFE TODAY

7. Based on your own experience, to what extent can you repeat all that David says to God in verse 2?

PSALM 31

SEEING WHAT'S THERE

1. Select a *key word, key phrase,* or *key sentence* in each stanza of this psalm.

2. Imagine yourself coming to visit David on the day he is writing this psalm. How might he answer if you said to him, "David, you seem troubled; what's on your mind and heart today?"

3. What specific requests does David make to God in this psalm?

4. What commitment does David make in verse 7, and how fully can you explain the reasons for his commitment?

CAPTURE THE ESSENCE

5. Remember again the description of David as "a man after God's own heart." What are the most significant things this psalm reveals about David's heart? What are his desires, his longings, and his commitments?

FOR LIFE TODAY

6. If God had written this psalm only for you, which words or phrases do you think He might have underlined, and why?

PSALM 32

SEEING WHAT'S THERE

1. If the word *blessed* means "happy," then what clues does this psalm give about the best way to happiness?

2. What different words are used in this psalm to mean *sin?*

3. What commands are presented in this psalm?

4. Identify a *key word, key phrase,* or *key sentence* in each stanza of this psalm.

CAPTURE THE ESSENCE

5. From the evidence you see in this psalm, how would you summarize what David knows about *sin* and *forgiveness?*

6. Why do you think David concludes this psalm the way he does with the commands in verse 11? How does ending tie in to the rest of the psalm?

7. After studying Psalms 28—32, what title would you give to each of them?

8. What is the best evidence you see in Psalms 28—32 of total honesty and openness while praying to God?

FOR LIFE TODAY

9. Remember again the promise in 1 John 1:9—that *if we confess our sins,* God will forgive us and cleanse us from unrighteousness. What parts of this psalm can serve as a model and inspiration for the way you confess your personal sins?

10. Look again at verses 8-9. In practical terms, how can you avoid what David speaks of in verse 9?

11. Which verse in this psalm do you think God would like you to understand best?

12. As you scan Psalms 28—32, which verse or passage most closely reflects your own spiritual and emotional feelings at this time?

FOR GOING DEEPER

Who will appreciate Psalm 32 most? Those who have been forgiven much, or those who have been forgiven little? Look in Luke 7:36-50 at an incident in the life of Jesus in which he spoke much about forgiveness. Then compare that passage with Psalm 32. In what each passage teaches, how are they most alike, and how are they most different?

PSALM 33

Startup: Talk together any times in your life when you've especially enjoyed worshiping God in a new and different way. What were the circumstances that brought this about?

SEEING WHAT'S THERE

1. What commands are God's people given in verses 1-3?

2. Choose a *key word, key phrase,* or *key sentence* in each stanza of this psalm.

3. Jesus tells us to "seek first the kingdom of God and His righteousness" (Matthew 6:33). From what you see in verses 4-5, what does God especially want us to understand about His righteousness?

4. What words or phrases in this psalm tell us the most about God's *character?*

5. How accurate would verses 20-21 be as a description of your church?

PSALM 34

1. For useful background to this psalm, look together at the events of David's life recorded in 1 Samuel 21:10-15.

2. What commitments does David make in this psalm?

3. What commands are given to us in this verses 8-9? How would you explain these in your own words?

4. What would you say are the strongest promises given in this psalm?

5. What possible fears on David's part are revealed in this psalm?

6. Select a *key word, key phrase,* or *key sentence* in each stanza of this psalm.

7. From what you see in this psalm, how would you summarize what David knows about God's character?

8. Look at what David says about loving life in verse 12. How strong is your love for life at this time? Use a scale of one to ten (one = "much weaker than ever," ten = "much stronger than ever") to help you decide.

9. What to you are the most important reasons to love life?

10. If you were to rephrase some or all of this psalm as an expression of your own heart to God at this time, how would you begin it? What would be "verse 1" in your own personal "Psalm 34"?

PSALM 35

1. Choose a *key word, key phrase,* or *key sentence* in each stanza of this psalm.

2. What specific requests does David make to God in this psalm?

3. What specific commitments does David express in this psalm?

4. What do you think were the chief *motives* behind David's words spoken out against his enemies?

5. Discuss how much you agree or disagree with this statement: David considered *his* enemies to be *God's* enemies, and that is why he so boldly asked God to bring about their ruin.

6. From the evidence you see in this psalm, what did David *expect* from God, and what did he think God expected from him?

7. After studying Psalms 33—35, what title would you give to each of them?

8. What is the best evidence you see in Psalms 33—35 of total honesty and openness while praying to God?

9. As you scan Psalms 33—35, which verse or passage most closely reflects your own spiritual and emotional feelings at this time?

PSALM 36

Startup: In the way we read and study the Bible, what kind of old mental habits or faulty assumptions can most easily block the Psalms from coming alive in our minds and hearts?

1. What particular request does David make of God in verse 10?

2. What specific images does David use in praising God in verses 5-9?

3. Identify a *key word, key phrase,* or *key sentence* in each stanza of this psalm.

4. Jesus tells us to "seek first the kingdom of God and His righteousness" (Matthew

6:33). From what you see in this psalm, what does God especially want us to understand about His righteousness?

CAPTURE THE ESSENCE

5. What are the most significant truths this psalm reveals about *God*, and what are the most significant truths it reveals about *us?*

FOR LIFE TODAY

6. Of all that you see in this psalm, what one truth are you most thankful for, because of its personal significance to you?

PSALM 37

SEEING WHAT'S THERE

1. How many times do you see the phrase "inherit the earth" or "inherit the land" in this psalm? How would you restate this phrase in your own words, and what clues do you think it offers about the central message of this psalm?

2. What commands do you see in verses 3-8?

3. What additional commands do you see in verses 27, 34, and 37?

4. How many times do you see the word *will* used in this psalm? Each time it's used, decide what this sentence tells you most about the future.

5. What are the strongest promises from God which you see in this psalm?

6. Choose a *key word, key phrase,* or *key sentence* in each stanza of this psalm.

FOR LIFE TODAY

7. Look again at the commands in verses 3-8. Which of them would you say are the easiest for most Christians today to obey? And which are the easiest to *dis-obey?*

8. Look again at the commands in verse 27. In practical terms, how do you think God most wants you to obey these words?

9. Review the guidelines for our thought-life given in Philippians 4:8 — "Whatever is true, whatever is noble, whatever is right, whatever is pure, whatever is lovely, whatever is admirable — if anything is excellent or praiseworthy — *think about such things."* What food for thought can you find in Psalm 37 that especially strikes you as being *true,* or *noble,* or *right,* or *pure,* or *lovely,* or *admirable,* or *excellent,* or *praiseworthy?*

PSALM 38

SEEING WHAT'S THERE

1. Select a *key word, key phrase,* or *key sentence* in each stanza of this psalm.

2. What fears and concerns does David reveal in this psalm?

3. What specific requests does David make to God in this psalm?

4. Look closely at verse 15. What confidence and what commitment does this verse reflect on David's part?

CAPTURE THE ESSENCE

5. From what you see in this psalm, how would you evaluate David's relationship with God? What does God mean to him in his everyday life? What does he depend on God for?

6. After studying Psalms 36—38, what title would you give to each of them?

FOR LIFE TODAY

7. Again, recall the promise in 1 John 1:9 — that *if we confess our sins,* God will forgive us and cleanse us from unrighteousness. What words or phrases in this psalm can serve as a model and inspiration for the way you confess your personal sins?

8. Look again at the requests David makes in this psalm. How relevant and appropriate would these requests be in a time when things were going well for you (which evidently was not the case for David when he wrote this psalm)?

9. As you scan Psalms 36—38, which verse or passage most closely reflects your own spiritual and emotional feelings at this time?

10. What is the best evidence you see in Psalms 36—38 of total honesty and openness while praying to God?

PSALM 39

Startup: Discuss how often you think about the shortness of our life on earth. What kind of circumstances will bring this topic to your mind?

SEEING WHAT'S THERE

1. Imagine yourself coming to visit David on the day he is writing this psalm. How might he answer if you said to him, "David, you seem troubled; what's on your mind and heart today?"

2. What requests does David make to God in this psalm?

3. Choose a *key word, key phrase,* or *key sentence* in each stanza of this psalm.

FOR LIFE TODAY

4. Look again at David's experience in verses 1-3. In what ways, if any, have you experienced something similar?

PSALM 40

SEEING WHAT'S THERE

1. Identify a *key word, key phrase,* or *key sentence* in each stanza of this psalm.

2. In this psalm, what acts of God does David acknowledge? What does he say God has already done?

3. What does David still want God to do?

4. If the word *blessed* means "happy," then what clues does this psalm give about the best way to happiness?

5. What fears on David's part are revealed in the last half of this psalm?

CAPTURE THE ESSENCE

6. From the evidence you see in this psalm, how would you describe David's relationship with God? What does God mean to him in his everyday life? What does he depend on God for?

7. Again, what verses in this psalm do you think would most impress the boy Jesus as He heard them read and discussed in the Temple in Jerusalem, and what questions or comments do you suppose He might have spoken to the teachers there?

FOR LIFE TODAY

8. To what extent would you say the words in verse 8 are an accurate reflection of your own heart at this time in life?

9. If you were to rephrase some or all of this psalm as an expression of your own heart to God at this time, how would you begin it? What would be "verse 1" in your own personal "Psalm 40"?

FOR GOING DEEPER

Restate in your own words what David expressed about his knowledge of God in verses 6-8. How does this compare with the words Jesus spoke in Matthew 9:13 and 12:7? (Look also at Hebrews 10:5-10.)

PSALM 41

SEEING WHAT'S THERE

1. If the word *blessed* means "happy," then what clues does this psalm give about the best way to happiness?

2. What specific promises does God impart to us in verses 1-3?

3. Choose a *key word, key phrase,* or *key sentence* in each stanza of this psalm.

CAPTURE THE ESSENCE

4. What patterns and principles does this psalm offer for teaching us how to pray when we're experiencing pain, trouble, or loneliness?

5. From what you see in this psalm, how would you summarize what David knows about God's character?

6. After studying Psalms 39—41, what title would you give to each of them?

7. What is the best evidence you see in Psalms 39—41 of total honesty and openness while praying to God?

FOR LIFE TODAY

8. As you scan Psalms 39—41, which verse or passage most closely reflects your own spiritual and emotional feelings at this time?

FOR GOING DEEPER

9. Discuss together the prophetic fulfillment of verse 9 which you see in John 13:18, Luke 22:21, and Matthew 26:23.

PSALM 42

Startup: What's the thirstiest you can ever recall being?

SEEING WHAT'S THERE

1. Select a *key word, key phrase,* or *key sentence* in each stanza of this psalm.

2. What questions are asked in this psalm, and which one do you think is most important?

FOR LIFE TODAY

3. How strongly does verse 8 reflect your own experience of God at this time in your life, compared with times in your past? Use a scale of one to ten (one = "much less than ever," ten = "much more than ever") to help you decide.

PSALM 43

SEEING WHAT'S THERE

1. Choose a *key word, key phrase,* or *key sentence* in each stanza of this psalm.

2. What words of commitment are expressed in this psalm?

FOR LIFE TODAY

3. Notice how God is described in verse 4. What are the most significant ways in which God represents these same things to you, at this time in your life?

PSALM 44

SEEING WHAT'S THERE

1. Identify a *key word, key phrase,* or *key sentence* in each stanza of this psalm.

2. What are the most important things the psalmist remembers about God in the past?

3. What facts about the present does the psalmist summarize?

4. What hopes for the future does the psalmist express?

CAPTURE THE ESSENCE

5. Would you say this psalm reflects *strong* faith, or *weak* faith? What evidence can you give for your answer?

6. What help does this psalm offer for dealing with deep suffering in our lives?

7. In your own words, what would you say is revealed most about God's character and personality in verse 21?

FOR LIFE TODAY

8. At what times in life could you most identify with the words in verse 25?

PSALM 45

SEEING WHAT'S THERE

1. Choose a *key word, key phrase,* or *key sentence* in each stanza of this psalm.

2. In Matthew 6:33, Jesus tells us to "seek first the kingdom of God and His righteousness." What can you learn about God's kingdom in this psalm?

CAPTURE THE ESSENCE

3. Once more, what verses in this psalm do you think would most impress the 12-year-old Jesus as He heard them read and discussed in the Temple in Jerusalem, and what questions or comments do you suppose He might have spoken to the teachers there?

4. After studying Psalms 42—45, what title would you give to each of them?

5. What is the best evidence you see in Psalms 42—45 of total honesty and openness while praying to God?

FOR LIFE TODAY

6. As you scan Psalms 42—45, which verse or passage most closely reflects your own spiritual and emotional feelings at this time?

FOR GOING DEEPER

To further explore how the life and ministry of Jesus the Messiah was foretold in the Psalms, compare verses 6-7 with Hebrews 1:8-9. See also Luke 1:32-33 and Philippians 2:9.

PSALM 46

Startup: If you've been in an earthquake before, tell what the experience was like.

SEEING WHAT'S THERE

1. Select a *key word, key phrase,* or *key sentence* in each stanza of this psalm.

2. What is the only command expressed in this psalm?

CAPTURE THE ESSENCE

3. In your own words, how would you explain the reason for the confidence expressed in this psalm?

4. What words or phrases in this psalm tell us the most about God's *character?*

FOR LIFE TODAY

5. How strongly do the words of verses 7 and 11 reflect your own experience of God at this time in your life, compared with times in your past? Use a scale of one to ten (one = "much less than ever," ten = "much more than ever") to help you decide.

PSALM 47

SEEING WHAT'S THERE

1. What commands are given in this psalm, and who are they given to?

2. Jesus tells us to "seek first the kingdom of God and His righteousness" (Matthew 6:33). What would you say this psalm teaches most about God's kingdom?

3. Select a *key word, key phrase,* or *key sentence* in each stanza of this psalm.

CAPTURE THE ESSENCE

4. From what you see in this psalm, what is it that God wants us to understand most about Himself?

PSALM 48

SEEING WHAT'S THERE

1. What conclusion does the psalmist arrive at in verse 14? And how exactly do you think he arrived at that conclusion?

2. What commands are given in verses 12-13, and what do you think is the reason for those commands?

3. Choose a *key word, key phrase,* or *key sentence* in each stanza of this psalm.

CAPTURE THE ESSENCE

4. How would you explain the confidence which is expressed in verse 14? On what basis does the psalmist arrive at this conclusion?

5. From what you see in this psalm, would you say that God wants to be considered *primarily* as the God of His people Israel, or as the God of the whole earth? Explain your answer.

FOR LIFE TODAY

6. Which verse in this psalm do you think God would like you to understand best?

PSALM 49

SEEING WHAT'S THERE

1. What commands are given in the opening verses of this psalm, and who are they given to?

2. Identify a *key word, key phrase,* or *key sentence* in each stanza of this psalm.

CAPTURE THE ESSENCE

3. In your own words, how would you explain the meaning of verses 7-9?

4. What exactly is the basis for the confident claim in verse 15?

5. How would you describe in your own words the people spoken of in verses 16-20?

FOR LIFE TODAY

6. What would you say are the most important things God wants us to understand from this psalm about *life,* and about *death?*

7. With what degree of confidence can you repeat the words of verse 15? If you

know these words are true for you, *how do you know it?*

PSALM 50

SEEING WHAT'S THERE

1. What does God most want us to understand about His character in this psalm?

2. What specific commands does God give us in this psalm?

3. What specific warnings does God give in this psalm?

4. Jesus tells us to "seek first the kingdom of God and His righteousness" (Matthew 6:33). What would you say this psalm teaches most about God's righteousness?

5. Choose a *key word, key phrase,* or *key sentence* in each stanza of this psalm.

CAPTURE THE ESSENCE

6. If this psalm was the only Scripture you had, how would you use it to help explain to someone else what God is like?

7. After studying Psalms 46—50, what title would you give to each of them?

FOR LIFE TODAY

8. Review the guidelines for our thought-life given in Philippians 4:8—"Whatever is true, whatever is noble, whatever is right, whatever is pure, whatever is lovely, whatever is admirable—if anything is excellent or praiseworthy—*think about such things.*" What food for thought can you find in Psalm 50 that especially strikes you as being *true,* or *noble,* or *right,* or *pure,* or *lovely,* or *admirable,* or *excellent,* or *praiseworthy?*

9. As you scan Psalms 46—50, which verse or passage most closely reflects your own spiritual and emotional feelings at this time?

PSALM 51

Startup: What have been some of the most difficult confessions of sin which you have had to make?

SEEING WHAT'S THERE

1. For the background to this psalm, review together the tragic events of David's life recorded in 2 Samuel 11—12.

2. How would you summarize what David asks God for in this psalm?

3. Jesus tells us to "seek first the kingdom of God and His righteousness" (Matthew 6:33). From what you see in verses 13-19, what does God especially want us to understand about His righteousness?

4. What would you say is the *key word, key phrase,* or *key sentence* in each stanza of this psalm?

CAPTURE THE ESSENCE

5. From what you see in this psalm, what are the most important things David understands about God's personality and character?

6. From what you see in this psalm, how would David define the words *repentance* and *forgiveness?*

FOR LIFE TODAY

7. Remember again the promise in 1 John 1:9—that *if we confess our sins,* God will forgive us and cleanse us from unrighteousness. What words or phrases in this psalm can serve as a model and inspiration for the way you confess your personal sins?

8. From what you see in this psalm, discuss together how you would complete this sentence: What God really wants from me is…

PSALM 52

SEEING WHAT'S THERE

1. For useful background to this psalm, look together at the time of David's life recorded in 1 Samuel 22:6-23.

2. What words of prophecy does David speak in verses 5-7?

3. Select a *key word, key phrase,* or *key sentence* in each stanza of this psalm.

4. What would you say God most wants us to understand from this psalm about what is *right* and what is *wrong?*

CAPTURE THE ESSENCE

5. From what you see in this psalm, how would you describe David's relationship with God? What does God mean to him in his everyday life? What does he depend on God for?

FOR LIFE TODAY

6. Look again at the picture David gives of his present and future life in verse 8. To what extent is this a picture of your life as well?

PSALM 53

SEEING WHAT'S THERE

1. Compare this psalm with Psalm 14. What are the biggest differences you see in these two psalms?

2. What question does David ask in this psalm?

3. Identify a *key word, key phrase,* or *key sentence* in each stanza of this psalm.

CAPTURE THE ESSENCE

4. From what you see in verse 2, what conclusions can you make about God's character and personality?

5. What does David understand about God's plan and purpose for His people?

6. How has God responded to David's longing in verse 6?

FOR LIFE TODAY

7. Which verse in this psalm do you think God would like you to understand best?

PSALM 54

SEEING WHAT'S THERE

1. For useful background to this psalm, look together at the time of David's life recorded in 1 Samuel 23:15-29.

2. Choose a *key word, key phrase,* or *key sentence* in each stanza of this psalm.

3. What exactly does David ask God for in this psalm?

4. What commitment does David make to God at the end of this psalm, and what does he say is his reason for making it?

CAPTURE THE ESSENCE

5. From the evidence you see in this psalm, how would you describe David's relationship with God? What does God mean to him in his everyday life? What does he depend on God for?

6. After studying Psalms 51—54, what title would you give to each of them? (Use this exercise to help you focus on what you believe is the essential message in each psalm.)

7. What is the best evidence you see in Psalms 51—54 of total honesty and openness while praying to God?

FOR LIFE TODAY

8. How strongly does verse 4 reflect your own experience of God at this time in your life, compared with times in your past? Use a scale of one to ten (one = "much less than ever," ten = "much more than ever") to help you decide.

9. Scan Psalms 51—54, and find the verse or passage which most closely reflects your own spiritual and emotional feelings at this time.

10. Recall again Paul's reminder in Romans 15:4 that the Old Testament Scriptures can give us patience and perseverance, as well as comfort and encouragement. In your own life, how do you see the Psalms living up to Paul's description? In what ways, if any, is this book meeting your personal needs for both *perseverance* and *encouragement?*

Psalm 55

Startup: What would you say is the key that allows danger and distress in our lives to lead to more meaningful prayer and worship?

SEEING WHAT'S THERE

1. What is David's prophecy in verses 19 and 23?

2. What command and promises are combined in verse 22?

3. How would you summarize what David asks God for in this psalm?

4. Select a *key word, key phrase,* or *key sentence* in each stanza of this psalm.

CAPTURE THE ESSENCE

5. What patterns and principles does this psalm offer for teaching us how to pray when we're experiencing trouble or hurt?

6. From the evidence you see in this psalm, how would you describe David's relationship with God? What does God mean to him in his everyday life? What does he depend on God for?

FOR LIFE TODAY

7. What would you say are the most practical ways to obey the command in verse 22?

Psalm 56

SEEING WHAT'S THERE

1. For useful background to this psalm, look together at the time of David's life recorded in 1 Samuel 21:10-15.

2. What commitments does David make in this psalm?

3. Identify a *key word, key phrase,* or *key sentence* in each stanza of this psalm.

CAPTURE THE ESSENCE

4. From what you see in this psalm, what are the most important things David understands about God's personality and character?

5. From what you see in this psalm, how would you describe David's basic *mindset* or *attitude* in life?

FOR LIFE TODAY

6. Look at the commitments David makes in this psalm. Have you also made these same commitments? If so, to what extent do you want to renew them now?

Psalm 57

SEEING WHAT'S THERE

1. For useful background to this psalm, look together at the events of David's life recorded in 1 Samuel 24.

2. What commitments does David make in this psalm?

3. Select a *key word, key phrase,* or *key sentence* in each stanza of this psalm.

4. What exactly does David *praise* God for in this psalm?

CAPTURE THE ESSENCE

5. From what you've seen in this psalm and others, how would you describe David's personality?

FOR LIFE TODAY

6. If you were to rephrase some or all of this psalm as an expression of your own heart to God at this time, how would you begin it? What would be "verse 1" in your own personal "Psalm 57"?

7. In Isaiah 55:10-11, God reminds us that He sends rain and snow from the sky to water the earth and to nurture life. In the same way, God says that He sends His words to accomplish specific purposes. From your study so far, what would you suggest are *God's* primary purposes for the book of Psalms in the lives of Christians today?

Psalm 58

SEEING WHAT'S THERE

1. In your own words, how would you summarize the prophecy David speaks in verses 9-11?

2. What does David request from God in this psalm?

3. Choose a *key word, key phrase,* or *key sentence* in each stanza of this psalm.

CAPTURE THE ESSENCE

4. What do you think were the chief *motives* behind David's words against his enemies in verses 6-8?

5. From what you see in this psalm, what does David know about God's character?

Psalm 59

SEEING WHAT'S THERE

1. For useful background to this psalm, look together at the events of David's life recorded in 1 Samuel 19.

2. What specific requests does David make to God in this psalm?

3. What specific commitments does David express in this psalm? And how fully can you explain the reasons for this commitment?

4. What phrases does David use to describe God in verses 9 and 17?

5. Identify a *key word, key phrase,* or *key sentence* in each stanza of this psalm.

CAPTURE THE ESSENCE

6. From the evidence you see in this psalm, how would you describe David's relationship with God? What does God mean to him in his everyday life? What does he depend on God for?

7. What patterns and principles does this psalm offer for teaching us how to pray when we're experiencing trouble, danger, or pain?

8. After studying Psalms 55—59, what title would you give to each of them?

9. What is the best evidence you see in Psalms 55—59 of total honesty and openness while praying to God?

FOR LIFE TODAY

10. To what extent would you say David's words in verse 17 are an accurate reflection of your own heart at this time in life?

11. As you scan Psalms 55—59, which verse or passage most closely reflects your own spiritual and emotional feelings at this time?

Psalm 60

Startup: Can you recall a time when you felt rejected by God? If so, what brought on that feeling?

SEEING WHAT'S THERE

1. Select a *key word, key phrase,* or *key sentence* in each stanza of this psalm.

2. What specific requests are made to God in this psalm?

CAPTURE THE ESSENCE

3. How would you explain the meaning of God's words in verses 6-8?

4. What help does this psalm offer for dealing with deep suffering in our lives?

5. Remember again the description of David as "a man after God's own heart." What are the most significant things this psalm reveals about David's heart? What are his desires, his longings, and his commitments?

FOR LIFE TODAY

6. In what significant ways in your own life have you discovered the truth of verses 11-12?

PSALM 61

SEEING WHAT'S THERE

1. Identify a *key word, key phrase,* or *key sentence* in each stanza of this psalm.

2. What specific requests does David make before God in this psalm?

3. What longing does David express in this psalm?

4. What specific commitment does David make before God in this psalm?

CAPTURE THE ESSENCE

5. Notice the last phrase in verse 5. What does it mean to fear God's *name?*

6. Also in verse 5, notice the heritage or inheritance that David speaks of. What do you think this is?

7. Once again, recall the Bible's description of David as "a man after God's own heart." What are the most significant things this psalm reveals about David's heart? What are his desires, his longings, his commitments?

8. From the evidence you see in this psalm, what would you say David considered to be the most important things in life?

FOR LIFE TODAY

9. If you were to rephrase some or all of this psalm as an expression of your own heart to God at this time, how would you begin it? What would be "verse 1" in your own personal "Psalm 61"?

PSALM 62

SEEING WHAT'S THERE

1. What does David want us to understand most about God in this psalm?

2. Choose a *key word, key phrase,* or *key sentence* in each stanza of this psalm.

CAPTURE THE ESSENCE

3. In your own words, what would you say is revealed most about God's character and personality in verses 11-12?

4. Are you convinced that David's words in this psalm represent his *heart*-knowledge, and not just *head*-knowledge? If so, what convinces you?

5. Look at David's conclusion in the last line of this psalm. How do you think David came to this conclusion?

FOR LIFE TODAY

6. Look again at David's conclusion at the end of verse 12. What difference do you think this truth makes in the life of someone who wholeheartedly believes it?

PSALM 63

SEEING WHAT'S THERE

1. For useful background to this psalm, look together at the time of David's life recorded in 2 Samuel 15:23-30, 16:13-14, and 17:27-29.

2. What commitments does David make in verses 3-5? And what are his reasons for making these commitments?

3. What specific prophecies does David make in verses 9-11?

4. Select a *key word, key phrase,* or *key sentence* in each stanza of this psalm.

CAPTURE THE ESSENCE

5. From the evidence you see in this psalm, how would you describe David's relationship with God? What does God mean to him in his everyday life? What does he depend on God for?

FOR LIFE TODAY

6. If you were to rephrase some or all of this psalm as an expression of your own heart to God at this time, how would you begin it? What would be "verse 1" in your own personal "Psalm 63"?

PSALM 64

SEEING WHAT'S THERE

1. Identify a *key word, key phrase,* or *key sentence* in each stanza of this psalm.

2. How would you summarize what David asks God for in this psalm?

3. What words of prophecy does David speak in verses 7-9?

4. From what you see in this psalm, how would you summarize what David knows about God's character?

CAPTURE THE ESSENCE

5. What patterns and principles does this psalm offer for teaching us how to pray when we're experiencing trouble or hurt?

FOR LIFE TODAY

6. Think again about David's reminder in verse 10. What are the most important ways for you to heed these words at this time in your life?

PSALM 65

SEEING WHAT'S THERE

1. Select a *key word, key phrase,* or *key sentence* in each stanza of this psalm.

2. What exactly does David *praise* God for in this psalm?

3. If the word *blessed* means "happy," then what clues does this psalm give about the best way to happiness?

4. If this psalm was the only Scripture you had, how would you use it to explain to someone else what God is like?

CAPTURE THE ESSENCE

5. What would you say God wants us to understand most from this psalm (especially verses 9-13) about the earth and our environment?

6. After studying Psalms 60—65, what title would you give to each of them?

7. What is the best evidence you see in Psalms 60—65 of total honesty and openness while praying to God?

FOR LIFE TODAY

8. To what extent would you say the words in verse 4 are an accurate reflection of your own church's experience at this time?

9. Review the guidelines for our thought-life given in Philippians 4:8—"Whatever is true, whatever is noble, whatever is right, whatever is pure, whatever is lovely, whatever is admirable—if anything is excellent or praiseworthy— *think about such things.*" What food for thought can you find in Psalm 65 that especially strikes you as being *true,* or *noble,* or *right,* or *pure,* or *lovely,* or *admirable,* or *excellent,* or *praiseworthy?*

10. As you scan Psalms 60—65, which verse or passage most closely reflects your own spiritual and emotional feelings at this time?

PSALM 66

Startup: Can you recall a time when you literally shouted out praise to God? What were the circumstances?

SEEING WHAT'S THERE

1. What specific commands are given in this psalm, and who are they given to?

2. What specific commitments are expressed in this psalm?

3. Choose a *key word, key phrase,* or *key sentence* in each stanza of this psalm.

CAPTURE THE ESSENCE

4. In your own words, what would you say is revealed most about God's character and personality in verse 7?

FOR LIFE TODAY

5. Look again at the description in verse 10. What are the most significant ways God has tested you?

PSALM 67

SEEING WHAT'S THERE

1. What vision for the future is revealed in verses 6-7?

CAPTURE THE ESSENCE

2. What helpful perspectives does this psalm offer about evangelism?

3. From what you see in this psalm, would you say that God wants to be considered *primarily* as the God of His people Israel, or as the God of the whole earth? Explain your answer.

FOR LIFE TODAY

4. In what ways, if any, do the words in verses 6-7 reflect your own personal vision for the future?

5. In what ways can this psalm serve as a model for the way you pray for non-Christians?

PSALM 68

SEEING WHAT'S THERE

1. In this psalm, what acts of God does David acknowledge? What does he say God has already done?

2. Summarize all the prophecies that David gives in the last half of this psalm. Which would you say have already been fulfilled, and which are still awaiting fulfillment?

3. What requests does David make of God in verses 28-30?

4. How would you summarize the commands given in verses 4, 26, and 32-34?

5. Identify a *key word, key phrase,* or *key sentence* in each stanza of this psalm.

CAPTURE THE ESSENCE

6. From all that you see in this psalm, what are the most important things David understands about God's personality and character?

7. After studying Psalms 66—68, what title would you give to each of them?

FOR LIFE TODAY

8. If God had written this psalm only for you, which words or phrases do you think He might have underlined, and why?

9. As you scan Psalms 66—68, which verse or passage most closely reflects your own spiritual and emotional feelings at this time?

FOR GOING DEEPER

To further explore how the life and ministry of Jesus the Messiah was foretold in the Psalms, compare verse 18 with Ephesians 4:8-10.

PSALM 69

Startup: Have you ever been close to drowning? If so, what can you remember from the experience?

SEEING WHAT'S THERE

1. Select a *key word, key phrase,* or *key sentence* in each stanza of this psalm.

2. What specific requests does David make to God in this psalm?

3. What commitment does David make in verse 30, and why does he make it?

CAPTURE THE ESSENCE

4. From the evidence you see in this psalm, how would you describe David's relationship with God? What does God mean to him in his everyday life? What does he depend on God for?

5. In this psalm, what instruction does the Lord give us about what *faith in God* really means?

6. What do you think were the chief *motives* behind David's words against his enemies in verses 22-28?

7. Again, imagine yourself being present in the temple in Jerusalem as the twelve-year-old Jesus hears this psalm read and discussed by the Jewish teachers. What verses in this psalm do you think would most impress Him, and what questions or comments do you suppose He might have spoken?

FOR LIFE TODAY

8. When in your life have you most been able to identify with David's words in verse 3?

Except for Psalm 22, this psalm is quoted more frequently in the New Testament than any other. What parts of this psalm do you see as a foreshadowing of the suffering of Christ? (For helpful background, look at Matthew 27:34 and 27:48, John 2:15-17, 15:23-25, and 19:28-30, and Acts 1:15-22.)

PSALM 70

SEEING WHAT'S THERE

1. What exactly does David ask God for in this psalm?

2. Choose a *key word, key phrase,* or *key sentence* in each stanza of this psalm.

CAPTURE THE ESSENCE

3. What patterns and principles does this psalm offer for teaching us how to pray when we're experiencing trouble or hurt?

4. From the evidence you see in this psalm, how would you describe David's relationship with God? What does God mean to him in his everyday life? What does he depend on God for?

FOR LIFE TODAY

5. At this time in life, how fully and sincerely can you identify with David's words in the first line of verse 5?

PSALM 71

SEEING WHAT'S THERE

1. Which phrases here give clues about the age of this psalm's writer?

2. What specific requests does this writer make of God in this psalm?

3. What specific commitments does the psalmist make?

4. Jesus tells us to "seek first the kingdom of God and His righteousness" (Matthew 6:33). From what you see in verses 14-19, what does God especially want us to understand about His righteousness?

5. Identify a *key word, key phrase,* or *key sentence* in each stanza of this psalm.

CAPTURE THE ESSENCE

6. How would you explain the confidence which is expressed in verses 20-21? On what basis does the psalmist arrive at this conclusion?

FOR LIFE TODAY

7. With the words of this psalm in mind, describe what you want your life to be like at age 65 (or at 75 or 85).

PSALM 72

SEEING WHAT'S THERE

1. How would you summarize what Solomon asks God for in this psalm?

2. How does Solomon describe the nature of the king's rule in this psalm?

3. Select a *key word, key phrase,* or *key sentence* in each stanza of this psalm.

CAPTURE THE ESSENCE

4. From what you see in verses 17-19 of this psalm, would you say that God wants to be considered *primarily* as the God of His people Israel, or as the God of the whole earth? Explain your answer.

5. Again, what verses in this psalm do you think would most impress the boy Jesus as He heard them read and discussed in the Temple in Jerusalem, and what questions or comments do you suppose He might have spoken to the teachers there?

6. After studying Psalms 69—72, what title would you give to each of them?

7. What is the best evidence you see in Psalms 69—72 of total honesty and openness while praying to God?

FOR LIFE TODAY

8. As you scan Psalms 69—72, which verse or passage most closely reflects your own spiritual and emotional feelings at this time?

PSALM 73

Startup: Describe which of these situations would bother you the most: (a) all the wealthy people in your community became wicked, or (b) all the wicked people in your community became wealthy.

SEEING WHAT'S THERE

1. What conclusion in verse 1 is Asaph's starting point for this psalm?

2. What danger does Asaph mention in verses 2-3?

3. Look at the conclusions Asaph makes about the wicked in verses 4-12. What evidence do you see that Asaph understood both their outward behavior and their inner motives?

4. After observing the wicked, what conclusion did Asaph arrive at about himself in verse 13-14?

5. What did it take for Asaph to get his focus *off* the wicked, and *on* to God?

6. In verses 18-28, what were the most important truths Asaph realized when his focus was on God?

7. What commitment does Asaph make at the end of this psalm?

8. Choose a *key word, key phrase,* or *key sentence* in each stanza of this psalm.

CAPTURE THE ESSENCE

9. From the evidence you see in this psalm, how would you describe Asaph's relationship with God? What does God mean to him in his everyday life? What does he depend on God for?

10. What would you say God wants us to understand most from this psalm about what is *right* and what is *wrong?*

11. What would you say God wants us to understand most from verses 23-28 about His presence with us?

FOR LIFE TODAY

12. Which phrases in verses 23-28 are the most meaningful to you in your own relationship with God?

13. Review the guidelines for our thought-life given in Philippians 4:8—"Whatever is true, whatever is noble, whatever is right, whatever is pure, whatever is love-ly, whatever is admirable—if anything is excellent or praiseworthy—*think about such things."* What food for thought can you find in Psalm 73 that especially strikes you as being *true,* or *noble,* or *right,* or *pure,* or *lovely,* or *admirable,* or *excellent,* or *praiseworthy?*

PSALM 74

SEEING WHAT'S THERE

1. This psalm divides easily into two major parts, each with very different moods. Which verse would you say marks the major turning point in the structure of this psalm?

2. What questions does Asaph ask in this psalm?

3. What requests does Asaph make to God?

4. How would you summarize Asaph's greatest fears at this time, as revealed in this psalm?

5. What does Asaph remember most about God in verses 12-17?

6. Jesus tells us to "seek first the kingdom of God and His righteousness" (Matthew 6:33). From what you see in verses 12-17, what does God especially want us to understand about His kingdom?

7. Identify a *key word, key phrase,* or *key sentence* in each stanza of this psalm.

CAPTURE THE ESSENCE

8. What help does this psalm offer for dealing with deep suffering in our lives?

9. From what you see in verses 16-17, what conclusions can you make about God's character and personality?

FOR LIFE TODAY

10. Look again at verses 22-23. What is God's *cause* today, and who are His enemies?

PSALM 75

SEEING WHAT'S THERE

1. Asaph begins the psalm by giving thanks to God. From what you see in this psalm, what is Asaph most thankful for?

2. What commitments does Asaph make in the closing verses of this psalm?

3. Select a *key word, key phrase,* or *key sentence* in each stanza of this psalm.

CAPTURE THE ESSENCE

4. From what you see in this psalm, what is it that God wants us to understand most about Himself?

5. After studying Psalms 73—75, what title would you give to each of them?

6. What is the best evidence you see in Psalms 73—75 of total honesty and openness while praying to God?

FOR LIFE TODAY

7. Which verse in this psalm do you think God would like you to understand best?

8. As you scan Psalms 73—75, which verse or passage most closely reflects your own spiritual and emotional feelings at this time?

PSALM 76

Startup: Talk together about times in your life when you have most needed to understand God's power.

SEEING WHAT'S THERE

1. What are God's people commanded to do in verse 11?

2. Choose a *key word, key phrase,* or *key sentence* in each stanza of this psalm.

CAPTURE THE ESSENCE

3. Look especially at verse 10. How would you explain its meaning in your own words?

FOR LIFE TODAY

4. In what ways, if any, would you interpret verse 11 as applying to your own life today? How do you feel you should respond to this command?

5. In Jeremiah 23:29, God says that His Word is like fire, and like a hammer. He can use the Scriptures to burn away unclean thoughts and desires in our hearts. He can also use Scripture to hit hard like a hammer, with the power to crush our spiritual hardness. From your study of the Psalms, how do you most want to see the "fire-and-hammer" power of God's Word at work in your own life?

PSALM 77

SEEING WHAT'S THERE

1. What questions does Asaph ask in this psalm? And how do you think God would answer each one?

2. Identify a *key word, key phrase,* or *key sentence* in each stanza of this psalm.

CAPTURE THE ESSENCE

3. In your own words, what would you say is revealed most about God's character and personality in verses 13-20?

FOR LIFE TODAY

4. How can this psalm serve as a model and inspiration for seeking God's help in times of trouble?

5. If you were to rephrase some or all of this psalm as an expression of your own heart to God at this time, how would you begin it? What would be "verse 1" in your own personal "Psalm 77"?

PSALM 78

SEEING WHAT'S THERE

1. What commitments does Asaph make in the opening verses of this psalm?

2. How would you summarize the most important events this psalm mentions from Israel's history?

3. Besides God, only one other individual is mentioned in this psalm's review of Israel's history. Who is that person? (The names Jacob, Israel, and Ephraim refer here to a nation and a tribe.)

4. Select a *key word, key phrase,* or *key sentence* in each stanza of this psalm.

5. Is this psalm best described as a celebration of Israel's history, or as a word of warning from Israel's history?

6. After studying Psalms 76—78, what title would you give to each of them?

7. What is the best evidence you see in Psalms 76—78 of total honesty and openness while praying to God?

FOR LIFE TODAY

8. If it's true that *the past is a lesson for the future,* then what would you say are the most important lessons for God's people today to learn from this psalm?

9. As you scan Psalms 76—78, which verse or passage most closely reflects your own spiritual and emotional feelings at this time?

PSALM 79

Startup: What is the most helpless you've ever felt in life?

SEEING WHAT'S THERE

1. Identify a *key word, key phrase,* or *key sentence* in each stanza of this psalm.

2. What exactly does Asaph ask God for in this psalm?

3. In verse 9, what reason does Asaph give in asking for God's help?

4. What vision for the future does Asaph see in verse 13?

5. How would you describe the mood or tone of this psalm?

CAPTURE THE ESSENCE

6. What help does this psalm offer for dealing with deep suffering in our lives?

7. What does it mean to call on God's *name,* as mentioned in verse 6?

FOR LIFE TODAY

8. When you ask for God's help, how important is it to have the same motives which Asaph gives in verse 9?

PSALM 80

SEEING WHAT'S THERE

1. What question does Asaph ask in verse 4?

2. What specific requests does Asaph make to God in this psalm?

3. How does Asaph make reference to God's *hand* and God's *face* in his prayers?

4. Choose a *key word, key phrase,* or *key sentence* in each stanza of this psalm.

CAPTURE THE ESSENCE

5. What help does this psalm offer for dealing with deep suffering in our lives?

FOR LIFE TODAY

6. Notice again the words and phrases spoken in prayer in verses 17-19. Which of these phrases, if any, would you like to use more in your prayers?

PSALM 81

SEEING WHAT'S THERE

1. What words of promise does God speak in this psalm?

2. Select a *key word, key phrase,* or *key sentence* in each stanza of this psalm.

CAPTURE THE ESSENCE

3. From what you see in this psalm, how would you summarize the quality of life which God wants His people to experience?

FOR LIFE TODAY

4. If God had written this psalm only for you, which words or phrases do you think He might have underlined, and why?

PSALM 82

SEEING WHAT'S THERE

1. In verse 1, who might these "rulers" or "gods" be whom the Lord addresses?

2. What question does God ask them in verse 2?

3. What commands does God give in verses 3-4?

4. What observations does God make about His hearers in verse 5?

5. What words of prophecy does God speak in verses 6-7?

6. What concluding prayer does Asaph make in verse 8, and how would you explain it in your own words?

7. Identify a *key word, key phrase,* or *key sentence* in each stanza of this psalm.

CAPTURE THE ESSENCE

8. After studying Psalms 79—82, what title would you give to each of them?

9. What is the best evidence you see in Psalms 79—82 of total honesty and openness while praying to God?

FOR LIFE TODAY

10. As you scan Psalms 79—82, which verse or passage most closely reflects your own spiritual and emotional feelings at this time?

PSALM 83

Startup: Can you recall a time in your life when God seemed severely silent? What were the circumstances?

SEEING WHAT'S THERE

1. Select a *key word, key phrase,* or *key sentence* in each stanza of this psalm.

2. How would you summarize what Asaph asks God for in this psalm?

CAPTURE THE ESSENCE

3. What help does this psalm offer God's people for dealing with deep suffering in their lives?

4. What do you think were the chief *motives* behind Asaph's words against his enemies in verses 9-17? (See especially verse 16.)

PSALM 84

SEEING WHAT'S THERE

1. If the word *blessed* means "happy," then what clues does this psalm give about the best way to happiness?

2. Choose a *key word, key phrase,* or *key sentence* in each stanza of this psalm.

CAPTURE THE ESSENCE

3. What are the most important things verse 11 communicates about God's character and personality?

FOR LIFE TODAY

4. Consider how strongly you desire to know God better, then ask yourself this question: What are the truths revealed in this psalm which He may want me to understand more deeply at this time in my life?

PSALM 85

SEEING WHAT'S THERE

1. What questions are asked in this psalm?

2. What requests does the psalmist make in verses 4 and 7?

3. What commitment does the psalmist make in verse 8?

4. In verses 10-11, what picture does the psalmist want to engrave in our minds?

5. Jesus tells us to "seek first the kingdom of God and His righteousness" (Matthew 6:33). What would you say this psalm teaches most about God's righteousness?

6. Identify a *key word, key phrase,* or *key sentence* in each stanza of this psalm.

CAPTURE THE ESSENCE

7. What would you say is the basis for the confident conclusion expressed by the psalmist in verses 12-13?

FOR LIFE TODAY

8. If it's true that "you become what you think," then what are the most important thoughts from this psalm to plant firmly in your mind?

PSALM 86

SEEING WHAT'S THERE

1. Select a *key word, key phrase,* or *key sentence* in each stanza of this psalm.

2. What specific requests does David make to God in this psalm?

3. What commitments does David make in this psalm?

4. What vision for the future does David see in verse 9?

CAPTURE THE ESSENCE

5. Notice the last phrase in verse 11. What do you think it means to fear God's *name?*

6. From all that you see in this psalm, what are the most important things David understands about God's personality and character?

7. Are you convinced that David's words in this psalm represent his *heart*-knowledge, and not just *head*-knowledge? If so, what convinces you?

8. After studying Psalms 83 — 86, what title would you give to each of them?

9. What is the best evidence you see in Psalms 83 — 86 of total honesty and openness while praying to God?

FOR LIFE TODAY

10. In your own life, how strongly can you echo David's words in verses 12-13? Is this an accurate reflection of your own commitment and your own experience?

11. If you were to rephrase some or all of this psalm as an expression of your own heart to God at this time, how would you begin it? What would be "verse 1" in your own personal "Psalm 86"?

12. Review again the guidelines for our thought-life given in Philippians 4:8 — "Whatever is true, whatever is noble, whatever is right, whatever is pure, whatever is lovely, whatever is admirable — if anything is excellent or praiseworthy — *think about such things.*" What food for thought can you find in Psalm 86 that especially strikes you as being *true,* or *noble,* or *right,* or *pure,* or *lovely,* or *admirable,* or *excellent,* or *praiseworthy?*

13. As you scan Psalms 83 — 86, which verse or passage most closely reflects your own spiritual and emotional feelings at this time?

PSALM 87

Startup: What images come to your mind when you think of Jerusalem?

SEEING WHAT'S THERE

1. What are the most important perspectives this psalm gives us about Zion, the city of God?

CAPTURE THE ESSENCE

2. From what you see in this psalm, would you say that God wants to be considered *primarily* as the God of His people Israel, or as the God of the whole earth? Explain your answer.

PSALM 88

SEEING WHAT'S THERE

1. The preface to this psalm lists the author as "Heman the Ezrahite." For helpful background on this psalmist, look at 1 Chronicles 15:16-19, 16:39-42, and 25:1 and 25:4-5. What were Heman's responsibilities?

2. How would you describe the mood or tone of this psalm? Is that mood sustained throughout the entire psalm, or does a change occur somewhere?

3. Choose a *key word, key phrase,* or *key sentence* in each stanza of this psalm.

FOR LIFE TODAY

4. Which verse in this psalm do you think God would like you to understand best?

PSALM 89

SEEING WHAT'S THERE

1. The preface to this psalm lists the author as "Ethan the Ezrahite." For helpful background on this psalmist, look at 1 Chronicles 15:16-19. What were the responsibilities of Ethan and the other musicians?

2. Identify a *key word, key phrase,* or *key sentence* in each stanza of this psalm.

3. This psalm divides easily into two major parts, each with very different moods. Which verse would you say marks the major turning point in the structure of this psalm?

4. What specific commitments does the psalmist make in verses 1-2?

5. What promises from God does the psalmist recall in verses 3-4 and 19-37?

6. What questions does the psalmist ask in verses 46-49?

7. What is the final request the psalmist makes?

8. Jesus tells us to "seek first the kingdom of God and His righteousness" (Matthew 6:33). From what you see in verses 14-16, what does God especially want us to understand about His righteousness?

CAPTURE THE ESSENCE

9. Restate in your own words what you believe are the most important truths revealed about God's character and personality in verses 6-18.

10. Again, what verses in this psalm do you think would most impress the 12-year-old Jesus as He heard them read and discussed in the Temple in Jerusalem, and what questions or comments do you suppose He might have spoken to the teachers there?

11. After studying Psalms 87—89, what title would you give to each of them?

12. What is the best evidence you see in Psalms 87—89 of total honesty and openness while praying to God?

FOR LIFE TODAY

13. Evaluate how well verses 15-16 describe your own relationship with God at this time in your life.

14. As you scan Psalms 87—89, which verse or passage most closely reflects your own spiritual and emotional feelings at this time?

FOR GOING DEEPER

To further explore how the life and ministry of Jesus the Messiah was foretold in the Psalms, compare verses 3-4 and 35-36 with Luke 1:31-33.

PSALM 90

Startup: Discuss how much you agree or disagree with this statement: You don't really know how to live until you really know you're going to die.

SEEING WHAT'S THERE

1. Select a *key word, key phrase,* or *key sentence* in each stanza of this psalm.

2. What specific requests does Moses make to God in this psalm?

CAPTURE THE ESSENCE

3. From all that you see in this psalm, what are the most important things Moses understands about God's personality and character?

4. From what you see in this psalm, how would you describe Moses' relationship with God? What does God mean to him in his everyday life? What does he depend on God for?

5. Which events in the life of Moses do you think may have had the most influence upon the writing of this psalm? In what ways can you detect their influence, as you examine the wording of this psalm?

FOR LIFE TODAY

6. Look again at verse 12. In practical terms, what is it that Moses is asking God to teach him? And what would this mean practically in your life, if God taught this to you?

PSALM 91

SEEING WHAT'S THERE

1. How many times do you see the word *will* used in this psalm? Each time it's used, decide how closely you believe this sentence describes your own future.

2. Choose a *key word, key phrase,* or *key sentence* in each stanza of this psalm.

3. In the final three verses of this psalm, what specific promises does God make toward the person who loves and acknowledges Him?

CAPTURE THE ESSENCE

4. What does this psalm say most about the security we can have in the Lord?

FOR LIFE TODAY

5. Consider how strongly you desire to know God better, then ask yourself this question: What are the truths revealed about Him in this psalm which He may want me to understand more deeply at this time in my life?

FOR GOING DEEPER

Notice God's promise of answered prayer in verse 15. What conditions do you see attached to that promise here in this psalm? What other requirements, if any, do you see in these passages—Psalm 66:18-19, Isaiah 59:1-2, Jeremiah 29:12-13, Matthew 7:7-8, Mark 11:25, John 14:13-14, 15:7, and 16:23-24, and James 1:5-6 and 4:3.

PSALM 92

SEEING WHAT'S THERE

1. Identify a *key word, key phrase,* or *key sentence* in each stanza of this psalm.

2. What vision for the future is revealed in verses 12-15?

CAPTURE THE ESSENCE

3. What would you say the writer of this psalm is most thankful for at this time in his life?

FOR LIFE TODAY

4. Think again about verses 1-3. In your own experience, why is it truly "good" to praise God in word and song?

5. What would you say are the most important lessons a new Christian could learn from this psalm about *joy?*

6. In what ways, if any, do the words in 12-15 reflect your own personal vision for the future?

PSALM 93

SEEING WHAT'S THERE

1. Choose a *key word, key phrase,* or *key sentence* in each stanza of this psalm.

2. In Matthew 6:33, Jesus tells us to "seek first the kingdom of God and His righteousness." What would you say this psalm teaches most about God's kingdom?

CAPTURE THE ESSENCE

3. Summarize in your own words what you believe are the most important truths revealed about God's character and personality in this psalm.

PSALM 94

SEEING WHAT'S THERE

1. What questions are asked in this psalm?

2. What specific requests are made to God in this psalm?

3. If the word *blessed* means "happy," then what clues does verse 12 give about the best way to happiness?

4. Select a *key word, key phrase,* or *key sentence* in each stanza of this psalm.

CAPTURE THE ESSENCE

5. What help does this psalm offer for dealing with deep suffering in our lives?

6. From what you see in verses 17-19, how would you describe the relationship with God which this psalmist enjoyed? How do you think he attained a relationship of this quality?

7. After studying Psalms 90—94, what title would you give to each of them?

8. What is the best evidence you see in Psalms 90—94 of total honesty and openness while praying to God?

9. How strongly does verse 22 reflect your own experience of God at this time in your life, compared with times in your past? Use a scale of one to ten (one = "much less than ever," ten = "much more than ever") to help you decide.

10. As you scan Psalms 90—94, which verse or passage most closely reflects your own spiritual and emotional feelings at this time?

PSALM 95

Startup: You've probably heard someone described before as a "hard" person. What does that description bring to mind?

SEEING WHAT'S THERE

1. How many reasons for praising and thanking God can you find in this psalm?

2. What are God's people told *not* to do in this psalm?

3. For helpful background on verse 8-10, what can you discover in Exodus 17:1-7?

4. Choose a *key word, key phrase,* or *key sentence* in each stanza of this psalm.

CAPTURE THE ESSENCE

5. What are the most significant truths this psalm reveals about *God,* and what are the most significant truths it reveals about *us?*

FOR LIFE TODAY

6. In what ways do we sometimes "harden our hearts" when God speaks, as we're told not to do in verses 7-8? What would you say helps most to "soften" our hearts?

FOR GOING DEEPER

Review verses 7-11, then look at how this passage is quoted in Hebrews 3:7—4:11. What are the major lessons which the author of Hebrews draws from this passage?

For further background on Psalm 95:7-11, what can you discover in Numbers 20:1-13 and 28:13-14, and Deuteronomy 32:50-52?

PSALM 96

SEEING WHAT'S THERE

1. Who is this psalm addressed to?

2. In your own words, how would you explain the commands given in verses 7-10?

3. What vision for the future is presented in verses 12-13?

4. Identify a *key word, key phrase,* or *key sentence* in each stanza of this psalm.

5. In Matthew 6:33, Jesus tells us to "seek first the kingdom of God and His righteousness." What does this psalm teach about God's kingdom and God's righteousness?

CAPTURE THE ESSENCE

6. What does God want us to understand most about Himself from this psalm?

7. From what you see in this psalm, would you say that God wants to be considered *primarily* as the God of His people Israel, or as the God of the whole earth? Explain your answer.

PSALM 97

SEEING WHAT'S THERE

1. We're told in verse 10 to "hate evil." What good reasons for doing just that are given in this psalm?

2. Recall again the command from Jesus to "seek first the kingdom of God and His righteousness" (Matthew 6:33). From what you see in this psalm, what does God especially want us to understand about His kingdom and His righteousness?

3. Select a *key word, key phrase,* or *key sentence* in each stanza of this psalm.

CAPTURE THE ESSENCE

4. This psalm does not include the phrase "the fear of the Lord," but how might you use this psalm any way to define what that phrase means?

5. Notice the awesome and fearful picture of God which is given with stormy imagery in verses 2-5—and yet the rest of this psalm focuses especially on the *joy* of God's people (as in verses 1, 8, and 11-

12). What is the relationship between this joy, and the awesome, consuming power of the Lord?

PSALM 98

SEEING WHAT'S THERE

1. What commands are given in verses 1 and 4?

2. What acts of God are acknowledged in verses 2-3? What does the psalmist say God has already done?

3. Choose a *key word, key phrase,* or *key sentence* in each stanza of this psalm.

CAPTURE THE ESSENCE

4. What are the most important things this psalm communicates about God's character and personality?

PSALM 99

SEEING WHAT'S THERE

1. What specific commands are given twice in this psalm?

2. What is the stated *reason* for these commands?

3. Remember again the command from Jesus to "seek first the kingdom of God and His righteousness" (Matthew 6:33). From what you see in this psalm, what does God especially want us to understand about His kingdom?

4. Select a *key word, key phrase,* or *key sentence* in each stanza of this psalm.

CAPTURE THE ESSENCE

5. Summarize in your own words what you believe are the most important truths revealed about God's character and personality in this psalm.

FOR LIFE TODAY

6. How could you use verses 6-8 to help teach a new Christian *how to pray* and *how to get answers to prayer?*

PSALM 100

SEEING WHAT'S THERE

1. How many specific commands are given to God's people in this psalm? And which one, if any, would you say is the most important?

2. What *reason* for these commands is given in verse 5?

3. Identify a *key word, key phrase,* or *key sentence* in each stanza of this psalm.

CAPTURE THE ESSENCE

4. In your own words, what are the most significant truths this psalm reveals about *God,* and what are the most significant truths it reveals about *us?*

FOR LIFE TODAY

5. From what you see in this psalm, discuss together how you would complete this sentence: *What God really wants from me is…*

PSALM 101

SEEING WHAT'S THERE

1. Choose a *key word, key phrase,* or *key sentence* in each stanza of this psalm.

2. What specific *commitments* does David make to God in this psalm?

3. How many times do you see the word *will* in this psalm?

CAPTURE THE ESSENCE

4. From what you see in this psalm, how would you describe David's basic *mindset* or *attitude* in life?

5. After studying Psalms 95—101, what title would you give to each of them?

FOR LIFE TODAY

6. Review once more the commitments David makes in this psalm. Which of these have you already made in your life? Which of them would you like to make or to renew at this time?

7. As you scan Psalms 95—101, which verse or passage most closely reflects your own spiritual and emotional feelings at this time?

PSALM 102

Startup: Discuss how being ill—physically or emotionally—influences your mental attitude toward life.

SEEING WHAT'S THERE

1. What requests does this psalmist make to God in the opening verses of this psalm?

2. What do verses 3-11 reveal about the psalmist at this time?

3. What important words of prophecy are made in verses 12-17, 21-22, and 28?

4. What does the psalmist say about God's creation in verses 25-26?

5. What would you say is the *key word, key phrase,* or *key sentence* in each stanza of this psalm?

CAPTURE THE ESSENCE

6. What help does this psalm offer for dealing with deep suffering in our lives?

7. What would you say God wants us to understand most about Himself in verses 12 and 27?

FOR LIFE TODAY

8. Remember again the promise in 1 John 1:9—that *if we confess our sins,* God will forgive us and cleanse us from unrighteousness. What words or phrases in this psalm can serve as a model and inspiration for the way you confess your personal sins?

FOR GOING DEEPER

Notice how verses 25-27 are applied to Jesus Christ in Hebrews 1:10-12. Taking these passages together, what do they teach us about the work and nature of Christ?

PSALM 103

SEEING WHAT'S THERE

1. What command is repeated several times in both the opening and closing verses of this psalm?

2. Select a *key word, key phrase,* or *key sentence* in each stanza of this psalm.

3. In Matthew 6:33, Jesus tells us to "seek first the kingdom of God and His righteousness." What does this psalm teach about God's kingdom? And what does it teach about God's righteousness?

CAPTURE THE ESSENCE

4. Imagine yourself with David as he is writing this psalm. How do you think he would answer if you interrupted him to quietly ask, "David, what are you most thankful to God for today?"

5. From all that you see in this psalm, how would you summarize what David knows about God's character?

FOR LIFE TODAY

6. What would you say are the most important lessons a new Christian could learn from this psalm about *intimacy with God?*

7. Notice again how often we're told to praise God in this psalm. On a typical day, how often would you say you offer up praise to God?

8. Review the guidelines for our thought-life given in Philippians 4:8—"Whatever is true, whatever is noble, whatever is right, whatever is pure, whatever is lovely, whatever is admirable—if anything is excellent or praiseworthy—*think about such things."* What food for thought can you find in Psalm 103 that especially strikes you as being *true,* or *noble,* or *right,* or *pure,* or *lovely,* or *admirable,* or *excellent,* or *praiseworthy?*

PSALM 104

SEEING WHAT'S THERE

1. Identify a *key word, key phrase,* or *key sentence* in each stanza of this psalm.

CAPTURE THE ESSENCE

2. If this psalm was the only Scripture you had, how would you use it to help explain to someone else what God is like?

3. From what you see in this psalm, how would you describe the *work* God does?

4. What would you say God wants us to understand most from this psalm about the earth and our environment?

5. After studying Psalms 102—104, what title would you give to each of them? (Use this exercise to help you focus on what you believe is the essential message in each psalm.)

6. What is the best evidence you see in Psalms 102—104 of total honesty and openness while praying to God?

FOR LIFE TODAY

7. From what you see in this psalm, what motivates you most to want to worship God?

8. Consider how strongly you desire to know God better, then ask yourself this question: *What are the truths revealed about Him in this psalm which He may want me to understand more deeply at this time in my life?*

9. As you scan Psalms 102—104, which verse or passage most closely reflects your own spiritual and emotional feelings at this time?

10. Recall again Paul's reminder in Romans 15:4 that the Old Testament Scriptures can give us patience and perseverance, as well as comfort and encouragement. In your own life, how do you see the Psalms living up to Paul's description? In what ways, if any, is this book meeting your personal needs for both *perseverance* and *encouragement?*

PSALM 105

Startup: If God asked you, "What are the three things you're most thankful for these days?"—how would you answer?

SEEING WHAT'S THERE

1. How many separate things are we told to do in verses 1-5?

2. How would you summarize the most important events this psalm mentions from Israel's history?

3. Choose a *key word, key phrase,* or *key sentence* in each stanza of this psalm.

CAPTURE THE ESSENCE

4. What is the covenant referred to in verses 8-11?

FOR LIFE TODAY

5. Look again at what we are told to do in verses 1-5. Which of these are the easiest for you to do consistently? Which are the most difficult?

6. If it's true that *the past is a lesson for the future,* then what would you say are the most important lessons for God's people today to learn from this psalm?

PSALM 106

SEEING WHAT'S THERE

1. What requests does the psalmist make in his prayer in verses 4-5, and what are his stated reasons for these requests?

2. What prayer does the psalmist add in verse 47, and what is his stated reason there?

3. How would you summarize the most important events this psalm mentions from Israel's history?

4. How many individuals are mentioned by name in this psalm? What is the most important thing you know about each one?

5. If the word *blessed* means "happy" (as in verse 2), then what clues does this psalm give about the best way to happiness?

6. Select a *key word, key phrase,* or *key sentence* in each stanza of this psalm.

7. After studying Psalms 105 and 106, what title would you give to each of them?

FOR LIFE TODAY

8. Once again, if it's true that *the past is a lesson for the future,* then what are the most important lessons for God's people today to learn from this psalm?

9. As you scan Psalms 105 and 106, which verse or passage most closely reflects your own spiritual and emotional feelings at this time?

FOR GOING DEEPER

For more information about Dathan and Abiram (mentioned in verse 17), look together at Numbers 16:1-35. What is your impression of these men? For more on Phinehas (verses 30-31), look also at Numbers 25:10-13 and 31:6. What's the best way to describe him?

PSALM 107

Startup: How would you define the word *miracle?*

SEEING WHAT'S THERE

1. What is the command given in the opening line of this psalm, and what is the stated reason for it?

2. What command is repeated in verses 8, 15, 21, and 31?

3. What pictures of God are given in verses 9 and 16?

4. What need was experienced by the people described in verses 4-7, and how did God meet that need?

5. What need was experienced by the people described in verses 10-14, and how did God meet that need?

6. What need was experienced by the people described in verses 17-20, and how did God meet that need?

7. What need was experienced by the people described in verses 23-30, and how did God meet that need?

8. What miraculous actions of God are described in verses 33-41?

9. What final command is given to conclude the psalm in verse 43?

10. Select a *key word, key phrase,* or *key sentence* in each stanza of this psalm.

CAPTURE THE ESSENCE

11. As we think about this psalm, what do you think God desires most for us to realize about Himself?

FOR LIFE TODAY

12. Does God still do today the kinds of things mentioned in Psalm 107? If so, what evidence can you give?

PSALM 108

SEEING WHAT'S THERE

1. Compare this psalm with Psalms 57 and 60. Which passages from those passages are seen also in this psalm?

2. What commitments does David make in this psalm?

3. Identify a *key word, key phrase,* or *key sentence* in each stanza of this psalm.

CAPTURE THE ESSENCE

4. From the evidence you see in this psalm, how would you describe David's relationship with God? What does God mean to him in his everyday life? What does he depend on God for?

FOR LIFE TODAY

5. To what extent would you say the opening words in verse 1 are an accurate reflection of your own heart at this time in life?

PSALM 109

SEEING WHAT'S THERE

1. Choose a *key word, key phrase,* or *key sentence* in each stanza of this psalm.

2. What fears and concerns on David's part are revealed in this psalm?

3. What specific requests does David make to God in this psalm?

4. What words of prophecy does David speak in verses 28-29?

5. What commitment does David make in verses 30-31, and what is his stated reason for this commitment?

CAPTURE THE ESSENCE

6. What do you think were the chief *motives* behind David's words against his enemies in this psalm?

7. What patterns and principles does this psalm offer God's people for teaching them how to pray when experiencing trouble or hurt?

8. From what you see in this psalm, how would you summarize what David knows about God's character?

9. After studying Psalms 107—109, what title would you give to each of them?

10. What is the best evidence you see in Psalms 107—109 of total honesty and openness while praying to God?

FOR LIFE TODAY

11. In your own life, have you ever experienced the presence of God in the way described in verse 31?

12. As you scan Psalms 107—109, which verse or passage most closely reflects your own spiritual and emotional feelings at this time?

PSALM 110

Startup: What images come to your mind when you think of the Lord as a warrior?

SEEING WHAT'S THERE

1. What words of prophecy does David speak in this psalm?

2. Select a *key word, key phrase,* or *key sentence* in each stanza of this psalm.

CAPTURE THE ESSENCE

3. How would you explain the picture of the Lord given in verse 7?

FOR GOING DEEPER

To further explore how the life and ministry of Jesus the Messiah was foretold in the Psalms, compare verse 1 with Matthew 22:41-46, and verse 4 with Hebrews 6:20 and 7:1-28.

PSALM 111

SEEING WHAT'S THERE

1. Notice the phrase that opens this psalm. How many times do you see this phrase used in Psalms 111-117?

2. What commitment is expressed in verse 1 of this psalm?

3. In this psalm, what acts of God does the psalmist acknowledge? What does he say God has already done?

4. Identify a *key word, key phrase,* or *key sentence* in each stanza of Psalm 111.

CAPTURE THE ESSENCE

5. From what you see in this psalm, what is it that God wants us to understand most about Himself?

FOR LIFE TODAY

6. Of all that you see in this psalm, what one truth are you most thankful for, because of its personal significance to you?

Psalm 112

SEEING WHAT'S THERE

1. If the word *blessed* means "happy," then what clues does this psalm give about the best way to happiness?

2. How many different promises are made in this psalm to the man who fears the Lord?

3. In contrast, what specific promises are given to the wicked in verse 10?

4. Select a *key word, key phrase,* or *key sentence* in each stanza of this psalm.

FOR LIFE TODAY

5. Review the guidelines for our thought-life given in Philippians 4:8— "Whatever is true, whatever is noble, whatever is right, whatever is pure, whatever is lovely, whatever is admirable—if anything is excellent or praiseworthy— *think about such things."* What food for thought can you find in Psalm 112 that especially strikes you as being *true,* or *noble,* or *right,* or *pure,* or *lovely,* or *admirable,* or *excellent,* or *praiseworthy?*

Psalm 113

SEEING WHAT'S THERE

1. What reasons for praising God are given in this psalm?

2. Choose a *key word, key phrase,* or *key sentence* in each stanza of this psalm.

CAPTURE THE ESSENCE

3. What would you say are the correct answers to the questions asked in verses 5-6?

FOR LIFE TODAY

4. Which word or phrase in this psalm do you think God would like you to understand best?

Psalm 114

SEEING WHAT'S THERE

1. What single command is given in this psalm, and who is it given to?

2. Identify a *key word, key phrase,* or *key sentence* in each stanza of this psalm.

3. What historical events are referred to in this psalm? (Find them in Exodus 14 and 17, Numbers 20, and Joshua 3 and 4.)

CAPTURE THE ESSENCE

4. After studying Psalms 110—114, what title would you give to each of them?

FOR LIFE TODAY

5. As you scan Psalms 110—114, which verse or passage most closely reflects your own spiritual and emotional feelings at this time?

Psalm 115

Startup: What comes to mind when you think of the word *idols?*

SEEING WHAT'S THERE

1. What statements of faith are made in verses 12-13?

2. What are the major points made in the description of idols in verses 2-8?

3. Select a *key word, key phrase,* or *key sentence* in each stanza of this psalm.

CAPTURE THE ESSENCE

4. In your own words, what would you say is revealed most about God's character and personality in verse 3?

5. How would you explain verse 16 in your own words?

FOR LIFE TODAY

6. Look again at the words of blessing in verses 12-13. In what ways would you say these words apply to you, and what difference do they make?

7. What would you say are the most dangerous idols to avoid in your life?

PSALM 116

SEEING WHAT'S THERE

1. Identify a *key word, key phrase,* or *key sentence* in each stanza of this psalm.

2. What has God done for the writer of this psalm?

3. What kind of trouble was the psalmist in, and how serious was it?

4. In response to what God has done, what commitments has the psalmist made to God?

5. How many times do you see the phrase "the name of the Lord" in this psalm? In your own words, what definition would you give for this phrase so that it captures as fully as possible all that the psalmist means by it?

CAPTURE THE ESSENCE

6. Based on the evidence you see in this psalm, how would you define *love for God?*

7. What qualities in God's personality come through strongest in this psalm?

8. What insight does the truth in verse 15 offer about the value of your *life* to God?

FOR LIFE TODAY

9. In what ways do the words of verse 7 apply to you?

10. What motivation and encouragement does this psalm offer you to be a man or woman of prayer?

FOR GOING DEEPER

How would you compare the message of this psalm with the words of Jesus in Matthew 10:28-33?

PSALM 117

Startup: What memorable example can you give in your life of something big coming in a small package?

SEEING WHAT'S THERE

1. What two reasons are given in this psalm for everyone on earth to praise God?

CAPTURE THE ESSENCE

2. How do you see this psalm reflecting the major themes of the entire Bible?

3. Again and again in Scripture, God's *love* and *faithfulness* are presented together, as they are here in verse 2. What do you think God wants to communicate to us through this?

FOR LIFE TODAY

4. How does the message of this psalm relate to the *motives* we should have for sharing the gospel with others?

5. Psalm 117 is the middle chapter in the Bible—there are 594 chapters in front of it, and 594 chapters to follow. It's also the *smallest* chapter in the Bible. But of course, big things sometimes come in small packages. How have you seen that truth in your life?

PSALM 118

SEEING WHAT'S THERE

1. What command is given in both the opening and closing verses of this psalm, and what is the stated reason for it?

2. The psalmist says in verse 8 that taking refuge in the Lord is better than trusting in man. From this psalm, how can you tell that this writer is speaking from experience?

3. Look at the scene described in verses 19-21. What images does this scene call to mind?

4. Which lines from this psalm can you recall being quoted in the New Testament?

5. Choose a *key word, key phrase,* or *key sentence* in each stanza of this psalm.

CAPTURE THE ESSENCE

6. What exactly is the victory (or victories) which this psalm celebrates?

7. Which of these themes would you say is the most prominent in this psalm: thanksgiving, security, or perseverance?

8. The psalm concludes with an acknowledgment of God's love. How do you see His love in this psalm?

9. After studying Psalms 115—118, what title would you give to each of them?

10. What is the best evidence you see in Psalms 115—118 of total honesty and openness while praying to God?

11. In Matthew 26:30 we learn that Jesus and the disciples sang a "hymn" after their meal together on the night He was betrayed and arrested. The hymn may well have been something from Psalms 113—118, since these psalms were often sung by the Jews at Passover time. Look back over these six psalms, and find the passages which you think would be most personally meaningful to Jesus that night.

FOR LIFE TODAY

12. How often does your *confidence* lead to *thanksgiving to God?* If your answer is "Not often enough," which of these diagnoses best fits your situation: (a) shortage of confidence; (b) shortage of the *right* confidence—confidence in God; (c) taking for granted the source of your right confidence, instead of expressing appreciation.

13. On a scale of one to ten, rate your life according to how much *confidence* you experience in everyday life, in each of these areas: (a) physical safety; (b) ability to carry out daily work; (c) ability to depend on friends and neighbors; (d) ability to depend on other family members; (e) ability to depend on God.

14. As you scan Psalms 115—118, which verse or passage most closely reflects your own spiritual and emotional feelings at this time?

FOR GOING DEEPER

Look again at verses 22-26, then explore the following New Testament references to see how these verses find fulfillment there: Matthew 21:8-11 and 21:42-46, Luke 13:34-35, Acts 4:8-12, Ephesians 2:20, and 1 Peter 2:6-8. Taken together, how do these passages enrich our understanding of our Lord Jesus Christ?

PSALM 119:1-88

Startup: Do you have a true *passion* in life? If so, what is it?

SEEING WHAT'S THERE

1. Psalm 119 has been called the key to the book of Psalms. What exactly does this psalm include that would make it this significant?

2. What words or phrases in this psalm are used as names for God's Word? What can you find out about the meaning of each of these terms?

3. If the word *blessed* means "happy," then what clues about the best way to happiness are found in the opening verses of this psalm?

4. What good examples do you see in these verses of prayers addressed directly to God? What kinds of things does the psalmist pray for?

5. What good examples do you see in these verses of specific *commitments* which the psalmist makes? And what does he give as his reasons for making these commitments?

6. What *choice* does the psalmist describe in verse 30?

7. What would you say are the *key words, key phrases,* or *key sentences* for each stanza in the first half of this psalm (through verse 88)?

CAPTURE THE ESSENCE

8. Tell which of these statements best describes the writer of this psalm, and why: (a) he lived a life of truth; (b) he lived a life of freedom; (c) he lived a life of suffering.

9. What would you say this psalmist understands best about God?

10. What is the best evidence you see in these verses that the psalmist is absolutely devoted to the Lord?

11. In the first half of the psalm, look for places where the psalmist speaks of suf-

fering he experienced. What seem to be the reasons behind this suffering?

12. What instruction would you say the Lord gives us in these verses about what *faith in God* really means?

13. Discuss how much you agree or disagree with this statement: It is impossible for us to have the kind of devotion to God's Word taught in Psalm 119 unless we truly see God Himself in the pages of Scripture.

14. Is it possible to become devoted to God's Word in a way that is more legalistic than godly? If so, how do we avoid that?

15. What motivates you most to spend time in the Bible?

16. In the first half of this Psalm, which verses or passages reflect most closely your own spiritual and emotional feelings at this time?

Look back at Psalm 19:7-11, and compare that passage with what you see here in Psalm 119? Are the messages of these two passages essentially the same? Or are there some key differences?

Also, keep the image in Psalm 119:32 in mind as you look at Hebrews 12:1 and 1 Corinthians 9:24. How do these three verses fit together?

PSALM 119:89-176

1. What are most important commitments which the psalmist makes in the last half of this psalm? And what are his *reasons* for making these commitments?

2. What good examples do you see in these verses of prayers addressed directly to God? What kinds of things does the psalmist pray for?

3. In what verses do you see the writer of this psalm expressing his failures and weaknesses?

4. Focus especially on the last three verses (174-176), as a summary of the entire psalm. How would you restate these verses in your own words?

5. What would you say is the *key word, key phrase,* or *key sentence* for each stanza in verses 89-176?

6. What common truth do you see in verses 86, 138, and 151? How would you state this truth in your own words? What do you think would best help Christians today to better comprehend this truth?

7. Notice the increasing number of places in the final half of the psalm where the psalmist speaks of suffering he experienced. What seem to be the reasons for this suffering?

8. What is the best evidence you see in these verses that the psalmist is absolutely devoted to the Lord?

9. What instruction do you see in these verses about what *faith in God* really means?

10. What would you say God wants us to understand most about Himself in verses 151-152?

11. In your own words, what would you say God wants us to understand most about Himself in verse 160?

12. After studying Psalm 119, what title would you give to it, to best reflect its essential message?

13. What is the best evidence you see in Psalm 119 of total honesty and openness while praying to God?

14. The writer of this psalm was focused on all of Scripture. Think about the entire Bible as you discuss your answer to this question: What receives the most emphasis in the Scriptures—God's rules, or God's promises?

15. In what kind of circumstances in life might it be hardest for us to believe firmly in the truths about God which we are taught in verses 137-138?

16. In the last half of this psalm (verses 89-176), what motivates you most to want to spend time in the Bible?

17. Scan verses 89-176 in this psalm, and find the verses or passages that most closely reflect your own spiritual and emotional feelings at this time.

FOR GOING DEEPER

If Psalm 119 were the only Scripture portion available to us, what major biblical doctrines would we still be able to discover?

PSALM 120

Startup: What images come to your mind when you think of the word *peace?*

SEEING WHAT'S THERE

1. What request does the psalmist make in this psalm?

2. What word of prophecy does he make?

3. Identify a *key word, key phrase,* or *key sentence* in each stanza of this psalm.

CAPTURE THE ESSENCE

4. What patterns and principles does this psalm offer for teaching us how to pray when we're experiencing trouble or hurt?

FOR LIFE TODAY

5. What do you think the psalmist means by the description he gives himself at the beginning of verse 7? And how accurate would those words be as a description of you?

PSALM 121

SEEING WHAT'S THERE

1. What specific promises are conveyed to God's people in verses 3-8?

2. Select a *key word, key phrase,* or *key sentence* in each stanza of this psalm.

CAPTURE THE ESSENCE

3. From what you see in this psalm, what is it that God wants us to understand most about Himself?

FOR LIFE TODAY

4. From what you see in this psalm, what *expectations* can you rightly have of God? What can we truly rely on God to do?

PSALM 122

SEEING WHAT'S THERE

1. What commitment does David make in the final verses of this psalm?

2. What command is given in verse 6?

3. Identify a *key word, key phrase,* or *key sentence* in each stanza of this psalm.

CAPTURE THE ESSENCE

4. Remember again the description of David as "a man after God's own heart." What are the most significant things this psalm reveals about David's heart? What are his desires, his longings, and his commitments?

FOR LIFE TODAY

5. Notice again David's words of prayer for Jerusalem in verses 6-9. How can this serve as a model and inspiration for the way you pray for God's people today?

PSALM 123

SEEING WHAT'S THERE

1. What specific request is made to God in this psalm, and what is the reason for it?

2. Choose a *key word, key phrase,* or *key sentence* in each stanza of this psalm.

FOR LIFE TODAY

3. If you were to rephrase some or all of this psalm as an expression of your own heart to God at this time, how would you begin it? What would be "verse 1" in your own personal "Psalm 123"?

Psalm 124

SEEING WHAT'S THERE

1. What reasons for praising God does David give in this psalm?

2. Select a *key word, key phrase,* or *key sentence* in each stanza of this psalm.

CAPTURE THE ESSENCE

3. From what you see in this psalm, how would you summarize what David knows about God's character?

4. As you think about the situation presented in verses 7-8, what parallels do you see with what *has* happened or *is* happening in your family or church, or in your personal life?

Psalm 125

SEEING WHAT'S THERE

1. What request does the psalmist make in verse 4?

2. What word of prophecy does the psalmist give in verse 5?

3. Identify a *key word, key phrase,* or *key sentence* in each stanza of this psalm.

CAPTURE THE ESSENCE

4. In your own words, how would you explain what God wants us to understand about our lives in verses 1-2?

5. In your own words, what would you say God wants us to understand most about Himself in verse 2?

6. From what you see in this psalm, would you say that God wants to be considered *primarily* as the God of His people Israel, or as the God of the whole earth? Explain your answer.

FOR LIFE TODAY

7. Consider how strongly you desire to know God better, then ask yourself this question: What are the truths revealed about Him in this psalm which He may want me to understand more deeply at this time in my life?

Psalm 126

SEEING WHAT'S THERE

1. What specific request does the psalmist make here?

2. What promises are conveyed to God's people in verses 5-6?

3. Select a *key word, key phrase,* or *key sentence* in each stanza of this psalm.

FOR LIFE TODAY

4. How true is verse 3 as a statement about your church today?

Psalm 127

SEEING WHAT'S THERE

1. How would you summarize what Solomon teaches us about our work in verses 1-2?

2. In how many ways are children described in verses 3 and 4?

3. Choose a *key word, key phrase,* or *key sentence* in each stanza of this psalm.

CAPTURE THE ESSENCE

4. From only the evidence you see in this psalm, what would you say Solomon considered to be the most important things in life?

5. From what you see in this psalm, what are the most important things Solomon understands about God's personality and character?

FOR LIFE TODAY

6. If God had written this psalm only for you, which words or phrases do you think He might have underlined, and why?

Psalm 128

1. What specific promises are made in this chapter to those who fear the Lord?

2. Identify a *key word, key phrase,* or *key sentence* in each stanza of this psalm.

CAPTURE THE ESSENCE

3. What kind of impression do you get from this psalm about what is truly important in life?

FOR LIFE TODAY

4. What would you say this psalm indicates or implies about a person's *work,* a person's *family,* and a person's *country?*

5. Why does God want us to *fear* Him?

6. How can this psalm serve as a model and inspiration for the way you pray for others?

FOR GOING DEEPER

Consider together how the following verses from the book of Proverbs shed light on the meaning of Psalm 128 reflected in these proverbs: 3:7-8, 9:10-12, and 14:26-27.

Psalm 129

SEEING WHAT'S THERE

1. Select a *key word, key phrase,* or *key sentence* in each stanza of this psalm.

CAPTURE THE ESSENCE

2. What help does this psalm offer for dealing with deep suffering in our lives?

3. After studying Psalms 120—129, what title would you give to each of them?

4. What is the best evidence you see in Psalms 120—129 of total honesty and openness while praying to God?

FOR LIFE TODAY

5. To what extent is verse 4 true about your own experience? What "cords" of wickedness has he freed you from?

6. As you scan Psalms 120—129, which verse or passage most closely reflects your own spiritual and emotional feelings at this time?

Psalm 130

Startup: Recall a time in life when you desperately wanted morning to come. What were the circumstances?

SEEING WHAT'S THERE

1. What prophetic promise about the Lord is given to us in verse 8?

2. What image of waiting and trusting in God is given in verses 5-6?

3. Identify a *key word, key phrase,* or *key sentence* in each stanza of this psalm.

CAPTURE THE ESSENCE

4. In your own words, what would you say God wants us to understand most about Himself in verse 7?

FOR LIFE TODAY

5. Recall again the promise in 1 John 1:9 —that *if we confess our sins,* God will forgive us and cleanse us from unrighteousness. What words or phrases in this psalm can serve as a model and inspiration for the way you confess your personal sins?

Psalm 131

CAPTURE THE ESSENCE

1. From the evidence you see in this psalm, how would you describe David's relationship with God? What does God mean to him in his everyday life? What does he depend on God for?

FOR LIFE TODAY

2. If you were to rephrase some or all of this psalm as an expression of your own heart to God at this time, how would you begin it? What would be "verse 1" in your own personal "Psalm 131"?

PSALM 132

SEEING WHAT'S THERE

1. What specific requests are made to God in this psalm?

2. What commitment from David is recorded in verses 3-5?

3. What commitments from the Lord are recorded in verses 11-18?

4. Choose a *key word, key phrase,* or *key sentence* in each stanza of this psalm.

CAPTURE THE ESSENCE

5. From what you see in this psalm, how would you describe the character of David?

6. Once more, what verses in this psalm do you think would most impress the 12-year-old Jesus as He heard them read and discussed in the Temple in Jerusalem, and what questions or comments do you suppose He might have spoken to the teachers there?

PSALM 133

Startup: What are your best memories of feeling unified with other Christians?

SEEING WHAT'S THERE

1. David gives two images in this psalm to portray the goodness and pleasantness of brotherly love. The first is that of the anointing oil of Israel's priests, flowing down on Aaron's head and robe. Look together at the following verses in Exodus to see how they enrich the meaning of this picture: 29:7, 30:22-33, and 40:12-16.

2. The second picture in this psalm of the goodness and pleasantness of brotherly love is that of the dew of Mount Hermon (an often snow-covered mountain, and Israel's tallest, in the far north of the country) falling upon Mount Zion, the hill on which Jerusalem was located. Why do you think this would have been an appealing image to the people who first heard this psalm from David?

CAPTURE THE ESSENCE

3. Why do you think David chose these two pictures in particular to convey the blessedness of brotherly unity?

FOR LIFE TODAY

4. Discuss how much you agree or disagree with this statement: Most people in my church truly understand the precious value of brotherly unity.

5. Discuss how much you agree or disagree with this statement: Most people in this Bible study discussion group truly understand the precious value of brotherly unity.

6. Look together at the way the theme of this psalm is turned into a command in these New Testament: Romans 12:10, 1 Thessalonians 4:9-10, Hebrews 13:1, and 1 Peter 1:22. What's the easiest part about obeying these commands? And what's the hardest part?

7. On a scale of one to ten (one = "not at all," ten = "very much"), how would you rate the truth of the following statement: "I am truly enjoying unity with other Christian believers in my life today."

FOR GOING DEEPER

Do you have the right expectations and understanding of Christian unity? Decide on a *definition* of true Christian unity that fits the following passages: John 17:11,21; Acts 4:32; Romans 12:4-5, 14:1, and 15:5-7; 1 Corinthians 1:10 and 10:16-17; Ephesians 4:3-7 and 4:13; and Philippians 1:27 and 2:1-4.

PSALM 134

SEEING WHAT'S THERE

1. What commands are made in this short psalm?

2. Who are these commands given to?

PSALM 135

SEEING WHAT'S THERE

1. How many times in this psalm do you see a command to praise the Lord?

2. What statement of faith for God's people does the psalmist express in verse 14?

3. Select a *key word, key phrase,* or *key sentence* in each stanza of this psalm.

CAPTURE THE ESSENCE

4. In your own words, what would you say is revealed most about God's character and personality in this psalm?

5. Notice the word *name* in verses 1 and 13. How would you say God would like us to define that word, in the way it's used about Him in this psalm?

FOR LIFE TODAY

6. Consider how strongly you desire to know God better, then ask yourself this question: What are the truths revealed about Him in this psalm which He may want me to understand more deeply at this time in my life?

PSALM 136

SEEING WHAT'S THERE

1. What events does this psalm mention from Israel's history?

CAPTURE THE ESSENCE

2. Think carefully about the phrase that is repeated in all the verses of this psalm. Why is it critically important for God's people to understand the truth of this phrase? What happens when they do *not* understand that truth?

3. From what you see in this psalm, how would you complete this statement: "I know God is a God of love because He…"

4. After studying Psalms 130—136, what title would you give to each of them?

5. What is the best evidence you see in Psalms 130—136 of total honesty and openness while praying to God?

FOR LIFE TODAY

6. As you scan Psalms 130—136, which verse or passage most closely reflects your own spiritual and emotional feelings at this time?

PSALM 137

Startup: What's the most homesick you can ever recall feeling?

SEEING WHAT'S THERE

1. How would you describe the mood or tone of verses 1-6?

2. Identify a *key word, key phrase,* or *key sentence* in each stanza of this psalm.

CAPTURE THE ESSENCE

3. Discuss how much you agree or disagree with this statement: For the psalmist who wrote these words, devotion to Jerusalem is the same as devotion to God.

4. What help does this psalm offer for dealing with deep suffering in our lives?

5. What do you think were the chief *motives* behind the words in verses 8-9?

6. From what you see in this psalm, would you say that God wants to be considered *primarily* as the God of His people Israel, or as the God of the whole earth? Explain your answer.

PSALM 138

SEEING WHAT'S THERE

1. What commitments does David make in verses 1 and 2?

2. At the end of verse 2, David speaks of how greatly God has honored or exalted or magnified His word. In what specific ways has God done this?

3. Identify all the reasons David gives in this psalm for *praising* the Lord.

4. Choose a *key word, key phrase,* or *key sentence* in each stanza of this psalm.

CAPTURE THE ESSENCE

5. From the evidence you see in this psalm, how would you describe David's relationship with God? What does God mean to him in his everyday life? What does he depend on God for?

6. Restate in your own words what you believe are the most important truths re-

vealed about God's character and personality in verse 6.

7. Are you convinced that David's words in this psalm represent his *heart*-knowledge, and not just *head*-knowledge? If so, what convinces you?

FOR LIFE TODAY

8. Look again at verse 8. How appropriate are these words as a statement about your own life, and what does this statement mean to you in practical terms?

PSALM 139

SEEING WHAT'S THERE

1. In this psalm, what specific things does David say God knows about him?

2. Select a *key word, key phrase,* or *key sentence* in each stanza of this psalm.

CAPTURE THE ESSENCE

3. From what you see in this psalm, how would you summarize what David knows about God's character?

4. Explain your answer to this question: Which of these qualities in David does this psalm reveal most: his courage, his wisdom, or his integrity?

FOR LIFE TODAY

5. Do you really *want* to be known by God to the degree David talks about in this psalm?

6. Look again at verse 23. How willing are you to be tried and tested by God?

7. Discuss your thoughts on this question: Which is more important—to know God well, or to be known well by God?

PSALM 140

SEEING WHAT'S THERE

1. Identify a *key word, key phrase,* or *key sentence* in each stanza of this psalm.

2. How would you summarize what David asks God for in this psalm?

3. What statement of faith does David make in verse 13?

CAPTURE THE ESSENCE

4. From what you see in this psalm, how would you describe David's basic *mindset* or *attitude* in life?

5. After studying Psalms 137—140, what title would you give to each of them?

6. What is the best evidence you see in Psalms 137—140 of total honesty and openness while praying to God?

FOR LIFE TODAY

7. What patterns and principles does this psalm offer for teaching us how to pray when we're experiencing trouble or hurt?

8. As you scan Psalms 137—140, which verse or passage most closely reflects your own spiritual and emotional feelings at this time?

PSALM 141

Startup: Can you recall a time when you felt deliberately trapped by someone else?

SEEING WHAT'S THERE

1. Select a *key word, key phrase,* or *key sentence* in each stanza of this psalm.

2. What specific requests does David make to God in this psalm?

3. What words of prophecy does David speak in verses 6 and 7?

CAPTURE THE ESSENCE

4. What patterns and principles does this psalm offer for teaching us how to pray when we're experiencing temptation or trouble or hurt?

5. From what you see in this psalm, how would you describe David's relationship with God? What does God mean to him in his everyday life? What does he depend on God for?

6. If God had written this psalm only for you, which words or phrases do you think He might have underlined, and why?

PSALM 142

SEEING WHAT'S THERE

1. For useful background to this psalm, look together at the time of David's life described in 1 Samuel 22:1-2.

2. How would you summarize what David asks God for in this psalm?

3. What vision for the future does David express in the last half of verse 7?

4. Choose a *key word, key phrase,* or *key sentence* in each stanza of this psalm.

CAPTURE THE ESSENCE

5. What patterns and principles does this psalm offer for teaching us how to pray when we're experiencing trouble or hurt?

6. From the evidence you see in this psalm, how would you describe David's relationship with God? What does God mean to him in his everyday life? What does he depend on God for?

FOR LIFE TODAY

7. To what extent do the words in the first half of verse 7 reflect your own prayer and longing at this time in life?

8. In what ways, if any, do the words in the last half of verse 7 reflect your own personal vision for the future?

PSALM 143

SEEING WHAT'S THERE

1. Identify a *key word, key phrase,* or *key sentence* in each stanza of this psalm.

2. What specific requests does David make to God in this psalm?

3. In verses 5-6, how do David's actions reflect the longings of his heart?

4. Remember again the description of David as "a man after God's own heart." What are the most significant things this psalm reveals about David's heart? What are his desires, his longings, and his commitments?

CAPTURE THE ESSENCE

5. From what you see in this psalm, how would you describe David's basic *mindset* or *attitude* in life?

FOR LIFE TODAY

6. Once more, recall the promise in 1 John 1:9—that *if we confess our sins,* God will forgive us and cleanse us from unrighteousness. What words or phrases in this psalm can serve as a model and inspiration for the way you confess your personal sins?

PSALM 144

SEEING WHAT'S THERE

1. Select a *key word, key phrase,* or *key sentence* in each stanza of this psalm.

2. What exactly does David ask God for in this psalm?

3. What commitment does David make in verses 9-10?

4. What vision for the future does David express in verses 12-14?

CAPTURE THE ESSENCE

5. Imagine yourself with David as he is writing this psalm. How do you think he would answer if you interrupted him to quietly ask, "David, what are you most thankful to God for today?"

6. Review verses 1-4. What are the most significant truths this passage reveals about *God,* and what are the most significant truths it reveals about *us?*

7. If you were to rephrase some or all of this psalm as an expression of your own heart to God at this time, how would you begin it? What would be "verse 1" in your own personal "Psalm 144"?

PSALM 145

SEEING WHAT'S THERE

1. What specific commitments does David make in both the opening lines and the closing lines of this psalm?

2. What vision for the future does David outline in verses 4-12?

3. Identify a *key word, key phrase,* or *key sentence* in each stanza of this psalm.

4. In Matthew 6:33, Jesus tells us to "seek first the kingdom of God and His righteousness." What does this psalm teach about God's kingdom? And what does it teach about God's righteousness?

CAPTURE THE ESSENCE

5. From all that you see in this psalm, what are the most important things David understands about God's personality and character?

6. After studying Psalms 141—145, what title would you give to each of them?

7. What is the best evidence you see in Psalms 141—145 of total honesty and openness while praying to God?

FOR LIFE TODAY

8. From what you see in this psalm, what motivates you most to want to give praise to God?

9. Review the guidelines for our thought-life given in Philippians 4:8—"Whatever is true, whatever is noble, whatever is right, whatever is pure, whatever is lovely, whatever is admirable—if anything is excellent or praiseworthy—*think about such things.*" What food for thought can you find in Psalm 145 that especially strikes you as being *true,* or *noble,* or *right,* or *pure,* or *lovely,* or *admirable,* or *excellent,* or *praiseworthy?*

10. As you scan Psalms 141—145, which verse or passage most closely reflects your own spiritual and emotional feelings at this time?

PSALM 146

Startup: How would you define the word *praise?*

SEEING WHAT'S THERE

1. Notice the phrase that opens this psalm. How many times do you see this phrase used in Psalms 146-150?

2. If the word *blessed* means "happy," then what clues does Psalm 146 give about the best way to happiness?

3. Choose a *key word, key phrase,* or *key sentence* in each stanza of this psalm.

CAPTURE THE ESSENCE

4. From what you see in this psalm, what is it that God wants us to understand most about Himself?

FOR LIFE TODAY

5. What would you say are the most important lessons a new Christian could learn from this psalm about God's sovereign control over all circumstances?

PSALM 147

SEEING WHAT'S THERE

1. Select a *key word, key phrase,* or *key sentence* in each stanza of this psalm.

2. In verses 19-20, what factor is emphasized in the uniqueness of Israel as a nation?

CAPTURE THE ESSENCE

3. From what you see in this psalm, what is it that God wants us to understand most about Himself?

FOR LIFE TODAY

4. Which phrase or sentence in this psalm do you think God would like you to understand best?

PSALM 148

SEEING WHAT'S THERE

1. *Who* and *what* are told to praise God in this psalm?

2. Identify a *key word, key phrase,* or *key sentence* in each stanza of this psalm.

CAPTURE THE ESSENCE

3. How would you explain the meaning of verse 14?

PSALM 149

SEEING WHAT'S THERE

1. What big reasons for praising God are given in this psalm?

2. In verse 1, what do you think is the best way to define the phrase "new song"?

3. Select a *key word, key phrase,* or *key sentence* in each stanza of this psalm.

FOR LIFE TODAY

4. Look again at verse 1. What's the latest "new song" which you have sung in praise to God?

PSALM 150

SEEING WHAT'S THERE

1. In this psalm, *where* is God to be praise, *why* is He to be praised, *how* is He to be praised, and *who* is to praise Him?

2. Choose a *key word, key phrase,* or *key sentence* in each stanza of this psalm.

CAPTURE THE ESSENCE

3. What especially makes Psalm 150 an appropriate closing chapter to the Psalms?

4. After studying Psalms 146—150, what title would you give to each of them?

FOR LIFE TODAY

5. Scan Psalms 146—150, and find the verse or passage which most closely reflects your own spiritual and emotional feelings at this time.

PSALMS:
THE BIG PICTURE

(Discuss again the questions in the "Overview," plus the questions below.)

1. For getting the most from the book of Psalms, one of the best guidelines is found in 2 Timothy 3:16-17, words which Paul wrote with the Old Testament first in view. He said that *all* Scripture is of great benefit to (a) teach us, (b) rebuke us, (c) correct us, and (d) train us in righteousness. Paul added that these Scriptures completely equip the person of God "for every good work." As you think seriously about those guidelines, in which of these areas do you especially see the usefulness of the Psalms?

2. Look together at each of these passages, and discuss which one you believe is the best candidate for "KEY VERSE" in the book of Psalms—the one which brings into sharpest focus what this book is most about: 19:14, 29:2, 95:1, 145:21, or 150:6.

3. SEARCH FOR THE SAVIOR—There are many words, images, and themes that point to Jesus Christ. Which of these have made the strongest impression on you?

4. Based especially on your own experience, complete this statement in the way that's most meaningful to you: I believe it's important for Christians to read and explore the Psalms because…

5. If Psalms were the only book in the Old Testament, in what ways would it still make a good introduction to the message of Jesus in the New Testament?

Proverbs

OVERVIEW

(Discuss these OVERVIEW questions both at the beginning of your study of Proverbs, then again after you've studied all 31 chapters. Your answers may change significantly once you've looked more closely at the entire book.)

Startup: Talk together about what you recall as being some of the best advice you received in your youth.

SEEING WHAT'S THERE

1. Before launching into a closer look at Proverbs, how would you summarize what you already know about this book?

2. What similarity do you see in the opening verses of all these chapters in Proverbs—2, 3, 4, 5, 7, and 13? What does this tell you about the nature and purpose of this book?

3. What information do you see in the opening verses of all these chapters in Proverbs about who wrote this book—1, 10, 25, 30, and 31?

4. Look also at the list of "Questions to Ask as You Begin Your Study of Each Book" on page 9.

CAPTURE THE ESSENCE

5. The words *wise* and *wisdom* occur more often in Proverbs than in any other book of the Bible. From what you see in the following verses, what would you say God wants us to understand most about wisdom from this book—2:6, 3:19, 9:10, 11:2, 14:8, 14:33, and 15:33?

6. From what you see in the following verses, describe the difference, if any, between *wisdom* and *knowledge*—1:7, 2:6, 2:10, 3:19-20, 9:10, 14:6, 21:11, 24:5, and 30:3. From the biblical point of view, is it possible to have knowledge without wisdom? Is it possible to have wisdom without knowledge?

FOR LIFE TODAY

7. The book of Proverbs has been called "Laws of Heaven for Life upon Earth," "The Behavior of the Believer," "The Way to Wisdom," and "The Nature of True Wisdom." With that reputation for this book, what kinds of answers and guidelines and solutions would you like to gain as you examine Proverbs more closely?

8. From what you see in 2:1-6, what would be a good personal prayer to offer to God as you study this book?

9. As you think first about *who God is,* and second about *what the Bible is,* how strongly would you rate your present desire to understand better the book of Proverbs? Use a scale of one to ten (one = "no desire at all," ten = "extremely intense desire") to help you decide.

10. When you get to heaven, if you have a long talk with Solomon and he asks you, "What was most helpful to you in the book of Proverbs?" how would you like to be able to answer him?

FOR GOING DEEPER

Look at the two psalms written by Solomon, 72 and 127. What do you learn from these chapters about Solomon's character, his wisdom, and his values?

PROVERBS 1

SEEING WHAT'S THERE

1. From what you see in verses 1-6, how would you summarize in your own words the overall *purpose* for this book?

2. From what you see in verse 3, answer the following question in your own words: What would a person's life look like on the outside if he or she truly understood and lived out the principles found in Proverbs?

3. From what you see in verses 7 and 29, how would you explain in your own words the importance of "the fear of the Lord" in providing true knowledge?

4. What picture of wisdom's blessings does Solomon give us in verse 9?

5. What specific things are we warned *not* to do in verses 10-19, and what reasons are given for the warnings?

6. How is wisdom portrayed to us in verses 20-21?

7. *Who* does wisdom speak to in verses 22-27, and what basic message does she have for them?

8. How would you state in your own words the message of warning and promise in verses 32-33?

CAPTURE THE ESSENCE

9. From what you see in this chapter, discuss which one of these statements you most agree with: (a) Our primary motive for learning wisdom should be the desire to improve our lives. (b) Our primary motive for learning wisdom should be the desire to show more love toward other people. (c) Our primary motive for learning wisdom should be the desire to please God.

FOR LIFE TODAY

10. If it's true that "you become what you think," then what are the most important thoughts from this chapter to plant firmly in your mind?

11. From what you see in this chapter, how would you describe the *quality of life* which God wants you to experience?

FOR GOING DEEPER

How do you see the wisdom of Jesus Christ presented in these passages—Luke 2:52, Mark 6:2, 1 Corinthians 1:24 and 1:30, and Colossians 2:2-3?

PROVERBS 2

SEEING WHAT'S THERE

1. What specific promises are made in verse 5, and what conditions for that promise are outlined in verses 1-4?

2. What additional promises are made in verses 9-12, and verse 16?

3. What summary promises are given in verses 20-21?

4. In contrast, what specific judgment is promised to the wicked in verse 22?

CAPTURE THE ESSENCE

5. From what you see in this chapter, what in your opinion are wisdom's best benefits?

6. In your own words, what would you say is revealed most about God's character and personality in verses 6-8?

7. Look back to 1:1-7, where Solomon gives the overall purpose for this book. How does he begin accomplishing that purpose in chapter 2?

FOR LIFE TODAY

8. In light of how you're doing spiritually in your life today, which verse in this chapter do you think is the most important at this time—and why?

FOR GOING DEEPER

If we are lacking in wisdom, what are we told to do first in James 1:5? How does this step of action compare to what we are told to do here in Proverbs 2:2-6?

PROVERBS 3

Startup: Discuss how much you agree or disagree with this statement: *Everything* you do in life relates directly to a *relationship* you have with someone else.

SEEING WHAT'S THERE

1. What specific commands do you see in verses 1-12?

2. What specific benefits of wisdom are listed in verses 13-18?

3. What specific promises are made in verses 21-26?

4. What specific things are we told *not* to do in verses 25-32?

5. What guidelines for good relationships do you see in verses 27-30?

CAPTURE THE ESSENCE

6. From what you've learned so far in Proverbs about the meaning of wisdom, would you say true wisdom is more of a *skill,* more of a *philosophy,* or more of an *attitude?* Explain your answer.

7. In your own words, what would you say God wants us to understand most about Himself in verses 19-20?

8. Notice the references to long life and prosperity in verses 2 and 16, then discuss how much you agree or disagree with each of the following statements: (a) Anyone who doesn't follow the guidelines of wisdom presented in Proverbs is doomed to poverty and to death at an early age. (b) The guidelines in Proverbs are the God-appointed pathway to prosperity and long life, but God has higher perspectives and purposes that will sometimes require His children to forego such earthly success. (c) It is only because of God's mercy that wicked people sometimes live long and prosperous lives on earth, yet they will not escape His judgment in eternity. (d) True prosperity and true "long life" can be found only in heaven.

FOR LIFE TODAY

9. From what you see in this chapter, discuss together how you would complete this sentence: What God really wants from me is…

FOR GOING DEEPER

Look again at verses 11-12. How is the teaching of this passage amplified in Hebrews 12:4-11? What larger lessons are developed there from this passage?

Proverbs 3:34 is also developed further in the New Testament. Look at James 4:6-7 and 1 Peter 5:5-6. What was on the minds of James and Peter as they studied this verse in Proverbs?

PROVERBS 4

SEEING WHAT'S THERE

1. In verses 3-8, what specific commands did Solomon receive from his father?

2. What specific promises are given in verses 9-12? Which of these do you feel is the most important?

3. What additional commands are presented in verses 13-15, and in 20-27? Which one does Solomon indicate as being the most important?

CAPTURE THE ESSENCE

4. What images come to your mind as you think carefully about verses 7-9?

5. Look also at the picture Solomon presents in verses 18-19. In what ways would you say that these verses could serve as a summary of the entire Bible?

6. Why do you think Solomon places such emphasis on the command in verse 23?

FOR LIFE TODAY

7. In verse 7, Solomon mentions a *cost* associated with wisdom. In your own life, what do you think that cost includes?

8. Look at the promises made in verses 11-12. In your own life, what do you feel are potentially the most dangerous ways that you could stumble and fall?

9. In Romans 15:4, Paul reminds us that the Old Testament Scriptures can give us patience and perseverance on one hand, as well as comfort and encouragement on the other. In your own life, how do you see this book of Proverbs living up to Paul's description? In what ways, if any, is it meeting your personal needs for both *perseverance* and *encouragement?*

What did Jesus have to say about wisdom in these passages—Luke 7:33-35, 11:31, and 21:14-15?

PROVERBS 5

Startup: If God asked you, "What are the three things you're most thankful for these days?"—how would you answer?

SEEING WHAT'S THERE

1. How would you summarize the warning given in this chapter?

2. In what ways would you say the adulteress described in this chapter serves also as a picture of *all* evil?

3. What positive command is given in verse 15?

4. How would you describe in your own words the picture of married joy in verses 15-19?

5. In verse 21, what reason is given for maintaining marriage purity?

CAPTURE THE ESSENCE

6. What to you are the most powerful reasons given in this chapter for avoiding adultery?

7. In your own words, what would you say God wants us to understand most about Himself in verse 21?

8. If the adulteress in this chapter is seen also as a picture of all evil, then how might you interpret verses 15-19?

9. What kind of death do you think is spoken of in verse 23?

FOR LIFE TODAY

10. If you're married, are you being completely faithful to your husband or wife? How do you think God views your faithfulness to your marriage partner at this time?

11. How do you think God views your faithfulness toward *Him* at this time?

FOR GOING DEEPER

Look again at the picture of married pleasure and joy described in verses 15-19. Then scan through the Song of Solomon to see how many times these same images and themes are presented.

PROVERBS 6

SEEING WHAT'S THERE

1. In your own words, how would you explain both the problem and the solution described in verses 1-5?

2. How would you summarize the main point being made in verses 6-11?

3. What negative trait or traits are we warned against in verses 12-15?

4. According to verses 16-19, what specifically does God hate? Which one thing, if any, do you think He hates the most? (Support your answer with other Scriptures.)

5. What specific commands are given in verses 20-21, and how do they relate to what you've seen before in Proverbs?

6. How would you explain in your own words the promises given in verses 22-24?

7. What specific reasons for avoiding adultery are given in verses 25-35?

CAPTURE THE ESSENCE

8. What insight do you find in verses 1-5 about the balance between being generous and being a good steward of your financial resources?

9. Look again at what verse 8 says about ants. There are other creatures, of course, which gather and store food in summer in preparation for winter. What might be the significance of Solomon using *ants* to make his point, instead of something else?

10. Look again at verses 16-19. In this list of things which God hates, which ones are mostly *attitudes,* and which are mostly *actions?*

FOR LIFE TODAY

11. Can you recall a time when a financial promise you made got you into trouble? How would the teachings in verses 1-5 relate to that situation?

12. In the list in verses 16-19 of things which God hates, which are the ones

that *you* hate the most, in yourself or in others?

FOR GOING DEEPER

Notice the poetic Hebrew style in which numbers are used in verse 16. For other interesting examples of this, turn together to Proverbs 30, and look at the four lists which begin in verses 15, 18, 21, and 29.

PROVERBS 7

SEEING WHAT'S THERE

1. What specific commands are given in verses 1-4, and how do they relate to what you've seen in earlier chapters of Proverbs?

2. At the end of this chapter (verses 24-27), what reasons does Solomon give for avoiding the adulteress, and how does this relate to what you've seen earlier in Proverbs?

3. Think through the story presented in verses 6-23. How would you present this story to a child just entering junior high school?

CAPTURE THE ESSENCE

4. Why do you think Solomon in this chapter returns to the theme of the adulteress, which we also saw in chapters 5 and 6?

5. Once again, suppose the adulteress was viewed as being also a picture of all seductive evil. How would you then interpret all the elements of the story in verses 6-23?

6. Look once more at Solomon's words in 1:1-7. How would you say this chapter helps Solomon fulfill his stated purpose for this book?

FOR LIFE TODAY

7. In practical terms, how can you go about obeying the guidelines in verse 25? What does this verse mean when applied to your own situation?

PROVERBS 8

Startup: What would you say are the five most important choices you've made in life?

SEEING WHAT'S THERE

1. Chapter 8 has been called the key to the book of Proverbs. What does this chapter include that could make it this significant?

2. What specific commands does wisdom give us in this chapter?

3. What does wisdom offer us in verses 4-5?

4. How are the *words* of wisdom described in verses 6-9?

5. Look at the choice mentioned in verses 10-11. Would you say that this is meant to be a one-time choice, or a continual choosing? What reasons can you give for your answer?

6. What specific benefits of wisdom are presented in verses 14-21? How do these relate to what you've seen earlier in Proverbs?

7. What do you think is the main point God is making by including verses 22-31 in the Bible?

8. If the word *blessed* means "happy," then what reliable clues do verses 32-36 give about the best way to happiness?

CAPTURE THE ESSENCE

9. What do you think God wants us to understand most from verses 12 and 13?

10. What do you think God most wants us to understand about the word *blessed* in verses 32 and 34? How does He want us to define this word?

11. If this chapter was the only portion of Scripture you had access to, how would you use it to define *wisdom* from God's point of view?

12. Imagine yourself being present in the temple in Jerusalem as the twelve-year-old Jesus hears this chapter read and discussed by the rabbis there. In Luke 2:46 we read that He was listening to these teachers and asking them questions. What verses from this chapter do you think would most impress the boy Jesus,

and what questions or comments do you suppose He might have spoken?

FOR LIFE TODAY

13. Look again at the choice set forth in verses 10-11. In practical terms, what does that choice mean in your life?

14. If God had written this chapter only for you, which words or phrases do you think He might have underlined, and why?

15. How well would verse 34 serve as a portrait of you?

PROVERBS 9

SEEING WHAT'S THERE

1. Compare carefully the two invitations presented in this chapter, and the way each one is presented—the first in verses 1-6, the second in verses 13-17. What are the biggest similarities and the biggest differences you see in these invitations?

2. What are the most important *contrasts* presented in verses 7-9?

3. What are the most important points made in verses 10-12, and how do they relate to what you've seen earlier in Proverbs?

4. Look carefully at verse 18. What is the main theme of this verse? Where in the earlier chapters of Proverbs have you also seen this theme?

CAPTURE THE ESSENCE

5. Which verse here in chapter 9 would you choose as the best *climax* to all you've seen so far in the book of Proverbs?

6. Focus again on 1:1-7, where Solomon presents his purpose for this book. How does this chapter help him accomplish that purpose?

FOR LIFE TODAY

7. Consider again verses 7-9. Which words or phrases in this passage reflect most closely the way *you* respond to criticism?

8. Looking back over the totality of your life, which of the invitations presented in this chapter have you responded to most often?

FOR GOING DEEPER

What are the most important truths about wisdom presented in James 3:13-18? What similarities do you see between what is taught in that passage and what is taught in Proverbs 9?

PROVERBS 10

Startup: In the way we read and study the Bible, what kind of old mental habits or faulty assumptions can most easily block this book of Proverbs from coming alive in our minds and hearts?

SEEING WHAT'S THERE

1. For each proverb in this chapter, decide what topic or topics it most addresses. Then make a list of all the topics covered in this chapter, and which verse numbers to list under each one. Which of these topics, if any, would you consider to be the most prominent in this chapter? Which would you consider to be most important?

2. What contrasts do you see presented in this chapter between the righteous and the wicked?

CAPTURE THE ESSENCE

3. Would you say the truths in this chapter apply only to Christians, or to believers and unbelievers alike?

4. Scripturally speaking, what would you say is the difference between a *proverb* and a *promise*?

5. In Proverbs 9:10, Solomon says that *fearing God* is the starting point for wisdom. Review carefully the attitudes and behaviors that are taught in this chapter. In which of them is it easiest for you to see reverence for God as the underlying motive or foundation? In which of them is it more difficult to see that foundation?

FOR LIFE TODAY

6. Suppose you heard a voice from heaven saying to you, "Don't get over-ambitious and try to apply too much from this chapter to your life right now. Just pick

one thing to focus on, and apply it well." What one thing would you choose?

FOR GOING DEEPER

How is the teaching in verse 12 reflected in 1 Peter 4:8-10?

PROVERBS 11

SEEING WHAT'S THERE

1. For each proverb in this chapter, decide what topic or topics it most addresses. Then make a list of all the topics covered in this chapter, and which verse numbers to list under each one. Which of these topics, if any, would you consider to be the most prominent in this chapter? Which would you consider to be most important?

2. What further contrasts do you see in this chapter between the righteous and the wicked?

CAPTURE THE ESSENCE

3. How would you define the word *righteousness*, from what you see in this chapter?

FOR LIFE TODAY

4. The word *wisdom* as used in Proverbs has been defined essentially as "skill"— the skill needed to live a productive life that pleases God. As you look back over chapters 10 and 11 in Proverbs, what areas of skill are taught here that you would most like to see "sharpened" in your own life?

5. If you were asked to give a five-minute talk from chapters 10 and 11 before a local high school assembly—to give them a taste of biblical advice—which verses from these chapters would you choose to talk about? Keeping in mind the age and interests of your audience, what are the main points you would make, and what true-life examples would you use to illustrate your points?

6. Suppose also that you were asked to give a five-minute presentation from chapters 10 and 11 to a class of second-graders. Again, which verses from these chapters would you choose to talk about? Once more keeping in mind the age and inter-

ests of this different audience, what are the main points you would make, and what true-life examples would you use to illustrate your points?

FOR GOING DEEPER

Look again at the last verse in this chapter. How does the apostle Peter expound on the meaning of this verse in 1 Peter 4:17-19?

PROVERBS 12

Startup: What do you consider the three most important values for being successful in today's world?

SEEING WHAT'S THERE

1. For each proverb in this chapter, decide what topic or topics it most addresses. Then make a list of all the topics covered in this chapter, and which verse numbers to list under each one. Which of these topics, if any, would you consider to be the most prominent in this chapter? Which would you consider to be most important?

2. What further contrasts do you see in this chapter between the righteous and the wicked?

CAPTURE THE ESSENCE

3. Recall again Solomon's statement that *fearing God* is the starting point for wisdom. Review carefully the attitudes and behaviors that are taught in this chapter. In which of them is it easiest for you to see reverence for God as the underlying motive or foundation? In which of them is it more difficult to see that foundation?

FOR LIFE TODAY

4. Suppose that at the end of this chapter, Solomon added this line: "If you remember only one thing from this chapter, let it be this:…" How do you think he would complete that sentence, especially if he had *you* in mind?

5. In Isaiah 55:10-11, God reminds us that He sends rain and snow from the sky to water the earth and to nurture life. In the same way, God says that He sends His words to accomplish specific purposes. From your study so far, what would you

suggest are *God's* primary purposes for the book of Proverbs in the lives of Christians today?

PROVERBS 13

SEEING WHAT'S THERE

1. For each proverb in this chapter, decide what topic or topics it most addresses. Then make a list of all the topics covered in this chapter, and which verse numbers to list under each one. Which of these topics, if any, would you consider to be the most prominent in this chapter? Which would you consider to be most important?

2. What further contrasts do you see in this chapter between the righteous and the wicked?

CAPTURE THE ESSENCE

3. What would you say are the most important things this chapter teaches about poverty and wealth?

FOR LIFE TODAY

4. Remember again that the word *wisdom* as used in Proverbs has been defined essentially as "skill"—the skill needed to live a productive life that pleases God. As you look back over chapters 12 and 13 in Proverbs, what areas of skill are taught here that you would most like to see "sharpened" in your own life?

5. Again, suppose you were asked to give a five-minute talk from chapters 12 and 13 before a local high school assembly, to give them a taste of biblical advice. Which verses from these chapters would you choose to talk about? What are the main points you would make, and what true-life examples would you use to illustrate your points?

6. And once more suppose that you were also asked to give a five-minute presentation from chapters 12 and 13 to a class of second-graders. Again, which verses from these chapters would you choose to talk about with these younger children? What are the main points you would make, and what true-life examples would you use to illustrate your points?

PROVERBS 14

Startup: What aspects of reality in their lives do you think people today find it hardest to face up to? What are the most common ways in which they deceive themselves?

SEEING WHAT'S THERE

1. For each proverb in this chapter, decide what topic or topics it most addresses. Then make a list of all the topics covered in this chapter, and which verse numbers to list under each one. Which of these topics, if any, would you consider to be the most prominent in this chapter? Which would you consider to be most important?

2. What further contrasts do you see in this chapter between the righteous and the wicked?

CAPTURE THE ESSENCE

3. In Matthew 6:33, Jesus tells us to "seek first the kingdom of God and His righteousness." What guidelines from God for kings or rulers can you find in this chapter? (See especially verses 28 and 35.) And what conclusions could you make from them about the *Lord's* kingship and kingdom?

4. What leadership principles would you draw from these same verses?

FOR LIFE TODAY

5. Which proverb in this chapter do you think God would most like you to understand and apply at this time?

6. What do you think are the most likely obstacles that could keep you personally from seeking and learning all that God wants you to in this book of Proverbs?

Proverbs 15

SEEING WHAT'S THERE

1. For each proverb in this chapter, decide what topic or topics it most addresses. Then make a list of all the topics covered in this chapter, and which verse numbers to list under each one. Which of these topics, if any, would you consider to be the most prominent in this chapter? Which would you consider to be most important?

2. What contrasts do you see in this chapter between right and wrong ways of speaking?

CAPTURE THE ESSENCE

3. In your own words, what would you say is revealed most about God's character and personality in verses 3, 11, and 25-26?

4. What part would you say this chapter plays in helping to fulfill Solomon's purpose for this book, as expressed in 1:1-7?

FOR LIFE TODAY

5. Once again, focus on the essential definition of the word *wisdom* as "skill"—the skill needed to live a productive life that pleases God. As you look back over chapters 14 and 15 in Proverbs, what areas of skill are taught here that you would most like to see "sharpened" in your own life?

6. Suppose again that you were asked to give a five-minute talk before a local high school assembly to give them a taste of biblical advice. Which verses from chapters 14 and 15 would you choose to talk about? What are the main points you would make, and what true-life examples would you use to illustrate your points?

7. Imagine also that you were asked to give a five-minute presentation to a class of second-graders. Again, which verses from chapters 14 and 15 would you choose to talk about? What are the main points you would make, and what true-life examples would you use to illustrate your points?

Proverbs 16

Startup: If today you could change instantly and permanently some area of your inner life—some attitude or mental tendency or thought pattern—what would you change?

SEEING WHAT'S THERE

1. For each proverb in this chapter, decide what topic or topics it most addresses. Then make a list of all the topics covered in this chapter, and which verse numbers to list under each one. Which of these topics, if any, would you consider to be the most prominent in this chapter? Which would you consider to be most important?

CAPTURE THE ESSENCE

2. From what you see in verses 1-4, what are the most important things Solomon understands about God's personality and character?

3. Recall again the command Jesus gave us to "seek first the kingdom of God and His righteousness." What guidelines from God for kings or rulers can you find in this chapter? (See especially verses 10 and 12-15.) And what conclusions could you make from them about the *Lord's* kingship and kingdom? What leadership principles would you draw from these same verses?

FOR LIFE TODAY

4. In practical terms, what would you say is the best way for you to carry out the command in verse 3 at this time?

PROVERBS 17

SEEING WHAT'S THERE

1. For each proverb in this chapter, decide what topic or topics it most addresses. Then make a list of all the topics covered in this chapter, and which verse numbers to list under each one. Which of these topics, if any, would you consider to be the most prominent in this chapter? Which would you consider to be most important?

CAPTURE THE ESSENCE

2. Recall again Solomon's statement that *fearing God* is the starting point for wisdom. Review carefully the attitudes and behaviors that are taught in this chapter. In which of them is it easiest for you to see reverence for God as the underlying motive or foundation? In which of them is it more difficult to see that foundation?

3. In your own words, what would you say God wants us to understand most about Himself in verse 3?

FOR LIFE TODAY

4. In light of how you're doing spiritually in your life today, which proverb in this chapter do you think is the most important at this time—and why?

PROVERBS 18

SEEING WHAT'S THERE

1. For each proverb in this chapter, decide what topic or topics it most addresses. Then make a list of all the topics covered in this chapter, and which verse numbers to list under each one. Which of these topics, if any, would you consider to be the most prominent in this chapter? Which would you consider to be most important?

CAPTURE THE ESSENCE

2. In your own words, what would you say God wants us to understand most about Himself in verse 10?

FOR LIFE TODAY

3. Recall again that the word *wisdom* means "skill"—the skill needed to live a pro-

ductive life that pleases God. As you look back over chapters 16—18 in Proverbs, what areas of skill are taught here that you would most like to see "sharpened" in your own life?

4. Prepare again to give a five-minute talk from this chapter before an assembly of high-schoolers, this time from chapters 16—18. Which verses would you choose to talk about? What main points would you make, and what true-life examples would you use to illustrate those points?

5. Prepare also for a five-minute presentation to second-graders. Which verses from chapters 16—18 would you choose to talk about, what main points would you make, and what true-life examples would you use to illustrate those points?

FOR GOING DEEPER

Look again at verse 10, and at the power of God's name. What reasons can you discover for this power in the following verses—Exodus 3:13-15, Psalm 52:9, Matthew 6:9, and Philippians 2:9-10.

PROVERBS 19

Startup: In what situations in life is it most difficult for you to practice patience?

SEEING WHAT'S THERE

1. For each proverb in this chapter, decide what topic or topics it most addresses. Then make a list of all the topics covered in this chapter, and which verse numbers to list under each one. Which of these topics, if any, would you consider to be the most prominent in this chapter? Which would you consider to be most important?

2. How would you explain verse 21 in your own words?

CAPTURE THE ESSENCE

3. Remember again Christ's command to "seek first the kingdom of God and His righteousness." What guidelines from God for kings or rulers can you find in this chapter? (See especially verses 6 and 12.) And what conclusions could you

make from them about the *Lord's* kingship and kingdom?

4. What leadership principles would you
draw from these same verses?

FOR LIFE TODAY

5. Suppose that at the end of this chapter,
Solomon added this line: "If you remember only one thing from this chapter, let
it be this:…" How do you think he
would complete that sentence, especially
if he had *you* in mind?

PROVERBS 20

SEEING WHAT'S THERE

1. For each proverb in this chapter, decide
what topic or topics it most addresses.
Then make a list of all the topics covered
in this chapter, and which verse numbers
to list under each one. Which of these
topics, if any, would you consider to be
the most prominent in this chapter?
Which would you consider to be most
important?

CAPTURE THE ESSENCE

2. Review carefully verse 27, then state in
your own words what you believe God
wants us to understand most about
Himself from these words.

3. Recall again the command of Jesus to
"seek first the kingdom of God and His
righteousness." What guidelines from
God for kings or rulers can you find in
this chapter? (See especially verses 2, 8,
26, and 28.) What conclusions could
you make from these verses about the
Lord's kingship and kingdom?

4. What leadership principles would you
draw from these same verses?

FOR LIFE TODAY

5. Which proverb in this chapter do you
think God would most like you to understand and apply at this time?

PROVERBS 21

SEEING WHAT'S THERE

1. For each proverb in this chapter, decide
what topic or topics it most addresses.
Then make a list of all the topics covered
in this chapter, and which verse numbers
to list under each one. Which of these
topics, if any, would you consider to be
the most prominent in this chapter?
Which would you consider to be most
important?

CAPTURE THE ESSENCE

2. Restate in your own words what you believe are the most important truths revealed about God's character and personality in verses 1-3, and also in 30-31.

FOR LIFE TODAY

3. Look again at verse 3. In light of the
principle given here, and the way God is
working in your life, what specific *actions*
on your part in the immediate future do
you think would be most pleasing and
acceptable to Him?

4. Remember again that the word *wisdom*
means the skill needed to live a productive life that pleases God. As you look
back over chapters 19—21 in Proverbs,
what areas of skill are taught here that
you would most like to see "sharpened"
in your own life?

5. Prepare again to give a five-minute talk
from this chapter before an assembly of
high-schoolers, this time from chapters
19—21. Which verses would you
choose to talk about? What main points
would you make, and what true-life examples would you use to illustrate those
points?

6. Prepare also for a five-minute presentation to second-graders. Which verses
from chapters 19—21 would you
choose to talk about, what main points
would you make, and what true-life examples would you use to illustrate those
points?

PROVERBS 22

Startup: What things would you like most to be said about you at your funeral?

SEEING WHAT'S THERE

1. For each proverb in this chapter, decide what topic or topics it most addresses. Then make a list of all the topics covered in this chapter, and which verse numbers to list under each one. Which of these topics, if any, would you consider to be the most prominent in this chapter? Which would you consider to be most important?

CAPTURE THE ESSENCE

2. Notice what is said in verse 19 about trusting God. How exactly does the book of Proverbs help to build our faith in God?

3. Recall once more how Jesus tells us to "seek first the kingdom of God and His righteousness." What guidelines from God for kings or rulers can you find in this chapter? (See especially verse 11.) And what conclusions could you make from them about the *Lord's* kingship and kingdom?

FOR LIFE TODAY

4. If God had written this chapter only for you, which words or phrases do you think He might have underlined, and why?

PROVERBS 23

SEEING WHAT'S THERE

1. For each proverb in this chapter, decide what topic or topics it most addresses. Then make a list of all the topics covered in this chapter, and which verse numbers to list under each one. Which of these topics, if any, would you consider to be the most prominent in this chapter? Which would you consider to be most important?

CAPTURE THE ESSENCE

2. Recall again Solomon's statement that *fearing God* is the starting point for wisdom. Review carefully the attitudes and behaviors that are taught in this chapter. In which of them is it easiest for you to see reverence for God as the underlying motive or foundation? In which of them is it more difficult to see that foundation?

FOR LIFE TODAY

3. In light of how you're doing spiritually in your life today, which proverb in this chapter do you think is the most important at this time—and why?

PROVERBS 24

SEEING WHAT'S THERE

1. For each proverb in this chapter, decide what topic or topics it most addresses. Then make a list of all the topics covered in this chapter, and which verse numbers to list under each one. Which of these topics, if any, would you consider to be the most prominent in this chapter? Which would you consider to be most important?

CAPTURE THE ESSENCE

2. Review carefully verses 11-12, then state in your own words what you believe God wants us to understand most about Himself from this passage.

FOR LIFE TODAY

3. Focus again on this definition for the word *wisdom*—the skill needed to live a productive life that pleases God. As you look back over chapters 22—24 in Proverbs, what areas of skill are taught here that you would most like to see "sharpened" in your own life?

4. Prepare again to give a five-minute talk from this chapter before an assembly of high-schoolers, this time from chapters 22—24. Which verses would you choose to talk about? What main points would you make, and what true-life examples would you use to illustrate those points?

5. Prepare also for a five-minute presentation to second-graders. Which verses from chapters 22—24 would you choose to talk about, what main points would you make, and what true-life examples would you use to illustrate those points?

How is the teaching in verses 21-22 developed further in 1 Peter 2:13-17 (especially as summed up in 1 Peter 2:17)?

PROVERBS 25

Startup: What is the most interesting thing you've read in the Bible in the past week?

SEEING WHAT'S THERE

1. For each proverb in this chapter, decide what topic or topics it most addresses. Then make a list of all the topics covered in this chapter, and which verse numbers to list under each one. Which of these topics, if any, would you consider to be the most prominent in this chapter? Which would you consider to be most important?

CAPTURE THE ESSENCE

2. In what important ways would you say this chapter helps to fulfill Solomon's purpose for this book, as expressed in 1:1-7?

FOR LIFE TODAY

3. If God had written this chapter only for you, which words or phrases do you think He might have underlined, and why?

FOR GOING DEEPER

Look again at verses 21-22, then notice how Paul uses this passage in Romans 12:20. What deeper lesson from this proverb does Paul develop in Romans 12:21?

PROVERBS 26

SEEING WHAT'S THERE

1. For each proverb in this chapter, decide what topic or topics it most addresses. Then make a list of all the topics covered in this chapter, and which verse numbers to list under each one. Which of these topics, if any, would you consider to be the most prominent in this chapter? Which would you consider to be most important?

CAPTURE THE ESSENCE

2. From what you see in this chapter, how would you think God would want us to define the word *fool?*

FOR LIFE TODAY

3. Think again of *wisdom* as the skill needed to live a productive life that pleases God. As you look back over chapters 25 and 26 in Proverbs, what areas of skill are taught here that you would most like to see "sharpened" in your own life? Which of these topics, if any, would you consider to be the most prominent in this chapter? Which would you consider to be most important?

4. Prepare again to give a five-minute talk from this chapter before an assembly of high-schoolers, this time from chapters 25 and 26. Which verses would you choose to talk about? What main points would you make, and what true-life examples would you use to illustrate those points?

5. Prepare also for a five-minute presentation to second-graders. Which verses from chapters 25 and 26 would you choose to talk about, what main points would you make, and what true-life examples would you use to illustrate those points?

FOR GOING DEEPER

Look again at verse 11. Peter quotes this passage in 2 Peter 2:22. From what you see at the beginning of that chapter, who is Peter talking about?

PROVERBS 27

Startup: What things would you say you are most looking forward to in your earthly future?

SEEING WHAT'S THERE

1. For each proverb in this chapter, decide what topic or topics it most addresses. Then make a list of all the topics covered in this chapter, and which verse numbers to list under each one. Which of these topics, if any, would you consider to be the most prominent in this chapter? Which would you consider to be most important?

CAPTURE THE ESSENCE

2. Recall again Solomon's statement that *fearing God* is the starting point for wisdom. Review carefully the attitudes and behaviors that are taught in this chapter. In which of them is it easiest for you to see reverence for God as the underlying motive or foundation? In which of them is it more difficult to see that foundation?

FOR LIFE TODAY

3. Suppose that at the end of this chapter, Solomon added this line: "If you remember only one thing from this chapter, let it be this:…" How do you think he would complete that sentence, especially if he had *you* in mind?

FOR GOING DEEPER

Compare verse 1 with what James says in James 4:13-16. How closely do the teachings in these passages match one another?

PROVERBS 28

SEEING WHAT'S THERE

1. For each proverb in this chapter, decide what topic or topics it most addresses. Then make a list of all the topics covered in this chapter, and which verse numbers to list under each one. Which of these topics, if any, would you consider to be the most prominent in this chapter? Which would you consider to be most important?

CAPTURE THE ESSENCE

2. What leadership principles would you draw from verses 2, 3, and 16?

FOR LIFE TODAY

3. Which proverb in this chapter do you think God would most like you to understand and apply at this time?

4. In Jeremiah 23:29, God says that His Word is like fire, and like a hammer. He can use the Scriptures to burn away unclean thoughts and desires in our hearts. He can also use Scripture to hit hard like a hammer, with the power to crush our spiritual hardness. From your study in this book of Proverbs, how do you most want to see the "fire-and-hammer" power of God's Word at work in your own life?

PROVERBS 29

SEEING WHAT'S THERE

1. For each proverb in this chapter, decide what topic or topics it most addresses. Then make a list of all the topics covered in this chapter, and which verse numbers to list under each one. Which of thcsc topics, if any, would you consider to be the most prominent in this chapter? Which would you consider to be most important?

CAPTURE THE ESSENCE

2. What leadership principles would you draw from verses 4, 12, 14, and 26?

FOR LIFE TODAY

3. Once more, think of *wisdom* as the skill needed to live a productive life that pleases God. As you look back over

chapters 27—29 in Proverbs, what areas of skill are taught here that you would most like to see "sharpened" in your own life?

4. Prepare again to give a five-minute talk from this chapter before an assembly of high-schoolers, this time from chapters 27—29. Which verses would you choose to talk about? What main points would you make, and what true-life examples would you use to illustrate those points?

5. Prepare also for a five-minute presentation to second-graders. Which verses from chapters 27—29 would you choose to talk about, what main points would you make, and what true-life examples would you use to illustrate those points?

PROVERBS 30

Startup: What is one significant area in which you want to grow personally in the next several months?

SEEING WHAT'S THERE

1. What does Agur say about himself in verses 2-3? And why do you think he says this? (You may find clues in the verses that follow.)

2. Look at verses 5-6. What command are we given in verse 6?

3. What specific requests does Agur make in verses 7-9, and what reasons for these does he give?

CAPTURE THE ESSENCE

4. In your own words, what would you say God wants us to understand most about Himself in verses 4-5?

5. Of all the images and concepts presented in verses 11-33, which stand out most to you?

FOR LIFE TODAY

6. How strongly does the last line in verse 5 reflect your own experience of God at this time in your life, compared with times in your past? Use a scale of one to ten (one = "much less than ever," ten = "much more than ever") to help you decide.

FOR GOING DEEPER

Look again at the command in verse 6. Then look at Deuteronomy 4:1-2 and Revelation 22:18-19. Would you say that the same point is being made in all of these passages? Why or why not?

PROVERBS 31

SEEING WHAT'S THERE

1. In the sayings of King Lemuel (verses 1-9), what specific commands do you see?

2. What warnings are given in those verses?

3. In your own words, how would you describe the *beauty* of verses 10-31? What makes this passage so impressive?

4. In the portrait given us in verses 10-31, how many positive character traits are presented about this woman?

5. What specific relationships in the woman's life are referred to in this passage?

CAPTURE THE ESSENCE

6. What leadership principles would you draw from verses 1-9?

7. Would you say that verses 10-31 are included here as something primarily for women, primarily for men, or equally for both? What reasons would you give for your answer?

8. What would you say is the major point God is making by including verses 10-31 in the Bible?

9. In what important ways would you say this chapter helps to fulfill the purpose for this book, as expressed in 1:1-7?

FOR LIFE TODAY

10. From what you see in this chapter, discuss together how you would complete this sentence: What God really wants from me is…

PROVERBS:
THE BIG PICTURE

(Discuss again the questions in the "Overview," plus the questions below.)

1. For getting the most from the book of Proverbs, one of the best guidelines is found in 2 Timothy 3:16-17, words which Paul wrote with the Old Testament foremost in mind. He said that *all* Scripture is of great benefit to (a) teach us, (b) rebuke us, (c) correct us, and (d) train us in righteousness. Paul added that these Scriptures completely equip the person of God "for every good work." As you think seriously about those guidelines, in which of these areas do you especially see the usefulness of Proverbs?

2. Look together at each of these passages, and discuss which one you believe is the best candidate for "KEY VERSE" in the book of Proverbs—the one which brings into sharpest focus what this book is most about: 1:5-7, 3:5-6, 4:23, 8:13, or 9:10.

3. SEARCH FOR THE SAVIOR—What words, images, or themes in Proverbs have reminded you most of Jesus?

4. Based especially on your own experience, complete this statement in the way that's most meaningful to you: I believe it's important for Christians to read and explore the book of Proverbs because…

5. If Proverbs were the only book in the Old Testament, in what ways would it still make a good introduction to the message of Jesus in the New Testament?

Ecclesiastes

OVERVIEW

(Discuss these OVERVIEW questions both at the beginning of your study of Ecclesiastes, then again after you've studied all twelve chapters. Your answers may change significantly once you've looked more closely at the entire book.)

Startup: Talk together about times in your life when you've especially learned that things which are pleasurable for the moment do not necessarily provide lasting pleasure. What were the circumstances that taught you this lesson?

SEEING WHAT'S THERE

1. Before launching into a closer look at Ecclesiastes, how would you summarize what you already know about this book?

2. From what you see in the following verses, how would you summarize the kind of teaching that the book of Ecclesiastes appears to give about *happiness* or *joy*— 2:26, 3:12, 5:19, 7:14, and 11:9.

3. Find the most prominent activity that reoccurs in the following verses—2:24, 3:13, 4:9, 5:19, 8:15, and 10:15. What clues could this offer about the central message of Ecclesiastes?

4. Look at the word that is repeated in 1:2. Then scan the rest of the book to see how often it reoccurs. What do you know about the meaning of this word as it is used here in Ecclesiastes?

5. What do you learn in 11:9 and 12:1 about the intended audience for this book?

6. What evidence do the following passages provide in helping us identify the author of this book—1:1, 1:12-13, 2:1-9, and 12:9-10?

7. Compare verse 1:2 with verses 12:13-14. From these statements at the beginning and end of Ecclesiastes, what conclusions can you draw about the purpose and nature of this book?

8. Look also at the list of "Questions to Ask as You Begin Your Study of Each Book" on page 9.

FOR LIFE TODAY

9. The book of Ecclesiastes has been called "Ancient Wisdom for Modern Man," "The Folly of Forgetting God," "A Wise Man Believes in God," and "The Futile Thinking and Living of the Natural Man." With that reputation for this book, what kinds of answers and guidelines and solutions would you like to gain as you examine it more closely?

10. From what you see in 12:13, what would be a good personal prayer to offer to God as you study this book?

11. As you think first about *who God is,* and second about *what the Bible is,* how strongly would you rate your present desire to understand better the book of Ecclesiastes? Use a scale of one to ten (one = "no desire at all," ten = "extremely intense desire") to help you decide.

12. When you get to heaven, if you have a long talk with Solomon and he asks you, "What was most helpful to you in Ecclesiastes?" how would you like to be able to answer him?

ECCLESIASTES 1

SEEING WHAT'S THERE

1. What two questions are asked in this chapter?

2. In your own words, how would you summarize the author's conclusions and observations in this chapter?

3. Look also on page 8 at the list of "Questions to Ask as You Study Each Chapter." You may want to look again at this list for each chapter in Ecclesiastes.

FOR LIFE TODAY

4. Proverbs 2:1-5 tells about the sincere person who truly longs for wisdom and understanding, and who searches the Scriptures for it—as if it were buried treasure. That person, Solomon says, will come to understand the fear of the Lord, and discover the knowledge of God. As you begin exploring the book of Ecclesiastes, what "buried treasure" would you like God to help you find here—to show you what God and His wisdom are really like? If you have this desire, how would you express it in your own words?

ECCLESIASTES 2

SEEING WHAT'S THERE

1. In this chapter, what aspects of life does the author explore in order to find true meaning in life?

2. How many times is God mentioned in this chapter, and what information is given about Him?

CAPTURE THE ESSENCE

3. What conclusions can you make from verses 17-26 about the right perspectives to have about our work?

4. From what you see in verses 24-26, summarize the most significant perspectives this passage offers about *God,* as well as the most important things it says about *us.*

5. In this chapter, what are the best verses that show the author's faith in God?

FOR GOING DEEPER

Look again at verses 24-26, then compare them with the New Testament teaching in 1 Corinthians 10:31 and Colossians 3:17. Would you say these passages all agree with one another? Why or why not?

ECCLESIASTES 3

SEEING WHAT'S THERE

1. What three questions are asked in this chapter?

2. How many times is God mentioned in this chapter, and what information is given about Him?

3. Review carefully the list of life's activities and experiences in verses 1-8. Can you think of significant aspects of human life which are not included here?

4. Look at the first half of verse 11. How would you rephrase this statement in your own words?

5. Now focus at the last half of verse 11. If this statement is true, *why* is it true? What are the best reasons you can give, from your own understanding?

6. What *motive* or *purpose* on God's part is revealed in verse 14?

7. Ecclesiastes is considered by some to be one of the most puzzling books in the Bible. From what you've seen so far in this book, what unanswered questions do you have about it?

CAPTURE THE ESSENCE

8. What evidence, if any, have you found for the following statement as an accurate summary of what this book teaches: *Although life is filled with frustrations, we can still enjoy our circumstances and find the strength to handle whatever comes our way.*

9. From what you see in verses 1-8, discuss how much you agree or disagree with this statement: *Timing is everything.*

10. From what you see in verses 10-15, what are the most important things Solomon understands about God's personality and character?

11. Look again at the first statement in verse 11, and compare it with verses 18-21. Is the statement in verse 11 true only about human beings? If so, how significant is it as a major indication of the difference

between human beings and all other life on earth?

12. Imagine yourself being present in the temple in Jerusalem as the twelve-year-old Jesus hears this chapter read and discussed by the rabbis there. In Luke 2:46 we read that He was listening to these teachers and asking them questions. What verses from this chapter do you think would most impress the boy Jesus, and what questions or comments do you suppose He might have spoken?

FOR LIFE TODAY

13. Look again at the list in verses 1-8, and think about the season of life which *you* are in right now. Which of the phrases in this list are most appropriate for where you are now?

14. Review the guidelines for our thought-life given in Philippians 4:8 — "Whatever is true, whatever is noble, whatever is right, whatever is pure, whatever is lovely, whatever is admirable — if anything is excellent or praiseworthy — *think about such things.*" What food for thought can you find in this chapter that especially strikes you as being *true*, or *noble*, or *right*, or *pure*, or *lovely*, or *admirable*, or *excellent*, or *praiseworthy?*

15. If you decided to write a fresh "Purpose Statement" for your life, what ideas or phrases from Ecclesiastes 1 — 3 would you include?

16. In this chapter, what words or phrases are the best evidence for the author's faith in God?

ECCLESIASTES 4

Startup: What kind of work do you enjoy most?

SEEING WHAT'S THERE

1. What two questions are asked in this chapter?

2. In one sentence, how would you summarize what this chapter teaches?

3. From what you've seen so far, would you describe the writing style in Ecclesiastes as somewhat cool and objective, or more heated and passionate? What does this writing style tell us about the author of the book?

CAPTURE THE ESSENCE

4. Discuss how much you agree or disagree with this statement: It is impossible to understand the meaning of life in this world unless you look *outside* this world.

FOR LIFE TODAY

5. What evidence have you seen so far in this book that God has a plan and purpose for your life?

FOR GOING DEEPER

The books of Ecclesiastes and Job both wrestle with universal questions about the meaning of life. How similar would you say these books are in writing style and tone? To help you answer, compare what you've seen so far in Ecclesiastes with passages in Job such as chapters 3, 10, 27, and 31. Which book would you say is more emotional?

ECCLESIASTES 5

SEEING WHAT'S THERE

1. Which two verses in this chapter include a question?

2. How many things are we told *not* to do in this chapter?

3. How many times is God mentioned in this chapter, and what information is given about Him?

CAPTURE THE ESSENCE

4. From what you see in verses 17-19, summarize the most significant perspectives this passage offers about *God,* as well as the most important things it says about *us.*

5. From what God gives in verse 19, what could we conclude about His *purpose* for our lives?

6. In this chapter, what are the best verses that show the author's faith in God?

7. Which of the following three statements do you see as the best description of Ecclesiastes, and why? (a) This book's message is how to live a life of faith. (b) This book shows us that a God-centered approach to life is better than a self-centered approach to life. (c) This book encourages us to get rid of all excess worldly possessions.

FOR LIFE TODAY

8. In Romans 15:4, Paul reminds us that the Old Testament Scriptures can give us patience and perseverance on one hand, as well as comfort and encouragement on the other. In your own life, how do you see this book of Ecclesiastes living up to Paul's description? In what ways, if any, is it meeting your personal needs for both *perseverance* and *encouragement?*

FOR GOING DEEPER

How well would you say the observations in verses 18-20 fit with what Jesus says in Matthew 6:25-34?

ECCLESIASTES 6

SEEING WHAT'S THERE

1. What questions are asked in this chapter? And which of them, if any, are questions that *you* have asked before?

CAPTURE THE ESSENCE

2. From what God gives and withholds in verses 1-2, what might we conclude about God's *sovereignty* over our lives, and about His *purpose* for our lives?

3. Again recalling the description of Ecclesiastes as one of the most puzzling books in the Bible, what unanswered questions do you have about what you've seen so far in this book?

FOR LIFE TODAY

4. If you decided to write a fresh "Purpose Statement" for your life, what ideas or phrases from Ecclesiastes 4—6 would you include?

ECCLESIASTES 7

Startup: In the past week, what's one of the best examples of *wisdom* you've seen in someone else's conduct?

SEEING WHAT'S THERE

1. How many times is God mentioned in this chapter, and what information is given about Him?

CAPTURE THE ESSENCE

2. Look at the last statement in verse 14. If this statement is true, *why* would you say it is true? And if it is true, how does it mean we should look at the future and plan for the future?

3. In other parts of the Bible, what evidence do you see that support the conclusions given in verse 29?

ECCLESIASTES 8

SEEING WHAT'S THERE

1. What *warnings*—either direct or implied—do you see in verses 9-13?

2. In this chapter, what words or phrases are the best evidence for the author's faith in God?

CAPTURE THE ESSENCE

3. Look closely at verses 16-17, then tell how much you agree or disagree with this statement: Ecclesiastes urges us to forget human philosophy and the kind of serious thinking that goes with it.

FOR LIFE TODAY

4. In Isaiah 55:10-11, God reminds us that He sends rain and snow from the sky to water the earth and to nurture life. In the same way, God says that He sends His words to accomplish specific purposes. From your study so far, what would you suggest are *God's* primary purposes for the book of Ecclesiastes in the lives of Christians today?

FOR GOING DEEPER

Compare verse 12 with Paul's words in Romans 8:28. What similarities and what differences do you see in what is taught in each of these verses?

ECCLESIASTES 9

SEEING WHAT'S THERE

1. How many times is God mentioned in this chapter, and what information is given about Him?

CAPTURE THE ESSENCE

2. How would you summarize the author's conclusions and observations in this chapter?

ECCLESIASTES 10

SEEING WHAT'S THERE

1. How would you summarize the author's conclusions and observations in this chapter?

CAPTURE THE ESSENCE

2. Recalling once more the description of Ecclesiastes as one of the most puzzling books in the Bible, what unanswered questions do you have about what you've seen so far in this book?

FOR LIFE TODAY

3. If you decided to write a fresh "Purpose Statement" for your life, what ideas or phrases from Ecclesiastes 7—10 would you include?

ECCLESIASTES 11

Startup: What things in life get easier as you grow older, and what things get more difficult?

SEEING WHAT'S THERE

1. How many times is God mentioned in this chapter, and what information is given about Him?

2. In this chapter, what are the best verses that show the author's faith in God?

CAPTURE THE ESSENCE

3. In your own words, what would you say God wants us to understand most about Himself in verse 5?

ECCLESIASTES 12

SEEING WHAT'S THERE

1. Chapter 12 has been called the key to the book of Ecclesiastes. What does this chapter include that could make it this significant?

2. How many times is God mentioned in this chapter, and what information is given about Him?

3. How would you summarize the author's conclusions and observations in this chapter?

CAPTURE THE ESSENCE

4. From what you've seen in Ecclesiastes, what would the author of this book say is the best way to please God: (a) to *withdraw* from worldly matters and focus instead on spiritual matters and concerns, or (b) to *transform* worldly matters and concerns into spiritual matters and concerns? Explain your reasons for your answer.

FOR LIFE TODAY

5. If you decided to write a fresh "Purpose Statement" for your life, what ideas or phrases from Ecclesiastes 11 and 12 would you include?

FOR GOING DEEPER

Look closely at James 4:13-17 and at 1 John 2:15-17. Which phrases in these New Testament passages would best reflect what is taught in the book of Ecclesiastes?

ECCLESIASTES:
THE BIG PICTURE

(Discuss again the questions in the "Overview," plus the questions below.)

1. What would you say is the major point God is making by including this book in the Bible?

2. For getting the most from the book of Ecclesiastes, one of the best guidelines is found in 2 Timothy 3:16-17, words which Paul wrote with the Old Testament first in view. He said that *all* Scripture is of great benefit to (a) teach us, (b) rebuke us, (c) correct us, and (d) train us in righteousness. Paul added that these Scriptures completely equip the person of God "for every good work." As you think seriously about those guidelines, in which of these areas do you especially see the usefulness of Ecclesiastes?

3. Look together at each of these passages, and discuss which one you believe is the best candidate for "KEY VERSE" in the book of Ecclesiastes—the one which brings into sharpest focus what this book is most about: 1:2-3, 2:24 or 12:13-14.

4. SEARCH FOR THE SAVIOR—What words, images, or themes in Ecclesiastes have reminded you most of Jesus?

5. If Ecclesiastes were the only book in the Old Testament, in what ways would it still make a good introduction to the message of Jesus in the New Testament?

6. Based especially on your own experience, complete this statement in the way that's most meaningful to you: I believe it's important for Christians to read and explore the book of Ecclesiastes because…

Song of Solomon
(Song of Songs)

OVERVIEW

(Discuss these OVERVIEW questions both at the beginning of your study of the Song of Solomon, then again after you've studied all eight chapters. Your answers may change significantly once you've looked more closely at the entire book.)

Startup: Talk together about any married couple you've known in which the husband and wife's relationship with one another especially impressed you as being close and enjoyable.

SEEING WHAT'S THERE

1. Before launching into a closer look at the Song of Solomon, how would you summarize what you already know about this book?

2. Find the most prominent word that reoccurs in the following verses—1:2, 2:4, 3:5, 4:10, and 8:6-7. How would you define this word, according to what it appears to mean here in the Song of Solomon?

3. Look also at the list of "Questions to Ask as You Begin Your Study of Each Book" on page 9.

FOR LIFE TODAY

4. The Song of Solomon has been called "The Book of Heavenly Love," "The Art of Adoration," "The Greatest Love Song," and "The Glorification of Wedded Love." With that reputation for this book, what kinds of answers and guidelines and solutions would you like to gain as you examine it more closely?

5. When you get to heaven, if you have a long talk with Solomon and he asks you, "What was most helpful to you in the Song of Solomon?" how would you like to be able to answer him?

6. As you think first about *who God is,* and second about *what the Bible is,* how strongly would you rate your present desire to understand better the Song of Solomon? Use a scale of one to ten (one = "no desire at all," ten = "extremely intense desire") to help you decide.

SONG OF SOLOMON 1

SEEING WHAT'S THERE

1. From what you see in this chapter, how would you describe the passion of married love? What does this passion think and say and do?

FOR LIFE TODAY

2. Proverbs 2:1-5 tells about the sincere person who truly longs for wisdom and understanding, and who searches the Scriptures for it—as if it were buried treasure. That person, Solomon says, will come to understand the fear of the Lord, and discover the knowledge of God. As you begin exploring the Song of Solomon, what "buried treasure" would you like God to help you find here—to show you what God and His wisdom are really like? If you have this desire, how would you express it in your own words?

Song of Solomon 2

SEEING WHAT'S THERE

1. Again from what you see in this chapter, describe the passion of married love. What does this passion think and say and do?

Song of Solomon 3

SEEING WHAT'S THERE

1. Again for this chapter, describe how you see the passion of married love portrayed here. What does it think and say and do?

FOR LIFE TODAY

2. In Isaiah 55:10-11, God reminds us that He sends rain and snow from the sky to water the earth and to nurture life. In the same way, God says that He sends His words to accomplish specific purposes. From your study so far, what would you suggest are *God's* primary purposes for the Song of Solomon in the lives of Christians today?

Song of Solomon 4

SEEING WHAT'S THERE

1. Again for this chapter, describe how you see the passion of married love portrayed here. What does this passion think and say and do?

CAPTURE THE ESSENCE

2. Throughout Scripture, God uses marriage as a picture of His own love-relationship with His people, and Christ's love-relationship with the Church. With this in mind, think about the images and themes you've seen so far in the Song of Solomon. In what ways do you think we can apply these to the Lord's relationship with us?

Song of Solomon 5

SEEING WHAT'S THERE

1. Describe how you see the passion of married love portrayed in chapter 5. What does it think and say and do?

2. How would you summarize what you have read so far in this book?

FOR LIFE TODAY

3. In light of how you're doing in your own married life today, which passages in this book so far have helped you most to deepen and value your passion for your spouse?

Song of Solomon 6

SEEING WHAT'S THERE

1. Again for chapter 6, describe how you see the passion of married love portrayed here. What does it think and say and do?

Song of Solomon 7

SEEING WHAT'S THERE

1. For chapter 7 as well, describe how you see the passion of married love portrayed here. What does this passion think and say and do?

SONG OF SOLOMON 8

SEEING WHAT'S THERE

1. Once more, describe the passion of married love from what you see in this chapter. What does this passion think and say and do?

CAPTURE THE ESSENCE

2. What is the best evidence you see in this chapter that the passion of married love is both *good* and *enjoyable*?

3. Recall again how God throughout Scripture uses marriage as a picture of His own love-relationship with His people, and Christ's love-relationship with the Church. With this in mind, think about the images and themes you've seen in the last half of the Song of Solomon. In what ways do you think we can apply these to the Lord's relationship with us?

FOR LIFE TODAY

4. Which passages in this book best reflect your own passion for your spouse?

SONG OF SOLOMON:
THE BIG PICTURE

(Discuss again the questions in the "Overview," plus the questions below.)

1. For getting the most from the Song of Solomon, one of the best guidelines is found in 2 Timothy 3:16-17, words which Paul wrote with the Old Testament first in view. He said that *all* Scripture is of great benefit to (a) teach us, (b) rebuke us, (c) correct us, and (d) train us in righteousness. Paul added that these Scriptures completely equip the person of God "for every good work." As you think seriously about those guidelines, in which of these areas do you especially see the usefulness of the Song of Solomon?

2. Imagine that you were helping to produce a film based on the Song of Solomon. Describe the kinds of scenery, supporting characters, background music, lighting effects, etc., which you would use to help portray the central message of this book.

3. Look together at each of these passages, and discuss which one you believe is the best candidate for "KEY VERSE" in the Song of Solomon—the one which brings into sharpest focus what this book is most about: 6:3, 7:10, or 8:7.

4. What would you say is the main theme (or themes) in the Song of Solomon?

5. SEARCH FOR THE SAVIOR—What words, images, or themes in the Song of Solomon have reminded you most of Jesus?

6. Based especially on your own experience, complete this statement in the way that's most meaningful to you: I believe it's important for Christians to read and explore the Song of Solomon because…

Isaiah

OVERVIEW

(Discuss these OVERVIEW questions both at the beginning of your study of Isaiah, then again after you've studied all 66 chapters. Your answers may change significantly once you've looked more closely at the entire book.)

Startup: Talk together about this question: From what you know of the Old Testament, what character qualities would be especially useful to a person whom God called to be a prophet?

SEEING WHAT'S THERE

1. Before launching into a closer look at Isaiah, how would you summarize what you already know about this book?

2. Find the most prominent phrase that re-occurs in the following verses—30:15, 31:1, 37:23, 40:25-26, 41:14-16, 48:17, and 54:5. (See also a similar and important wording in 29:23.) From the way you see it used in these passages, what comments would you make about the significance of this phrase? What does God want us to understand most from it?

3. Find the most prominent word that re-occurs in the following verses—12:2-3, 25:9, 33:6, 49:6, 51:5-6, and 61:10. How would you define this word, according to what it means here in Isaiah?

4. Look also at the list of "Questions to Ask as You Begin Your Study of Each Book" on page 9.

FOR LIFE TODAY

5. The book of Isaiah has been titled "Return, Repent, and Be Renewed," "God's Message in Troubled Times," and "The Coming Savior and Israel's King," while Isaiah himself has been called "The Messianic Prophet" and "The Evangelical Prophet." With that reputation for this book, what kinds of answers and guidelines and solutions would you like to gain as you examine it more closely?

6. As you think first about *who God is,* and second about *what the Bible is,* how strongly would you rate your present desire to understand better the book of Isaiah? Use a scale of one to ten (one = "no desire at all," ten = "extremely intense desire") to help you decide.

7. From what you see in God's words in 55:10-11, what would be a good personal prayer to offer to God as you study this book?

8. When you get to heaven, if you have a long talk with Isaiah and he asks you, "What was most helpful to you in my book?" how would you like to be able to answer him?

ISAIAH 1

SEEING WHAT'S THERE

1. What to you are the most powerful images presented through the words of this chapter?

2. What specific sins and failures are pointed out in this chapter?

3. What specific commands does God give?

4. What invitation does God extend to His people, beginning in verse 18?

5. What specific warnings does He give?

6. What promises does He make?

7. Look also on page 8 at the list of "Questions to Ask as You Study Each Chapter." You may want to look again at this list for each chapter in Isaiah.

CAPTURE THE ESSENCE

8. Many times we rob ourselves of the discovery of deeper truths in Scripture because we see a passage and say to ourselves, "I already know that." For what teachings in this chapter might it be easiest for Christians to fall into that trap?

9. In your own words, how would you summarize what this chapter tells us most about God's *purpose* and *plan* for His people?

10. Imagine yourself being present in the temple in Jerusalem as the twelve-year-old Jesus hears this chapter read and discussed by the rabbis there. In Luke 2:46 we read that He was listening to these teachers and asking them questions. What verses from this chapter do you think would most impress the boy Jesus, and what questions or comments do you suppose He might have spoken?

FOR LIFE TODAY

11. Proverbs 2:1-5 tells about the sincere person who truly longs for wisdom and understanding, and who searches the Scriptures for it—as if it were buried treasure. That person, Solomon says, will come to understand the fear of the Lord, and discover the knowledge of God. As you begin exploring the book of Isaiah, what "buried treasure" would you like God to help you find here—to show you what God and His wisdom are really like? If you have this desire, how would you express it in your own words?

FOR GOING DEEPER

Restate in your own words the basic principle which God is communicating in verses 11-17. How does this compare with the words Jesus spoke in Matthew 9:13 and 12:7?

ISAIAH 2

SEEING WHAT'S THERE

1. As in chapter 1, discuss again what to you are the most memorable images presented through the words of this chapter. (Ask this question for each chapter in Isaiah.)

2. What vision of a future day does Isaiah see in verses 1-4?

3. What does Isaiah ask God's people to do in verse 5?

4. What sins and failures are outlined in verses 6-9?

5. Look closely at verses 6-21. What are the strongest features in this vision of the future?

CAPTURE THE ESSENCE

6. In your own words, how would you summarize the most important truths revealed in this chapter about God's purpose and plans for His people?

FOR LIFE TODAY

7. Look again at the last line in verse 5. In practical terms, what would doing that mean for you at this time in your life?

FOR GOING DEEPER

In what ways is John's vision of the New Jerusalem in Revelation 21 a fulfillment of Isaiah's prophetic words in the first four verses of this chapter?

ISAIAH 3

Startup: What's more important to you: freedom, or security?

SEEING WHAT'S THERE

1. What would you say is the brightest promise in this chapter? The most piercing accusation? And the strongest picture of punishment and disaster?

FOR LIFE TODAY

2. Which verse in this chapter do you think God would like you to understand best?

ISAIAH 4

SEEING WHAT'S THERE

1. In your own words, what would you say is the brightest promise in this chapter? The most powerful vision of a future day? And the sharpest picture of punishment and disaster?

ISAIAH 5

Startup: What do you enjoy most, if anything, about gardening or farming?

SEEING WHAT'S THERE

1. As you explore these words to God's people, what would you say is the brightest promise here? The most fearful warning? The most powerful vision of a future day? The most painful accusation? And the sharpest picture of punishment and disaster?

2. How would you describe God's heart for His people, as revealed in this chapter?

CAPTURE THE ESSENCE

3. With verse 2 in mind, discuss how much you agree or disagree with this statement: More than anything else, *righteousness* is the "good fruit" which God wants most to harvest in my life.

ISAIAH 6

SEEING WHAT'S THERE

1. What exactly does Isaiah see and hear in verses 1-4, and what does Isaiah say in response in verse 5?

2. What does the angel do and say in verses 6-7?

3. What does the Lord ask in verse 8, and how does Isaiah answer?

4. What specific commands does God give Isaiah in verses 9-10, and for what stated reasons?

5. In verses 11-13, what question does Isaiah ask, and how would you explain God's answer?

CAPTURE THE ESSENCE

6. From what you see in Isaiah's words in this chapter, what are the most important things he understands about God's personality and character?

7. After Isaiah's response of dread in verse 5, how would you explain the boldness with which he responded to God's question in verse 8? What dramatic change had occurred within Isaiah from verse 5 to verse 8?

8. Notice again the last thing the angel says to Isaiah in verse 7. Is this true also of you? If so, how would you compare your next step of response with Isaiah's next response in verse 8? Is God "sending" you to someone in some way? If so, how would you explain it?

FOR GOING DEEPER

Note carefully what the apostle observes in John 12:39-41 after quoting from verse 10. What does John reveal about the identity of the One who sits on the throne in verses 1-4?

ISAIAH 7

Startup: When you get to heaven, and you meet Isaiah, what's the first question you'd like to ask him?

SEEING WHAT'S THERE

1. As He speaks through Isaiah, what specific commands does God give King Ahaz in verses 4-11? And what is Ahaz's response in verse 12?

2. How would you explain the sign God gives in verses 14-16?

3. What pictures of disaster and punishment does God show Ahaz in verses 18-25?

CAPTURE THE ESSENCE

4. Again, imagine yourself being present in the temple in Jerusalem as the twelve-year-old Jesus hears this chapter read and discussed by the Jewish teachers. What verses in this chapter do you think would most impress Him, and what questions or comments do you suppose He might have spoken?

FOR GOING DEEPER

Discuss together the prophetic fulfillment of verse 14 which you see in Matthew 1:18-25 and Luke 1:26-38. Why is the fact of Jesus' virgin birth an important truth for us to know and believe?

ISAIAH 8

SEEING WHAT'S THERE

1. Summarize what happens to Isaiah in verses 1-4.

2. What accusations and words of disaster and punishment does God speak in verses 6-8?

3. What does God command Isaiah to do in verses 11-12?

4. In your own words, how would you explain what God reveals about Himself in verses 13-15?

5. What commitment does Isaiah make in verse 17?

6. How would you explain the words of warning from Isaiah in verses 19-22?

FOR LIFE TODAY

7. Choose one of these sentences, and complete it as fully and candidly as you would like: (a) What I see and understand in this chapter is important to my life because… OR: (b) What I see and understand in this chapter does NOT seem important to my life at this time, because…

ISAIAH 9

SEEING WHAT'S THERE

1. Remember to discuss here (and throughout this book) what to you are the most memorable images presented through the words of Isaiah in this chapter.

2. As you read this chapter, what would you say is the brightest promise here? The most fearful warning? The most powerful vision of a future day? The most painful accusation? And the sharpest picture of punishment and disaster?

CAPTURE THE ESSENCE

3. Look again at verses 2-7. As a prophetic passage about the coming Messiah, what does this Scripture teach us about the *character* and the *ministry* of Jesus Christ?

4. With verse 6 in mind, discuss how much you agree or disagree with this statement: It is impossible to be God's *child* unless we first become *childlike*.

5. In light of how you're doing spiritually in your life today, which verse in this chapter do you think is the most important at this time—and why?

FOR GOING DEEPER

Compare verses 1-2 with the way Matthew quotes this passage in Matthew 4:15-16. What "great light" did Isaiah foresee dawning on this northern corner of Israel?

ISAIAH 10

Startup: If you were allowed to write three new laws for your community, what would they be about?

SEEING WHAT'S THERE

1. As you study Isaiah's words here, what would you say is the brightest promise in this chapter? The most fearful warning? The most urgent command? The most powerful vision of a future day? The most painful accusation? And the sharpest picture of punishment and disaster?

CAPTURE THE ESSENCE

2. What does God reveal most about His own character in this chapter?

ISAIAH 11

SEEING WHAT'S THERE

1. As you reflect on Isaiah's message for God's people in this chapter, what would you say is the brightest promise it contains? The most powerful vision of a future day? And the sharpest picture of punishment and disaster?

CAPTURE THE ESSENCE

2. As a prophetic passage about the coming Messiah, what does this chapter teach us most about the *character* and the *ministry* of Jesus Christ?

3. Think again about the picture in verses 6-9. Then discuss how much you agree or disagree with this statement: God gave us this picture of peace so we can strive to bring it about here on earth.

FOR LIFE TODAY

4. In Philippians 4:8 we're given the following command: "Whatever is true, whatever is noble, whatever is right, whatever is pure, whatever is lovely, whatever is admirable—if anything is excellent or praiseworthy—*think about such things.*" What food for thought can you find in this chapter that especially strikes you as being *true,* or *noble,* or *right,* or *pure,* or *lovely,* or *admirable,* or *excellent,* or *praiseworthy?*

FOR GOING DEEPER

Look again at the references to the "Root" of Jesse in verses 1 and 10. What additional titles are linked with this one in Revelation 5:5-6?

ISAIAH 12

SEEING WHAT'S THERE

1. What future praise and thanksgiving will come from the lips of God's people, according to verses 1-4?

2. What promise does God make in verse 3, and how would you express it in your own words?

3. What commands does God give His people in verses 5-6, and what reason for these commands?

FOR LIFE TODAY

4. How genuinely can you say now the words in verses 1, 2, and 4?

5. What fulfillment in your own life do you already see of the promise in verse 3?

FOR GOING DEEPER

In what ways does Zephaniah 3:14-17 echo the heavenly "melodies" ringing through the songs of worship in this chapter?

ISAIAH 13

Startup: In the way we read and study the Bible, what kind of old mental habits or faulty assumptions can most easily block this book of Isaiah from coming alive in our minds and hearts?

SEEING WHAT'S THERE

1. As you ponder Isaiah's words in this chapter, what would you say is the most powerful vision of a future day? And the sharpest picture of punishment and disaster?

ISAIAH 14

SEEING WHAT'S THERE

1. As you think about Isaiah's prophecy in this chapter, what would you say is the brightest promise here? The most urgent command? The most powerful vision of a future day? The most painful accusation? And the sharpest picture of punishment and disaster?

CAPTURE THE ESSENCE

2. Restate in your own words what you believe are the most important truths revealed about God's character and personality in verses 24-27.

ISAIAH 15

SEEING WHAT'S THERE

1. What would you say is the sharpest picture of punishment and disaster in this chapter?

ISAIAH 16

SEEING WHAT'S THERE

1. As you reflect on this chapter, what would you say is the brightest promise it expresses? The most painful accusation? And the sharpest picture of punishment and disaster?

ISAIAH 17

SEEING WHAT'S THERE

1. What would you say is the most powerful vision of a future day in this chapter? The most painful accusation? And the sharpest picture of punishment and disaster?

ISAIAH 18

SEEING WHAT'S THERE

1. In your own words, what would you say is the most powerful vision of a future day in this chapter?

ISAIAH 19

Startup: Can you recall the first time you looked *down* on clouds, either from an airplane or from a high mountain? How did the experience impress you?

SEEING WHAT'S THERE

1. As you explore these words to God's people, what would you say is the brightest promise here? The most powerful vision of a future day? The most painful accusation? And the sharpest picture of punishment and disaster?

CAPTURE THE ESSENCE

2. What does God reveal most about His own character in this chapter?

3. From what you see in this chapter, would you say that God wants to be considered *primarily* as the God of His people Israel, or as the God of the whole earth? Explain your answer.

Isaiah 20

SEEING WHAT'S THERE

1. What specific commands did the Lord give Isaiah? What were these a sign of?

Isaiah 21

SEEING WHAT'S THERE

1. As you read this chapter, what would you say is the most urgent command here? The most powerful vision of a future day? And the sharpest picture of punishment and disaster?

2. In verses 3 and 4, how is Isaiah affected by the vision he sees? Why do you think he responds this way?

FOR GOING DEEPER

Verses 6-9 speak of a lookout in a watchtower, scanning the horizon for news of Israel's enemy. The prophet Habakkuk also proclaimed himself a "watchman." Look at Habakkuk 3:16-19 for a description of a watchman's heart.

Isaiah 22

SEEING WHAT'S THERE

1. Here, as well as for each chapter in this book, remember to discuss what to you are the most memorable images presented through Isaiah's words.

2. As you study Isaiah's words here, what would you say is the most fearful warning in this chapter? The most powerful vision of a future day? The most painful accusation? And the sharpest picture of punishment and disaster?

FOR LIFE TODAY

3. In what ways, if any, would you say that verses 12-13 might accurately describe God's people today, especially those in your church?

Isaiah 23

SEEING WHAT'S THERE

1. As you reflect on Isaiah's message for God's people in this chapter, what would you say is the brightest promise it contains? The most painful accusation? And the sharpest picture of punishment and disaster?

CAPTURE THE ESSENCE

2. What do we see most about God's character in this chapter, especially in verse 9?

Isaiah 24

Startup: What kind of images have you had in your mind about the end of the world?

SEEING WHAT'S THERE

1. As you reflect on Isaiah's message for God's people in this chapter, what would you say is the brightest promise it contains? The most powerful vision of a future day? The most painful accusation? And the sharpest picture of punishment and disaster?

FOR GOING DEEPER

With the worldwide devastation and judgment described in chapter 24 still fresh in your mind, turn over to 2 Peter 3:10-5. What counsel does the apostle Peter offer those who see God's righteous judgment hovering on the horizon?

Isaiah 25

SEEING WHAT'S THERE

1. What specific points of praise ring out from Isaiah's voice in this chapter?

2. What acts of God does Isaiah acknowledge? What does he say God has already done?

3. What specific promises are imparted to all people in verses 6-9?

4. What words of judgment are pronounced in verses 10-12?

CAPTURE THE ESSENCE

5. From what you see in this chapter, what is it that God wants us to understand most about Himself?

FOR LIFE TODAY

6. In light of how you're doing spiritually in your life today, which verse in this chapter do you think is the most important at this time—and why?

Isaiah 26

SEEING WHAT'S THERE

1. In this vision of the future for God's people, what do they praise Him for? What do they ask God for? What do they confess or acknowledge? What hope do they express?

CAPTURE THE ESSENCE

2. Songs are often a way to express and release deep emotions. What emotions are behind the song in this chapter?

FOR LIFE TODAY

3. In what ways would you say that verses 8, 12, and 13 might accurately describe God's people today, especially those in your church?

Isaiah 27

SEEING WHAT'S THERE

1. As you ponder Isaiah's words in this chapter, what would you say is the brightest promise here? The most powerful vision of a future day? And the sharpest picture of punishment and disaster?

FOR LIFE TODAY

2. In Romans 15:4, Paul reminds us that the Old Testament Scriptures can give us patience and perseverance on one hand, as well as comfort and encouragement on the other. In your own life, how do you see this book of Isaiah living up to Paul's description? In what ways, if any, is it meeting your personal needs for both *perseverance* and *encouragement?*

Isaiah 28

Startup: Do you think of the Bible more as an instruction manual, a letter from a friend, a philosophical essay, or a book of classical literature?

SEEING WHAT'S THERE

1. As you think about Isaiah's prophecy in this chapter, what would you say is the brightest promise here? The most fearful warning? The most urgent command? The most powerful vision of a future day? And the most painful accusation?

CAPTURE THE ESSENCE

2. What does God reveal most about His character in this chapter?

3. Again, imagine yourself being present in the temple in Jerusalem as the twelve-year-old Jesus hears this chapter read and discussed by the Jewish teachers. What verses in this chapter do you think would most impress Him, and what questions or comments do you suppose He might have spoken?

FOR GOING DEEPER

Compare the words of verse 16 with what is taught in 1 Peter 2:4-8. How do Peter's words increase your understanding and appreciation of Isaiah's words?

ISAIAH 29

SEEING WHAT'S THERE

1. As you reflect on this chapter, what would you say is the brightest promise it expresses? The most fearful warning? The most powerful vision of a future day? The most painful accusation? And the sharpest picture of punishment and disaster?

ISAIAH 30

SEEING WHAT'S THERE

1. What would you say is the brightest promise in this chapter? The most fearful warning? The most powerful vision of a future day? The most painful accusation? And the sharpest picture of punishment and disaster?

CAPTURE THE ESSENCE

2. In your own words, what would you say God wants us to understand most about His salvation in verse 15?

3. What would you say God wants us to understand most about Himself in verses 18 and 27-28?

FOR LIFE TODAY

4. If God had written this chapter only for you, which words or phrases do you think He might have underlined, and why?

ISAIAH 31

SEEING WHAT'S THERE

1. In your own words, what would you say is the brightest promise in this chapter? The most fearful warning? The most urgent command? The most powerful vision of a future day? And the sharpest picture of punishment and disaster?

CAPTURE THE ESSENCE

2. From all that you see in this chapter, what are the most important things God wants us to understand about His personality and character?

ISAIAH 32

SEEING WHAT'S THERE

1. As you explore these words to God's people, what would you say is the brightest promise here? The most urgent command? The most powerful vision of a future day? And the sharpest picture of punishment and disaster?

CAPTURE THE ESSENCE

2. What would you say God wants us to understand most from this chapter about what is right and what is wrong?

3. In Matthew 6:33, Jesus tells us to "seek first the kingdom of God and His righteousness." What can you learn about God's *righteousness* in this chapter, especially in verses 17?

FOR LIFE TODAY

4. Look again at verse 17. How present is this righteousness—and these effects—in *your* life?

ISAIAH 33

SEEING WHAT'S THERE

1. As you read this chapter, what would you say is the brightest promise here? The most fearful warning? The most powerful vision of a future day? And the sharpest picture of punishment and disaster?

2. What specific requests are made to God in verse 2?

CAPTURE THE ESSENCE

3. Review verse 22, then state in your own words what you believe God wants us to understand most about Himself from this passage.

4. What more do you learn in this chapter about the meaning of *righteousness?*

5. Now that you're halfway through Isaiah, how would you summarize the most important teachings in this book?

FOR LIFE TODAY

6. Look again at verse 2. How often would these words be an accurate reflection of your own heart's desire, and your own prayer to God?

ISAIAH 34

Startup: What comes to your mind when you think of the word *vengeance*?

SEEING WHAT'S THERE

1. As you study Isaiah's words here, what would you say is the most urgent command in this chapter? The most powerful vision of a future day? And the sharpest picture of punishment and disaster?

CAPTURE THE ESSENCE

2. Discuss how much you agree or disagree with this statement: When God destroys, it is always in order to save.

ISAIAH 35

SEEING WHAT'S THERE

1. As you reflect on Isaiah's message for God's people in this chapter, what would you say is the brightest promise it contains? The most urgent command? And the most powerful vision of a future day?

FOR LIFE TODAY

2. From what you see in this chapter, how would you describe the *quality of life* which God wants His people to experience? In practical terms, how would you describe the quality of life which He wants *you* to experience?

3. Look ahead to 55:10-11, where God reminds us that He sends rain and snow from the sky to water the earth and to nurture life. In the same way, God says that He sends His words to accomplish specific purposes. From your study so far, what would you suggest are *God's* primary purposes for the book of Isaiah in the lives of Christians today?

FOR GOING DEEPER

The writer of Hebrews quotes from verses 3-4 here in Isaiah 35. Examine that quotation in Hebrews 12:12. For what purpose do each of these biblical writers use this strong exhortation?

ISAIAH 36

Startup: Describe a time in your life when you truly felt you had your back against the wall. Describe the circumstances—and how you got out of the difficulty.

SEEING WHAT'S THERE

1. How would you summarize the situation facing Hezekiah?

ISAIAH 37

SEEING WHAT'S THERE

1. How does Hezekiah respond to the crisis? What are the most important things he says in his prayer to the Lord?

2. In His words spoken through Isaiah, how does God answer Hezekiah's prayer? What are the most important things God communicates about Himself to Hezekiah?

ISAIAH 38

SEEING WHAT'S THERE

1. How does God reveal Himself to Hezekiah in this chapter? What are the most important things He wants Hezekiah to learn?

ISAIAH 39

SEEING WHAT'S THERE

1. What would you say is the major point God is making by including this chapter in the Bible?

FOR GOING DEEPER

How does the graphic description in 2 Kings 25:1-21 heighten your awareness of Isaiah's dark prediction to King Hezekiah here in verses 3-8?

ISAIAH 40

Startup: In what experiences in life have you most sensed God's majesty and greatness?

SEEING WHAT'S THERE

1. What would you say is the most tender encouragement in this chapter? The most powerful vision of a future day? And the deepest glimpse into God's character?

2. With chapter 40, we begin a major new division in the book of Isaiah. What are the most important teachings you've seen so far in this book?

3. Here again, as well as for each chapter in this book, remember to discuss what to you are the most memorable images presented through Isaiah's words.

CAPTURE THE ESSENCE

4. From what you see in this chapter, what is it that God wants us to understand most about Himself?

5. In this chapter, what does God want us to understand most about His purpose and plan for His people?

6. Once more, what verses in this chapter do you think would most impress the 12-year-old Jesus as He heard it read and discussed in the Temple in Jerusalem, and what questions or comments do you suppose He might have spoken to the teachers there?

FOR LIFE TODAY

7. Review again the guidelines for our thought-life given in Philippians 4:8— "Whatever is true, whatever is noble, whatever is right, whatever is pure, whatever is lovely, whatever is admirable—if anything is excellent or praiseworthy— *think about such things.*" What food for thought can you find in this chapter that especially strikes you as being *true,* or *noble,* or *right,* or *pure,* or *lovely,* or *admirable,* or *excellent,* or *praiseworthy?*

8. Consider how strongly you desire to know God better, then ask yourself this question: *What are the truths revealed about Him in this chapter which He may want me to understand more deeply at this time in my life?*

FOR GOING DEEPER

Isaiah heard the prophetic echo of a distant voice here in verses 3-8. Take time to consider the mission of one who claimed to *be* that voice, in John 1:19-27.

ISAIAH 41

SEEING WHAT'S THERE

1. In your own words, what would you say is the brightest promise in this chapter? The most tender encouragement? The most powerful vision of a future day? The most painful accusation? And the deepest glimpse into God's character?

CAPTURE THE ESSENCE

2. In your own words, what would you say is revealed most about God's character and personality in verses 9-10?

3. In verses 8-16, what does God want us to understand most about His purpose and plan for His people?

FOR LIFE TODAY

4. Which verse in this chapter do you think God would like you to understand best?

ISAIAH 42

Startup: What images come to mind when you think of the word *servant?*

SEEING WHAT'S THERE

1. As you explore these words to God's people, what would you say is the brightest promise here? The most urgent command? The most powerful vision of a future day? The most painful accusation? The sharpest picture of punishment and disaster? And the deepest glimpse into God's character?

2. In what specific ways in this chapter does God show His concern for the entire world?

CAPTURE THE ESSENCE

3. Look again at verses 1-7. As a prophetic passage about the coming Messiah, what does this Scripture teach us about the *character* and the *ministry* of Jesus Christ?

4. In your own words, what would you say is revealed most about God's character and personality in verse 8?

5. What aspects of God's character and personality would you say He wants us to understand most from verses 13-17?

FOR GOING DEEPER

Look again at the description of the Lord's "servant" in verses 1-4. What distinctive of that divine servant does the gospel writer underline in Luke 4:14-19?

ISAIAH 43

SEEING WHAT'S THERE

1. As you read this chapter, what would you say is the brightest promise here? The most tender encouragement? The most urgent command? The most powerful vision of a future day? The most painful accusation? The sharpest picture of punishment and disaster? And the deepest glimpse into God's character?

2. What does God remind His people of in verses 16-17?

3. What is the "new thing" God is doing in verse 19?

4. What does God give in verse 21 as His *reason* for forming the nation of Israel?

CAPTURE THE ESSENCE

5. In your own words, how would you summarize the most important truths revealed in verses 1-7 about God's purpose and plans for His people?

6. Review carefully verses 10-13, then state in your own words what you believe God wants us to understand most about Himself from this passage.

7. What aspects of God's character and personality would you say He wants us to realize most from verses 22-28?

ISAIAH 44

Startup: What would you say are the most powerful idols in our society today?

SEEING WHAT'S THERE

1. As you study Isaiah's words here, what would you say is the brightest promise in this chapter? The most tender encouragement? The most urgent command? The most powerful vision of a future day? The most painful accusation? And the deepest glimpse into God's character?

CAPTURE THE ESSENCE

2. In verses 1-5, what does God want us to understand most about His purpose and plan for His people?

3. In your own words, what would you say is revealed most about God's character and personality in verses 6-8 and verse 24?

ISAIAH 45

SEEING WHAT'S THERE

1. As you reflect on Isaiah's message for God's people in this chapter, what would you say is the brightest promise it contains? The most fearful warning? The most urgent command? The most powerful vision of a future day? And the deepest glimpse into God's character?

CAPTURE THE ESSENCE

2. From what you see in this chapter, what is it that God wants us to understand most about Himself?

3. What words or phrases in this chapter tell us the most about God's *purpose* and *plan* for His people?

FOR GOING DEEPER

Consider verses 1-2 alongside the first chapter of Ezra. What was at least one of the tasks for which the gentile King Cyrus was "anointed" by the Lord?

ISAIAH 46

Startup: What expectations do you have about your old age? How do you picture your lifestyle at that time?

SEEING WHAT'S THERE

1. As you ponder Isaiah's words in this chapter, what would you say is the brightest promise here? The most tender encouragement? The most urgent command? The most powerful vision of a future day? And the deepest glimpse into God's character?

CAPTURE THE ESSENCE

2. What aspects of God's character is He emphasizing to us in verses 9-10?

3. What aspects of God's plan and purpose for His people is He emphasizing to us in verses 3-4 and again in verses 12-13?

ISAIAH 47

SEEING WHAT'S THERE

1. As you think about Isaiah's prophecy in this chapter, what would you say is the most fearful warning here? The most painful accusation? And the sharpest picture of punishment and disaster?

ISAIAH 48

SEEING WHAT'S THERE

1. As you reflect on this chapter, what would you say is the most powerful vision of a future day expressed here? The most painful accusation? And the deepest glimpse into God's character?

CAPTURE THE ESSENCE

2. Summarize in your own words what you believe God wants us to understand most about Himself from this chapter.

3. What words or phrases in this chapter tell us the most about God's purpose and plan for His people?

FOR GOING DEEPER

Notice how the Lord identifies himself to his people in verses 12-13. What similarities do you see here to the way the Lord Jesus identified himself to John—and ultimately the church—in Revelation 1:4-8 and 1:17-19?

ISAIAH 49

Startup: What day in your life did you work harder than any other?

SEEING WHAT'S THERE

1. What would you say is the brightest promise in this chapter? The most tender encouragement? The most powerful vision of a future day?

CAPTURE THE ESSENCE

2. In your own words, how would you summarize the most important truths revealed in verses 8-26 about God's purpose and plans for His people?

FOR GOING DEEPER

What insights do you gain when you compare the note of sorrow in the divine servant's voice in verses 3-4 with the lament of the Lord Jesus in Matthew 23:37-39?

ISAIAH 50

SEEING WHAT'S THERE

1. In your own words, what would you say is the most powerful vision of a future day in this chapter? And the deepest glimpse into God's character?

CAPTURE THE ESSENCE

2. In your own words, what would you say is revealed most about God's character and personality in verses 2-3?

3. Look again at verses 4-7. As a prophetic passage about the coming Messiah, what does this Scripture teach us about the *character* and the *ministry* of Jesus Christ?

FOR GOING DEEPER

Discuss together the prophetic fulfillment of verse 6 which you see in Matthew 26:67 and 27:30, and Mark 14:65. Why do you think God put prophecies of Christ's suffering like this into the Old Testament, since at the time Jesus suffered and died, practically everyone failed to notice how He was fulfilling these prophecies?

ISAIAH 51

Startup: How good is your hearing?

SEEING WHAT'S THERE

1. As you explore these words to God's people, what would you say is the brightest promise here? The most tender encouragement? The most urgent command? The most powerful vision of a future day? The sharpest picture of punishment and disaster? And the deepest glimpse into God's character?

CAPTURE THE ESSENCE

2. In this chapter, what does God want us to understand most about His purpose and plan for His people?

3. Review carefully verses 12-16, then state in your own words what you believe God wants us to understand most about Himself from this passage.

ISAIAH 52

SEEING WHAT'S THERE

1. As you read this chapter, what would you say is the brightest promise here? The most urgent command? The most powerful vision of a future day? And the deepest glimpse into God's character?

CAPTURE THE ESSENCE

2. In verses 1-12, what does God want us to understand most about His purpose and plan for His people?

3. Look again at verses 13-15. As a prophetic passage about the coming Messiah, what does this Scripture teach us about the *character* and the *ministry* of Jesus Christ?

ISAIAH 53

SEEING WHAT'S THERE

1. Chapter 53 has been called the key to the book of Isaiah. What does this chapter include that could make it this significant?

2. How many descriptions can you list for the Person this chapter describes? What is He like, what exactly does He do, and why does He do it?

CAPTURE THE ESSENCE

3. This chapter is quoted more frequently in the New Testament than any other Old Testament passage. If you had never read or heard about the New Testament, which parts of the gospel could you still learn from this chapter?

4. As a prophetic passage about the coming Messiah, what does this chapter teach us especially about the *character* and the *ministry* of Jesus Christ?

FOR LIFE TODAY

5. In how many phrases and verses in this chapter do you see *yourself?*

FOR GOING DEEPER

Read verses 1-3 alongside the first 13 verses of John 1. What common themes emerge when you consider these passages together?

ISAIAH 54

Startup: Can you recall a time in life when you felt as if God had His face turned away from you? What were the circumstances?

SEEING WHAT'S THERE

1. As you study Isaiah's words here, what would you say is the brightest promise in this chapter? The most tender encouragement? The most urgent command? The most powerful vision of a future day? And the deepest glimpse into God's character?

CAPTURE THE ESSENCE

2. In your own words, what would you say God wants us to understand most about Himself in verses 5-10?

3. What words or phrases in this chapter tell us the most about God's purpose and plan for His people?

ISAIAH 55

SEEING WHAT'S THERE

1. As you reflect on Isaiah's message for God's people in this chapter, what would you say is the brightest promise it contains? The most urgent command? And the deepest glimpse into God's character?

CAPTURE THE ESSENCE

2. Restate in your own words what you believe are the most important truths revealed about God's character and personality in verses 8-11.

3. What words or phrases in this chapter tell us the most about God's purpose and plan for His people?

4. Once more, what verses in this chapter do you think would most impress the 12-year-old Jesus as He heard it read and discussed in the Temple in Jerusalem, and what questions or comments do you suppose He might have spoken to the teachers there?

FOR LIFE TODAY

5. Once more, look over the guidelines for our thought-life given in Philippians 4:8 —"Whatever is true, whatever is noble, whatever is right, whatever is pure, whatever is lovely, whatever is admirable—if anything is excellent or praiseworthy— *think about such things."* What food for thought can you find in this chapter that especially strikes you as being *true,* or *noble,* or *right,* or *pure,* or *lovely,* or *admirable,* or *excellent,* or *praiseworthy?*

FOR GOING DEEPER

As you consider God's gracious invitation in verses 1-7, take time to reread the account of Jesus with the Samaritan woman in John 4:1-38. In what sense does the gospel account parallel this passage in Isaiah?

ISAIAH 56

SEEING WHAT'S THERE

1. As you ponder Isaiah's words in this chapter, what would you say is the brightest promise here? The most urgent command? And the most painful accusation?

CAPTURE THE ESSENCE

2. How does this chapter help us understand what God most *desires* for His people?

FOR LIFE TODAY

3. In Jeremiah 23:29, God says that His Word is like fire, and like a hammer. He can use the Scriptures to burn away unclean thoughts and desires in our hearts. He can also use Scripture to hit hard like a hammer, with the power to crush our spiritual hardness. From your study in this book of Isaiah, how do you most want to see the "fire-and-hammer" power of God's Word at work in your own life?

ISAIAH 57

SEEING WHAT'S THERE

1. As you think about Isaiah's prophecy in this chapter, what would you say is the brightest promise here? The most tender encouragement? The most powerful vision of a future day? The most painful accusation? The sharpest picture of punishment and disaster? And the deepest glimpse into God's character?

CAPTURE THE ESSENCE

2. Review verses 14-21. What are the most significant truths this passage reveals about *God,* and what are the most significant truths it reveals about *us?*

ISAIAH 58

Startup: What experiences have you had in fasting?

SEEING WHAT'S THERE

1. As you reflect on this chapter, what would you say is the brightest promise it expresses? The most powerful vision of a future day? The most painful accusation? And the deepest glimpse into God's character?

CAPTURE THE ESSENCE

2. What would you say God wants us to understand most from this chapter about what is right and what is wrong?

FOR LIFE TODAY

3. In what ways, if any, would you say that verses 1-4 might accurately describe God's people today, especially those in your church?

4. If everyone in your church thoroughly understood this chapter, and they all had a passion for living out its truth in their lives, what kind of practical changes do you think would result?

ISAIAH 59

SEEING WHAT'S THERE

1. Remember again in each chapter in this book to discuss what to you are the most memorable images presented through Isaiah's words.

2. What sins and weaknesses and failures on the part of God's people does Isaiah confess and acknowledge in this chapter?

3. In verses 15-17, what acts of God does Isaiah acknowledge? What does he say God has already done?

4. What vision of a future day is revealed in verses 18 and 19?

5. What astonishing promises does God make in verses 20-21?

CAPTURE THE ESSENCE

6. From all that you see in this chapter, what is it that God wants us to understand most about Himself?

FOR LIFE TODAY

7. In what ways, if any, would you say that this chapter (especially verses 3-11) might accurately describe God's people today, especially those in your church?

FOR GOING DEEPER

Ponder the prophet's damning indictment of man's sin in 59:1-15, and then consider God's solution to man's dilemma in verses 16-20. How does this parallel Paul's statement of dilemma and divine remedy in Romans 3:9-26?

ISAIAH 60

SEEING WHAT'S THERE

1. What would you say is the brightest promise in this chapter? The most urgent command? And the most powerful vision of a future day?

CAPTURE THE ESSENCE

2. In this chapter, what does God want us to understand most about His purpose and plan for His people?

ISAIAH 61

Startup: What images or situations come to mind when you think of being *brokenhearted?*

SEEING WHAT'S THERE

1. In your own words, what would you say is the brightest promise in this chapter? The most powerful vision of a future day? And the deepest glimpse into God's character?

CAPTURE THE ESSENCE

2. What words or phrases in this chapter tell us the most about God's purpose and plan for His people?

FOR LIFE TODAY

3. If it's true that "you become what you think," then what are the most important thoughts from this chapter to plant firmly in your mind?

FOR GOING DEEPER

The Lord Jesus read aloud verse 1 and half of verse 2 when he stood up to read the Scriptures in his hometown of Nazareth, as recorded in Luke 4:16-20. In what sense did he proclaim himself the fulfillment of those words? Why might he have *ended* the reading of that passage at the precise point where he did?

ISAIAH 62

SEEING WHAT'S THERE

1. As you explore these words to God's people, what would you say is the brightest promise here? The most tender encouragement? The most urgent command? And the most powerful vision of a future day?

CAPTURE THE ESSENCE

2. How does this chapter help us understand what God most *desires* for His people?

ISAIAH 63

SEEING WHAT'S THERE

1. As you read this chapter, what would you say is the most tender encouragement here? The most powerful vision of a future day? The most painful accusation? The sharpest picture of punishment and disaster? And the deepest glimpse into God's character?

2. Look closely at the prayer in verses 15-19. What questions are presented to God? What requests are made in the opening line of verse 15, and in the last half of verse 17?

CAPTURE THE ESSENCE

3. From all that you see in this chapter, what are the most important things God wants us to realize about Himself?

ISAIAH 64

SEEING WHAT'S THERE

1. Consider carefully each line of the prayer in this chapter. What specific requests are made of God in verses 2 and 9?

2. How is God's character acknowledged in this prayer?

3. What sins and failures are acknowledged on the part of God's people?

FOR LIFE TODAY

4. What parts of the prayer in this chapter would be especially appropriate as a message to God from your church?

FOR GOING DEEPER

Look together at the way verse 4 is quoted by Paul in 1 Corinthians 2:9-10. Taken together, what do these passages tell us about God's character?

ISAIAH 65

Startup: What have been some of the biggest *surprises* in your life?

SEEING WHAT'S THERE

1. As you study Isaiah's words here, what would you say is the brightest promise in this chapter? The most powerful vision of a future day? The most painful accusation? And the deepest glimpse into God's character?

CAPTURE THE ESSENCE

2. In this chapter, what does God want us to understand most about His purpose and plan for His people?

FOR GOING DEEPER

Keeping in mind verses 1-3 from this chapter, explore Paul's extended comments on Israel and the Gentiles in Romans 10:16—11:27. How does the Paul build and expand on the Lord's poignant statement of Israel's stubborn unbelief here in Isaiah?

Isaiah 66

SEEING WHAT'S THERE

1. As you reflect on Isaiah's message for God's people in this chapter, what would you say is the brightest promise it contains? The most urgent command? The most powerful vision of a future day? The most painful accusation? The sharpest picture of punishment and disaster? And the deepest glimpse into God's character?

CAPTURE THE ESSENCE

2. In your own words, what would you say God wants us to understand most about Himself in verses 1-2?

3. What words or phrases in this chapter tell us the most about God's purpose and plan for His people?

Isaiah:
The Big Picture

(Discuss again the questions in the "Overview," plus the questions below.)

1. For getting the most from the book of Isaiah, one of the best guidelines is found in 2 Timothy 3:16-17, words which Paul wrote with the Old Testament first in view. He said that *all* Scripture is of great benefit to (a) teach us, (b) rebuke us, (c) correct us, and (d) train us in righteousness. Paul added that these Scriptures completely equip the person of God "for every good work." As you think seriously about those guidelines, in which of these areas do you especially see the usefulness of Isaiah?

2. Imagine that you were helping to produce a film based on the ministry of Isaiah the prophet. Describe the kinds of scenery, supporting characters, background music, lighting effects, etc., that you would use to help portray the central message of his book.

3. Look together at each of these passages, and discuss which one you believe is the best candidate for "KEY VERSE" in the book of Isaiah—the one which brings into sharpest focus what this book is most about: 9:6-7, 53:5, or 53:6.

4. SEARCH FOR THE SAVIOR—There are many words, images, and themes in Isaiah that point to Jesus. Which of these have made the strongest impression on you?

5. If Isaiah were the only book in the Old Testament, in what ways would it still make a good introduction to the message of Jesus in the New Testament?

6. Based especially on your own experience, complete this statement in the way that's most meaningful to you: I believe it's important for Christians to read and explore the book of Isaiah because…

Jeremiah

OVERVIEW

(Discuss these OVERVIEW questions both at the beginning of your study of Jeremiah, then again after you've studied all 52 chapters. Your answers may change significantly once you've looked more closely at the entire book.)

Startup: Talk together about this question: What do you consider the three most important values for being successful in today's world?

SEEING WHAT'S THERE

1. Before launching into a closer look at Jeremiah, how would you summarize what you already know about this book?

2. Find the most prominent word that re-occurs in the following verses—3:1, 4:1, 8:4-5, and 24:7. What clues could this word offer about the central message of Jeremiah?

3. Notice the word that is repeated in the following verses—11:20, 17:9-10, 24:7, and 29:13. What *progression* do you see in the way this concept is presented as you move through these verses in Jeremiah?

4. Find another frequently used word in each of the following verses—3:21, 9:1, 9:10, 13:17, 22:10, 31:9, 31:15-16, 41:6, 48:5, and 48:32. What does this show about the *emotion* of this book?

5. Look also at the list of "Questions to Ask as You Begin Your Study of Each Book" on page 9.

FOR LIFE TODAY

6. The book of Jeremiah has been called "The Book of Horror and Hope," "A Warning about Captivity," "Death Throes of a Decadent Nation," "God's Final Effort to Save Jerusalem," "Repent or Be Punished," and "Jerusalem's Judgment and Coming Glory," while Jeremiah himself has been called "The Weeping Prophet." With that reputation for this book, what kinds of answers and guidelines and solutions would you like to gain as you examine it more closely?

7. As you think first about *who God is,* and second about *what the Bible is,* how strongly would you rate your present desire to understand better the book of Jeremiah? Use a scale of one to ten (one = "no desire at all," ten = "extremely intense desire") to help you decide.

8. From what you see in God's words in 23:29, what would be a good personal prayer to offer to God as you study this book?

9. When you get to heaven, if you have a long talk with Jeremiah and he asks you, "What was most helpful to you in my book?" how would you like to be able to answer him?

Jeremiah 1

SEEING WHAT'S THERE

1. What does God tell Jeremiah in verse 5, and how does Jeremiah respond in verse 6?

2. From what God tells him in verses 7-9, what conclusions could Jeremiah make about his future ministry?

3. In verses 14-16, what specific sin does God accuse Israel of, and what punishment does He announce?

4. In verses 17-19, what specific commands and what specific promises does Jeremiah receive from God?

5. Look also on page 8 at the list of "Questions to Ask as You Study Each Chapter." You may want to look again at this list for each chapter in Jeremiah.

CAPTURE THE ESSENCE

6. How would you summarize what Jeremiah learns most about God in this chapter?

FOR LIFE TODAY

7. Proverbs 2:1-5 tells about the sincere person who truly longs for wisdom and understanding, and who searches the Scriptures for it—as if it were buried treasure. That person, Solomon says, will come to understand the fear of the Lord, and discover the knowledge of God. As you begin exploring the book of Jeremiah, what "buried treasure" would you like God to help you find here—to show you what God and His wisdom are really like? If you have this desire, how would you express it in your own words?

FOR GOING DEEPER

How would you compare and contrast Jeremiah's divine "commissioning service" in verses 4-19 with that of Moses in Exodus 3:1—4:17?

Jeremiah 2

SEEING WHAT'S THERE

1. Chapter 2 has been called the key to the book of Jeremiah. What does this chapter include that could make it this significant?

2. What to you are the most powerful images presented through the words of this chapter?

3. What would you say is the most painful accusation in this chapter? And the sharpest picture of punishment and disaster?

FOR LIFE TODAY

4. In what ways, if any, would you say that verses 31-32 might accurately describe God's people today, especially those in your church?

Jeremiah 3

SEEING WHAT'S THERE

1. As in the previous chapter, discuss again what to you are the most powerful images presented through the words of this chapter. (Ask this question for each chapter in Jeremiah.)

2. In your own words, what would you say is the brightest promise in this chapter? The most tender encouragement? The most urgent command? The most painful accusation? And the sharpest picture of punishment and disaster?

3. What confession and repentance do you see beginning halfway through verse 22?

FOR LIFE TODAY

4. In what ways, if any, would you say that verses 21-22 might accurately describe God's people today? In what ways might it describe your church today?

JEREMIAH 4

SEEING WHAT'S THERE

1. As you explore these words to God's people, what would you say is the brightest promise here? The most urgent command? The most powerful vision of a future day? The most painful accusation? The sharpest picture of punishment and disaster? And the deepest glimpse into God's character?

2. In verse 19, how is Jeremiah affected by what God is revealing to him? Why do you think he responds this way?

FOR LIFE TODAY

3. Choose one of these sentences, and complete it as fully and candidly as you would like. (a) What I see and understand in this chapter is important to my life because... OR: (b) What I see and understand in this chapter does NOT seem important to my life at this time, because...

JEREMIAH 5

SEEING WHAT'S THERE

1. As you read this chapter, what would you say is the most painful accusation here? The sharpest picture of punishment and disaster? And the deepest glimpse into God's character?

CAPTURE THE ESSENCE

2. From what you see in verse 22, what conclusions can you make about God's character and personality?

FOR LIFE TODAY

3. In what ways, if any, would you say this chapter might accurately describe God's people today, especially those in your church?

JEREMIAH 6

Startup: How do you think God views the spiritual health of our own nation today?

SEEING WHAT'S THERE

1. As you study Jeremiah's words here, what would you say is the most fearful warning in this chapter? The most urgent command? The most powerful vision of a future day? The most painful accusation? The sharpest picture of punishment and disaster? And the deepest glimpse into God's character?

2. What does the Lord tell Jeremiah in verses 27-30? Express this in your own words?

CAPTURE THE ESSENCE

3. From what you see in verse 16, what does God desire for His people?

4. Discuss how much you agree or disagree with this statement: When it comes to repentance before God, there is no such thing as being too late.

JEREMIAH 7

SEEING WHAT'S THERE

1. As you reflect on Jeremiah's message for God's people, what would you say is the most urgent command in this chapter? The most painful accusation? The sharpest picture of punishment and disaster? And the deepest glimpse into God's character?

2. In verse 9 alone, how many of the Ten Commandments were the Israelites guilty of breaking? (You can refer back to the list of the commandments in Exodus 20.)

FOR LIFE TODAY

3. In what ways, if any, would you say that verses 8-11 might accurately describe God's people today, especially those in your church?

FOR GOING DEEPER

Restate in your own words the basic principle which God is communicating in verses 21-23. How does this compare with the words Jesus spoke in Matthew 9:13 and 12:7?

JEREMIAH 8

SEEING WHAT'S THERE

1. As you ponder Jeremiah's words, what would you say is the most powerful vision of a future day in this chapter? The most painful accusation? The sharpest picture of punishment and disaster? And the deepest glimpse into God's character?

2. What is the people's response in verses 14-16, and in verse 20?

3. What is Jeremiah's response in verses 18-19, and 21-22?

CAPTURE THE ESSENCE

4. Imagine yourself being present in the temple in Jerusalem as the twelve-year-old Jesus hears this chapter read and discussed by the rabbis there. In Luke 2:46 we read that He was listening to these teachers and asking them questions. What verses from this chapter do you think would most impress the boy Jesus, and what questions or comments do you suppose He might have spoken?

FOR GOING DEEPER

Look again at verses 21-22. What word-pictures and statements that deepen our understanding of this truth can you find in Jeremiah 30:12-17?

JEREMIAH 9

SEEING WHAT'S THERE

1. What emotions and concerns does Jeremiah reveal in verses 1-2 and verse 10?

2. What accusations and warnings does the Lord make in verses 3-9, and what word of judgment in verse 11?

3. What questions does Jeremiah ask in verse 12, and how does God answer him?

4. Remember to discuss here (and throughout this book) what to you are the most powerful images presented through the words of Jeremiah in this chapter.

CAPTURE THE ESSENCE

5. From what you see in verse 24, how would you explain in your own words what God most wants us to know about Him?

FOR LIFE TODAY

6. Look again at verse 24. Which of these three—wisdom, strength, or riches—would you most likely be tempted to boast about?

7. In practical terms, how can you live out in your own life what God says in verse 24?

JEREMIAH 10

SEEING WHAT'S THERE

1. Review carefully verses 6-16, then state in your own words what you believe God wants us to understand most about Himself from this passage.

2. In verses 17-18, what does God tell the people to do, and for what reason?

3. How would you explain Jeremiah's response in verses 19-20?

4. What requests does Jeremiah make to God in verses 23-25?

JEREMIAH 11

Startup: In the way we read and study the Bible, what kind of old mental habits or faulty assumptions can most easily block this book of Jeremiah from coming alive in our minds and hearts?

SEEING WHAT'S THERE

1. As you think about Jeremiah's prophecy, what would you say is the most fearful warning in this chapter? The most painful accusation? And the sharpest picture of punishment and disaster?

2. What does God command Jeremiah to do in verse 14?

3. What developments in Jeremiah's circumstances are recorded in this chapter?

CAPTURE THE ESSENCE

4. From what you see in Jeremiah's words in verse 20, what are the most important things he understands about God's personality and character?

FOR LIFE TODAY

5. How consistently do you find yourself truly thinking about and wanting to please God at this time in your life, com-

pared with times in your past? Use a scale of one to ten (one = "much less consistent than ever," ten = "much more consistent than ever") to help you decide.

JEREMIAH 12

SEEING WHAT'S THERE

1. How would you summarize Jeremiah's questions in verses 1-4, and God's answers in verses 5-6?

2. As you reflect on verses 7-17, what would you say is the brightest promise this passage expresses? The most fearful warning? The most powerful vision of a future day? And the sharpest picture of punishment and disaster?

CAPTURE THE ESSENCE

3. How would you summarize what Jeremiah learns most about God in this chapter?

FOR GOING DEEPER

In verses 1-4, Jeremiah complains about the apparent prosperity and security of the wicked. Compare his words of perplexity and indignation with similar sentiments from Job (Job 21:4-21), Asaph (Psalm 73), and Habakkuk (Habakkuk 1:2-4).

JEREMIAH 13

SEEING WHAT'S THERE

1. What commands does God give Jeremiah in the opening verses of this chapter?

2. What would you say is the most fearful warning in this chapter? The most urgent command? The most powerful vision of a future day? The most painful accusation? And the sharpest picture of punishment and disaster?

JEREMIAH 14

SEEING WHAT'S THERE

1. In verses 1-6, how does God portray the drought that comes to Judah?

2. What does God command Jeremiah to do in verses 11-12?

3. Look at Jeremiah's prayers in verses 7-9 and 13-22. What are his *questions* to God, what are his *confessions* to God, and what are his *requests* to God?

JEREMIAH 15

SEEING WHAT'S THERE

1. What specific words of judgment and disaster does God speak in verses 1-9?

2. What complaint does Jeremiah make in verse 10, and what promise is contained in God's response in verse 11?

3. What does Jeremiah say to God in verses 15-18, and what do these words reveal about Jeremiah's character as well as his circumstances at this time?

4. How does God answer Jeremiah in verses 19-21?

CAPTURE THE ESSENCE

5. How would you summarize what Jeremiah learns most about God in this chapter?

FOR LIFE TODAY

6. What can you learn most from Jeremiah's example in this chapter about trusting God?

JEREMIAH 16

Startup: If you're married, what have you learned most about your spouse in the last few months?

SEEING WHAT'S THERE

1. What command does God give Jeremiah in verse 2?

2. In the remainder of the chapter, what would you say is the brightest promise expressed here? The most urgent command? The most powerful vision of a future day? The most painful accusation? The sharpest picture of punishment and

disaster? And the deepest glimpse into God's character?

JEREMIAH 17

SEEING WHAT'S THERE

1. Here, as well as for each chapter in this book, remember to discuss what to you are the most powerful images presented through Jeremiah's words.

2. In verses 1-13, what would you say is the brightest promise here? The most fearful warning? The most painful accusation? The sharpest picture of punishment and disaster? And the deepest glimpse into God's character?

3. Look at Jeremiah's prayer in verses 12-18. What does he praise God for? And what does he ask God for?

4. In verses 19-27, how would you summarize what God commands about the Sabbath?

CAPTURE THE ESSENCE

5. Review verses 9-10. What are the most significant truths this passage reveals about *God*, and what are the most significant truths it reveals about *us*?

6. From what you see in verses 12-18, what are the most important things that Jeremiah understands about God's personality and character?

FOR LIFE TODAY

7. Look again at verses 7-8. How strongly does this passage reflect your own experience of God at this time in your life, compared with times in your past? Use a scale of one to ten (one = "much less than ever," ten = "much more than ever") to help you decide.

FOR GOING DEEPER

Consider again the directives in verses 19-27. After the destruction of Jerusalem, the exile of its people, and the eventual return of the exiles, the same issue resurfaces in Nehemiah 13:15-22. What similarities do you see in the two situations—separated as they are by so many years?

JEREMIAH 18

SEEING WHAT'S THERE

1. What does Jeremiah hear and see in verses 1-4?

2. In verses 5-17, what would you say is the most urgent command here? The most painful accusation? The sharpest picture of punishment and disaster? And the deepest glimpse into God's character?

3. Look at the words of Jeremiah's enemies in verse 18, and Jeremiah's prayer to God in verses 19-23. What does Jeremiah ask God for, and on what basis does he make these requests?

CAPTURE THE ESSENCE

4. From verses 5-11, what important conclusions can you make about God's character and personality?

FOR LIFE TODAY

5. Look ahead to 23:29, where God says that His Word is like fire, and like a hammer. He can use the Scriptures to burn away unclean thoughts and desires in our hearts. He can also use Scripture to hit hard like a hammer, with the power to crush our spiritual hardness. From your study in this book of Jeremiah, how do you most want to see the "fire-and-hammer" power of God's Word at work in your own life?

JEREMIAH 19

SEEING WHAT'S THERE

1. As you study Jeremiah's words here, what would you say is the most powerful vision of a future day in this chapter? The most painful accusation? And the sharpest picture of punishment and disaster?

JEREMIAH 20

SEEING WHAT'S THERE

1. What changes in Jeremiah's circumstances are recorded in this chapter? In Jeremiah's next prayer to God, what does the prophet reveal about the inner struggle he is undergoing along with his outward struggle?

CAPTURE THE ESSENCE

2. From what you see in Jeremiah's words in verses 7-18, what are the most important things that Jeremiah understands about God's personality and character?

3. How would you evaluate Jeremiah's character and personality at this time?

FOR LIFE TODAY

4. At what times in life have you most been able to identify with Jeremiah's prayer in this chapter?

5. In Romans 15:4, Paul reminds us that the Old Testament Scriptures can give us patience and perseverance on one hand, as well as comfort and encouragement on the other. In your own life, how do you see this book of Jeremiah living up to Paul's description? In what ways, if any, is it meeting your personal needs for both *perseverance* and *encouragement?*

JEREMIAH 21

Startup: What two or three problems, if solved, would make the most difference in your life today?

SEEING WHAT'S THERE

1. Summarize the events of this chapter. What messages does Jeremiah have for King Zedekiah, and for the people of Jerusalem?

FOR LIFE TODAY

2. In Isaiah 55:10-11, God reminds us that He sends rain and snow from the sky to water the earth and to nurture life. In the same way, God says that He sends His words to accomplish specific purposes. From your study so far, what would you suggest are *God's* primary purposes for the book of Jeremiah in the lives of Christians today?

JEREMIAH 22

SEEING WHAT'S THERE

1. As you reflect on Jeremiah's message for God's people in this chapter, what would you say is the most fearful warning it contains? The most urgent command? The most painful accusation? And the sharpest picture of punishment and disaster?

JEREMIAH 23

SEEING WHAT'S THERE

1. As you ponder Jeremiah's words in this chapter, what would you say is the brightest promise here? The most fearful warning? The most urgent command? The most powerful vision of a future day? The most painful accusation? The sharpest picture of punishment and disaster? And the deepest glimpse into God's character?

CAPTURE THE ESSENCE

2. Look again at verses 5-6. As a prophetic passage about the coming Messiah, what does this Scripture teach us about the character and ministry of Jesus?

3. What aspects of God's character and personality would you say He wants us to understand most from verses 23-24?

FOR GOING DEEPER

In what ways do you see the truth of verses 9-14 reflected also in Jeremiah 6:13-15?

JEREMIAH 24

SEEING WHAT'S THERE

1. As you think about Jeremiah's prophecy in this chapter, what would you say is the brightest promise here? And the sharpest picture of punishment and disaster?

JEREMIAH 25

Startup: What images come to mind first when you think of the word *guilt?*

SEEING WHAT'S THERE

1. As you reflect on this chapter, what would you say is the most powerful vision of a future day it expresses? The most painful accusation? The sharpest picture of punishment and disaster? And the deepest glimpse into God's character?

CAPTURE THE ESSENCE

2. With verses 11 and 12 in mind, discuss how much you agree or disagree with this statement: God's discipline has limitations, but God's judgment does not.

FOR GOING DEEPER

In verses 15-38, focus again on the "cup of God's wrath," especially in verse 28. Then use the following passages to trace this theme through Scripture: Jeremiah 49:12 and 51:7, Isaiah 51:17, Ezekiel 23:31-34, and Revelation 14:10 and 16:19.

JEREMIAH 26

SEEING WHAT'S THERE

1. What developments in Jeremiah's life are recorded in this chapter? What impresses you most about the prophet in this chapter?

JEREMIAH 27

SEEING WHAT'S THERE

1. What would you say is the brightest promise in this chapter? The most fearful warning? The most urgent command? The most painful accusation? The sharpest picture of punishment and disaster? And the deepest glimpse into God's character?

CAPTURE THE ESSENCE

2. Now that you're halfway through Jeremiah, how would you summarize the most important teachings in this book?

JEREMIAH 28

SEEING WHAT'S THERE

1. How would you describe the confrontation in this chapter between Jeremiah and the false prophet Hananiah?

JEREMIAH 29

SEEING WHAT'S THERE

1. In Jeremiah's letter to the captives in Babylon (verses 4-23), what would you say is the brightest promise here? The most urgent command? The most painful accusation? And the sharpest picture of punishment and disaster?

CAPTURE THE ESSENCE

2. In Jeremiah's letter, what does God want us to understand most about His *purpose* and *plan* for His people?

JEREMIAH 30

Startup: What images come to mind first when you think of the word *restore?*

SEEING WHAT'S THERE

1. As you explore these words to God's people, what would you say is the brightest promise here? The most urgent command? The most powerful vision of a future day? And the sharpest picture of punishment and disaster?

CAPTURE THE ESSENCE

2. In this chapter, what does God want us to understand most about His purpose and plan for His people?

3. Again, imagine yourself being present in the temple in Jerusalem as the twelve-year-old Jesus hears this chapter read and discussed by the Jewish teachers. What verses in this chapter do you think would most impress Him, and what questions or comments do you suppose He might have spoken?

FOR LIFE TODAY

4. In verse 9, notice Jeremiah's words about serving God. If God were to write down a list of the ways in which you truly served Him in the past week, what do you think would be on that list?

JEREMIAH 31

SEEING WHAT'S THERE

1. Here again, as well as for each chapter in this book, remember to discuss what to you are the most powerful images presented through Jeremiah's words.

2. Look at the last three words in verse 14. How many times do you see this phrase repeated in this chapter? If this phrase is a way to emphasize what was just spoken by God, then what are the statements that God is emphasizing in this chapter?

3. How many *promises from God* can you find in this chapter? Which of them do you feel are the most important?

4. Look especially at God's stunning promises in verses 31-34. This passage is considered the high point of Jeremiah's

prophecies. From what you see in these verses, why would that be so?

CAPTURE THE ESSENCE

5. Again in this chapter, what does God want us to understand most about His purpose and plan for His people?

6. In your own words, what would you say is revealed most about God's character and personality in this chapter?

FOR LIFE TODAY

7. Look again at verses 31-34. To what extent are God's promises there also His promises to you? What *expectations* can you rightly have of God because of them? What can you truly rely on God to do?

FOR GOING DEEPER

Consider again the major truth expressed in verses 29-30. How do Deuteronomy 24:16 and Ezekiel 18:1-20 expand your understanding of this truth?

JEREMIAH 32

Startup: In a hundred-mile radius from where you are now, where is the last place you would want to buy property?

SEEING WHAT'S THERE

1. What are the biggest developments in Jeremiah's situation in this chapter?

2. In verses 17-25, what points of praise does Jeremiah offer in his prayer? And what doubts or uncertainty does he reveal?

3. What does God emphasize in His answer to Jeremiah's prayer, beginning in verse 26?

4. What specific promises does God make about God's people in verses 37-44?

CAPTURE THE ESSENCE

5. From what you see in Jeremiah's prayer in verses 17-25, what are the most important things he understands about God's personality and character?

6. What aspects of God's character and personality would you say He wants us to understand most from verse 27?

7. Look carefully at verses 39-40. To what extent would you say that these verses reflect the experience of your church?

JEREMIAH 33

SEEING WHAT'S THERE

1. What are the most significant promises from God in this chapter, and how would you explain their importance?

CAPTURE THE ESSENCE

2. In this chapter, what does God want us to understand most about His purpose and plan for His people?

3. Look closely at verses 14-16. As a prophetic passage about the coming Messiah, what does this Scripture teach us about the *character* and the *ministry* of Jesus Christ?

FOR LIFE TODAY

4. In light of how you're doing spiritually in your life today, which verse in this chapter do you think is the most important at this time—and why?

5. Review the guidelines for our thought-life given in Philippians 4:8—"Whatever is true, whatever is noble, whatever is right, whatever is pure, whatever is lovely, whatever is admirable—if anything is excellent or praiseworthy—*think about such things.*" What food for thought can you find in this chapter that especially strikes you as being *true,* or *noble,* or *right,* or *pure,* or *lovely,* or *admirable,* or *excellent,* or *praiseworthy?*

FOR GOING DEEPER

Consider again the Lord's magnificent promise to his servant in verse 3. How do these additional Scriptures underline the emphasis in this passage?—Psalms 105:1 and 145:18, Isaiah 55:6 and 58:9, and Matthew 7:7-11.

JEREMIAH 34

Startup: What would you rather do—die in battle (and die free), or live the rest of your life as a prisoner of a cruel enemy?

SEEING WHAT'S THERE

1. How would you summarize Jeremiah's message to King Zedekiah in this chapter?

2. What accusations does the Lord make against His people in the last half of this chapter, and what punishment does He promise?

JEREMIAH 35

SEEING WHAT'S THERE

1. What do you think is the main point God is making by including this chapter in the Bible?

FOR GOING DEEPER

Look again at the inspiring story of the Recabites in this chapter. For further insight into the heart of this clan's zealous founder, read 2 Kings 10:15-28.

JEREMIAH 36

SEEING WHAT'S THERE

1. How would you summarize what happens to Jeremiah in this chapter?

2. EYE FOR DETAIL—*From what you recall seeing in chapter 36, try answering the following question without looking at your Bibles:* Why did Baruch go to the temple and read aloud the words of Jeremiah's prophecies, rather than Jeremiah himself? (See verses 5-6.)

JEREMIAH 37

Startup: What images come to mind first when you think of the word *suffering?*

SEEING WHAT'S THERE

1. How would you summarize the crisis Jeremiah faces in this chapter? What is most needed from him at this time?

2. EYE FOR DETAIL— *From what you recall seeing in chapter 37, try answering the following question without looking at your Bibles:* Why did the Babylonian army withdraw from its siege of Jerusalem at this time? (See verse 5.)

JEREMIAH 38

SEEING WHAT'S THERE

1. What are the most important decisions and choices that are made in this chapter, and how would you analyze each one?

2. EYE FOR DETAIL— *From what you recall seeing in chapter 38, try answering the following question without looking at your Bibles:* After Jeremiah was pulled out of the muddy cistern, where was he taken? (See verse 13.)

FOR GOING DEEPER

In chapters 37 and 38, look carefully at the course King Zedekiah followed in his treatment of the prophet Jeremiah. What portrait emerges of Judah's last monarch? How well would you say James 1:5-8 serves as an epitaph for this man?

JEREMIAH 39

Startup: When you get to heaven, and you meet Jeremiah, what's the first question you'd like to ask him?

SEEING WHAT'S THERE

1. How would you summarize the political and military developments in this chapter?

2. In the final verses of this chapter, what promise does God extend to the man who pulled Jeremiah out of the cistern in chapter 38?

FOR GOING DEEPER

Details of King Zedekiah's fate, recorded in verses 1-7, were prophesied by Ezekiel to captive Jews in faraway Babylon. What additional insights about this historical event do you learn as you consider Ezekiel 12:1-14?

JEREMIAH 40

SEEING WHAT'S THERE

1. In this chapter, what are the most important developments in the stories of Jeremiah and Judah?

JEREMIAH 41

SEEING WHAT'S THERE

1. To review, retrace your way through the last few chapters. What has happened since Jeremiah was placed in prison?

2. What further developments occur in this chapter?

JEREMIAH 42

SEEING WHAT'S THERE

1. How would you summarize the promises and warnings God gives in this chapter to the people remaining in Judah?

JEREMIAH 43

SEEING WHAT'S THERE

1. What are the most important decisions and choices that are made in this chapter, and how would you analyze each one?

JEREMIAH 44

Startup: What do you see as the most important decision you'll be making in the next month?

SEEING WHAT'S THERE

1. From what you see in this chapter, how would you evaluate the spiritual health of the Jews now living in Egypt with Jeremiah?

FOR GOING DEEPER

In light of what you see happening in verses 2-6, what deeper significance do you find in Deuteronomy 13:6-11?

JEREMIAH 45

SEEING WHAT'S THERE

1. How would you explain the answer God gives to Baruch's complaint in this chapter?

FOR LIFE TODAY

2. Look at the question at the beginning of verse 5. If God asked you this question today, how would you answer?

JEREMIAH 46

Startup: What do you expect to be your greatest opportunities in the coming year? And how do you think you can best prepare for them?

SEEING WHAT'S THERE

1. Remember again in each chapter in this book to discuss what to you are the most powerful images presented through Jeremiah's words.

2. As you read this chapter, what would you say is the brightest promise here? The most urgent command? The most powerful vision of a future day? The most painful accusation? And the sharpest picture of punishment and disaster?

JEREMIAH 47

SEEING WHAT'S THERE

1. As you study Jeremiah's words here, what would you say is the most powerful vision of a future day in this chapter? And the sharpest picture of punishment and disaster?

JEREMIAH 48

SEEING WHAT'S THERE

1. As you reflect on Jeremiah's message for God's people in this chapter, what would you say is the brightest promise it contains? The most fearful warning? The most urgent command? The most powerful vision of a future day? The most painful accusation? And the sharpest picture of punishment and disaster?

FOR GOING DEEPER

As you consider the lament of the Lord for Moab in verses 31-32 and 36, what additional glimpses into God's heart and character do you gain from Ezekiel 18:32, Lamentations 3:33, and 2 Peter 3:9?

JEREMIAH 49

SEEING WHAT'S THERE

1. As you ponder Jeremiah's words in this chapter, what would you say is the brightest promise here? The most urgent command? The most powerful vision of a future day? The most painful accusation? And the sharpest picture of punishment and disaster?

JEREMIAH 50

Startup: What images come to your mind first when you think of *Babylon*?

SEEING WHAT'S THERE

1. As you think about Jeremiah's prophecy in this chapter, what would you say is the brightest promise here? The most urgent command? The most powerful vision of a future day? The most painful accusation? And the sharpest picture of punishment and disaster?

CAPTURE THE ESSENCE

2. What aspects of God's character and personality would you say He wants us to understand most from verse 19?

JEREMIAH 51

SEEING WHAT'S THERE

1. As you reflect on this chapter, what would you say is the most urgent command it expresses? The most powerful vision of a future day? The most painful accusation? The sharpest picture of punishment and disaster? And the deepest glimpse into God's character?

CAPTURE THE ESSENCE

2. Restate in your own words what you believe are the most important truths revealed about God's character and personality in verses 15-19.

JEREMIAH 52

SEEING WHAT'S THERE

1. How would you summarize the events surrounding the final fall of Jerusalem to Nebuchadnezzar?

FOR LIFE TODAY

2. Think back on all that has happened to the people of Israel in the book of Jeremiah. If it's true that *the past is a lesson for the future,* then what would you say are the most important lessons for God's people today to learn from these events?

FOR GOING DEEPER

Review Jeremiah's description of the temple's destruction in verses 12-23. Compare this judgment with God's warning in 1 Kings 9:1-9 to King Solomon, hundreds of years before, when the "paint was still wet" on the new temple.

JEREMIAH:
THE BIG PICTURE

(Discuss again the questions in the "Overview," plus the questions below.)

1. For getting the most from the book of Jeremiah, one of the best guidelines is found in 2 Timothy 3:16-17, words which Paul wrote with the Old Testament first in view. He said that *all* Scripture is of great benefit to (a) teach us, (b) rebuke us, (c) correct us, and (d) train us in righteousness. Paul added that these Scriptures completely equip the person of God "for every good work." As you think seriously about those guidelines, in which of these areas do you especially see the usefulness of Jeremiah?

2. Imagine that you were helping to produce a film based on the life and ministry of the prophet Jeremiah. Describe the kinds of scenery, supporting characters, background music, lighting effects, etc., which you would use to help portray the central message of his book.

3. Look together at each of these passages, and discuss which one you believe is the best candidate for "KEY VERSE" in the book of Jeremiah — the one which brings into sharpest focus what this book is most about: 2:19, 7:23-24, or 8:11-12.

4. SEARCH FOR THE SAVIOR — What words, images, or themes in Jeremiah have reminded you most of Jesus?

5. If Jeremiah were the only book in the Old Testament, in what ways would it still make a good introduction to the message of Jesus in the New Testament?

6. Based especially on your own experience, complete this statement in the way that's most meaningful to you: I believe it's important for Christians to read and explore the book of Jeremiah because...

Lamentations

OVERVIEW

(Discuss these OVERVIEW questions both at the beginning of your study of Lamentations, then again after you've studied all five chapters. Your answers may change significantly once you've looked more closely at the entire book.)

Startup: Talk together about this question: What have you learned about how to help and comfort someone who is experiencing profound grief?

SEEING WHAT'S THERE

1. Before launching into a closer look at Lamentations, how would you summarize what you already know about this book?

2. Find the theme that reoccurs in the following verses—1:2, 1:6, 2:18, and 3:48. What clues would you say this offers about the central message of Lamentations?

3. Look also at the list of "Questions to Ask as You Begin Your Study of Each Book" on page 9.

FOR LIFE TODAY

4. The book of Lamentations has been titled "The Book of Tears" and "A Funeral Dirge over Jerusalem's Desolation." With that reputation for this book, what kinds of answers and guidelines and solutions would you like to gain as you examine it more closely?

5. As you think first about *who God is,* and second about *what the Bible is,* how strongly would you rate your present desire to understand better the book of Lamentations? Use a scale of one to ten (one = "no desire at all," ten = "extremely intense desire") to help you decide.

6. From what you see in 3:24, what would be a good personal prayer to offer to God as you study this book?

LAMENTATIONS 1

SEEING WHAT'S THERE

1. Listen carefully to the words cried out in this chapter. What exactly has happened? What has been lost, and why? What requests are made to God? What observations are made about Him? What confession is expressed?

2. Look also on page 8 at the list of "Questions to Ask as You Study Each Chapter." You may want to look again at this list for each chapter in Lamentations.

FOR LIFE TODAY

3. Proverbs 2:1-5 tells about the sincere person who truly longs for wisdom and understanding, and who searches the Scriptures for it—as if it were buried treasure. That person, Solomon says, will come to understand the fear of the Lord, and discover the knowledge of God. As you begin exploring the book of Lamentations, what "buried treasure" would you like God to help you find here—to show you what God and His wisdom are really like? If you have this desire, how would you express it in your own words?

LAMENTATIONS 2

SEEING WHAT'S THERE

1. What cries come forth from the author in this chapter? What does he say that God has done? How does he view God? What suffering is occurring? What is Jerusalem now like?

LAMENTATIONS 3

SEEING WHAT'S THERE

1. In this chapter, how does the author continue to express his grief? What does he say God has done to him? What hope and faith does he express? How is God's love described? What does the writer say the people of Jerusalem must do now? What requests are made to God, and why?

2. What evidence for heartfelt repentance do you see in this chapter?

CAPTURE THE ESSENCE

3. From what you see in verses 19-26, what are the most important things God wants us to understand about *hope?* How would you use this passage to help you define what hope truly is, from the Bible's point of view?

4. Imagine yourself being present in the temple in Jerusalem as the twelve-year-old Jesus hears this chapter read and discussed by the rabbis there. In Luke 2:46 we read that He was listening to these teachers and asking them questions. What verses from this chapter do you think would most impress the boy Jesus, and what questions or comments do you suppose He might have spoken?

FOR LIFE TODAY

5. Look again at verses 21-27, and verse 40. What principles and guidelines do these verses offer us today for dealing with grief and loss?

6. In Romans 15:4, Paul reminds us that the Old Testament Scriptures can give us patience and perseverance on one hand, as well as comfort and encouragement on the other. In your own life, how do you see this book of Lamentations living up to Paul's description? In what ways, if any, is it meeting your personal needs for both *perseverance* and *encouragement?*

FOR GOING DEEPER

Consider Jeremiah's dramatic word picture of a nation sinking into sin and judgment in verses 55-60. Now, in Jeremiah 38:6-13, review the real-life situation that may have inspired the prophet's illustration.

LAMENTATIONS 4

SEEING WHAT'S THERE

1. How is Jerusalem described? How extensive and how deep is her suffering?

FOR LIFE TODAY

2. In Isaiah 55:10-11, God reminds us that He sends rain and snow from the sky to water the earth and to nurture life. In the same way, God says that He sends His words to accomplish specific purposes. From your study so far, what would you suggest are *God's* primary purposes for the book of Lamentations in the lives of Christians today?

LAMENTATIONS 5

SEEING WHAT'S THERE

1. What requests are made to God? How is Jerusalem's suffering further described? What questions are asked to God?

2. What evidence for heartfelt repentance do you see in this chapter?

FOR LIFE TODAY

3. Look again at verse 15. When joy is gone from your life, how similar are your own emotions and thoughts to what is expressed in Lamentations? What principles do you see in this book for enduring the time of sadness?

LAMENTATIONS:
THE BIG PICTURE

(Discuss again the questions in the "Overview," plus the questions below.)

1. For getting the most from the book of Lamentations, one of the best guidelines is found in 2 Timothy 3:16-17, words which Paul wrote with the Old Testament first in view. He said that *all* Scripture is of great benefit to (a) teach us, (b) rebuke us, (c) correct us, and (d) train us in righteousness. Paul added that these Scriptures completely equip the person of God "for every good work." As you think seriously about those guidelines, in which of these areas do you especially see the usefulness of Lamentations?

2. Look together at each of these passages, and discuss which one you believe is the best candidate for "KEY VERSE" in the book of Lamentations—the one which brings into sharpest focus what this book is most about: 1:1, 2:5-6, 2:11, or 3:22-23.

3. SEARCH FOR THE SAVIOR—What words, images, or themes in Lamentations have reminded you most of Jesus?

4. Based especially on your own experience, complete this statement in the way that's most meaningful to you: I believe it's important for Christians to read and explore the book of Lamentations because...

5. If Lamentations were the only book in the Old Testament, in what ways would it still make a good introduction to the message of Jesus in the New Testament?

Ezekiel

OVERVIEW

(Discuss these OVERVIEW questions both at the beginning of your study of Ezekiel, then again after you've studied all 48 chapters. Your answers may change significantly once you've looked more closely at the entire book.)

Startup: Talk together about people you've known who especially impressed you as being unafraid to speak up at any time as a witness for Jesus Christ.

SEEING WHAT'S THERE

1. Before launching into a closer look at Ezekiel, how would you summarize what you already know about this book?

2. Find the most prominent phrase that re-occurs in the following verses—6:13-14, 7:9, 12:15-16, 12:20, 20:25-26, 20:41-44, 36:37-38, and 37:13-14. What does this phrase show about God's *purpose* for His people? And how do these passages indicate that God will accomplish this purpose?

3. Look also at the list of "Questions to Ask as You Begin Your Study of Each Book" on page 9.

FOR LIFE TODAY

4. The book of Ezekiel has been titled "The Book of Glory Lost and Regained," "God's Message to the Captives," "Future Restoration of Israel and the Land," and "The Role of Divine Discipline." With that reputation for this book, what kinds of answers and guidelines and solutions would you like to gain as you examine it more closely?

5. When you get to heaven, if you have a long talk with Ezekiel and he asks you, "What was most helpful to you in my book?" how would you like to be able to answer him?

6. As you think first about *who God is,* and second about *what the Bible is,* how strongly would you rate your present desire to understand better the book of Ezekiel? Use a scale of one to ten (one = "no desire at all," ten = "extremely intense desire") to help you decide.

7. From what you see in God's promise to His people in 11:19-20, what would be a good personal prayer to offer to God as you study this book?

EZEKIEL 1

SEEING WHAT'S THERE

1. As you explore this chapter, imagine that you are Ezekiel, and God is "invading" your world with these visions. How would this experience affect you? What would these visions mean to you?

2. Look also on page 8 at the list of "Questions to Ask as You Study Each Chapter." You may want to look again at this list for each chapter in Ezekiel.

CAPTURE THE ESSENCE

3. From what happens in this chapter, what things would you say were most important for Ezekiel to understand about God? How might these visions change or deepen his view God?

FOR LIFE TODAY

4. Proverbs 2:1-5 tells about the sincere person who truly longs for wisdom and understanding, and who searches the Scriptures for it—as if it were buried treasure. That person, Solomon says, will come to understand the fear of the Lord, and discover the knowledge of God. As you begin exploring the book of Ezekiel, what "buried treasure" would you like God to help you find here—to show you what God and His wisdom are really like? If you have this desire, how would you express it in your own words?

FOR GOING DEEPER

Compare Ezekiel's remarkable vision in verses 4-14 with that of the apostle John in Revelation 4. What similarities do you see in these visions, separated by hundreds of years?

EZEKIEL 2

SEEING WHAT'S THERE

1. What is Ezekiel's mission assignment? And how difficult does it appear to be?

EZEKIEL 3

SEEING WHAT'S THERE

1. What will God do for Ezekiel to equip him for his task? Where did God's Spirit take Ezekiel? What specific words of warning does God give? And what does God tell Ezekiel to do?

CAPTURE THE ESSENCE

2. From what happens in chapters 2—3, what things would you say were most important for Ezekiel to understand about God? And what things were most important for Ezekiel to understand about himself?

FOR LIFE TODAY

3. If God had written this chapter only for you, which words or phrases do you think He might have underlined, and why?

EZEKIEL 4

CAPTURE THE ESSENCE

1. How would you summarize the meaning of what Ezekiel is asked to do in this chapter, as well as in chapter 5?

EZEKIEL 5

SEEING WHAT'S THERE

1. What words of judgment does God pronounce against His people? What is His plan and purpose for them?

Ezekiel 6

SEEING WHAT'S THERE

1. What are the *reasons* for God's wrath and judgment? How is God's heart involved? What does He want His people to remember?

FOR LIFE TODAY

2. Consider how strongly you desire to know God better, then ask yourself this question: *What truths are revealed in this chapter about what it means to know God? And what do these principles mean for me personally?*

Ezekiel 7

SEEING WHAT'S THERE

1. What are the tragic words sounding forth from God in this chapter? What does God want His people to understand now?

Ezekiel 8

SEEING WHAT'S THERE

1. How does God show His power and control in Ezekiel's life—and in Israel's life? Where does Ezekiel go, and what does God let him see? Why is God angry?

Ezekiel 9

SEEING WHAT'S THERE

1. How does the punishment begin? How does Ezekiel respond when he sees the killing, and how does God answer him?

Ezekiel 10

SEEING WHAT'S THERE

1. What happens now to God's glory? What does Ezekiel see once more?

Ezekiel 11

SEEING WHAT'S THERE

1. What encounter does God place Ezekiel in? And what words of judgment and insight does He give Ezekiel to say? Ezekiel is terrified by something he sees—but how does God answer the prophet's agonized question? What startling promise does God make known?

CAPTURE THE ESSENCE

2. How would you answer this question: In the way we live our lives before God, should we count more on God's grace, or more on His holiness?

FOR LIFE TODAY

3. Look again at the gifts God promises in verse 19. Have you received these gifts? And is verse 20 a reflection of you at this time in your life?

FOR GOING DEEPER

As you think about the Lord's promise in verses 16-17, what additional insight do you gain from linking this passage with Jeremiah 24:1-7?

Ezekiel 12

SEEING WHAT'S THERE

1. What does God tell Ezekiel to do? And what do the prophet's actions symbolize?

CAPTURE THE ESSENCE

2. In this chapter, what would you say God wants us to understand most about His purpose and plan for His people?

EZEKIEL 13

SEEING WHAT'S THERE

1. What is God's judgment upon the false prophets? What does God say about the terrible damage they have done? What commitment does God make to His people?

EZEKIEL 14

SEEING WHAT'S THERE

1. How will God deal with those who set up idols in their hearts? And what will God do to the nation that disobeys Him? What does God say about Noah, Daniel, and Job?

FOR LIFE TODAY

2. Look again at verse 3. What idols today are demanding to be set up in our hearts?

EZEKIEL 15

SEEING WHAT'S THERE

1. How will God be like fire to people who have already been burned?

EZEKIEL 16

SEEING WHAT'S THERE

1. What is the tragic story God tells to reveal His heart? What does it reveal also about His people?

CAPTURE THE ESSENCE

2. What does this chapter reveal especially about God's *motives* and *purposes* in the way He deals with His people?

EZEKIEL 17

SEEING WHAT'S THERE

1. Another story is told. What does it reveal about double unfaithfulness?

EZEKIEL 18

SEEING WHAT'S THERE

1. What does God claim ownership of? Is the guilt of a father shared by his son? Does a righteous father guarantee a righteous son? Who is to live and who is to die? Is God unfair?

CAPTURE THE ESSENCE

2. In your own words, what are the most significant truths this chapter reveals about *God,* and what are the most significant truths it reveals about *us?*

EZEKIEL 19

SEEING WHAT'S THERE

1. Why does God grieve for the princes of Israel?

FOR LIFE TODAY

2. In Isaiah 55:10-11, God reminds us that He sends rain and snow from the sky to water the earth and to nurture life. In the same way, God says that He sends His words to accomplish specific purposes. From your study so far, what would you suggest are *God's* primary purposes for the book of Ezekiel in the lives of Christians today?

EZEKIEL 20

SEEING WHAT'S THERE

1. What does the long story of Israel's rebellion look like from God's point of view? What are God's purpose and plan for these people? What promises does God make to them, and what are His reasons for those promises?

FOR LIFE TODAY

2. Consider again how strongly you desire to know God better, then ask yourself this question: *What truths are revealed in this chapter about what it means to know God? And what do these principles mean for me personally?*

EZEKIEL 21

SEEING WHAT'S THERE

1. What destiny has God appointed for Babylon?

EZEKIEL 22

SEEING WHAT'S THERE

1. What punishment will there be for a city of bloodshed? What punishment will there be for princes who shed blood? Who will be thrown into the furnace of God's wrath? What did God look for first before pouring out His wrath?

FOR LIFE TODAY

2. Look in verse 30. Are there situations where God is still looking for such a person as the one described there? If so, could *you* be that person?

FOR GOING DEEPER

In verse 23, the Lord instructs Ezekiel to prophesy against Israel's apathetic, reckless priests. Review Malachi 1:6—2:9, then answer this question: Did the priests who served *after* the exile—back in Jerusalem in a rebuilt temple—fulfill their responsibilities any better?

EZEKIEL 23

SEEING WHAT'S THERE

1. Who are the two prostitutes in this chapter, and what is their story?

CAPTURE THE ESSENCE

2. How does this chapter help us understand what God most desires from His people?

EZEKIEL 24

SEEING WHAT'S THERE

1. What is the cooking pot, and what will go into it? Ezekiel's wife dies, but why is Ezekiel not permitted to mourn for her?

CAPTURE THE ESSENCE

2. Now that you're halfway through Ezekiel, how would you summarize the most important teachings in this book?

EZEKIEL 25

SEEING WHAT'S THERE

1. What specific words of judgment does God have against Israel's enemies?

FOR GOING DEEPER

For a deeper understanding of the judgment against these blood brothers of the Jews (verses 12-14), trace the Edomites' hostility through the following Scriptures: Numbers 20:14-21, 1 Samuel 14:47, 2 Samuel 8:13-14, 1 Kings 11:14-22, 2 Kings 8:20-22, 2 Chronicles 28:16-17, Jeremiah 49:7-22, Amos 1:11-12, and the book of Obadiah.

EZEKIEL 26

SEEING WHAT'S THERE

1. What is God's special word of judgment against Tyre? Why is Tyre singled out for this?

EZEKIEL 27

SEEING WHAT'S THERE

1. What was Tyre's glory? And now, what is Tyre's shame?

EZEKIEL 28

SEEING WHAT'S THERE

1. How does God confront the pride and corruption of the king of Tyre? And what are God's promises to Israel?

EZEKIEL 29

SEEING WHAT'S THERE

1. Why is God against Pharaoh and Egypt? What will God do to them? Who does the Nile belong to—God, or Pharaoh?

EZEKIEL 30

SEEING WHAT'S THERE

1. Why does God ask for wailing and mourning for Egypt? And who breaks Pharaoh's arms?

EZEKIEL 31

SEEING WHAT'S THERE

1. What is the meaning of this story of a cedar tree?

EZEKIEL 32

SEEING WHAT'S THERE

1. How is Pharaoh like a monster? And how will he be caught and broken?

EZEKIEL 33

SEEING WHAT'S THERE

1. How is Ezekiel a watchman? What warning is he now to give? Jerusalem has fallen—but what further disaster is coming?

FOR LIFE TODAY

2. In Romans 15:4, Paul reminds us that the Old Testament Scriptures can give us patience and perseverance on one hand, as well as comfort and encouragement on the other. In your own life, how do you see this book of Ezekiel living up to Paul's description? In what ways, if any, is it meeting your personal needs for both *perseverance* and *encouragement?*

FOR GOING DEEPER

Ezekiel's prophesies were apparently entertaining (consider again verses 30-33), but the Lord wanted to see changed lives and hearts. What do Luke 6:46-49 and James 1:22-25 contribute to your understanding of these verses?

EZEKIEL 34

SEEING WHAT'S THERE

1. What does God say about shepherds and sheep? What must a good shepherd do? What will happen to shepherds who care only for themselves? What are God's promises to the sheep?

CAPTURE THE ESSENCE

2. What does God most want us to understand about Himself in this chapter?

3. Imagine yourself being present in the temple in Jerusalem as the twelve-year-old Jesus hears this chapter read and discussed by the rabbis there. In Luke 2:46 we read that He was listening to these teachers and asking them questions. What verses from this chapter do you think would most impress the boy Jesus, and what questions or comments do you suppose He might have spoken?

FOR LIFE TODAY

4. Review these guidelines for our thought-life in Philippians 4:8—"Whatever is true, whatever is noble, whatever is right, whatever is pure, whatever is lovely, whatever is admirable—if anything is excellent or praiseworthy—*think about such things.*" What food for thought can you find in this chapter that especially strikes you as being *true,* or *noble,* or *right,* or *pure,* or *lovely,* or *admirable,* or *excellent,* or *praiseworthy?*

5. What do you think are the best ways for applying the principles of this chapter to leadership in your church? Which concepts in this chapter should the leaders of a church understand most?

FOR GOING DEEPER

Review verses 23-31, then look together at Matthew 14:13-21. To what degree could you say that Ezekiel's prophecy finds fulfillment in this gospel passage?

EZEKIEL 35

SEEING WHAT'S THERE

1. What is God's word of judgment upon Mount Seir and Edom?

EZEKIEL 36

SEEING WHAT'S THERE

1. What does God say to the mountains of Israel? What promises does God give for their future?

2. What exactly is God's concern for His *name?* And how does that concern translate into promises for Israel?

3. What new gift will God give to the people of Israel? What will this gift accomplish?

CAPTURE THE ESSENCE

4. In this chapter, what does God want us to understand most about His purpose and plan for His people?

FOR GOING DEEPER

Compare what you see in verses 26-27 with Ezekiel 11:19-20 and Jeremiah 31:27-28. How are these passages most alike, and how are they different?

EZEKIEL 37

SEEING WHAT'S THERE

1. Chapter 37 has been called the key to the book of Ezekiel. What does this chapter include that could make it this significant?

2. What is the valley of dry bones, and what happens there? What does that mean for God's people? What further promises does God make to them?

CAPTURE THE ESSENCE

3. In this chapter, what does God want us to understand most about His purpose and plan for His people?

FOR LIFE TODAY

4. Look at the covenant described in verse 26? Are you a partner in that covenant? What do you know of God's peace?

EZEKIEL 38

SEEING WHAT'S THERE

1. Who invades Israel in this chapter? While Israel is dwelling in safety, what massive invader comes like a cloud to plunder and loot? When God's anger is aroused, what happens?

EZEKIEL 39

SEEING WHAT'S THERE

1. What will God do to this invader, and for what purpose? What will God do for the sake of His name? What will be God's message to every bird and wild animal? What will all this mean for Israel? What will God do for His people?

CAPTURE THE ESSENCE

2. In this chapter, what does God want us to understand most about His purpose and plan for His people?

FOR LIFE TODAY

3. In Jeremiah 23:29, God says that His Word is like fire, and like a hammer. He can use the Scriptures to burn away unclean thoughts and desires in our hearts. He can also use Scripture to hit hard like a hammer, with the power to crush our spiritual hardness. From your study in this book of Ezekiel, how do you most want to see the "fire-and-hammer" power of God's Word at work in your own life?

EZEKIEL 40

SEEING WHAT'S THERE

1. Where does God take Ezekiel now, and what does the prophet see and hear? What details does he see of the new temple, beginning at the east gate?

EZEKIEL 41

SEEING WHAT'S THERE

1. What details does Ezekiel see of the temple's outer sanctuary, and the Most Holy Place within?

FOR GOING DEEPER

Look again in verses 3-4 at the description of the innermost room in the temple. Explore together how this same inner room was configured and furnished in the tabernacle built by Moses—in Exodus 26:33-34—and in the temple of Solomon—in 1 Kings 6:16, 6:23-28, 8:6-9, and Hebrews 9:3-5. For both the tabernacle and Solomon's temple, tell what differences you see from the description of the inner room here in Ezekiel's temple.

This inner room was also included in the temple which Herod built in Jerusalem, and which was there at the time of Jesus' ministry. Look at Matthew 27:50-51 to see what happened to the curtain that separated the Most Holy Place in this temple.

Finally, review Hebrews 9:3-9 and 10:19-22 to see how God's people today are to view this innermost room in God's dwelling place.

EZEKIEL 42

SEEING WHAT'S THERE

1. What details does Ezekiel see of the rooms for priests in the temple?

EZEKIEL 43

SEEING WHAT'S THERE

1. What does Ezekiel see and hear when the glory of God came to the temple? What details does Ezekiel see of the altar?

FOR GOING DEEPER

The foundational law for God's temple was *holiness*. As you ponder verses 10-12, what additional insights do you gain from Leviticus 19:1-2 and 1 Peter 1:15-16?

EZEKIEL 44

SEEING WHAT'S THERE

1. Ezekiel sees the glory of God filling the temple, and falls face down. What does God then tell him about those who will work in the temple?

CAPTURE THE ESSENCE

2. Since this temple shown to Ezekiel has never been built on earth, what do you think it represents? Is it earthly, or heavenly?

EZEKIEL 45

SEEING WHAT'S THERE

1. How is the new land of Israel divided? And what are the new offerings and feast days?

EZEKIEL 46

SEEING WHAT'S THERE

1. What will be the duties of the prince?

EZEKIEL 47

SEEING WHAT'S THERE

1. What is the new river like that flows beside the temple?

FOR GOING DEEPER

What similarities do you see in the beautiful rivers described in verses 1-12, Genesis 2:10, and Revelation 22:1-2? What might these waters symbolize?

EZEKIEL 48

SEEING WHAT'S THERE

1. How will the tribes of God's people be arranged in the new land? What will the gates of the new city be like, and what will the new city's name be?

EZEKIEL:
THE BIG PICTURE

(Discuss again the questions in the "Overview," plus the questions below.)

1. For getting the most from the book of Ezekiel, one of the best guidelines is found in 2 Timothy 3:16-17, words which Paul wrote with the Old Testament first in view. He said that *all* Scripture is of great benefit to (a) teach us, (b) rebuke us, (c) correct us, and (d) train us in righteousness. Paul added that these Scriptures completely equip the person of God "for every good work." As you think seriously about those guidelines, in which of these areas do you especially see the usefulness of Ezekiel?

2. Imagine that you were helping to produce a film based on the book of Ezekiel. Describe the kinds of scenery, supporting characters, background music, lighting effects, etc., which you would use to help portray the central message of this book.

3. Look together at each of these passages, and discuss which one you believe is the best candidate for "KEY VERSE" in the book of Ezekiel—the one which brings into sharpest focus what this book is most about: 1:1, 36:24-26, 36:33-35, or 37:14.

4. SEARCH FOR THE SAVIOR—What words, images, or themes in Ezekiel have reminded you most of Jesus?

5. If Ezekiel were the only book in the Old Testament, in what ways would it still make a good introduction to the message of Jesus in the New Testament?

6. Based especially on your own experience, complete this statement in the way that's most meaningful to you: I believe it's important for Christians to read and explore the book of Ezekiel because...

Daniel

OVERVIEW

(Discuss these OVERVIEW questions both at the beginning of your study of Daniel, then again after you've studied all twelve chapters. Your answers may change significantly once you've looked more closely at the entire book.)

Startup: Talk together about any experiences in which you especially felt like "a stranger in a strange land."

SEEING WHAT'S THERE

1. Before launching into a closer look at Daniel, how would you summarize what you already know about this book?

2. What simple description does Jesus give of Daniel in Matthew 24:15?

3. Bible teachers usually divide this book into two main parts. As you look over Daniel, where would you place the dividing point between the two major parts?

4. Look also at the list of "Questions to Ask as You Begin Your Study of Each Book" on page 9.

CAPTURE THE ESSENCE

5. Find the most prominent theme that reoccurs in the following verses—2:39-40, 2:44, 4:3, 4:34, 6:26, 7:14, and 7:27. From the way you see this truth presented in these passages, what would you say God wants us to understand most about it?

6. Notice what is said about Daniel by a messenger from God in 9:23, 10:11, and 10:19. Look also at the view of Daniel given in 5:12. If you knew Daniel while he was on earth, what do you think would most impress you about him?

FOR LIFE TODAY

7. The book of Daniel has been titled "The Book of Loyalty and Light," "The Book of God's Sovereignty," "The Key to All Biblical Prophecy," and "The Times of the Gentiles and Israel's Kingdom." The book has been described as "a battlefield between faith and unbelief," while Daniel himself has been called "A Man of Adventure" and "The Prophet Greatly Beloved." With that reputation for this book, what kinds of answers and guidelines and solutions would you like to gain as you examine it more closely?

8. From the example you see in Daniel's prayer in 2:19-23, what would be a good personal prayer to offer to God as you study this book?

9. As you think first about *who God is,* and second about *what the Bible is,* how strongly would you rate your present desire to understand better the book of Daniel? Use a scale of one to ten (one = "no desire at all," ten = "extremely intense desire") to help you decide.

10. When you get to heaven, if you have a long talk with Daniel and he asks you, "What was most helpful to you in my book?" how would you like to answer him?

DANIEL 1

Startup: What would you say are the most important *testings* which you have experienced—times when you knew others were watching to see whether you would succeed or fail?

SEEING WHAT'S THERE

1. Notice the historical facts mentioned in verses 1-2. What helpful background to these events do you find in 2 Kings 24 and 25, and Jeremiah 39?

2. What are the most important decisions and *choices* that are made in this chapter, and how would you analyze each one?

3. What would you say God wants us to understand most in this chapter about the character of Daniel and his three fellow Hebrews?

4. What is the best evidence you see in this chapter of God's sovereign power?

5. Which important details in this chapter do you think might be the easiest to overlook?

6. Look also on page 8 at the list of "Questions to Ask as You Study Each Chapter." You may want to look again at this list for each chapter in Daniel.

CAPTURE THE ESSENCE

7. How would you describe the character qualities of Daniel that are revealed in verses 8-13?

8. What would you say is Daniel's strongest motive in this chapter?

9. From what you see in this chapter, how do you think Daniel and his three friends would answer this question: What important challenges do you think you're going to face in the near future?

FOR LIFE TODAY

10. If God had written this chapter only for *you,* which words or phrases do you think He might have underlined, and why?

11. If this chapter were the only portion of Scripture you had access to, how could you use it to help answer this question: *What is the most powerful and effective way to improve my life?*

12. Proverbs 2:1-5 tells about the sincere person who truly longs for wisdom and understanding, and who searches the Scriptures for it—as if it were buried treasure. That person, Solomon says, will come to understand the fear of the Lord, and discover the knowledge of God. As you begin exploring the book of Daniel, what "buried treasure" would you like God to help you find—to show you what God and His wisdom are really like? If you have this desire, how would you express it in your own words?

DANIEL 2

SEEING WHAT'S THERE

1. Chapter 2 has been called the key to the book of Daniel. What does this chapter include that could make it this significant?

2. What are the most important *choices* that are made in this chapter, and how would you analyze each one?

3. How much was correct and how much was incorrect in the answer given to King Nebuchadnezzar in verses 10-11?

4. What brief descriptions would you use to characterize King Nebuchadnezzar, as you see him portrayed in this chapter?

5. Summarize in your own words the events that happened in Nebuchadnezzar's dream.

6. As you read about Nebuchadnezzar's dream, what's the strongest impression or image which it leaves in your mind?

7. What is the best evidence you see in this chapter of God's sovereign power?

8. EYE FOR DETAIL— *From what you recall seeing in chapters 1 and 2, try answering the following question without looking in your Bible:* Shadrach, Meshach, and Abednego were given those names when they came to Babylon; what were their original Hebrew names? (See 1:6-7.)

CAPTURE THE ESSENCE

9. Take a "walk" together through the incidents that happen in this chapter: Using your imagination, talk about the kinds of sights, smells, sounds, and feelings you might experience.

10. How would you describe the character qualities of Daniel that are revealed in this chapter?

11. From what you see in Daniel's prayer in verses 19-23, what are the most important things he understands about God's personality and character?

12. From what you see in this chapter, how do you think Daniel would answer this question: If Satan wanted to disqualify you as God's servant right now, what might be his most effective way to do that?

13. Imagine yourself being present in the temple in Jerusalem as the twelve-year-old Jesus hears this chapter read and discussed by the rabbis there. In Luke 2:46 we read that He was listening to these teachers and asking them questions. What verses from this chapter do you think would most impress the boy Jesus, and what questions or comments do you suppose He might have spoken?

FOR LIFE TODAY

14. What lessons can you draw from this chapter that will be good to remember when you face something that seems impossible?

15. How could you use this chapter to teach a new Christian about the power of prayer?

FOR GOING DEEPER

Compare verse 44 with Daniel 7:27, 1 Corinthians 15:24, and Revelation 11:15. From what you see in these passages, what does God want us to understand most about His kingdom?

DANIEL 3

Startup: What's the *hottest* environment you've ever been in?

SEEING WHAT'S THERE

1. What *choices* are made in this chapter by Shadrach, Meshach, and Abednego?

2. Which important details in this chapter do you think might be the easiest to overlook?

3. What is the best evidence you see in this chapter of God's sovereign power?

CAPTURE THE ESSENCE

4. Imagine that you are one of King Nebuchadnezzar's advisers, and you are present throughout the events described in verses 8-30. Using your imagination, talk about the kinds of sights, smells, sounds, and feelings you might experience.

5. What spiritual laws and forces do you see at work in this chapter?

6. From what you see in this chapter, how do you think Shadrach, Meshach, and Abednego would answer this question: What would you say are your greatest fears at this present time?

7. If the three young Hebrew men had decided to go ahead and worship King Nebuchadnezzar's statue, what excuses might they easily have given for that decision?

8. From what you see in verses 16-18, what was the most important truth these three men understood about God's nature and character?

9. Discuss how much you agree or disagree with this statement: It's always wrong to serve God in order to get some benefit from God in return.

10. In this chapter, what instruction does the Lord give us about what *faith in God* really means?

FOR LIFE TODAY

11. From what you see in this chapter, discuss together how you would complete this sentence: *What God really wants from me is…*

12. In Romans 15:4, Paul reminds us that the Old Testament Scriptures can give us patience and perseverance on one hand, as well as comfort and encouragement on the other. In your own life, how do you see this book of Daniel living up to Paul's description? In what ways, if any, is it meeting your personal needs for both *perseverance* and *encouragement?*

FOR GOING DEEPER

Compare the actions of Shadrach, Meshach, and Abednego with the New Testament guideline given in James 1:2-4. How well does the example of these three men serve to illustrate the passage in James?

DANIEL 4

SEEING WHAT'S THERE

1. Since no historical account can include *every* detail of the events it describes, review the story of Nebuchadnezzar in this chapter and notice which details *are* included. Think also about which details seem to be left out. What does this selection process tell you about what God wants us to understand most from this story?

2. What brief descriptions would you use to characterize King Nebuchadnezzar, as you see him portrayed in this chapter?

3. What does verse 19 reveal about Daniel's character?

4. What is the best evidence you see in this chapter of God's sovereign power?

5. If Nebuchadnezzar was reading this chapter aloud to you right now, which word or phrase do you think he would emphasize most?

6. EYE FOR DETAIL— *From what you recall seeing in chapters 3 and 4, try answering the following question without looking in your Bible:* What were Shadrach, Meshach, and Abednego wearing when they were thrown into the fiery furnace? (See 3:21.)

CAPTURE THE ESSENCE

7. What would you say is the major point that God is making by including in the Bible this incident about Nebuchadnezzar?

8. What insights does this chapter offer about *pride,* and about how to deal with it?

9. From what you see in Nebuchadnezzar's words in verses 34-37, what are the most important things he understands about God's personality and character?

FOR LIFE TODAY

10. Analyze carefully this chapter to answer this question: How many things, if any, can you find in common between your experience and that of Nebuchadnezzar?

11. Discuss how much you agree or disagree with this statement: The more freedom and power we have in this world, the harder it is for us to understand and yield to God's sovereign control in our lives.

FOR GOING DEEPER

Compare Nebuchadnezzar's experience with that of the rich man Jesus spoke about in Luke 12:16-21. How were their stories alike, and how were they different? Would you say that the chief moral lesson is the same in both these passages?

DANIEL 5

Startup: What was the most surprising or unusual banquet or dinner party you've ever attended, and what made it different?

SEEING WHAT'S THERE

1. Imagine that you are one of King Belshazzar's nobles attending the great banquet described in this chapter. Using your imagination, talk about the kinds of sights, smells, sounds, and feelings you might experience.

2. Humanly speaking, what would you say is the best thing anybody does in this chapter?

3. What is the worst or most questionable thing anybody does in this chapter?

4. What brief descriptions would you use to characterize King Belshazzar, as you see him portrayed in this chapter?

5. Which important details in this chapter do you think might be the easiest to overlook?

6. What is the best evidence you see in this chapter of God's sovereign power?

CAPTURE THE ESSENCE

7. What are the most important *choices* that are made in this chapter, and how would you analyze each one?

8. What spiritual laws and forces do you see at work in this chapter?

9. Look again at verses 22-23. What could the king have done to truly humble himself, and escape this charge?

10. Why do you think God chose to communicate in the way He did in this chapter?

FOR LIFE TODAY

11. Consider how strongly you desire to know God better, then ask yourself this question: What are the truths revealed about Him in Daniel which He may want me to understand more deeply at this time in my life?

12. In Isaiah 55:10-11, God reminds us that He sends rain and snow from the sky to water the earth and to nurture life. In the same way, God says that He sends His words to accomplish specific purposes. From your study so far, what would you suggest are *God's* primary purposes for the book of Daniel in the lives of Christians today?

DANIEL 6

SEEING WHAT'S THERE

1. So far in this book, what evidence (if any) have you seen of anything which Daniel clearly did wrong?

2. What is the best evidence you see here in chapter 6 of God's sovereign power?

3. What brief descriptions would you use to characterize King Darius, as you see him portrayed in this chapter?

4. In verse 3, notice how Daniel impressed the king. From what you know of Daniel, what would you say were the specific qualities that brought Daniel this high regard?

5. EYE FOR DETAIL— *From what you recall seeing in chapters 5 and 6, try answering the following question without looking in your Bible:* What three things did King Belshazzar promise to do for Daniel if he could read and interpret the writing on the wall? (See 5:16.)

CAPTURE THE ESSENCE

6. How would you describe the character qualities of Daniel that are revealed in this chapter?

7. From what you see in this chapter, how do you think Daniel would answer this question: How is your relationship with God right now?

8. How do you think Daniel would answer this question: If Satan wanted to disqualify you as God's servant right now, what might be his most effective way to do that?

9. From what you see in the message of King Darius in verses 25-27, what are the most important things Darius understands about God's personality and character?

10. Now that you're halfway through Daniel, how would you summarize the most important teachings in this book?

FOR LIFE TODAY

11. How would you compare *your* faith with what you see of Daniel's faith in this chapter?

12. If it's true that "you *become* what you *think,*" then what are the most impor-tant thoughts from this chapter to plant firmly in your mind?

13. In what kind of circumstances in life might it be hardest for us to believe firmly in the truths about God which we are taught in verse 27?

14. What would you say are the most important lessons a new Christian could learn from this chapter about *prayer?*

15. In Philippians 4:8 we're given this command: "Whatever is true, whatever is noble, whatever is right, whatever is pure, whatever is lovely, whatever is admirable—if anything is excellent or praiseworthy—*think about such things.*" What food for thought can you find in this chapter that especially strikes you as being *true,* or *noble,* or *right,* or *pure,* or *lovely,* or *admirable,* or *excellent,* or *praise-worthy?*

FOR GOING DEEPER

In what ways has Daniel's experience been like that of Joseph in the book of Genesis?

DANIEL 7

Startup: What aspects of biblical prophecy are the most interesting to you?

SEEING WHAT'S THERE

1. After reading through this chapter, which words or phrases or sentences here do you feel are the most difficult to understand?

2. What is the best evidence you see in this chapter of God's sovereign power?

3. In Matthew 6:33, Jesus tells us to "seek first the kingdom of God and His righteousness." What can you learn about God's kingdom in this chapter, especially in verses 22 and 27?

4. In this chapter, God reveals some of His future plans to Daniel. What would you say were the most important things God wanted Daniel to understand about these plans?

CAPTURE THE ESSENCE

5. Look at the name given in verses 9, 13, and 22 to the One whom Daniel sees. What is *right* to you about this name?

6. From the description of the vision in verses 9-14, what would you say are the most important things God wanted to communicate about Himself to Daniel?

7. If you talked with Daniel right after the events of this chapter, and you asked him to define the word *vision,* how do you think he would answer?

8. Again, imagine yourself being present in the temple in Jerusalem as the twelve-year-old Jesus hears this chapter read and discussed by the Jewish teachers. What verses in this chapter do you think would most impress Him, and what questions or comments do you suppose He might have spoken?

9. The last half of the book of Daniel (chapters 7—12) is concerned primarily with Daniel's prophetic visions. Think back on what you learned about Daniel in the first six chapters of the book. What would you say are the most important lessons from those chapters to keep in mind as you launch into the prophecy chapters of Daniel, in order to see them in the right perspective?

FOR LIFE TODAY

10. *Why* would you say God wants *you personally* to know the things revealed in this chapter?

11. In light of how you're doing spiritually in your life today, which verse in this chapter do you think is the most important at this time—and why?

FOR GOING DEEPER

Notice carefully the descriptive phrases in verse 13. Then compare these to what you see in Matthew 24:30 and 26:64, and Revelation 1:7 and 1:18. By seeing these phrases used this way in the New Testament, what do you think the Lord Jesus wants us to understand most about Himself?

DANIEL 8

SEEING WHAT'S THERE

1. In your own words, how would you summarize the events that occur in Daniel's vision in verses 1-14?

2. After reading through this chapter, which words or phrases or sentences used here would you most like to understand better?

3. In this chapter again, God reveals some of His future plans to Daniel. From the evidence you see in chapter 8, what were the most important things God wanted Daniel to understand about these plans?

4. What is the best evidence you see in this chapter of God's sovereign power?

5. Read again verse 13, then look ahead at similar wording that occurs in 9:27, 11:31, and 12:11. Compare these with the words of Jesus in Matthew 24:15. What connection do you see in these passages?

6. EYE FOR DETAIL— *From what you recall seeing in chapters 7 and 8, try answering the following question without looking in your Bible:* What was the very first thing Daniel saw in his first vision described in chapter 7? (See 7:2.)

CAPTURE THE ESSENCE

7. If you were asked to give a character reference for Daniel, what would you say about him?

8. In what ways does Daniel's vision in this chapter relate to the dream recorded in chapter 7?

9. Notice again verse 27. What explanation would you offer for why Daniel was affected in this way by what he had seen?

10. Imagine that you were helping to produce a film based on the book of Daniel. Describe the kinds of scenery, supporting characters, background music, lighting effects, etc., which you would use to help portray the central message of this book.

FOR LIFE TODAY

11. In Psalm 119:105, the psalmist describes God's Word as "a lamp unto my feet, and a light unto my path." As you've explored this book of Daniel, what is the brightest light it offers you for your personal path in life? What are the truths in this book that are most relevant to you at this time?

FOR GOING DEEPER

Look again at Gabriel's visit to Daniel in verses 15-26. Then compare it to Gabriel's other appearances in Scripture—in Daniel 9:21-27, and in Luke 1:11-20 and 1:26-38. What similarities do you find in these appearances and announcements?

DANIEL 9

Startup: When you get to heaven, and you meet Daniel, what's the first question you'd like to ask him?

SEEING WHAT'S THERE

1. God continues in this chapter to reveal some of His future plans to Daniel. From the evidence in chapter 9, what were the most important things God wanted Daniel to understand about these plans?

2. What do we especially learn from verse 24 about God's plan and purpose for His people?

3. What does verse 20 reveal about Daniel's life and character?

4. After reading through this chapter, which words or phrases or sentences here would you most like to understand better?

CAPTURE THE ESSENCE

5. How do you see this chapter pointing to God's plan of redemption for His people through Jesus Christ?

6. What do you think is meant by the words "cut off" in verse 26?

7. From what you see in Daniel's prayer in verses 4-19, what are the most important things he understands about God's personality and character?

8. How would you describe the character qualities of Daniel that are revealed in this chapter?

9. Once more, what verses in this chapter do you think would most impress the 12-year-old Jesus as He heard it read and discussed in the Temple in Jerusalem, and what questions or comments do you suppose He might have spoken to the teachers there?

FOR LIFE TODAY

10. What would you say are the most important lessons a new Christian could learn from this chapter about *prayer?*

11. If you had only this chapter in Scripture to refer to, how would you use it to help show someone what the Bible teaches about *sin?*

12. In Jeremiah 23:29, God says that His Word is like fire, and like a hammer. He can use the Scriptures to burn away unclean thoughts and desires in our hearts. He can also use Scripture to hit hard like a hammer, with the power to crush our spiritual hardness. From your study in this book of Daniel, how do you most want to see the "fire-and-hammer" power of God's Word at work in your own life?

FOR GOING DEEPER

In what ways do you see the truth of verse 24 reflected in 2 Corinthians 5:21 and Hebrews 9:11-12?

DANIEL 10

SEEING WHAT'S THERE

1. In your own words, how would you summarize the events that occur in Daniel's vision in this chapter?

2. What commands does the messenger from heaven give to Daniel in this chapter?

3. As you read this chapter, what's the strongest impression or image which it leaves in your mind?

4. What in this chapter do you think might be most surprising to a new Christian reading it for the first time?

5. What do we learn from verse 12 about prayer?

6. EYE FOR DETAIL— *From what you recall seeing in chapters 9 and 10, try answering the following question without looking in your Bible:* Which book of prophecy in the Old Testament Scriptures did Daniel say he had been reading? (See 9:2.)

CAPTURE THE ESSENCE

7. From what you see in this chapter, how do you think Daniel would answer this question: How is your relationship with God right now?

FOR LIFE TODAY

8. Notice again how Daniel was ministered to in this chapter, especially in verses 18-19. How realistic is it for us to expect the Lord to minister to us in this way today?

DANIEL 11

Startup: In the way we read and study the Bible, what kind of old mental habits or faulty assumptions can most easily block this book of Daniel from coming alive in our minds and hearts?

SEEING WHAT'S THERE

1. In your own words, how would you summarize the events that occur in Daniel's vision in this chapter?

2. What is the best evidence you see in this chapter of God's sovereign power?

CAPTURE THE ESSENCE

3. God continues in this chapter to reveal some of His future plans to Daniel. From the evidence in chapter 11, what were the most important things God wanted Daniel to understand about these plans?

4. What are the most important lessons for God's people which you see in verses 32-35?

FOR LIFE TODAY

5. Look again at verses 32-35. If you faced great persecution, how confident are you that your faith and obedience would be strong?

DANIEL 12

SEEING WHAT'S THERE

1. As you read this chapter, what's the strongest impression or image which it leaves in your mind?

2. What in this chapter do you think might be most interesting to someone who was reading the Bible for the first time?

3. What important facts does verse 2 give us about life?

4. How would you explain to a young child the words spoken to Daniel in verse 3?

5. EYE FOR DETAIL— *From what you recall seeing in chapters 11 and 12, try answering the following question without looking in your Bible:* How is the angel Michael described in this book? (See 12:1.)

CAPTURE THE ESSENCE

6. How would you compare this book of Daniel with what you know about the book of Revelation? In what ways do they support and complement one another?

7. From what you've seen in this book, how do you think Daniel would answer this question: What three things are you most thankful for these days?

8. What evidence have you seen in this book that Daniel truly *loved* God?

9. From all that you've seen in Daniel, what conclusions can you make about the nature and ministry of angels?

FOR LIFE TODAY

10. If this was the last book of the Bible you read before you died, which verses from it would you most like to be lingering in your mind as you said goodbye to this earth?

FOR GOING DEEPER

With the words of verse 2 in mind, compare what is taught about eternity there with what you see in Matthew 25:46 and John 5:28-29. What are the fundamental truths that are taught in all these passages?

DANIEL:
THE BIG PICTURE

(Discuss again the questions in the "Overview," plus the questions below.)

1. For getting the most from the book of Daniel, one of the best guidelines is found in 2 Timothy 3:16-17, words which Paul wrote with the Old Testament first in view. He said that *all* Scripture is of great benefit to (a) teach us, (b) rebuke us, (c) correct us, and (d) train us in righteousness. Paul added that these Scriptures completely equip the person of God "for every good work." As you think seriously about those guidelines, in which of these areas do you especially see the usefulness of Daniel?

2. What evidence have you seen in this book of anything which Daniel clearly did wrong?

3. Look together at each of these passages, and discuss which one you believe is the best candidate for "KEY VERSE" in the book of Daniel—the one which brings into sharpest focus what this book is most about: 2:20-22, 2:44, 5:21, or 7:14.

4. What would you say is the main theme (or themes) in the book of Daniel?

5. SEARCH FOR THE SAVIOR—What words, images, or themes in Daniel have reminded you most of Jesus?

6. If Daniel were the only book in the Old Testament, in what ways would it still make a good introduction to the message of Jesus in the New Testament?

7. Based especially on your own experience, complete this statement in the way that's most meaningful to you: I believe it's important for Christians to read and explore the book of Daniel because…

8. If everyone in your church thoroughly understood this book, and they all had a passion for living out its truth in their lives, what kind of practical changes do you think would result?

Hosea

OVERVIEW

(Discuss these OVERVIEW questions both at the beginning of your study of Hosea, then again after you've studied all fourteen chapters. Your answers may change significantly once you've looked more closely at the entire book.)

Startup: Talk together about times in your life when you've been especially impressed by someone's persistent, unconditional love —either toward you, or toward someone else.

SEEING WHAT'S THERE

1. Before launching into a closer look at Hosea, how would you summarize what you already know about this book?

2. Find the most prominent word that re-occurs in the following verses—3:5, 6:1, 7:10, and 14:1. What clues could this word offer about the central message of Hosea?

3. Look also at the list of "Questions to Ask as You Begin Your Study of Each Book" on page 9.

FOR LIFE TODAY

4. The book of Hosea has been titled "The Backslider's Book," "Broken Heart and Broken Home," "God's Faithfulness," "The Love of God for His Erring People," and "The Lord Loves Israel Despite Her Sin." With that reputation for this book, what kinds of answers and guidelines and solutions would you like to gain as you examine it more closely?

5. When you get to heaven, if you have a long talk with Hosea and he asks you, "What was most helpful to you in my book?" how would you like to be able to answer him?

6. As you think first about *who God is,* and second about *what the Bible is,* how strongly would you rate your present de-sire to understand better the book of Hosea? Use a scale of one to ten (one = "no desire at all," ten = "extremely intense desire") to help you decide.

7. From what you see in the last verse in this book (14:9), what would be a good personal prayer to offer to God as you study this book?

HOSEA 1

SEEING WHAT'S THERE

1. What did Hosea do in this chapter, at the Lord's command?

2. What punishment does God announce in this chapter?

3. What promise does God give the people of Judah?

CAPTURE THE ESSENCE

4. How exactly were Hosea's actions a pic-ture of God's relationship with His peo-ple?

FOR LIFE TODAY

5. Proverbs 2:1-5 tells about the sincere person who truly longs for wisdom and understanding, and who searches the Scriptures for it—as if it were buried treasure. That person, Solomon says, will come to understand the fear of the Lord, and discover the knowledge of God. As you explore the book of Hosea, what "buried treasure" would you like God to help you find here—to show you what God and His wisdom are really like? If you have this desire, how would you ex-press it in your own words?

HOSEA 2

SEEING WHAT'S THERE

1. What would you say is the brightest promise in this chapter? The most tender encouragement? The most fearful warning? The most urgent command? The most powerful vision of a future day? The most painful accusation? The sharpest picture of punishment and disaster? And the deepest glimpse into God's character?

CAPTURE THE ESSENCE

2. What words or phrases in this chapter tell us the most about God's purpose and plan for His people?

3. What words or phrases in this chapter tell us the most about God's character?

HOSEA 3

SEEING WHAT'S THERE

1. Chapter 3 has been called the key to the book of Hosea. What does this chapter include that could make it this significant?

CAPTURE THE ESSENCE

2. From what you've seen so far in this book, how would you complete this statement: "I know God is a God of love because He…"

HOSEA 4

SEEING WHAT'S THERE

1. In your own words, what would you say is the most painful accusation in this chapter? And the sharpest picture of punishment and disaster?

FOR LIFE TODAY

2. In what ways, if any, would you say that the words of this chapter might accurately describe God's people today, especially those in your church?

HOSEA 5

SEEING WHAT'S THERE

1. As you explore these words to God's people, what would you say is the most fearful warning here? The most urgent command? The most powerful vision of a future day? The most painful accusation? And the sharpest picture of punishment and disaster?

CAPTURE THE ESSENCE

2. From what you see in this chapter, how would you complete this statement: "I know God is a God of love because He…"

HOSEA 6

SEEING WHAT'S THERE

1. In verses 1-3, notice the people's words to one another about returning to the Lord. From what you see in verses 4, how does God regard these words?

CAPTURE THE ESSENCE

2. Look at how Jesus quotes the words of verse 6 in Matthew 9:13 and 12:7. Jesus said that the Pharisees did not know what these words mean. How would you express the meaning of these words?

FOR LIFE TODAY

3. In what ways, if any, would you say that the words of this chapter might accurately describe God's people today, especially those in your church?

4. With God's words in verse 6 in mind, how would you complete this sentence: What God really wants from me is…

HOSEA 7

SEEING WHAT'S THERE

1. As you read this chapter, what would you say is the most painful accusation here? The sharpest picture of punishment and disaster? And the deepest glimpse into God's character?

CAPTURE THE ESSENCE

2. From what you see in this chapter, how would you complete this statement: "I know God is a God of love because He…"

3. Now that you're halfway through Hosea, how would you summarize the most important teachings in this book?

FOR LIFE TODAY

4. In what ways, if any, would you say that this chapter might accurately describe God's people today, especially those in your church?

HOSEA 8

SEEING WHAT'S THERE

1. As you study Hosea's words here, what would you say is the most urgent command in this chapter? The most powerful vision of a future day? The most painful accusation? The sharpest picture of punishment and disaster? And the deepest glimpse into God's character?

FOR LIFE TODAY

2. In Isaiah 55:10-11, God reminds us that He sends rain and snow from the sky to water the earth and to nurture life. In the same way, God says that He sends His words to accomplish specific purposes. From your study so far, what would you suggest are *God's* primary purposes for the book of Hosea in the lives of Christians today?

HOSEA 9

SEEING WHAT'S THERE

1. As you reflect on Hosea's message for God's people in this chapter, what would you say is the most urgent command it contains? The most powerful vision of a future day? The most painful accusation? The sharpest picture of punishment and disaster? And the deepest glimpse into God's character?

CAPTURE THE ESSENCE

2. From what you see in this chapter, how would you complete this statement: "I know God is a God of love because He…"

HOSEA 10

SEEING WHAT'S THERE

1. As you ponder Hosea's words in this chapter, what would you say is the most urgent command here? The most powerful vision of a future day? The most painful accusation? And the sharpest picture of punishment and disaster?

HOSEA 11

SEEING WHAT'S THERE

1. As you think about Hosea's prophecy in this chapter, what would you say is the most powerful vision of a future day? The most painful accusation? The sharpest picture of punishment and disaster? And the deepest glimpse into God's character?

2. In God's relationship with His people, what *actions* and *emotions* on His part do you see in this chapter?

CAPTURE THE ESSENCE

3. How does this chapter help us understand what God most *desires* for His people?

4. From what you see in this chapter, how would you complete this statement: "I know God is a God of love because He…"

5. In Romans 15:4, Paul reminds us that the Old Testament Scriptures can give us patience and perseverance on one hand, as well as comfort and encouragement on the other. In your own life, how do you see this book of Hosea living up to Paul's description? In what ways, if any, is it meeting your personal needs for both *perseverance* and *encouragement?*

HOSEA 12

SEEING WHAT'S THERE

1. As you reflect on this chapter, what would you say is the most urgent command it expresses? The most powerful vision of a future day? The most painful accusation? The sharpest picture of punishment and disaster? And the deepest glimpse into God's character?

CAPTURE THE ESSENCE

2. With verse 5 in mind, how concerned would you say God is with His *reputation?* Explain your answer.

FOR LIFE TODAY

3. In Jeremiah 23:29, God says that His Word is like fire, and like a hammer. He can use the Scriptures to burn away unclean thoughts and desires in our hearts. He can also use Scripture to hit hard like a hammer, with the power to crush our spiritual hardness. From your study in this book of Hosea, how do you most want to see the "fire-and-hammer" power of God's Word at work in your own life?

HOSEA 13

SEEING WHAT'S THERE

1. In your own words, what would you say is the brightest promise in this chapter? The most urgent command? The most powerful vision of a future day? The most painful accusation? The sharpest picture of punishment and disaster? And the deepest glimpse into God's character?

CAPTURE THE ESSENCE

2. What aspects of God's character and personality would you say He wants us to understand most from verses 4-9?

3. From what you see in this chapter, how would you complete this statement: "I know God is a God of love because He…"

FOR GOING DEEPER

Look again at verse 14. How does Paul amplify the meaning of this verse in the way he quotes it in 1 Corinthians 15:54-57?

HOSEA 14

SEEING WHAT'S THERE

1. What would you say is the brightest promise in this chapter? The most urgent command? The most powerful vision of a future day? And the deepest glimpse into God's character?

CAPTURE THE ESSENCE

2. From what you see in verse 8, what conclusions can you make about God's character and personality?

3. What words or phrases in this chapter tell us the most about God's purpose and plan for His people?

4. Imagine yourself being present in the temple in Jerusalem as the twelve-year-old Jesus hears this book read and discussed by the rabbis there. In Luke 2:46 we read that He was listening to these teachers and asking them questions. What passages from this book do you think would most impress the boy Jesus, and what questions or comments do you suppose He might have spoken?

5. If God had written this chapter only for you, which words or phrases do you think He might have underlined, and why?

6. Review the guidelines for our thought-life given in Philippians 4:8 — "Whatever is true, whatever is noble, whatever is right, whatever is pure, whatever is lovely, whatever is admirable — if anything is excellent or praiseworthy — *think about such things.*" What food for thought have you found in the book of Hosea that especially strikes you as being *true,* or *noble,* or *right,* or *pure,* or *lovely,* or *admirable,* or *excellent,* or *praiseworthy?*

HOSEA:
THE BIG PICTURE

(Discuss again the questions in the "Overview," plus the questions below.)

1. For getting the most from the book of Hosea, one of the best guidelines is found in 2 Timothy 3:16-17, words which Paul wrote with the Old Testament first in view. He said that *all* Scripture is of great benefit to (a) teach us, (b) rebuke us, (c) correct us, and (d) train us in righteousness. Paul added that these Scriptures completely equip the person of God "for every good work." As you think seriously about those guidelines, in which of these areas do you especially see the usefulness of Hosea?

2. Imagine that you were helping to produce a film based on the life of Hosea. Describe the kinds of scenery, supporting characters, background music, lighting effects, etc., which you would use to help portray the central message of his book.

3. Look together at each of these passages, and discuss which one you believe is the best candidate for "KEY VERSE" in the book of Hosea — the one which brings into sharpest focus what this book is most about: 3:1, 4:1, 11:7-9, or 13:9-10.

4. What would you say is the main theme (or themes) in the book of Hosea?

5. SEARCH FOR THE SAVIOR — What words, images, or themes in Hosea have reminded you most of Jesus?

6. If Hosea were the only book in the Old Testament, in what ways would it still make a good introduction to the message of Jesus in the New Testament?

7. Based especially on your own experience, complete this statement in the way that's most meaningful to you: I believe it's important for Christians to read and explore the book of Hosea because…

Joel

OVERVIEW

(Discuss these OVERVIEW questions both at the beginning of your study of Joel, then again after you've studied all three chapters. Your answers may change significantly once you've looked more closely at the entire book.)

Startup: Talk together about this question: What kind of pictures come to your mind when you think of God's *power?*

SEEING WHAT'S THERE

1. Before launching into a closer look at Joel, how would you summarize what you already know about this book?

2. Find the phrase that reoccurs in the following verses—1:15, 2:11, 2:31, and 3:14. How would you restate this phrase in your own words, and what clues do you think it offers about the central message of this book?

3. Look also at the list of "Questions to Ask as You Begin Your Study of Each Book" on page 9.

FOR LIFE TODAY

4. The book of Joel has been titled "Prophecy of the Plague," "Judgment Precedes Spiritual Revival," "God Punishes and Restores," "The Book of God's Severity and Goodness," and "The Day of the Lord and the Judgment of Nations." With that reputation for this book, what kinds of answers and guidelines and solutions would you like to gain as you examine it more closely?

5. When you get to heaven, if you have a long talk with Joel and he asks you, "What was most helpful to you in my book?" how would you like to be able to answer him?

6. As you think first about *who God is,* and second about *what the Bible is,* how strongly would you rate your present de-sire to understand better the book of Joel? Use a scale of one to ten (one = "no desire at all," ten = "extremely intense desire") to help you decide.

7. From what you see in 2:12-13, what would be a good personal prayer to offer to God as you study this book?

JOEL 1

SEEING WHAT'S THERE

1. How does this chapter describe the locust invasion? And what response is called for from God's people in the last half of the chapter?

FOR LIFE TODAY

2. Proverbs 2:1-5 tells about the sincere person who truly longs for wisdom and understanding, and who searches the Scriptures for it—as if it were buried treasure. That person, Solomon says, will come to understand the fear of the Lord, and discover the knowledge of God. As you explore the book of Joel, what "buried treasure" would you like God to help you find here—to show you what God and His wisdom are really like? If you have this desire, how would you express it in your own words?

JOEL 2

1. What are God's people commanded to do in this chapter?

2. What specific promises are God's people given in this chapter?

CAPTURE THE ESSENCE

3. In your own words, what would you say is revealed most about God's character and personality in verses 10-14?

4. In verses 18-32, what does God want us to understand most about His purpose and plan for His people?

FOR LIFE TODAY

5. If God had written this chapter only for you, which words or phrases do you think He might have underlined, and why?

6. In Jeremiah 23:29, God says that His Word is like fire, and like a hammer. He can use the Scriptures to burn away unclean thoughts and desires in our hearts. He can also use Scripture to hit hard like a hammer, with the power to crush our spiritual hardness. From your study in this book of Joel, how do you most want to see the "fire-and-hammer" power of God's Word at work in your own life?

FOR GOING DEEPER

Look again at verses 28-33, then explore how this passage is applied in the New Testament in Acts 2:16-21 and Romans 10:12-13.

JOEL 3

SEEING WHAT'S THERE

1. What would you say is the brightest promise in this chapter? The most fearful warning? The most urgent command? The most powerful vision of a future day? The most painful accusation? The sharpest picture of punishment and disaster? And the deepest glimpse into God's character?

CAPTURE THE ESSENCE

2. From what you see in verses 14-17, what is it that God wants us to understand most about Himself?

3. Imagine yourself being present in the temple in Jerusalem as the twelve-year-old Jesus hears this book read and discussed by the rabbis there. In Luke 2:46 we read that He was listening to these teachers and asking them questions. What passages from this book do you think would most impress the boy Jesus, and what questions or comments do you suppose He might have spoken?

FOR LIFE TODAY

4. Consider how strongly you desire to know God better, then ask yourself this question: What are the truths revealed about Him in this chapter which He may want me to understand more deeply at this time in my life?

5. Review the guidelines for our thought-life given in Philippians 4:8—"Whatever is true, whatever is noble, whatever is right, whatever is pure, whatever is lovely, whatever is admirable—if anything is excellent or praiseworthy—*think about such things.*" What food for thought have you found in the book of Joel that especially strikes you as being *true,* or *noble,* or *right,* or *pure,* or *lovely,* or *admirable,* or *excellent,* or *praiseworthy?*

JOEL:

THE BIG PICTURE

(Discuss again the questions in the "Overview," plus the questions below.)

1. For getting the most from the book of Joel, one of the best guidelines is found in 2 Timothy 3:16-17, words which Paul wrote with the Old Testament first in view. He said that *all* Scripture is of great benefit to (a) teach us, (b) rebuke us, (c) correct us, and (d) train us in righteousness. Paul added that these Scriptures completely equip the person of God "for every good work." As you think seriously about those guidelines, in which of these areas do you especially see the usefulness of Joel?

2. Look together at each of these passages, and discuss which one you believe is the best candidate for "KEY VERSE" in the book of Joel—the one which brings into sharpest focus what this book is most about: 2:11, 2:12-13, 2:28-29, or 2:32.

3. What would you say is the main theme (or themes) in the book of Joel?

4. SEARCH FOR THE SAVIOR—What words, images, or themes in Joel have reminded you most of Jesus?

5. If Joel were the only book in the Old Testament, in what ways would it still make a good introduction to the message of Jesus in the New Testament?

6. Based especially on your own experience, complete this statement in the way that's most meaningful to you: I believe it's important for Christians to read and explore the book of Joel because…

Amos

OVERVIEW

(Discuss these OVERVIEW questions both at the beginning of your study of Amos, then again after you've studied all nine chapters. Your answers may change significantly once you've looked more closely at the entire book.)

Startup: Talk together about this question: In what important areas do Christians tend to become too *complacent* today? And what do you think causes this complacency?

SEEING WHAT'S THERE

1. Before launching into a closer look at Amos, how would you summarize what you already know about this book?

2. Find the most prominent theme that re-occurs in the following verses—2:7, 3:9, 4:1, 5:11-12, 8:4, and 8:6. From the way you see this theme presented in these passages, what comments would you make about its significance? What does God want us to understand most about it?

3. Look also at the list of "Questions to Ask as You Begin Your Study of Each Book" on page 9.

FOR LIFE TODAY

4. The book of Amos has been titled "Divine Punishment Follows Persistent Sin," "Warnings to Stop Sinning," "The Book of the Plumbline," and "God Is Just and Must Judge Sin." With that reputation for this book, what kinds of answers and guidelines and solutions would you like to gain as you examine it more closely?

5. When you get to heaven, if you have a long talk with Amos and he asks you, "What was most helpful to you in my book?" how would you like to be able to answer him?

6. As you think first about *who God is,* and second about *what the Bible is,* how strongly would you rate your present desire to understand better the book of Amos? Use a scale of one to ten (one = "no desire at all," ten = "extremely intense desire") to help you decide.

7. From what you see in the Lord's words to His people in 5:4, what would be a good personal prayer to offer to God as you study this book?

AMOS 1

SEEING WHAT'S THERE

1. What would you say is the most painful accusation in this chapter? And the sharpest picture of punishment and disaster?

2. Look also on page 8 at the list of "Questions to Ask as You Study Each Chapter." You may want to look again at this list for each chapter in Amos.

FOR LIFE TODAY

3. Proverbs 2:1-5 tells about the sincere person who truly longs for wisdom and understanding, and who searches the Scriptures for it—as if it were buried treasure. That person, Solomon says, will come to understand the fear of the Lord, and discover the knowledge of God. As you explore the book of Amos, what "buried treasure" would you like God to help you find here—to show you what God and His wisdom are really like? If you have this desire, how would you express it in your own words?

Amos 2

SEEING WHAT'S THERE

1. In your own words, what would you say is the most painful accusation in this chapter? And the sharpest picture of punishment and disaster?

FOR GOING DEEPER

Verses 1-3 describe the destruction of Israel's unneighborly neighbor to the southeast. What do the following passages teach about this nation bound for divine judgment?— Genesis 19:30-38, Numbers 22:1-8, Numbers 25:1-3, and 2 Kings 3:26-27.

Amos 3

SEEING WHAT'S THERE

1. As you explore these words to God's people, what would you say is the most powerful vision here of a future day? The most painful accusation? The sharpest picture of punishment and disaster? And the deepest glimpse into God's character?

Amos 4

SEEING WHAT'S THERE

1. As you read this chapter, what would you say is the most urgent command here? The most painful accusation? The sharpest picture of punishment and disaster? And the deepest glimpse into God's character?

CAPTURE THE ESSENCE

2. In your own words, what would you say God wants us to understand most about Himself in verses 12-13?

FOR LIFE TODAY

3. Which verse or phrase in this chapter do you think God would like you to understand best?

Amos 5

SEEING WHAT'S THERE

1. As you study Amos's words here, what would you say is the most fearful warning in this chapter? The most urgent command? The most powerful vision of a future day? The most painful accusation? And the sharpest picture of punishment and disaster?

CAPTURE THE ESSENCE

2. How does this chapter help us understand what God most desires from His people?

FOR LIFE TODAY

3. Look again at verse 24. In practical terms, how should Christians today go about obeying this command?

4. In Jeremiah 23:29, God says that His Word is like fire, and like a hammer. He can use the Scriptures to burn away unclean thoughts and desires in our hearts. He can also use Scripture to hit hard like a hammer, with the power to crush our spiritual hardness. From your study in this book of Amos, how do you most want to see the "fire-and-hammer" power of God's Word at work in your own life?

FOR GOING DEEPER

With the words of verses 21-24 ringing in your ears, look over at Malachi 1:10-14. What similarities do you see between these two sorrowful statements of the Lord—one before the exile of Israel and one after the exiles had returned?

Amos 6

SEEING WHAT'S THERE

1. As you reflect on Amos's message for God's people in this chapter, what would you say is the most fearful warning it contains? The most powerful vision of a future day? The most painful accusation? The sharpest picture of punishment and disaster? And the deepest glimpse into God's character?

Amos 7

SEEING WHAT'S THERE

1. How would you summarize the events of this chapter, and their significance?

CAPTURE THE ESSENCE

2. How would you summarize what Amos learns most about God in this chapter?

FOR GOING DEEPER

Experience again the dramatic conversation in verses 10-17. What similarities do you see between the rustic roots of an Amos and the unschooled power of a Peter and John as they faced their nation's rulers in Acts 4:8-13?

Amos 8

SEEING WHAT'S THERE

1. As you ponder Amos's words in this chapter, what would you say is the most powerful vision here of a future day? The most painful accusation? And the sharpest picture of punishment and disaster?

FOR LIFE TODAY

2. In Isaiah 55:10-11, God reminds us that He sends rain and snow from the sky to water the earth and to nurture life. In the same way, God says that He sends His words to accomplish specific purposes. From your study so far, what would you suggest are *God's* primary purposes for the book of Amos in the lives of Christians today?

Amos 9

SEEING WHAT'S THERE

1. Chapter 9 has been called the key to the book of Amos. What does this chapter include that could make it this significant?

2. As you think about Amos's prophecy in this chapter, what would you say is the brightest promise here? The most powerful vision of a future day? The sharpest picture of punishment and disaster? And the deepest glimpse into God's character?

CAPTURE THE ESSENCE

3. In this chapter, what does God want us to understand most about His purpose and plan for His people?

4. What aspects of God's character and personality would you say He wants us to understand most from verses 5-10?

5. Imagine yourself being present in the temple in Jerusalem as the twelve-year-old Jesus hears this book read and discussed by the rabbis there. In Luke 2:46 we read that He was listening to these teachers and asking them questions. What passages from this book do you think would most impress the boy Jesus, and what questions or comments do you suppose He might have spoken?

FOR LIFE TODAY

6. Of all that you see in this chapter, what one truth are you most thankful for, because of its personal significance to you?

7. Review the guidelines for our thought-life given in Philippians 4:8—"Whatever is true, whatever is noble, whatever is right, whatever is pure, whatever is lovely, whatever is admirable—if anything is excellent or praiseworthy—*think about such things.*" What food for thought have you found in the book of Joel that especially strikes you as being *true,* or *noble,* or *right,* or *pure,* or *lovely,* or *admirable,* or *excellent,* or *praiseworthy?*

8. In Romans 15:4, Paul reminds us that the Old Testament Scriptures can give us patience and perseverance on one hand, as well as comfort and encouragement on the other. In your own life, how do you see this book of Amos living up to

Paul's description? In what ways, if any, is it meeting your personal needs for both *perseverance* and *encouragement?*

AMOS:
THE BIG PICTURE

(Discuss again the questions in the "Overview," plus the questions below.)

1. For getting the most from the book of Amos, one of the best guidelines is found in 2 Timothy 3:16-17, words which Paul wrote with the Old Testament first in view. He said that *all* Scripture is of great benefit to (a) teach us, (b) rebuke us, (c) correct us, and (d) train us in righteousness. Paul added that these Scriptures completely equip the person of God "for every good work." As you think seriously about those guidelines, in which of these areas do you especially see the usefulness of Amos?

2. Look together at each of these passages, and discuss which one you believe is the best candidate for "KEY VERSE" in the book of Amos—the one which brings into sharpest focus what this book is most about: 3:1-2, 5:12, 5:24, 7:7-8, or 8:11-12.

3. What would you say is the main theme (or themes) in the book of Amos?

4. SEARCH FOR THE SAVIOR—What words, images, or themes in Amos have reminded you most of Jesus?

5. If Amos were the only book in the Old Testament, in what ways would it still make a good introduction to the message of Jesus in the New Testament?

6. Based especially on your own experience, complete this statement in the way that's most meaningful to you: I believe it's important for Christians to read and explore the book of Amos because...

Obadiah

Startup: Talk together about this question: When do you feel most like God's child?

OVERVIEW

1. Before launching into a closer look at Obadiah, how would you summarize what you already know about this book?

2. The book of Obadiah has been titled "A Nation's Doom" and "Sure Retribution for Merciless Pride." With that reputation for this book, what kinds of answers and guidelines and solutions would you like to gain as you examine it more closely?

3. As you think first about *who God is,* and second about *what the Bible is,* how strongly would you rate your present desire to understand better the book of Obadiah? Use a scale of one to ten (one = "no desire at all," ten = "extremely intense desire") to help you decide.

4. Look also at the list of "Questions to Ask as You Begin Your Study of Each Book" on page 9.

SEEING WHAT'S THERE

5. What exactly does God promise to do to Edom? And for what reasons?

6. How would you describe Edom's future, as revealed in this book?

CAPTURE THE ESSENCE

7. In verses 17-21, what does God want us to understand most about His purpose and plan for His people?

8. What would you say is the main theme (or themes) in the book of Obadiah?

9. What four-to-eight-word title would you give to this book, to best summarize its content and significance?

10. Which verse would you select as the key verse in Obadiah?

FOR LIFE TODAY

11. Think about the picture this book gives of how much God values and protects His people. How much does He love and value both you and your church? What are you convinced He will do to protect you?

OBADIAH: THE BIG PICTURE

12. When you get to heaven, if you have a long talk with Obadiah and he asks you, "What was most helpful to you in my book?" how would you like to be able to answer him?

13. For getting the most from the book of Obadiah, one of the best guidelines is found in 2 Timothy 3:16-17, words which Paul wrote with the Old Testament first in view. He said that *all* Scripture is of great benefit to (a) teach us, (b) rebuke us, (c) correct us, and (d) train us in righteousness. Paul added that these Scriptures completely equip the person of God "for every good work." As you think seriously about those guidelines, in which of these areas do you especially see the usefulness of Obadiah?

14. SEARCH FOR THE SAVIOR—What words, images, or themes in Obadiah remind you most of Jesus?

15. Based especially on your own experience, complete this statement in the way that's most meaningful to you: I believe it's important for Christians to read and explore the book of Obadiah because…

FOR GOING DEEPER

What do you discover about the history of the conflict between Edom and Israel in these passages—Genesis 25:19-26, Numbers 20:14-22, 2 Samuel 8:13-14, and 2 Kings 8:20-22?

Jonah

OVERVIEW

(Discuss these OVERVIEW questions both at the beginning of your study of Jonah, then again after you've studied all four chapters. Your answers may change significantly once you've looked more closely at the entire book.)

Startup: Talk together about times in your life when you've most needed to understand God's love for someone whom you didn't consider very lovable.

SEEING WHAT'S THERE

1. Before launching into a closer look at Jonah, how would you summarize what you already know about this book?

2. Scan the book together to find all the places where God speaks. What do these passages tell us about God's values and character?

3. Look for the places where Jonah speaks. What do you learn about Jonah's view of God, especially in verses 1:9, 2:9, and 4:2?

4. Imagine that you were helping to produce a film based on the book of Jonah. Describe the kinds of scenery, supporting characters, background music, lighting effects, etc., which you would use to help portray the central message of this book.

5. Look also at the list of "Questions to Ask as You Begin Your Study of Each Book" on page 9.

CAPTURE THE ESSENCE

6. Throughout this book, how do you see God's sovereign control of all circumstances?

7. Would you describe Jonah as a weak person or a strong person?

FOR LIFE TODAY

8. The book of Jonah has been titled "The Story of an Unwilling Prophet," "A Prophet Runs from God," "Israel's Mission to the Nations," "The Book of God's Mercy," "God's Concern for Gentiles," and "The Universal Sweep of Divine Grace." With that reputation for this book, what kinds of answers and guidelines and solutions would you like to gain as you examine it more closely?

9. When you get to heaven, if you have a long talk with Jonah and he asks you, "What was most helpful to you in my book?" how would you like to be able to answer him?

10. As you think first about *who God is,* and second about *what the Bible is,* how strongly would you rate your present desire to understand better the book of Jonah? Use a scale of one to ten (one = "no desire at all," ten = "extremely intense desire") to help you decide.

11. From the example you see in Jonah's words in 2:7, what would be a good personal prayer to offer to God as you study this book?

FOR GOING DEEPER

Jonah's name means "dove." Notice in the following passages how this word is used in other Old Testament Scriptures—Psalm 68:13 and 74:18-19, and Hosea 7:11. What clues do you see in these verses about the symbolism of this word, and what it might mean in understanding the book of Jonah?

Jonah 1

Startup: If you were given a week's vacation to visit anyone in the world, who would you go see?

SEEING WHAT'S THERE

1. What exactly were God's instructions to Jonah?

2. Do you think Jonah might have responded differently to God's instructions if he had been told to take a word of blessing to Nineveh?

CAPTURE THE ESSENCE

3. From what you see in this chapter, how would you describe Jonah's character?

4. From what you see in this chapter, how would you describe the character of the sailors on the ship with Jonah?

5. Look together at 4:2 to find the reason Jonah gives for running away from God. How would you explain this reason in your own words?

6. What does David say in Psalm 139:7-12 about running away from God?

FOR LIFE TODAY

7. Recall a time when you did not want to do something God wanted you to do. Describe the reasons…and the results.

8. Proverbs 2:1-5 tells about the sincere person who truly longs for wisdom and understanding, and who searches the Scriptures for it—as if it were buried treasure. That person, Solomon says, will come to understand the fear of the Lord, and discover the knowledge of God. As you explore the book of Jonah, what "buried treasure" would you like God to help you find—to show you what God and His wisdom are really like? If you have this desire, how would you express it in your own words?

Jonah 2

SEEING WHAT'S THERE

1. Are Jonah's words in this chapter a prayer of despair, a prayer of hope, or a mixture of the two?

CAPTURE THE ESSENCE

2. From what you see in Jonah's prayer in this chapter, what are the most important things he understands about God's personality and character?

3. What do you think was the reason for the hope Jonah expressed in his prayer?

4. What do you think is the true cause for the change that has come upon Jonah since the events of chapter 1?

5. Jonah says he will sacrifice to God a song of thanksgiving (verse 9). What all does Jonah have to be thankful for?

6. To see how Jesus compared Himself to Jonah, look carefully together at Matthew 12:38-40. In what ways could you say that the prayer of Jonah in this chapter was also the prayer of Jesus after He was crucified?

FOR LIFE TODAY

7. In what ways is this chapter a model prayer for Christians?

8. If Jonah could be thankful in his circumstances…what reasons do *you* have today for giving God a prayer of thanksgiving?

FOR GOING DEEPER

To explore how Jesus used Jonah's story in His ministry, look at Matthew 12:38-41 and 16:1-4, and at Luke 11:29-32.

Jonah 3

Startup: How long have you known about the story of Jonah? What are some of the earliest impressions this story left with you?

SEEING WHAT'S THERE

1. What were God's exact instructions to Jonah?

2. Summarize in your own words the response of the people and the king of Nineveh to God's words.

3. What does this chapter reveal to us about God's character?

4. In Isaiah 55:10-11, God reminds us that He sends rain and snow from the sky to water the earth and to nurture life. In the same way, God says that He sends His words to accomplish specific purposes. From your study so far, what would you suggest are *God's* primary purposes for the book of Jonah in the lives of Christians today?

JONAH 4

1. How would you describe Jonah's understanding—or lack of understanding—of God?

2. How did God respond to Jonah's anger?

3. Look back at the first three chapters. What clues do you find there for the way Jonah is acting in chapter 4?

4. Why do you think Jonah wanted to die (verse 3)?

5. What do you think God is trying to teach Jonah in this chapter?

6. After Jonah heard God's words in 4:10-11, what do you think most likely happened next?

7. Would you describe Jonah as a hero? Why or why not?

8. How would you summarize what Jonah learns most about God in this chapter?

9. Imagine yourself being present in the temple in Jerusalem as the twelve-year-old Jesus hears this book read and discussed by the rabbis there. In Luke 2:46 we read that He was listening to these teachers and asking them questions. What passages from this book do you think would most impress the boy Jesus, and what questions or comments do you suppose He might have spoken?

10. How does the message of this chapter relate to what we read in 2 Peter 3:9?

11. Is the question God asks in verse 4 a good one to ask whenever we feel anger? Are there times when the right answer to this question could be yes?

The book of Nahum describes God's later dealings with the city of Nineveh. How does Nahum 1:1-8 compare with what we see in the book of Jonah?

JONAH:
THE BIG PICTURE

(Discuss again the questions in the "Overview," plus the questions below.)

1. For getting the most from the book of Jonah, one of the best guidelines is found in 2 Timothy 3:16-17, words which Paul wrote with the Old Testament first in view. He said that *all* Scripture is of great benefit to (a) teach us, (b) rebuke us, (c) correct us, and (d) train us in righteousness. Paul added that these Scriptures completely equip the person of God "for every good work." As you think seriously about those guidelines, in which of these areas do you especially see the usefulness of Jonah?

2. Look together at each of these passages, and discuss which one you believe is the best candidate for "KEY VERSE" in the book of Jonah—the one which brings into sharpest focus what this book is most about: 2:8-9, 3:2, 4:2, or 4:11.

3. What would you say is the main theme (or themes) in the book of Jonah?

4. SEARCH FOR THE SAVIOR—What words, images, or themes in Jonah have reminded you most of Jesus?

5. If Jonah were the only book in the Old Testament, in what ways would it still make a good introduction to the message of Jesus in the New Testament?

6. Based especially on your own experience, complete this statement in the way that's most meaningful to you: I believe it's important for Christians to read and explore the book of Jonah because...

Micah

OVERVIEW

(Discuss these OVERVIEW questions both at the beginning of your study of Micah, then again after you've studied all seven chapters. Your answers may change significantly once you've looked more closely at the entire book.)

Startup: Talk together about this question: What kind of pictures come to your mind when you think of God's *judgment?*

SEEING WHAT'S THERE

1. Before launching into a closer look at Micah, how would you summarize what you already know about this book?

2. What thought or theme do you see repeated in these verses—1:2, 3:1, 6:1-2, and 6:9? What clues could this offer about the central message of Micah?

3. Look also at the list of "Questions to Ask as You Begin Your Study of Each Book" on page 9.

FOR LIFE TODAY

4. The book of Micah has been titled "How God Hates Sin But Loves the Sinner," "Personal and Social Righteousness," "Punishment and Kindness for God's People," "The Book of Doom and Glory," and "Bethlehem's King and Kingdom." With that reputation for this book, what kinds of answers and guidelines and solutions would you like to gain as you examine it more closely?

5. When you get to heaven, if you have a long talk with Micah and he asks you, "What was most helpful to you in my book?" how would you like to be able to answer him?

6. As you think first about *who God is,* and second about *what the Bible is,* how strongly would you rate your present desire to understand better the book of Micah? Use a scale of one to ten (one = "no desire at all," ten = "extremely intense desire") to help you decide.

7. From what you see in 6:8, what would be a good personal prayer to offer to God as you study this book?

MICAH 1

SEEING WHAT'S THERE

1. What specific sins are spoken against in verse 7?

2. As you reflect on this chapter, what would you say is the most urgent command it gives? The most powerful vision of a future day? The most painful accusation? And the sharpest picture of punishment and disaster?

3. Look also on page 8 at the list of "Questions to Ask as You Study Each Chapter." You may want to look again at this list for each chapter in Micah.

MICAH 2

SEEING WHAT'S THERE

1. What specific sins are spoken against in verses 1-2?

2. As you think about Micah's prophecy in this chapter, what would you say is the brightest promise here? The most fearful warning? The most urgent command? The most powerful vision of a future day? The most painful accusation? And the sharpest picture of punishment and disaster?

CAPTURE THE ESSENCE

3. From what you see in verse 7, what conclusions can you make about God's character and personality?

4. Which verse or phrase in this chapter do you think God would like you to understand best?

5. Proverbs 2:1-5 tells about the sincere person who truly longs for wisdom and understanding, and who searches the Scriptures for it—as if it were buried treasure. That person, Solomon says, will come to understand the fear of the Lord, and discover the knowledge of God. As you explore the book of Micah, what "buried treasure" would you like God to help you find here—to show you what God and His wisdom are really like? If you have this desire, how would you express it in your own words?

MICAH 3

SEEING WHAT'S THERE

1. What specific sins are spoken against in this chapter?

2. As you ponder Micah's words in this chapter, what would you say is the most urgent command here? The most powerful vision of a future day? The most painful accusation? And the sharpest picture of punishment and disaster?

MICAH 4

SEEING WHAT'S THERE

1. As you reflect on Micah's message for God's people in this chapter, what would you say is the brightest promise it contains? The most urgent command? The most powerful vision of a future day? And the sharpest picture of punishment and disaster?

CAPTURE THE ESSENCE

2. In this chapter, what does God want us to understand most about His purpose and plan for His people?

FOR LIFE TODAY

3. If God had written this chapter only for you, which words or phrases do you think He might have underlined, and why?

4. In Isaiah 55:10-11, God reminds us that He sends rain and snow from the sky to water the earth and to nurture life. In the same way, God says that He sends His words to accomplish specific purposes. From your study so far, what would you suggest are *God's* primary purposes for the book of Micah in the lives of Christians today?

MICAH 5

SEEING WHAT'S THERE

1. As you study Micah's words here, what would you say is the brightest promise in this chapter? The most powerful vision of a future day? And the sharpest picture of punishment and disaster?

2. What specific sins are spoken against in verses 12-14?

CAPTURE THE ESSENCE

3. What words or phrases in this chapter tell us the most about God's purpose and plan for His people?

4. Discuss together the prophetic fulfillment of verse 2 (and the expectation of it) which you see in Matthew 2:1-6 and Luke 2:1-20.

FOR LIFE TODAY

5. In Romans 15:4, Paul reminds us that the Old Testament Scriptures can give us patience and perseverance on one hand, as well as comfort and encouragement on the other. In your own life, how do you see this book of Micah living up to Paul's description? In what ways, if any, is it meeting your personal needs for both *perseverance* and *encouragement?*

MICAH 6

SEEING WHAT'S THERE

1. As you read this chapter, what would you say is the most urgent command here? The most powerful vision of a future day? The most painful accusation? The sharpest picture of punishment and disaster? And the deepest glimpse into God's character?

2. What specific sins are spoken against in verses 10-12?

CAPTURE THE ESSENCE

3. From what you see in verse 8, what conclusions can you make about God's character and personality?

FOR LIFE TODAY

4. Look again at verse 8, and think of it in light of your own relationship with God. How you would complete this sentence: What God really wants from me is...

5. In Jeremiah 23:29, God says that His Word is like fire, and like a hammer. He can use the Scriptures to burn away unclean thoughts and desires in our hearts. He can also use Scripture to hit hard like a hammer, with the power to crush our spiritual hardness. From your study in this book of Micah, how do you most want to see the "fire-and-hammer" power of God's Word at work in your own life?

FOR GOING DEEPER

Compare the "requirements" in verse 8 with what you see in Deuteronomy 11:12-13. What similarities do you see in these passages, and also what differences?

MICAH 7

SEEING WHAT'S THERE

1. Chapter 7 has been called the key to the book of Micah. What does this chapter include that could make it this significant?

2. What specific sins are spoken against in verse 3?

3. As you explore these words to God's people, what would you say is the brightest promise here? The most urgent command? The most powerful vision of a future day? The most painful accusation? The sharpest picture of punishment and disaster? And the deepest glimpse into God's character?

CAPTURE THE ESSENCE

4. What aspects of God's character and personality would you say He wants us to understand most from verses 18-20?

5. Imagine yourself being present in the temple in Jerusalem as the twelve-year-old Jesus hears this book read and discussed by the rabbis there. In Luke 2:46 we read that He was listening to these teachers and asking them questions. What passages from this book do you think would most impress the boy Jesus, and what questions or comments do you suppose He might have spoken?

FOR LIFE TODAY

6. Consider how strongly you desire to know God better, then ask yourself this question: What are the truths revealed about Him in this chapter which He may want me to understand more deeply at this time in my life?

7. Review the guidelines for our thought-life given in Philippians 4:8—"Whatever is true, whatever is noble, whatever is right, whatever is pure, whatever is lovely, whatever is admirable—if anything is excellent or praiseworthy—*think about such things.*" What food for thought have you found in the book of Micah that especially strikes you as being *true,* or *noble,* or *right,* or *pure,* or *lovely,* or *admirable,* or *excellent,* or *praiseworthy?*

MICAH:
THE BIG PICTURE

(Discuss again the questions in the "Overview," plus the questions below.)

1. For getting the most from the book of Micah, one of the best guidelines is found in 2 Timothy 3:16-17, words which Paul wrote with the Old Testament first in view. He said that *all* Scripture is of great benefit to (a) teach us, (b) rebuke us, (c) correct us, and (d) train us in righteousness. Paul added that these Scriptures completely equip the person of God "for every good work." As you think seriously about those guidelines, in which of these areas do you especially see the usefulness of Micah?

2. Look together at each of these passages, and discuss which one you believe is the best candidate for "KEY VERSE" in the book of Micah—the one which brings into sharpest focus what this book is most about: 1:2, 6:8, or 7:18.

3. What would you say is the main theme (or themes) in the book of Micah?

4. SEARCH FOR THE SAVIOR—What words, images, or themes in Micah have reminded you most of Jesus?

5. If Micah were the only book in the Old Testament, in what ways would it still make a good introduction to the message of Jesus in the New Testament?

6. Based especially on your own experience, complete this statement in the way that's most meaningful to you: I believe it's important for Christians to read and explore the book of Micah because...

Nahum

OVERVIEW

(Discuss these OVERVIEW questions both at the beginning of your study of Nahum, then again after you've studied all three chapters. Your answers may change significantly once you've looked more closely at the entire book.)

Startup: Talk together about this question: What kind of pictures come to your mind when you think of God's *holiness?*

SEEING WHAT'S THERE

1. Before launching into a closer look at Nahum, how would you summarize what you already know about this book?

2. Scan through the three chapters of Nahum to see how many times do you see the word *will* used in this book, in reference to God's actions.

3. Look also at the list of "Questions to Ask as You Begin Your Study of Each Book" on page 9.

FOR LIFE TODAY

4. The book of Nahum has been titled "God's Holiness Vindicated in Judgment," "The Book of Perversity and Penalty," and "A Wicked City's Doom." With that reputation for this book, what kinds of answers and guidelines and solutions would you like to gain as you examine it more closely?

5. When you get to heaven, if you have a long talk with Nahum and he asks you, "What was most helpful to you in my book?" how would you like to be able to answer him?

6. As you think first about *who God is,* and second about *what the Bible is,* how strongly would you rate your present desire to understand better the book of Nahum? Use a scale of one to ten (one = "no desire at all," ten = "extremely intense desire") to help you decide.

7. From what you see in 1:7, what would be a good personal prayer to offer to God as you study this book?

NAHUM 1

SEEING WHAT'S THERE

1. In this chapter, what does God specifically promise to do concerning Nineveh, and for what reasons?

CAPTURE THE ESSENCE

2. What aspects of God's character and personality would you say He wants us to understand most from verses 2-8?

NAHUM 2

SEEING WHAT'S THERE

1. In this chapter, what specific promises does God make concerning both Israel and Nineveh?

NAHUM 3

SEEING WHAT'S THERE

1. What sins in Nineveh are referred to in this chapter?

2. In this chapter, what specific promises does God make concerning Nineveh?

CAPTURE THE ESSENCE

3. Imagine yourself being present in the temple in Jerusalem as the twelve-year-old Jesus hears this book read and discussed by the rabbis there. In Luke 2:46 we read that He was listening to these teachers and asking them questions. What passages from this book do you think would most impress the boy Jesus, and what questions or comments do you suppose He might have spoken?

FOR LIFE TODAY

4. Review the guidelines for our thought-life given in Philippians 4:8—"Whatever is true, whatever is noble, whatever is right, whatever is pure, whatever is lovely, whatever is admirable—if anything is excellent or praiseworthy—*think about such things.*" What food for thought have you found in the book of Nahum that especially strikes you as being *true,* or *noble,* or *right,* or *pure,* or *lovely,* or *admirable,* or *excellent,* or *praiseworthy?*

NAHUM:
THE BIG PICTURE

(Discuss again the questions in the "Overview," plus the questions below.)

1. For getting the most from the book of Nahum, one of the best guidelines is found in 2 Timothy 3:16-17, words which Paul wrote with the Old Testament first in view. He said that *all* Scripture is of great benefit to (a) teach us, (b) rebuke us, (c) correct us, and (d) train us in righteousness. Paul added that these Scriptures completely equip the person of God "for every good work." As you think seriously about those guidelines, in which of these areas do you especially see the usefulness of Nahum?

2. Look together at each of these passages, and discuss which one you believe is the best candidate for "KEY VERSE" in the book of Nahum—the one which brings into sharpest focus what this book is most about: 1:2-3, 1:7-9, or 3:5-7.

3. What would you say is the main theme (or themes) in the book of Nahum?

4. SEARCH FOR THE SAVIOR—What words, images, or themes in Nahum have reminded you most of Jesus?

5. Based especially on your own experience, complete this statement in the way that's most meaningful to you: I believe it's important for Christians to read and explore the book of Nahum because...

Habakkuk

OVERVIEW

(Discuss these OVERVIEW questions both at the beginning of your study of Habakkuk, then again after you've studied all three chapters. Your answers may change significantly once you've looked more closely at the entire book.)

Startup: Talk together about times when you have most needed to understand God's sovereignty over all events and circumstances in your life.

SEEING WHAT'S THERE

1. Before launching into a closer look at Habakkuk, how would you summarize what you already know about this book?

2. Scan through the three chapters in Habakkuk to find those verses which you feel best reflect this prophet's personality.

3. Look also at the list of "Questions to Ask as You Begin Your Study of Each Book" on page 9.

FOR LIFE TODAY

4. The book of Habakkuk has been titled "Prophet with a Problem," "The Lord's Kingdom and People Will Triumph," "Learning How to Trust God," "The Mysteries of Providence," and "Justification by Faith as God's Way of Salvation." With that reputation for this book, what kinds of answers and guidelines and solutions would you like to gain as you examine it more closely?

5. When you get to heaven, if you have a long talk with Habakkuk and he asks you, "What was most helpful to you in my book?" how would you like to be able to answer him?

6. As you think first about *who God is,* and second about *what the Bible is,* how strongly would you rate your present desire to understand better the book of Habakkuk? Use a scale of one to ten (one = "no desire at all," ten = "extremely intense desire") to help you decide.

7. From the example you see in Habakkuk's words in 3:18-19, what would be a good personal prayer to offer to God as you study this book?

HABAKKUK 1

SEEING WHAT'S THERE

1. What are the questions that Habakkuk asks in this chapter?

CAPTURE THE ESSENCE

2. What do Habakkuk's questions reveal about his strongest values and concerns in life?

3. From what you see in Habakkuk's words in this chapter, what are the most important things he understands about God?

FOR LIFE TODAY

4. Which verse in this chapter do you think God would like you to understand best?

5. Proverbs 2:1-5 tells about the sincere person who truly longs for wisdom and understanding, and who searches the Scriptures for it—as if it were buried treasure. That person, Solomon says, will come to understand the fear of the Lord, and discover the knowledge of God. As you explore the book of Habakkuk, what "buried treasure" would you like God to help you find here—to show you what God and His wisdom are really like? If you have this desire, how would you express it in your own words?

FOR GOING DEEPER

Look in 2 Kings 23:4 — 24:5 for a description of the era in which Habakkuk prophesied. What discoveries can you make by comparing this with Habakkuk's complaint in verses 1-4 here in chapter 1?

HABAKKUK 2

SEEING WHAT'S THERE

1. What are the five "woes" that God announces in this chapter? Since all of them express something that displeases God, think about what is opposite to each one. For each statement, change the opening words ("Woe to him") to "Blessed is he," then reword the rest of the statement to present what *pleases* God, instead of what displeases Him.

2. What promises does God make in this chapter—statements in which He uses the word *will* to tell what He plans to do?

CAPTURE THE ESSENCE

3. How would you summarize what Habakkuk learns most about God in this chapter?

FOR LIFE TODAY

4. Which verse in this chapter do you think God would like you to understand best?

5. In Jeremiah 23:29, God says that His Word is like fire, and like a hammer. He can use the Scriptures to burn away unclean thoughts and desires in our hearts. He can also use Scripture to hit hard like a hammer, with the power to crush our spiritual hardness. From your study in this book of Habakkuk, how do you most want to see the "fire-and-hammer" power of God's Word at work in your own life?

HABAKKUK 3

SEEING WHAT'S THERE

1. What specific request does Habakkuk make in verse 2?

2. What does Habakkuk *praise* God for in this chapter?

3. What *commitments* does Habakkuk make in verses 16-18?

CAPTURE THE ESSENCE

4. From what you see in this chapter, what are the most important things that Habakkuk understands about God's personality and character?

5. Imagine yourself being present in the temple in Jerusalem as the twelve-year-old Jesus hears this book read and discussed by the rabbis there. In Luke 2:46 we read that He was listening to these teachers and asking them questions. What passages from this book do you think would most impress the boy Jesus, and what questions or comments do you suppose He might have spoken?

FOR LIFE TODAY

6. Think about Habakkuk's example in this chapter as you answer this question: What should Christians do when God brings down judgment upon the nation or society around them?

7. Which thoughts and words and phrases in Habakkuk's prayer would be right for you to use in *your* prayers to God at this time in your life?

8. From what you see in this chapter, discuss together how you would complete this sentence: What God really wants from me is...

9. Review the guidelines for our thought-life given in Philippians 4:8—"Whatever is true, whatever is noble, whatever is right, whatever is pure, whatever is lovely, whatever is admirable—if anything is excellent or praiseworthy—*think about such things.*" What food for thought have you found in the book of Habakkuk that especially strikes you as being *true,* or *noble,* or *right,* or *pure,* or *lovely,* or *admirable,* or *excellent,* or *praiseworthy?*

10. In Isaiah 55:10-11, God reminds us that He sends rain and snow from the sky to

water the earth and to nurture life. In the same way, God says that He sends His words to accomplish specific purposes. From your study so far, what would you suggest are *God's* primary purposes for the book of Habakkuk in the lives of Christians today?

HABAKKUK:
THE BIG PICTURE

(Discuss again the questions in the "Overview," plus the questions below.)

1. For getting the most from the book of Habakkuk, one of the best guidelines is found in 2 Timothy 3:16-17, words which Paul wrote with the Old Testament first in view. He said that *all* Scripture is of great benefit to (a) teach us, (b) rebuke us, (c) correct us, and (d) train us in righteousness. Paul added that these Scriptures completely equip the person of God "for every good work." As you think seriously about those guidelines, in which of these areas do you especially see the usefulness of Habakkuk?

2. What does this book teach us most about the judgment of God?

3. Look together at each of these passages, and discuss which one you believe is the best candidate for "KEY VERSE" in the book of Habakkuk—the one which brings into sharpest focus what this book is most about: 2:4, 3:2, or 3:17-19.

4. What would you say is the main theme (or themes) in the book of Habakkuk?

5. SEARCH FOR THE SAVIOR—What words, images, or themes in Habakkuk have reminded you most of Jesus?

6. Based especially on your own experience, complete this statement in the way that's most meaningful to you: I believe it's important for Christians to read and explore the book of Habakkuk because…

7. If Habakkuk were the only book in the Old Testament, in what ways would it still make a good introduction to the message of Jesus in the New Testament?

Zephaniah

OVERVIEW

(Discuss these OVERVIEW questions both at the beginning of your study of Zephaniah, then again after you've studied all three chapters. Your answers may change significantly once you've looked more closely at the entire book.)

Startup: What kind of pictures come to your mind when you think of the word *hope?*

SEEING WHAT'S THERE

1. Before launching into a closer look at Zephaniah, how would you summarize what you already know about this book?

2. Look also at the list of "Questions to Ask as You Begin Your Study of Each Book" on page 9.

FOR LIFE TODAY

3. The book of Zephaniah has been titled "Rescue and Blessings for the Remnant," "God Will Judge the World," "The Book of Wonder and Wrath," and "The Day of the Lord Must Precede Kingdom Blessing." With that reputation for this book, what kinds of answers and guidelines and solutions would you like to gain as you examine it more closely?

4. When you get to heaven, if you have a long talk with Zephaniah and he asks you, "What was most helpful to you in my book?" how would you like to be able to answer him?

5. As you think first about *who God is,* and second about *what the Bible is,* how strongly would you rate your present desire to understand better the book of Zephaniah? Use a scale of one to ten (one = "no desire at all," ten = "extremely intense desire") to help you decide.

6. From what you see in 3:17, what would be a good personal prayer to offer to God as you study this book?

ZEPHANIAH 1

SEEING WHAT'S THERE

1. As you explore these words to God's people, what would you say is the most fearful warning here? The most urgent command? The most powerful vision of a future day? The most painful accusation? And the sharpest picture of punishment and disaster?

ZEPHANIAH 2

SEEING WHAT'S THERE

1. As you read this chapter, what would you say is the brightest promise here? The most fearful warning? The most urgent command? The most powerful vision of a future day? The most painful accusation? And the sharpest picture of punishment and disaster?

FOR LIFE TODAY

2. In Isaiah 55:10 11, God reminds us that He sends rain and snow from the sky to water the earth and to nurture life. In the same way, God says that He sends His words to accomplish specific purposes. From your study so far, what would you suggest are *God's* primary purposes for the book of Zephaniah in the lives of Christians today?

ZEPHANIAH 3

SEEING WHAT'S THERE

1. Look at the picture given in verse 9 of the people of the world serving God. What do you think God most wants us to understand from this image? What kind of service to God would this be?

2. As you study Zephaniah's words in this chapter, what would you say is the brightest promise here? The most tender encouragement? The most urgent command? The most powerful vision of a future day? The most painful accusation? The sharpest picture of punishment and disaster? And the deepest glimpse into God's character?

CAPTURE THE ESSENCE

3. In this chapter, what does God want us to understand most about His purpose and plan for His people?

4. What aspects of God's character and personality would you say He wants us to understand most from verses 5 and 17?

5. Imagine yourself being present in the temple in Jerusalem as the twelve-year-old Jesus hears this book read and discussed by the rabbis there. In Luke 2:46 we read that He was listening to these teachers and asking them questions. What passages from this book do you think would most impress the boy Jesus, and what questions or comments do you suppose He might have spoken?

FOR LIFE TODAY

6. In light of how you're doing spiritually in your life today, what words in this chapter do you think are the most important to you at this time—and why?

7. Review the guidelines for our thought-life given in Philippians 4:8—"Whatever is true, whatever is noble, whatever is right, whatever is pure, whatever is lovely, whatever is admirable—if anything is excellent or praiseworthy—*think about such things.*" What food for thought have you found in the book of Zephaniah that especially strikes you as being *true,* or *noble,* or *right,* or *pure,* or *lovely,* or *admirable,* or *excellent,* or *praiseworthy?*

ZEPHANIAH: THE BIG PICTURE

(Discuss again the questions in the "Overview," plus the questions below.)

1. For getting the most from the book of Zephaniah, one of the best guidelines is found in 2 Timothy 3:16-17, words which Paul wrote with the Old Testament first in view. He said that *all* Scripture is of great benefit to (a) teach us, (b) rebuke us, (c) correct us, and (d) train us in righteousness. Paul added that these Scriptures completely equip the person of God "for every good work." As you think seriously about those guidelines, in which of these areas do you especially see the usefulness of Zephaniah?

2. Look together at each of these passages, and discuss which one you believe is the best candidate for "KEY VERSE" in the book of Zephaniah—the one which brings into sharpest focus what this book is most about: 1:12, 1:14-15, or 2:3.

3. What would you say is the main theme (or themes) in the book of Zephaniah?

4. SEARCH FOR THE SAVIOR—What words, images, or themes in Zephaniah have reminded you most of Jesus?

5. Based especially on your own experience, complete this statement in the way that's most meaningful to you: I believe it's important for Christians to read and explore the book of Zephaniah because…

6. If Zephaniah were the only book in the Old Testament, in what ways would it still make a good introduction to the message of Jesus in the New Testament?

Haggai

OVERVIEW

(Discuss these OVERVIEW questions both at the beginning of your study of Haggai, then again after you've studied both chapters. Your answers may change significantly once you've looked more closely at the entire book.)

Startup: Talk together about how you would number the correct priorities in a Christian's life.

SEEING WHAT'S THERE

1. Before launching into a closer look at Haggai, how would you summarize what you already know about this book?

2. Look also at the list of "Questions to Ask as You Begin Your Study of Each Book" on page 9.

FOR LIFE TODAY

3. The book of Haggai has been titled "First Things First," "The Temple Restored and the Kingdom Foretold," "The Builder's Book," and "God's Interests Deserve Top Priority." With that reputation for this book, what kinds of answers and guidelines and solutions would you like to gain as you examine it more closely?

4. When you get to heaven, if you have a long talk with Haggai and he asks you, "What was most helpful to you in my book?" how would you like to be able to answer him?

5. As you think first about *who God is,* and second about *what the Bible is,* how strongly would you rate your present desire to understand better the book of Haggai? Use a scale of one to ten (one = "no desire at all," ten = "extremely intense desire") to help you decide.

6. From what you see in the actions of the people of Israel in 1:12, what would be a good personal prayer to offer to God as you study this book?

HAGGAI 1

SEEING WHAT'S THERE

1. How does this chapter show the consequences of disobedience?

2. What are God's people challenged to do in this chapter?

FOR LIFE TODAY

3. Think again about verses 2 and 3. What would God say it is time for in *your* life?

4. In Jeremiah 23:29, God says that His Word is like fire, and like a hammer. He can use the Scriptures to burn away unclean thoughts and desires in our hearts. He can also use Scripture to hit hard like a hammer, with the power to crush our spiritual hardness. From your study in this book of Haggai, how do you most want to see the "fire-and-hammer" power of God's Word at work in your own life?

HAGGAI 2

SEEING WHAT'S THERE

1. How exactly does this chapter show the consequences of both obedience and disobedience?

2. What specific *encouragement* is given in this chapter?

3. What promises does God make in this chapter?

CAPTURE THE ESSENCE

4. Imagine yourself being present in the temple in Jerusalem as the twelve-year-old Jesus hears this book read and discussed by the rabbis there. In Luke 2:46

we read that He was listening to these teachers and asking them questions. What passages from this book do you think would most impress the boy Jesus, and what questions or comments do you suppose He might have spoken?

FOR LIFE TODAY

5. What encouragement do you think God most wants to give *you* today? How might He use the words of this chapter to do it?

6. Review the guidelines for our thought-life given in Philippians 4:8—"Whatever is true, whatever is noble, whatever is right, whatever is pure, whatever is lovely, whatever is admirable—if anything is excellent or praiseworthy—*think about such things.*"What food for thought have you found in the book of Haggai that especially strikes you as being *true,* or *noble,* or *right,* or *pure,* or *lovely,* or *admirable,* or *excellent,* or *praiseworthy?*

HAGGAI:
THE BIG PICTURE

(Discuss again the questions in the "Overview," plus the questions below.)

1. For getting the most from the book Haggai, one of the best guidelines is found in 2 Timothy 3:16-17, words which Paul wrote with the Old Testament first in view. He said that *all* Scripture is of great benefit to (a) teach us, (b) rebuke us, (c) correct us, and (d) train us in righteousness. Paul added that these Scriptures completely equip the person of God "for every good work." As you think seriously about those guidelines, in which of these areas do you especially see the usefulness of Haggai?

2. Imagine that you were helping to produce a film based on the book of Haggai. Describe the kinds of scenery, supporting characters, background music, lighting effects, etc., which you would use to help portray the central message of this book.

3. Look together at each of these passages, and discuss which one you believe is the best candidate for "KEY VERSE" in the book of Haggai—the one which brings into sharpest focus what this book is most about: 1:4, 1:7-8, or 2:7-9.

4. What would you say is the main theme (or themes) in the book of Haggai?

5. SEARCH FOR THE SAVIOR—What words, images, or themes in Haggai have reminded you most of Jesus?

6. If Haggai were the only book in the Old Testament, in what ways would it still make a good introduction to the message of Jesus in the New Testament?

7. Based especially on your own experience, complete this statement in the way that's most meaningful to you: I believe it's important for Christians to read and explore the book of Haggai because…

Zechariah

OVERVIEW

(Discuss these OVERVIEW questions both at the beginning of your study of Zechariah, then again after you've studied all fourteen chapters. Your answers may change significantly once you've looked more closely at the entire book.)

Startup: Remember back to what your life was like ten years ago. Then talk together about how easy it would have been back then to predict the most important things that would happen in your life in the next decade.

SEEING WHAT'S THERE

1. Before launching into a closer look at Zechariah, how would you summarize what you already know about this book?

2. Look also at the list of "Questions to Ask as You Begin Your Study of Each Book" on page 9.

FOR LIFE TODAY

3. The book of Zechariah has been titled "Looking Ahead," "Visions and a Coming King," "The Book of the Future," "The Nation God Remembers," and "The Lord Remembers His People Israel." With that reputation for this book, what kinds of answers and guidelines and solutions would you like to gain as you examine it more closely?

4. When you get to heaven, if you have a long talk with Zechariah and he asks you, "What was most helpful to you in my book?" how would you like to be able to answer him?

5. As you think first about *who God is,* and second about *what the Bible is,* how strongly would you rate your present desire to understand better the book of Zechariah? Use a scale of one to ten (one = "no desire at all," ten = "extremely intense desire") to help you decide.

6. From what you see in the words of the Lord in 1:3, what would be a good personal prayer to offer to God as you study this book?

ZECHARIAH 1

SEEING WHAT'S THERE

1. What would you say is the brightest promise in verses 1-6? The most fearful warning? The most urgent command? And the most painful accusation?

2. Discuss all the details you see in the visions in verses 7-21. As fully as you can, how would you explain the meaning and significance of each vision?

3. Look also on page 8 at the list of "Questions to Ask as You Study Each Chapter." You may want to look again at this list for each chapter in Zechariah.

FOR LIFE TODAY

4. Proverbs 2:1-5 tells about the sincere person who truly longs for wisdom and understanding, and who searches the Scriptures for it—as if it were buried treasure. That person, Solomon says, will come to understand the fear of the Lord, and discover the knowledge of God. As you begin exploring the book of Zechariah, what "buried treasure" would you like God to help you find here—to show you what God and His wisdom are really like? If you have this desire, how would you express it in your own words?

ZECHARIAH 2

SEEING WHAT'S THERE

1. Discuss all the details you see in Zechariah's vision in this chapter. As fully as you can, how would you explain the meaning and significance of this vision?

ZECHARIAH 3

SEEING WHAT'S THERE

1. Again, discuss all the details you see in Zechariah's vision in this chapter. As fully as you can, how would you explain the meaning and significance of this vision?

ZECHARIAH 4

SEEING WHAT'S THERE

1. Discuss all the details you see in Zechariah's vision in this chapter. As fully as you can, how would you explain the meaning and significance of this vision?

CAPTURE THE ESSENCE

2. How would you restate in your own words God's message to Zerubbabel in verse 6?

ZECHARIAH 5

SEEING WHAT'S THERE

1. Again discuss all the details you see in Zechariah's two visions in this chapter. As fully as you can, how would you explain the meaning and significance of each vision?

ZECHARIAH 6

SEEING WHAT'S THERE

1. Discuss all the details you see in Zechariah's vision in verses 1-8. As fully as you can, how would you explain the meaning and significance of this vision?

2. Look carefully at the Lord's words in verses 9-15. What exactly does He tell Zechariah to do, and for what purpose?

ZECHARIAH 7

SEEING WHAT'S THERE

1. As you reflect on this chapter, what would you say is the most urgent command it expresses? The most painful accusation? The sharpest picture of punishment and disaster? And the deepest glimpse into God's character?

CAPTURE THE ESSENCE

2. Now that you're halfway through Zechariah, how would you summarize the most important teachings in this book?

FOR LIFE TODAY

3. In Jeremiah 23:29, God says that His Word is like fire, and like a hammer. He can use the Scriptures to burn away unclean thoughts and desires in our hearts. He can also use Scripture to hit hard like a hammer, with the power to crush our spiritual hardness. From your study in this book of Zechariah, how do you most want to see the "fire-and-hammer" power of God's Word at work in your own life?

ZECHARIAH 8

SEEING WHAT'S THERE

1. As you think about Zechariah's prophecy in this chapter, what would you say is the brightest promise here? The most urgent command? The most powerful vision of a future day? And the deepest glimpse into God's character?

CAPTURE THE ESSENCE

2. In this chapter, what does God want us to understand most about His purpose and plan for His people?

FOR LIFE TODAY

3. If God had written this chapter only for you, which words or phrases do you think He might have underlined, and why?

ZECHARIAH 9

SEEING WHAT'S THERE

1. As you ponder Zechariah's words in this chapter, what would you say is the brightest promise here? The most urgent command? The most powerful vision of a future day? The sharpest picture of punishment and disaster? And the deepest glimpse into God's character?

CAPTURE THE ESSENCE

2. Look again at verse 9. As a prophetic passage about the coming Messiah, what does this Scripture teach us about the *character* and the *ministry* of Jesus Christ?

FOR GOING DEEPER

Discuss together the prophetic fulfillment of verse 9 which you see in Matthew 21:1-9 and John 12:12-16.

ZECHARIAH 10

SEEING WHAT'S THERE

1. As you reflect on Zechariah's message for God's people in this chapter, what would you say is the brightest promise it contains? The most tender encouragement? The most urgent command? The most powerful vision of a future day? The most painful accusation? And the deepest glimpse into God's character?

CAPTURE THE ESSENCE

2. How does this chapter help us understand what God most desires for His people?

FOR LIFE TODAY

3. In Isaiah 55:10-11, God reminds us that He sends rain and snow from the sky to water the earth and to nurture life. In the same way, God says that He sends His words to accomplish specific purposes. From your study so far, what would you suggest are *God's* primary purposes for the book of Zechariah in the lives of Christians today?

ZECHARIAH 11

SEEING WHAT'S THERE

1. Look over verses 4-17. How would you explain the meaning and significance of what Zechariah does here?

FOR LIFE TODAY

2. In Romans 15:4, Paul reminds us that the Old Testament Scriptures can give us patience and perseverance on one hand, as well as comfort and encouragement on the other. In your own life, how do you see this book of Zechariah living up to Paul's description? In what ways, if any, is it meeting your personal needs for both *perseverance* and *encouragement?*

ZECHARIAH 12

SEEING WHAT'S THERE

1. As you study Zechariah's words here, what would you say is the brightest promise in this chapter? The most powerful vision of a future day? And the sharpest picture of punishment and disaster?

CAPTURE THE ESSENCE

2. In your own words, what would you say God wants us to understand most about Himself in verse 1?

3. What words or phrases in this chapter tell us the most about God's purpose and plan for His people?

FOR GOING DEEPER

How was the meaning of verse 10 regarded by the apostle John in John 19:34-37?

ZECHARIAH 13

SEEING WHAT'S THERE

1. Which of the prophecies in this chapter would you say point most directly to Jesus Christ?

FOR GOING DEEPER

Review the Messianic prophecy in verse 7, then look at how Jesus used this passage in Matthew 26:31-35 and Mark 14:27-31.

ZECHARIAH 14

SEEING WHAT'S THERE

1. Chapter 14 has been called the key to the book of Zechariah. What does this chapter include that could make it this significant?

2. As you review the various prophecies in this chapter, which of them call to mind New Testament passages and teachings which you are familiar with?

CAPTURE THE ESSENCE

3. What are the most important things this chapter communicates about God's character and personality?

4. What are the most important things this chapter communicates about God's purpose and plans for His people?

5. Imagine yourself being present in the temple in Jerusalem as the twelve-year-old Jesus hears this book read and discussed by the rabbis there. In Luke 2:46 we read that He was listening to these teachers and asking them questions. What passages from this book do you think would most impress the boy Jesus, and what questions or comments do you suppose He might have spoken?

FOR LIFE TODAY

6. Review the guidelines for our thought-life given in Philippians 4:8—"Whatever is true, whatever is noble, whatever is right, whatever is pure, whatever is lovely, whatever is admirable—if anything is excellent or praiseworthy—*think about such things.*" What food for thought have you found in the book of Zechariah that especially strikes you as being *true,* or *noble,* or *right,* or *pure,* or *lovely,* or *admirable,* or *excellent,* or *praiseworthy?*

ZECHARIAH:
THE BIG PICTURE

(Discuss again the questions in the "Overview," plus the questions below.)

1. For getting the most from the book of Zechariah, one of the best guidelines is found in 2 Timothy 3:16-17, words which Paul wrote with the Old Testament first in view. He said that *all* Scripture is of great benefit to (a) teach us, (b) rebuke us, (c) correct us, and (d) train us in righteousness. Paul added that these Scriptures completely equip the person of God "for every good work." As you think seriously about those guidelines, in which of these areas do you especially see the usefulness of Zechariah?

2. Look together at each of these passages, and discuss which one you believe is the best candidate for "KEY VERSE" in the book of Zechariah—the one which brings into sharpest focus what this book is most about: 1:3, 8:3, or 9:9-10.

3. What would you say is the main theme (or themes) in the book of Zechariah?

4. SEARCH FOR THE SAVIOR—What words, images, or themes in Zechariah have reminded you most of Jesus?

5. If Zechariah were the only book in the Old Testament, in what ways would it still make a good introduction to the message of Jesus in the New Testament?

6. Based especially on your own experience, complete this statement in the way that's most meaningful to you: I believe it's important for Christians to read and explore the book of Zechariah because…

Malachi

OVERVIEW

(Discuss these OVERVIEW questions both at the beginning of your study of Malachi, then again after you've studied all four chapters. Your answers may change significantly once you've looked more closely at the entire book.)

Startup: Talk together about the kinds of things that help you most to restore a close relationship with God after a time of "drifting away" from Him.

SEEING WHAT'S THERE

1. Before launching into a closer look at Malachi, how would you summarize what you already know about this book?

2. Look also at the list of "Questions to Ask as You Begin Your Study of Each Book" on page 9.

FOR LIFE TODAY

3. The book of Malachi has been titled "The Gathering Gloom," "Final Judgment and Warning," "God Tells His People to Be Loyal," and "The Certainty of Judgment." With that reputation for this book, what kinds of answers and guidelines and solutions would you like to gain as you examine it more closely?

4. When you get to heaven, if you have a long talk with Malachi and he asks you, "What was most helpful to you in my book?" how would you like to be able to answer him?

5. As you think first about *who God is,* and second about *what the Bible is,* how strongly would you rate your present desire to understand better the book of Malachi? Use a scale of one to ten (one = "no desire at all," ten = "extremely intense desire") to help you decide.

MALACHI 1

SEEING WHAT'S THERE

1. What sins and failures does the Lord rebuke in this chapter?

2. Look also on page 8 at the list of "Questions to Ask as You Study Each Chapter." You may want to look again at this list for each chapter in Malachi.

CAPTURE THE ESSENCE

3. From all that you see in this chapter, what are the most important things God wants us to understand about His personality and character?

FOR LIFE TODAY

4. Which verse or phrase in this chapter do you think God would like you to understand best?

5. Proverbs 2:1-5 tells about the sincere person who truly longs for wisdom and understanding, and who searches the Scriptures for it—as if it were buried treasure. That person, Solomon says, will come to understand the fear of the Lord, and discover the knowledge of God. As you begin exploring the book of Malachi, what "buried treasure" would you like God to help you find here—to show you what God and His wisdom are really like? If you have this desire, how would you express it in your own words?

MALACHI 2

SEEING WHAT'S THERE

1. What sins and failures does the Lord rebuke in this chapter?

2. From what you see in this chapter, how would you summarize God's *expectations* for His people?

FOR LIFE TODAY

3. If God had written this chapter only for you, which words or phrases do you think He might have underlined, and why?

4. In Isaiah 55:10-11, God reminds us that He sends rain and snow from the sky to water the earth and to nurture life. In the same way, God says that He sends His words to accomplish specific purposes. From your study so far, what would you suggest are *God's* primary purposes for the book of Malachi in the lives of Christians today?

FOR GOING DEEPER

The returned exiles had returned to the shameful practice of divorcing their Israelite wives and marrying pagan women. As you consider verses 10-16, what do Matthew 5:31-32 and 19:4-9 contribute to your understanding of God's heart on this matter?

Also, compare what you see here in Malachi 2:11-12 with Nehemiah 13:23-29 and Ezra 9—10. From the way Ezra and Nehemiah responded to this problem, how well would you say they conformed to God's standards as presented here in Malachi?

MALACHI 3

SEEING WHAT'S THERE

1. What vision for a future day does the Lord reveal in verses 1-5? What does God promise to do?

2. What further sins does the Lord rebuke in verses 6-15?

3. In verses 16-17, how would you summarize in your own words the responses to one another between God and His people? And what promise does God extend in verse 18?

CAPTURE THE ESSENCE

4. What times and events in the life of Jesus would you say were in fulfillment of the prophecy spoken by Malachi in the first three verses of this chapter?

5. What words or phrases in this chapter tell us the most about God's *character*?

FOR LIFE TODAY

6. In light of how you're doing spiritually in your life today, which verse in this chapter do you think is the most important at this time—and why?

7. In Jeremiah 23:29, God says that His Word is like fire, and like a hammer. He can use the Scriptures to burn away unclean thoughts and desires in our hearts. He can also use Scripture to hit hard like a hammer, with the power to crush our spiritual hardness. From your study in this book of Malachi, how do you most want to see the "fire-and-hammer" power of God's Word at work in your own life?

FOR GOING DEEPER

Notice how Jesus used verse 1 in His ministry in Matthew 11:7-19 and Luke 7:24-27.

MALACHI 4

SEEING WHAT'S THERE

1. What vision for a future day is described in this chapter? How would you explain each detail?

CAPTURE THE ESSENCE

2. Imagine yourself being present in the temple in Jerusalem as the twelve-year-old Jesus hears this book read and discussed by the rabbis there. In Luke 2:46 we read that He was listening to these teachers and asking them questions. What passages from this book do you think would most impress the boy Jesus, and what questions or comments do you suppose He might have spoken?

FOR LIFE TODAY

3. Which verse or phrase in this chapter do you think God would like you to understand best?

4. Review the guidelines for our thought-life given in Philippians 4:8—"Whatever is true, whatever is noble, whatever is right, whatever is pure, whatever is lovely, whatever is admirable—if anything is excellent or praiseworthy—*think about such things.*" What food for thought have you found in the book of Malachi that especially strikes you as being *true,* or *noble,* or *right,* or *pure,* or *lovely,* or *admirable,* or *excellent,* or *praiseworthy?*

FOR GOING DEEPER

Read again the words of this last chapter in the Old Testament... then turn to Revelation 22:12-21, the last words in the New Testament. What similarities and differences do you see in these passages?

MALACHI:
THE BIG PICTURE

(Discuss again the questions in the "Overview," plus the questions below.)

1. For getting the most from the book of Malachi, one of the best guidelines is found in 2 Timothy 3:16-17, words which Paul wrote with the Old Testament first in view. He said that *all* Scripture is of great benefit to (a) teach us, (b) rebuke us, (c) correct us, and (d) train us in righteousness. Paul added that these Scriptures completely equip the person of God "for every good work." As you think seriously about those guidelines, in which of these areas do you especially see the usefulness of Malachi?

2. Look together at each of these passages, and discuss which one you believe is the best candidate for "KEY VERSE" in the book of Malachi—the one which brings into sharpest focus what this book is most about: 3:1, 4:1-2, or 4:5-6.

3. What would you say is the main theme (or themes) in the book of Malachi?

4. SEARCH FOR THE SAVIOR—What words, images, or themes in Malachi have reminded you most of Jesus?

5. If Malachi were the only book in the Old Testament, in what ways would it still make a good introduction to the message of Jesus in the New Testament?

6. Based especially on your own experience, complete this statement in the way that's most meaningful to you: I believe it's important for Christians to read and explore the book of Malachi because...

Topical Study Guide

USE THIS SECTION for a topical approach to your group's Bible study discussions. The subject areas here are listed alphabetically by topic. For each one you'll see a few brief but foundational discussion questions, plus a selection of illuminating Scripture passages to explore together. (Especially where a longer passage is indicated, you may want to refer to the questions listed for that Bible chapter in the main section of *The Complete Bible Discussion Guide.*)

CONFIDENCE

1. What thoughts and images come to mind when you think of the word *confidence?* In what situations have you felt most confident in life? When have you felt least confident?

2. Is *confidence* the same as *pride?* Is it the same as *boldness?* What would you say is the best definition for each word?

3. What do the following verses tell us about confidence? Take a fresh look at each passage, searching especially for (a) God's commands and standards to keep, (b) someone's example to learn from, (c) a promise from God to believe, (d) a warning to heed, or (e) a challenge to face.

   •2 Chronicles 26 •Psalm 27
   •Jeremiah 9:23-24 •Acts 27:21-25
   •2 Corinthians 5:6-10 •Philippians 1:6
   •2 Timothy 1:12 •Hebrews 10:35
   •1 John 2:28-29, 5:14-15

4. What vital, fundamental principles can you see in these passages (principles which are consistent with other Scriptures you know)?

5. Finally, answer these questions, especially in light of what you've observed in the passages above: (a) What does God want me to understand most about Himself? (b) What does God want me to understand most about others? (c) What does God want me to understand most about myself? And in light of all this, what would He have me *do?*

COUNSELING

1. How would you compare the meaning of the words *counsel, advice,* and *influence?*

2. Decide together how you would define the word *counselor.*

3. Discuss what guidelines and information the following verses offer us about counseling. Look in a fresh way at each passage, searching especially for (a) God's commands and standards to keep, (b) someone's example to learn from, (c) a promise from God to believe, (d) a warning to heed, or (e) a challenge to face.

   •Exodus 18 •1 Samuel 25:20-34
   •2 Samuel 15:32-34, 16:5–17:23
   •1 Kings 12:1-20
   •2 Chronicles 25:14-16
   •Proverbs 11:14, 13:10, 15:22, 24:6, 27:9

4. What vital, fundamental principles can you see in these passages (principles which are consistent with other Scriptures you know)?

5. In conclusion, answer these questions, especially in light of what you've ob-

served in the passages above: (a) What does God want me to understand most about Himself? (b) What does God want me to understand most about others? (c) What does God want me to understand most about myself? And in light of all this, what would He have me *do?*

DECISION MAKING

1. What would you say are the five most important decisions you have made in your life? What is the most important decision you expect to make in the next month?

2. Discuss how much you agree or disagree with this statement: There is no such thing as a situation in life in which you "have no choice."

3. Dig deeply in the following verses and decide how they relate to decision making. Take a fresh look at each passage, searching especially for (a) God's commands and standards to keep, (b) someone's example to learn from, (c) a promise from God to believe, (d) a warning to heed, or (e) a challenge to face.

   •Genesis 28:20-22
   •Numbers 13:30-33
   •Deuteronomy 30:19-20
   •Joshua 24:14-15 •Psalm 73:23-24, 86:11 •Isaiah 48:17 •Luke 14:16-33
   •Philippians 1:21-26
   •Hebrews 11:24-26

4. What vital, fundamental principles can you see in these passages (principles which are consistent with other Scriptures you know)?

5. In conclusion, answer these questions, especially in light of what you've observed in the passages above: (a) What does God want me to understand most about Himself? (b) What does God want me to understand most about others? (c) What does God want

me to understand most about myself? And in light of all this, what would He have me *do?*

DESIRE

1. What thoughts and images come to mind when you think of the word *desire?*

2. Discuss what you believe is the best definition for the word *desire.*

3. Discuss how the following verses relate to our desires. Look in a fresh way at each passage, searching especially for (a) God's commands and standards to keep, (b) someone's example to learn from, (c) a promise from God to believe, (d) a warning to heed, or (e) a challenge to face.

   •Psalm 37:4, 42:1-2, 73:25
   •Proverbs 4:23 •Luke 12:15

4. What vital, fundamental principles can you see in these passages (principles which are consistent with other Scriptures you know)?

5. Finally, answer these questions, especially in light of what you've observed in the passages above: (a) What does God want me to understand most about Himself? (b) What does God want me to understand most about others? (c) What does God want me to understand most about myself? And in light of all this, what would He have me *do?*

DISCIPLINE

1. What thoughts and images come to mind when you think of the word *discipline?* Are they negative, positive, or a mixture of both?

2. Decide together how you would define the word *discipline.*

3. Discuss how the following verses relate to discipline. Take a fresh look at each passage, searching especially for (a) God's commands and standards to keep, (b) someone's example to learn from, (c) a promise from God to believe, (d) a warning to heed, or (e) a challenge to face.

   •Proverbs 3:11-12, 6:23, 10:17, 12:1, 13:18, 20:30

4. What vital, fundamental principles can you see in these passages (principles which are consistent with other Scriptures you know)?

5. Finally, answer these questions, especially in light of what you've observed in the passages above: (a) What does God want me to understand most about Himself? (b) What does God want me to understand most about others? (c) What does God want me to understand most about myself? And in light of all this, what would He have me *do?*

EVANGELISM

1. What thoughts and images come to mind when you think of the word *evangelism?*

2. Decide together what you believe is the best definition for the word *evangelism.*

3. Discuss how the following verses relate to evangelism. Look in a fresh way at each passage, searching especially for (a) God's commands and standards to keep, (b) someone's example to learn from, (c) a promise from God to believe, (d) a warning to heed, or (e) a challenge to face.

•Psalm 73:27-28 •Matthew 5:13-16, 28:18-20 •Mark 16:15 •Acts 1:8
•2 Corinthians 5:16-21, 6:1-2
•Colossians 4:5-6
•Revelation 12:10-11

4. What vital, fundamental principles can you see in these passages (principles which are consistent with other Scriptures you know)?

5. In conclusion, answer these questions, especially in light of what you've observed in the passages above: (a) What does God want me to understand most about Himself? (b) What does God want me to understand most about others? (c) What does God want me to understand most about myself? And in light of all this, what would He have me *do?*

FAITH

1. What thoughts and images come to mind when you think of the word *faith?* What individuals in the Bible impress you most as being people of faith?

2. Decide together how you would define the word *faith.* How would you explain the meaning of this word to a child?

3. Discuss how the following verses relate to faith. Take a fresh look at each passage, searching especially for (a) God's commands and standards to keep, (b) someone's example to learn from, (c) a promise from God to believe, (d) a warning to heed, or (e) a challenge to face.

•Genesis 15 •Psalm 42:11, 125:1-2
•Proverbs 3:5-6, 29:25 •Jonah 3:3-5
•Mark 6:1-6 •Luke 7:1-10, 17:5-6
•John 20:24-29 •Romans 14:1-4
•Hebrews 11 •James 2:14-26

4. What vital, fundamental principles can you see in these passages (principles

which are consistent with other Scriptures you know)?

5. In conclusion, answer these questions, especially in light of what you've observed in the passages above: (a) What does God want me to understand most about Himself? (b) What does God want me to understand most about others? (c) What does God want me to understand most about myself? And in light of all this, what would He have me *do?*

FAMILY

1. How would you explain God's purpose for the family? How many purposes can you think of?

2. Discuss what you believe is the most useful definition for the word *family.*

3. Discuss how the following verses relate to the family. Take a fresh look at each passage, searching especially for (a) God's commands and standards to keep, (b) someone's example to learn from, (c) a promise from God to believe, (d) a warning to heed, or (e) a challenge to face.

   •Genesis 2:21-24 •Genesis 9:1
   •Genesis 18:19 •1 Samuel 1
   •Proverbs 17:6, 19:13-14, 19:26, 21:9, 22:6, 30:17 •Psalm 127:3-5
   •Ephesians 5:22–6:4

4. What vital, fundamental principles can you see in these passages (principles which are consistent with other Scriptures you know)?

5. In conclusion, answer these questions, especially in light of what you've observed in the passages above: (a) What does God want me to understand most about Himself? (b) What does God want me to understand most about others? (c) What does God want me to understand most about myself? And in light of all this, what would He have me *do?*

FELLOWSHIP

1. What thoughts and images come to mind when you think of the word *fellowship?*

2. Discuss what you consider to be the best definition for the word *fellowship.* Within the body of Christ, does it mean the same as the word *unity?* Is it possible to have fellowship without unity? Is it possible to have unity without fellowship?

3. Explore the following verses to find the biblical view of fellowship. Take a fresh look at each passage, searching especially for (a) God's commands and standards to keep, (b) someone's example to learn from, (c) a promise from God to believe, (d) a warning to heed, or (e) a challenge to face.

   •Psalm 133 •Matthew 18:15-20
   •John 17:20-23 •Acts 2:42-47
   •Romans 15:7 •2 Corinthians 6:14-18
   •Philippians 3:10 •1 John 1

4. What vital, fundamental principles can you see in these passages (principles which are consistent with other Scriptures you know)?

5. Finally, answer these questions, especially in light of what you've observed in the passages above: (a) What does God want me to understand most about Himself? (b) What does God want me to understand most about others? (c) What does God want me to understand most about myself? And in light of all this, what would He have me *do?*

FORGIVENESS

1. What thoughts and images come to mind when you think of the word *forgiveness?*

2. Decide together how you would define the word *forgiveness,* both from God's point of view (our forgiveness from Him), and our point of view (our forgiveness for one another). Should the word have the same meaning in each case?

3. Discuss how the following verses relate to forgiveness. Take a fresh look at each passage, searching especially for (a) God's commands and standards to keep, (b) someone's example to learn from, (c) a promise from God to believe, (d) a warning to heed, or (e) a challenge to face.

   •Leviticus 4:13-21 •Psalm 32
   •Proverbs 19:11 •Matthew 5:7,
   6:12-15 •Luke 6:37-38, 7:36-50,
   17:3-4 •Romans 12:17
   •Colossians 3:13 •Hebrews 10:1-18
   •1 John 1:9

4. What vital, fundamental principles can you see in these passages (principles which are consistent with other Scriptures you know)?

5. Finally, answer these questions, especially in light of what you've observed in the passages above: (a) What does God want me to understand most about Himself? (b) What does God want me to understand most about others? (c) What does God want me to understand most about myself? And in light of all this, what would He have me *do?*

FREEDOM

1. What thoughts and images come to mind when you think of the word *freedom?*

2. Decide together what you believe is the best definition for the word *freedom.*

3. Discuss how the following verses relate to freedom. Look in a fresh way at each passage, searching especially for (a) God's commands and standards to keep, (b) someone's example to learn from, (c) a promise from God to believe, (d) a warning to heed, or (e) a challenge to face.

   •John 8:31-36 •Romans 8:1-2
   •2 Corinthians 3:17 •Galatians 5:1-2
   •Colossians 1:13-14

4. What vital, fundamental principles can you see in these passages (principles which are consistent with other Scriptures you know)?

5. In conclusion, answer these questions, especially in light of what you've observed in the passages above: (a) What does God want me to understand most about Himself? (b) What does God want me to understand most about others? (c) What does God want me to understand most about myself? And in light of all this, what would He have me *do?*

FRIENDSHIP

1. What thoughts and images come to mind when you think of the word *friend?*

2. What would you say is the best definition for the word *friend?*

3. Discuss how the following verses relate to friendship. Look in a fresh way at each passage, searching especially for (a) God's commands and standards to keep, (b) someone's example to learn from, (c) a promise from God to believe, (d) a warning to heed, or (e) a challenge to face.

   •1 Samuel 18:1-4 •Job 2:11-13
   •Psalm 119:63 •Proverbs 17:17, 18:24, 27:6 •Ecclesiastes 4:9 •John 15:13-17
   •James 4:4

4. What vital, fundamental principles can you see in these passages (principles which are consistent with other Scriptures you know)?

5. In conclusion, answer these questions, especially in light of what you've observed in the passages above: (a) What does God want me to understand most about Himself? (b) What does God want me to understand most about others? (c) What does God want me to understand most about myself? And in light of all this, what would He have me *do?*

GENEROSITY

1. What thoughts and images come to mind when you think of the word *generosity?*

2. Decide together how you would define the word *generosity.*

3. Discuss what the following verses tell us about generosity. Take a fresh look at each passage, searching especially for (a) God's commands and standards to keep, (b) someone's example to learn from, (c) a promise from God to believe, (d) a warning to heed, or (e) a challenge to face.

   •Proverbs 3:9-10, 3:27-28, 11:25, 19:17, 22:9, 28:27 •Luke 6:38
   •2 Corinthians 8, 9 •Galatians 6:6-10
   •Philippians 4:12-19 •1 John 3:17-18

4. What vital, fundamental principles can you see in these passages (principles which are consistent with other Scriptures you know)?

5. In conclusion, answer these questions, especially in light of what you've observed in the passages above: (a) What does God want me to understand most about Himself? (b) What does God want me to understand most about others? (c) What does God want me to understand most about myself? And in light of all this, what would He have me *do?*

GENTLENESS

1. What thoughts and images come to mind when you think of the word *gentleness?* How well do you think most people understand this quality, which is also among the fruit of the Spirit (Galatians 5:22-23)?

2. Discuss what you believe is the best definition for the word *gentleness.*

3. Discuss what the following verses reveal about gentleness. Look in a fresh way at each passage, searching especially for (a) God's commands and stan-

dards to keep, (b) someone's example to learn from, (c) a promise from God to believe, (d) a warning to heed, or (e) a challenge to face.

• 2 Samuel 22:36 •Matthew 5:5, 11:28-30 •Galatians 6:1
• 1 Thessalonians 2:7

4. What vital, fundamental principles can you see in these passages (principles which are consistent with other Scriptures you know)?

5. In conclusion, answer these questions, especially in light of what you've observed in the passages above: (a) What does God want me to understand most about Himself? (b) What does God want me to understand most about others? (c) What does God want me to understand most about myself? And in light of all this, what would He have me *do*?

HOLINESS

1. What thoughts and images come to mind when you think of the words *holy* and *holiness?* Are these thoughts and images mostly positive, or mostly negative?

2. Discuss what you believe are the best definitions for the words *holy* and *holiness.* How would you explain the meaning of these words to a child?

3. Discuss how the following verses relate to holiness. Take a fresh look at each passage, searching especially for (a) God's commands and standards to keep, (b) someone's example to learn from, (c) a promise from God to believe, (d) a warning to heed, or (e) a challenge to face.

• Genesis 2:3 •Exodus 19:4-6
• Leviticus 11:44-45 •Romans 12:1-2
• 2 Corinthians 7:1 •Ephesians 1:4
• 1 Peter 1:13-25 •Revelation 22:11

4. What vital, fundamental principles can you see in these passages (principles

which are consistent with other Scriptures you know)?

5. Finally, answer these questions, especially in light of what you've observed in the passages above: (a) What does God want me to understand most about Himself? (b) What does God want me to understand most about others? (c) What does God want me to understand most about myself? And in light of all this, what would He have me *do*?

HONOR

1. What thoughts and images come to mind when you think of the word *honor?*

2. Discuss what you believe is the best definition for the word *honor.*

3. Discuss how the following verses relate to honor. Look in a fresh way at each passage, searching especially for (a) God's commands and standards to keep, (b) someone's example to learn from, (c) a promise from God to believe, (d) a warning to heed, or (e) a challenge to face.

• Genesis 41:39-44
• Numbers 27:18-20 •1 Samuel 2:30, 18:5 •Psalm 84:11 •Proverbs 15:33, 20:3, 21:21 •Daniel 2:46-49
• John 5:23, 12:26 •1 Timothy 1:17
• Ephesians 6:1-2

4. What vital, fundamental principles can you see in these passages (principles which are consistent with other Scriptures you know)?

5. Finally, answer these questions, especially in light of what you've observed in the passages above: (a) What does God want me to understand most about Himself? (b) What does God want me to understand most about others? (c) What does God want me to understand most about myself? And in light of all this, what would He have me *do*?

HUMILITY

1. What thoughts and images come to mind when you think of the words *proud* and *humble?* Think about people whom you consider to be humble. What do they do that causes you to think of them in that regard?

2. Decide together what you consider to be the best definition for the word *humble.* How would you explain the meaning of this word to a child?

3. Discuss how the following verses relate to humility. Take a fresh look at each passage, searching especially for (a) God's commands and standards to keep, (b) someone's example to learn from, (c) a promise from God to believe, (d) a warning to heed, or (e) a challenge to face.

   •1 Kings 21:27-29 •Psalm 25:8-9
   •Proverbs 3:7, 3:33-34 •Isaiah 6:5,
   57:15, 66:2 •Micah 6:8 •Matthew 5:3,
   11:25-30, 20:20-28 •Mark 1:4-8
   •Ephesians 4:1-2 •Philippians 2:1-8
   •Titus 3:1-2 •James 4:6-10

4. What vital, fundamental principles can you see in these passages (principles which are consistent with other Scriptures you know)?

5. In conclusion, answer these questions, especially in light of what you've observed in the passages above: (a) What does God want me to understand most about Himself? (b) What does God want me to understand most about others? (c) What does God want me to understand most about myself? And in light of all this, what would He have me *do?*

INTEGRITY

1. What thoughts and images come to mind when you think of the word *integrity?* How important is personal integrity to you at this time in your life, compared with times in your past? Use a scale of one to ten (one = "much less than ever," ten = "much more than ever") to help you decide.

2. Decide together what you believe is the best definition for the word *integrity.* How would you explain the meaning of this word to a child?

3. Discuss how the following verses relate to integrity. Take a fresh look at each passage, searching especially for (a) God's commands and standards to keep, (b) someone's example to learn from, (c) a promise from God to believe, (d) a warning to heed, or (e) a challenge to face.

   •Leviticus 19:35-36
   •Deuteronomy 16:19 •2 Kings 22:5-7
   •Nehemiah 13 •Psalm 41:11-12,
   78:72 •Proverbs 11:1, 11:3, 12:22,
   16:11, 20:7, 20:10 •Luke 3:12-14
   •2 Corinthians 8:20-21

4. What vital, fundamental principles can you see in these passages (principles which are consistent with other Scriptures you know)?

5. In conclusion, answer these questions, especially in light of what you've observed in the passages above: (a) What does God want me to understand most about Himself? (b) What does God want me to understand most about others? (c) What does God want me to understand most about myself? And in light of all this, what would He have me *do?*

JOY

1. What thoughts and images come to mind when you think of the word *joy?*

2. Decide together what you believe is the best definition for the word *joy.* Is it best described as an emotion, an attitude, a decision, an instinct, or a consequence?

3. Discuss how the following verses relate to joy. Take a fresh look at each passage, searching especially for (a) God's commands and standards to keep, (b) someone's example to learn from, (c) a promise from God to believe, (d) a warning to heed, or (e) a challenge to face.

   •1 Samuel 2:1 •Nehemiah 8:9-12
   •Psalm 68:1-3 •Ecclesiastes 2:1-11,
   3:12 •Isaiah 35 •Matthew 5:4
   •Luke 1:46-49, 15:3-10 •John 16:22
   •Acts 3:6-10 •Philippians 4:4
   •1 Thessalonians 5:16-18
   •1 Peter 1:6-9

4. What vital, fundamental principles can you see in these passages (principles which are consistent with other Scriptures you know)?

5. Finally, answer these questions, especially in light of what you've observed in the passages above: (a) What does God want me to understand most about Himself? (b) What does God want me to understand most about others? (c) What does God want me to understand most about myself? And in light of all this, what would He have me *do?*

LEADERSHIP

1. What qualities impress you most in a good leader? And what traits do you want to see least in a leader?

2. What exactly does a leader do? Discuss what you believe is the best definition for the word *leadership.*

3. Discuss how the following verses relate to leadership. Take a fresh look at each passage, searching especially for (a) God's commands and standards to keep, (b) someone's example to learn from, (c) a promise from God to believe, (d) a warning to heed, or (e) a challenge to face.

   •Exodus 18:24-26 •Joshua 1
   •1 Samuel 18:16 •Psalm 78:70-72
   •Proverbs 16:10, 20:8, 20:26, 20:28, 22:11, 28:3, 28:15-16, 29:4
   •Luke 22:24-30 •1 Timothy 3:1-13, 4:11-12

4. What vital, fundamental principles can you see in these passages (principles which are consistent with other Scriptures you know)?

5. Finally, answer these questions, especially in light of what you've observed in the passages above: (a) What does God want me to understand most about Himself? (b) What does God want me to understand most about others? (c) What does God want me to understand most about myself? And in light of all this, what would He have me *do?*

LOVE

1. What thoughts and images come to mind when you think of the word *love?*

2. Decide together what you believe is the best definition for the word *love.*

3. Discuss how the following verses relate to love. Aim especially toward a fresh view of each passage, as you search for (a) God's commands and standards to keep, (b) someone's example to learn from, (c) a promise from God to believe, (d) a warning to heed, or (e) a challenge to face.

   •Leviticus 19:18 •Deuteronomy 6:4-5
   •1 Samuel 18:1-4 •Proverbs 3:3-4,
   10:12, 17:9 •Matthew 10:37,
   25:34-36 •John 8:42 John 15:9-13
   •Romans 8:35-39, 12:9-10, 13:8-10
   •Galatians 5:13-15
   •Ephesians 3:17-19
   •1 Thessalonians 4:9-10
   •1 Timothy 1:5 •Hebrews 10:24-25
   •1 Peter 4:8 •1 John 2:15-17, 3:11-20,
   4:7-21, 5:3

4. What vital, fundamental principles can you see in these passages (principles which are consistent with other Scriptures you know)?

5. In conclusion, answer these questions, especially in light of what you've observed in the passages above: (a) What does God want me to understand most about Himself? (b) What does God want me to understand most about others? (c) What does God want me to understand most about myself? And in light of all this, what would He have me *do?*

MATURITY

1. What qualities and actions come to mind when you hear someone described as being "spiritual mature"?

2. Discuss what you believe is the best definition for the term *spiritual maturity.*

3. Discuss how the following verses relate to spiritual maturity. Take a fresh look at each passage, searching especially for (a) God's commands and standards to keep, (b) someone's example to learn from, (c) a promise from God to believe, (d) a warning to heed, or (e) a challenge to face.

   •Matthew 5:6 •Luke 2:40, 2:52
   •Romans 15:1 •1 Corinthians 13:11,
   14:20 •Colossians 1:9-12, 2:6-7
   •Hebrews 5:11-14 •2 Peter 1:3-8
   •1 John 2:12-14

4. What vital, fundamental principles can you see in these passages (principles which are consistent with other Scriptures you know)?

5. Finally, answer these questions, especially in light of what you've observed in the passages above: (a) What does God want me to understand most about Himself? (b) What does God want me to understand most about others? (c) What does God want me to understand most about myself? And in light of all this, what would He have me *do?*

MONEY AND POSSESSIONS

1. What thoughts and images come to mind when you think of the word *wealth?* Are they mostly negative, mostly positive, or a mixture of both?

2. What thoughts and images come to mind when you think of the word *poverty?* Are they mostly negative, mostly positive, or a mixture of both?

3. Discuss how the following verses relate to money and possessions. Look in a fresh way at each passage, searching especially for (a) God's commands and standards to keep, (b) someone's example to learn from, (c) a promise from God to believe, (d) a warning to heed, or (e) a challenge to face.

•Deuteronomy 8:17-19 •Psalm 23:1, 49, 112 •Proverbs 13:11, 18:11
•Luke 12:15-34, 16
•1 Timothy 6:3-10, 6:17-19

4. What vital, fundamental principles can you see in these passages (principles which are consistent with other Scriptures you know)?

5. In conclusion, answer these questions, especially in light of what you've observed in the passages above: (a) What does God want me to understand most about Himself? (b) What does God want me to understand most about others? (c) What does God want me to understand most about myself? And in light of all this, what would He have me *do?*

OBEDIENCE

1. What thoughts and images come to mind when you think of the word *obedience?*

2. Decide together what you believe is the best definition for the word *obedience.*

3. Discuss how the following verses relate to obedience. Take a fresh look at each passage, searching especially for (a) God's commands and standards to keep, (b) someone's example to learn from, (c) a promise from God to believe, (d) a warning to heed, or (e) a challenge to face.

•Genesis 12:1-4 •Exodus 19:5, 23:20-33 •Joshua 11:15
•1 Samuel 15:22-23 •Ezra 7:10
•Psalm 25:10, 40:8, 119:56-60

•Matthew 12:50 •Luke 17:7-10, 22:41-42 •John 13:15, 14:15, 14:23
•Acts 5:29 •Hebrews 10:26-29
•James 1:19-27 •1 John 5:2-3

4. What vital, fundamental principles can you see in these passages (principles which are consistent with other Scriptures you know)?

5. Finally, answer these questions, especially in light of what you've observed in the passages above: (a) What does God want me to understand most about Himself? (b) What does God want me to understand most about others? (c) What does God want me to understand most about myself? And in light of all this, what would He have me *do?*

PATIENCE

1. Discuss what you believe is the best definition for the word *patience.*

2. In general, how patient do you consider yourself at this time in your life, compared with times in your past? To help you decide, use a scale of one to ten (one = "much less patient than ever," ten = "much more patient than ever").

3. Discuss how the following verses relate to patience. Take a fresh look at each passage, searching especially for (a) God's commands and standards to keep, (b) someone's example to learn from, (c) a promise from God to believe, (d) a warning to heed, or (e) a challenge to face.

•Job 1–2 •Psalm 27:14, 40:1-3
•Ecclesiastes 7:8-9 •Romans 12:12
•2 Timothy 3:10-12 •Hebrews 6:12, 12:1-3 •James 5:7-8

4. What vital, fundamental principles can you see in these passages (principles which are consistent with other Scriptures you know)?

5. In conclusion, answer these questions, especially in light of what you've observed in the passages above: (a) What does God want me to understand most about Himself? (b) What does God want me to understand most about others? (c) What does God want me to understand most about myself? And in light of all this, what would He have me *do?*

PERSEVERANCE

1. What thoughts and images come to mind when you think of the word *perseverance?*

2. Decide together what you believe is the best definition for the word *perseverance.*

3. Discuss how the following verses relate to perseverance. Look in a fresh way at each passage, searching especially for (a) God's commands and standards to keep, (b) someone's example to learn from, (c) a promise from God to believe, (d) a warning to heed, or (e) a challenge to face.

   •Romans 15:4-5 •
   •1 Corinthians 15:58
   •Galatians 6:9-10 •2 Timothy 4:7-8
   •Hebrews 3:12-14, 6:10-12, 10:23, 10:35-36, 12:1-3 •James 1:3-4

4. What vital, fundamental principles can you see in these passages (principles which are consistent with other Scriptures you know)?

5. Finally, answer these questions, especially in light of what you've observed in the passages above: (a) What does God want me to understand most about Himself? (b) What does God want me to understand most about others? (c) What does God want me to understand most about myself? And in light of all this, what would He have me *do?*

PEACE

1. What thoughts and images come to mind when you think of the word *peace?*

2. Would you say that peace is essentially the absence of conflict — or is it rather the *presence* of something, something that drives conflict away? What really is *peace?*

3. Discuss how the following verses relate to peace. Take a fresh look at each passage, searching especially for (a) God's commands and standards to keep, (b) someone's example to learn from, (c) a promise from God to believe, (d) a warning to heed, or (e) a challenge to face.

   •Genesis 13 •Psalm 34:14, 119:165
   •Proverbs 14:30, 16:7 •Isaiah 2:1-5, 26:3 •Matthew 5:9 •Mark 9:50
   •John 14:27 •Romans 5:1-5, 12:18
   •Philippians 4:6-7 •Colossians 3:15

4. What vital, fundamental principles can you see in these passages (principles which are consistent with other Scriptures you know)?

5. Finally, answer these questions, especially in light of what you've observed in the passages above: (a) What does God want me to understand most about Himself? (b) What does God want me to understand most about others? (c) What does God want me to understand most about myself? And in light of all this, what would He have me *do?*

PRAYER

1. In general, how would you evaluate the consistency and intensity of your prayers at this time in your life, compared with times in your past? To help you decide, use a scale of one to ten (one = "much less consistent and intense than ever," ten = "much more consistent and intense than ever").

2. What do you believe is the best definition for the word *prayer?*

3. Discuss how the following verses relate to prayer. Take a fresh look at each passage, searching especially for (a) God's commands and standards to keep, (b) someone's example to learn from, (c) a promise from God to believe, (d) a warning to heed, or (e) a challenge to face.

   •Deuteronomy 4:7 •1 Samuel 12:23
   •1 Kings 18:36-37 •2 Chronicles 7:14
   •Nehemiah 2:4-5 •Psalm 5:3,
   34:17-18, 42:8, 50:14-15, 88:1,
   88:13, 142:1-7 •Daniel 9:1-23
   •Matthew 6:5-18, 7:7-8, 18:19-20,
   21:22, 26:39 •Mark 1:35
   •Luke 11:1-12, 18:1-8 •John 15:7-8
   •Ephesians 6:18 •Colossians 4:2
   •1 Thessalonians 5:17 •1 Timothy 2:8
   •Hebrews 10:19-22 •James 5:16
   •1 Peter 3:7, 4:7 •1 John 5:14

4. What vital, fundamental principles can you see in these passages (principles which are consistent with other Scriptures you know)?

5. Finally, answer these questions, especially in light of what you've observed in the passages above: (a) What does God want me to understand most about Himself? (b) What does God want me to understand most about others? (c) What does God want me to understand most about myself? And in light of all this, what would He have me *do?*

PURITY

1. What thoughts and images come to mind when you think of the word *purity?*

2. How would you express the best definition for the word *purity?*

3. Discuss how the following verses relate to purity. Look in a fresh way at each passage, searching especially for (a) God's commands and standards to keep, (b) someone's example to learn from, (c) a promise from God to believe, (d) a warning to heed, or (e) a challenge to face.

   •Psalm 24:3-4, 51:10 •Proverbs 20:9
   •Isaiah 6:5-7 •Zephaniah 3:9
   •Matthew 5:8 •Philippians 4:8
   •1 Timothy 5:2 •Titus 1:15-16,
   2:11-14 •Hebrews 10:22 •James 1:27,
   3:17 •1 John 3:2-3

4. What vital, fundamental principles can you see in these passages (principles which are consistent with other Scriptures you know)?

5. In conclusion, answer these questions, especially in light of what you've observed in the passages above: (a) What does God want me to understand most about Himself? (b) What does God want me to understand most about others? (c) What does God want me to understand most about myself? And in light of all this, what would He have me *do?*

PURPOSE

1. What thoughts and images would come to mind if you heard someone described as being very "purposeful"?

2. In a sentence or less, how would you summarize *your* purpose in life, and *God's* purpose in your life?

3. Discuss how the following verses relate to the theme of *purpose*. Take a fresh look at each passage, searching especially for (a) God's commands and standards to keep, (b) someone's example to learn from, (c) a promise from God to believe, (d) a warning to heed, or (e) a challenge to face.

   •Psalm 31:14-15, 37:5-6, 57:2, 119:175, 138:8, 143:10
   •Proverbs 4:25-27, 16:8-9
   •Jeremiah 10:23 •John 17:4, 19:30
   •Romans 8:28-30

4. What vital, fundamental principles can you see in these passages (principles which are consistent with other Scriptures you know)?

5. Finally, answer these questions, especially in light of what you've observed in the passages above: (a) What does God want me to understand most about Himself? (b) What does God want me to understand most about others? (c) What does God want me to understand most about myself? And in light of all this, what would He have me *do*?

REPENTANCE

1. What thoughts and images come to mind when you think of the word *repentance*?

2. Decide together what you believe is the best definition for the word *repentance*.

3. Discuss how the following verses relate to repentance. Take a fresh look at each passage, searching especially for (a) God's commands and standards to keep, (b) someone's example to learn from, (c) a promise from God to believe, (d) a warning to heed, or (e) a challenge to face.

   •Isaiah 55:6-7 •Hosea 14:1 •Amos 5:4
   •Matthew 3:1-12 •Mark 1:15

4. What vital, fundamental principles can you see in these passages (principles which are consistent with other Scriptures you know)?

5. In conclusion, answer these questions, especially in light of what you've observed in the passages above: (a) What does God want me to understand most about Himself? (b) What does God want me to understand most about others? (c) What does God want me to understand most about myself? And in light of all this, what would He have me *do*?

REWARD

1. What thoughts and images come to mind when you think of the word *reward*?

2. Discuss how much you agree or disagree with this statement: It is impossible to live a full Christian life without a true eagerness to receive the reward God promises to those who please Him.

3. Discuss how the following verses relate to the theme of *reward*. Take a fresh look at each passage, searching especially for (a) God's commands and standards to keep, (b) someone's exam-

ple to learn from, (c) a promise from God to believe, (d) a warning to heed, or (e) a challenge to face.

•2 Chronicles 15:7 •Psalm 4:8
•Daniel 12:3 •Matthew 19:28-30, 25:14-46 •Ephesians 6:7-8
•2 Timothy 4:7-8 •Hebrews 10:35-38
•1 Peter 3:9-12 •2 Peter 1:10-11

4. What vital, fundamental principles can you see in these passages (principles which are consistent with other Scriptures you know)?

5. Finally, answer these questions, especially in light of what you've observed in the passages above: (a) What does God want me to understand most about Himself? (b) What does God want me to understand most about others? (c) What does God want me to understand most about myself? And in light of all this, what would He have me *do?*

SELF-ACCEPTANCE

1. What thoughts and images come to mind when you think of the term *self-acceptance?*

2. Decide together what you believe is the best definition for *self-acceptance?*

3. Discuss how the following verses relate to self-acceptance. Look in a fresh way at each passage, searching especially for (a) God's commands and standards to keep, (b) someone's example to learn from, (c) a promise from God to believe, (d) a warning to heed, or (e) a challenge to face.

•Psalm 139:1-16 •Luke 9:23-26
•John 12:24-25 •2 Corinthians 5:21
•Ephesians 2:8-10 •1 Peter 5:7

4. What vital, fundamental principles can you see in these passages (principles which are consistent with other Scriptures you know)?

5. In conclusion, answer these questions, especially in light of what you've observed in the passages above: (a) What does God want me to understand most about Himself? (b) What does God want me to understand most about others? (c) What does God want me to understand most about myself? And in light of all this, what would He have me *do?*

SELF-CONTROL

1. What thoughts and images come to mind when you think of *self-control?* How would you define this term?

2. How strong is your self-control at this time in life, compared with times in your past? To help you decide, use a scale of one to ten (one = "much weaker than ever," ten = "much stronger than ever").

3. Discuss how the following verses relate to self-control. Take a fresh look at each passage, searching especially for (a) God's commands and standards to keep, (b) someone's example to learn from, (c) a promise from God to believe, (d) a warning to heed, or (e) a challenge to face.

•2 Timothy 1:7 •Titus 2:11-14
•1 Peter 1:13, 3:7

4. What vital, fundamental principles can you see in these passages (principles which are consistent with other Scriptures you know)?

5. In conclusion, answer these questions, especially in light of what you've observed in the passages above: (a) What does God want me to understand most about Himself? (b) What does God want me to understand most about others? (c) What does God want me to understand most about myself? And in light of all this, what would He have me *do?*

SERVANTHOOD

1. What thoughts and images come to mind when you think of the word *servant?* Are these mostly negative, mostly positive, or a good mixture of both?

2. Decide together what you believe is the best definition for the word *servant.*

3. Discuss how the following verses relate to servanthood. Look in a fresh way at each passage, searching especially for (a) God's commands and standards to keep, (b) someone's example to learn from, (c) a promise from God to believe, (d) a warning to heed, or (e) a challenge to face.

   •Matthew 20:28 •Luke 10:25-37
   •John 13:1-17, 15:15 •Romans 15:8
   •Ephesians 6:5-8 •Philippians 2:5-8

4. What vital, fundamental principles can you see in these passages (principles which are consistent with other Scriptures you know)?

5. In conclusion, answer these questions, especially in light of what you've observed in the passages above: (a) What does God want me to understand most about Himself? (b) What does God want me to understand most about others? (c) What does God want me to understand most about myself? And in light of all this, what would He have me *do?*

SPIRITUAL GIFTS

1. What thoughts and images come to mind when you think of the term *spiritual gifts?*

2. Discuss what you believe is the best definition for the term *spiritual gifts.*

3. Discuss how the following verses relate to spiritual gifts. Look in a fresh way at each passage, searching especially for (a) God's commands and standards to keep, (b) someone's example to learn from, (c) a promise from God to believe, (d) a warning to heed, or (e) a challenge to face.

   •John 16:13-15 •Romans 12:6-8
   •1 Corinthians 12, 14 •Galatians 5:22
   •Ephesians 4:11 •2 Timothy 1:6-7
   •1 Peter 4:11

4. What vital, fundamental principles can you see in these passages (principles which are consistent with other Scriptures you know)?

5. Finally, answer these questions, especially in light of what you've observed in the passages above: (a) What does God want me to understand most about Himself? (b) What does God want me to understand most about others? (c) What does God want me to understand most about myself? And in light of all this, what would He have me *do?*

SPIRITUAL WARFARE

1. What thoughts and images come to mind when you think of the term spiritual warfare? How would you describe your own experience in spiritual warfare? How often in a typical day do you think about it?

2. Decide together what you believe is the best definition for *spiritual warfare.*

3. Discuss how the following verses relate to spiritual warfare. Take a fresh look at each passage, searching especially for (a) God's commands and standards to keep, (b) someone's example to learn from, (c) a promise from God to believe, (d) a warning to heed, or (e) a challenge to face.

   •Psalm 44:6-8, 60:11-12
   •Proverbs 21:31 •Romans 12:19-21
   •Ephesians 6:10-18 •1 John 4:1-6

4. What vital, fundamental principles can you see in these passages (principles

which are consistent with other Scriptures you know)?

5. In conclusion, answer these questions, especially in light of what you've observed in the passages above: (a) What does God want me to understand most about Himself? (b) What does God want me to understand most about others? (c) What does God want me to understand most about myself? And in light of all this, what would He have me *do?*

STRENGTH

1. What thoughts and images come to mind first when you think of the word *strength?*

2. Would you call yourself "a strong Christian?" Would others call you that? Would God call you that? How strong are you at this time in life, compared with times in your Christian past? To help you decide, use a scale of one to ten (one = "much weaker than ever," ten = "much stronger than ever").

3. Discuss how the following verses relate to strength. Take a fresh look at each passage, searching especially for (a) God's commands and standards to keep, (b) someone's example to learn from, (c) a promise from God to believe, (d) a warning to heed, or (e) a challenge to face.

  •Joshua 1:6-9 •Nehemiah 8:10
  •Psalm 18:1-2, 28:7, 46, 59:9, 61:2-3, 73:26, 105:4 •Proverbs 18:10
  •Isaiah 12:2, 40:29-31, 41:10
  •Romans 8:31 •2 Corinthians 12:8-10
  •Ephesians 3:14-16, 6:10
  •Philippians 4:13 •2 Timothy 4:17-18

4. What vital, fundamental principles can you see in these passages (principles which are consistent with other Scriptures you know)?

5. Finally, answer these questions, especially in light of what you've observed in the passages above: (a) What does God want me to understand most about Himself? (b) What does God want me to understand most about others? (c) What does God want me to understand most about myself? And in light of all this, what would He have me *do?*

SUFFERING

1. What thoughts and images come to mind when you think of the word *suffering?*

2. Decide together how you would define *suffering,* as the Bible uses this word.

3. Discuss how the following verses relate to suffering. Look in a fresh way at each passage, searching especially for (a) God's commands and standards to keep, (b) someone's example to learn from, (c) a promise from God to believe, (d) a warning to heed, or (e) a challenge to face.

  •Matthew 5:10-12, 16:21-28
  •Romans 5:3-5
  •2 Corinthians 4:16-18, 6:3-10
  •Hebrews 10:32-34 •1 Peter 2:21-24, 4:12-19

4. What vital, fundamental principles can you see in these passages (principles which are consistent with other Scriptures you know)?

5. In conclusion, answer these questions, especially in light of what you've observed in the passages above: (a) What does God want me to understand most about Himself? (b) What does God want me to understand most about others? (c) What does God want me to understand most about myself? And in light of all this, what would He have me *do?*

SUCCESS

1. What thoughts and images come to mind when you hear someone described as being "very successful"?

2. Discuss how you would define the word *success,* on a personal level.

3. Discuss how the following verses relate to success. Take a fresh look at each passage, searching especially for (a) God's commands and standards to keep, (b) someone's example to learn from, (c) a promise from God to believe, (d) a warning to heed, or (e) a challenge to face.

   •Joshua 1:7-9 •Nehemiah 4
   •Ecclesiastes 4:13-16
   •Matthew 6:32-34 •Luke 12:13-21
   •Philippians 3:13-14

4. What vital, fundamental principles can you see in these passages (principles which are consistent with other Scriptures you know)?

5. In conclusion, answer these questions, especially in light of what you've observed in the passages above: (a) What does God want me to understand most about Himself? (b) What does God want me to understand most about others? (c) What does God want me to understand most about myself? And in light of all this, what would He have me *do?*

TEACHER

1. What are the most important teaching responsibilities you have at this time in life?

2. How you would describe the ideal teacher?

3. Discuss how the following verses relate to teaching. Look in a fresh way at each passage, searching especially for (a) God's commands and standards to keep, (b) someone's example to learn from, (c) a promise from God to believe, (d) a warning to heed, or (e) a challenge to face.

   •1 Samuel 12:23 •Ezra 7:10
   •Psalm 19:7-11, 32:8 •Proverbs 1:1-7
   •Colossians 1:28-29
   •1 Thessalonians 2:13
   •2 Timothy 2:24-26
   •Hebrews 5:12-13 •James 3:1-2

4. What vital, fundamental principles can you see in these passages (principles which are consistent with other Scriptures you know)?

5. Finally, answer these questions, especially in light of what you've observed in the passages above: (a) What does God want me to understand most about Himself? (b) What does God want me to understand most about others? (c) What does God want me to understand most about myself? And in light of all this, what would He have me *do?*

TEMPTATION

1. What thoughts and images come to mind when you think of the word *temptation?*

2. Discuss what you believe is the best definition for the word *temptation.* In what ways, if any, would you distinguish this term from the words *trial* and *testing?*

3. Discuss how the following verses relate to temptation. Take a fresh look at each passage, searching especially for (a) God's commands and standards to keep, (b) someone's example to learn from, (c) a promise from God to believe, (d) a warning to heed, or (e) a challenge to face.

   •Joshua 7:19-26 •Matthew 4:1-11, 26:40-41 •Luke 21:34-36
   •1 Corinthians 6:18-20, 10:13
   •2 Timothy 2:22 •James 4:7

4. What vital, fundamental principles can you see in these passages (principles which are consistent with other Scriptures you know)?

5. In conclusion, answer these questions, especially in light of what you've observed in the passages above: (a) What does God want me to understand most about Himself? (b) What does God want me to understand most about others? (c) What does God want me to understand most about myself? And in light of all this, what would He have me *do?*

UNITY

1. What thoughts and images come to mind when you think of the word *unity?*

2. Decide together what you believe is the best definition for the word *unity.*

3. Discuss how the following verses relate to unity. Take a fresh look at each passage, searching especially for (a) God's commands and standards to keep, (b) someone's example to learn from, (c) a promise from God to believe, (d) a warning to heed, or (e) a challenge to face.

   •Psalm 133 •Acts 2:42-47
   •Romans 15:5-6
   •1 Corinthians 12:12-31
   •Ephesians 4:3-13 •Colossians 3:15

4. What vital, fundamental principles can you see in these passages (principles which are consistent with other Scriptures you know)?

5. Finally, answer these questions, especially in light of what you've observed in the passages above: (a) What does God want me to understand most about Himself? (b) What does God want me to understand most about others? (c) What does God want me to understand most about myself? And in light of all this, what would He have me *do?*

WISDOM

1. What thoughts and images come to mind when you think of the word *wisdom?*

2. Decide together what you believe is the best definition for the word *wisdom.*

3. Discuss how the following verses relate to wisdom. Take a fresh look at each passage, searching especially for (a) God's commands and standards to keep, (b) someone's example to learn from, (c) a promise from God to believe, (d) a warning to heed, or (e) a challenge to face.

   •Psalm 51:6 •Proverbs 2:1-6, 4:5-12, 8:1-21, 9:10-12 •James 1:5, 3:13-17

4. What vital, fundamental principles can you see in these passages (principles which are consistent with other Scriptures you know)?

5. Finally, answer these questions, especially in light of what you've observed in the passages above: (a) What does God want me to understand most about Himself? (b) What does God want me to understand most about others? (c) What does God want me to understand most about myself? And in light of all this, what would He have me *do?*

WORK

1. As it pertains to your life, what does the word *work* mean most?

2. Decide together what you believe is the best definition for the word *work.*

3. Discuss how the following verses relate to work. Take a fresh look at each passage, searching especially for (a) God's commands and standards to keep, (b) someone's example to learn from, (c) a promise from God to believe, (d) a warning to heed, or (e) a challenge to face.

   •Proverbs 12:24, 18:9, 24:30-34
   •John 9:4 •Ephesians 2:10
   •1 Thessalonians 2:9, 4:11-12
   •2 Thessalonians 3:6-15

4. What vital, fundamental principles can you see in these passages (principles which are consistent with other Scriptures you know)?

5. In conclusion, answer these questions, especially in light of what you've observed in the passages above: (a) What does God want me to understand most about Himself? (b) What does God want me to understand most about others? (c) What does God want me to understand most about myself? And in light of all this, what would He have me *do?*

WORSHIP

1. What thoughts and images come to mind when you think of the word *worship?* When do you feel most that you are worshiping God? When is it most difficult to worship God?

2. Discuss what you believe is the best definition for the word *worship.*

3. Discuss how the following verses relate to worship. Look in a fresh way at each passage, searching especially for (a) God's commands and standards to keep, (b) someone's example to learn from, (c) a promise from God to believe, (d) a warning to heed, or (e) a challenge to face.

   •1 Kings 18:21-39 •Psalm 5:7, 27:8, 35:18, 57:8-11, 92:1-2, 95:1-7, 100, 113, 148, 150 •Matthew 4:10 •John 4:23-24 •Romans 1:21-25, 12:1-2 •Ephesians 3:20-21 •Colossians 3:16-17

4. What vital, fundamental principles can you see in these passages (principles which are consistent with other Scriptures you know)?

5. In conclusion, answer these questions, especially in light of what you've observed in the passages above: (a) What does God want me to understand most about Himself? (b) What does God want me to understand most about others? (c) What does God want me to understand most about myself? And in light of all this, what would He have me *do?*

Suggested Study Schedule

➤ GENESIS: *21 weeks* — one week for the overview and chapters 1–2; then one week each for chapters 3–5, 6–8, 9–11, 12–14, 15–17, 18–20, 21–22, 23–24, 25–26, 27–28, 29–30, 31–33, 34–36, 37–38, 39–41, 42–43, 44–45, and 46–47; and a final week for chapters 48–50 and the "Big Picture" summary.

➤ EXODUS: *12 weeks* — one week for the overview and chapters 1–2; then one week each for chapters 3–6, 7–10, 11–15, 16–18, 19–20, 21–23, 24–27, 28–31, and 32–34; and a final week for chapters 35–40 and the "Big Picture" summary.

➤ LEVITICUS: *7 weeks* — one week for the overview and chapters 1–7; then one week each for chapters 8–10, 11–15, 16, 17–22, and 23–25; and a final week for chapters 26–27 and the "Big Picture" summary.

➤ NUMBERS: *9 weeks* — one week for the overview and chapters 1–6; then one week each for chapters 7–10, 11–12, 13–15, 16–18, 19–21, 22–25, and 26–29; and a final week for chapters 30–36 and the "Big Picture" summary.

➤ DEUTERONOMY: *9 weeks* — one week for the overview and chapters 1–3; then one week each for chapters 4–5, 6–8, 9–11, 12–15, 16–19, 20–27, and 28–31; and a final week for chapters 32–34 and the "Big Picture" summary.

➤ JOSHUA: *11 weeks* — one week for the overview and chapter 1; then one week each for chapters 2–3, 4–5, 6, 7–8, 9, 10–12, 13–19, 20–21, and 22; and a final week for chapters 23–24 and the "Big Picture" summary.

➤ JUDGES: *7 weeks* — one week for the overview and chapters 1–3; then one week each for chapters 4–5, 6–8, 9–12, 13–16, and 17–18; and a final week for chapters 19–21 and the "Big Picture" summary.

➤ RUTH: *2 weeks* — one week for the overview and chapters 1–2; then a second week for chapters 3–4 and the "Big Picture" summary.

➤ 1 SAMUEL: *10 weeks* — one week for the overview and chapters 1–3; then one week each for chapters 4–7, 8–11, 12–15, 16–17, 18–19, 20–22, 23–25, and 26–28; and a final week for chapters 29–31 and the "Big Picture" summary.

➤ 2 SAMUEL: *9 weeks* — one week for the overview and chapters 1–4; then one week each for chapters 5–7, 8–10, 11–12, 13–14, 15–17, 18–20, and 21–22; and a final week for chapters 23–24 and the "Big Picture" summary.

➤ 1 KINGS: *7 weeks* — one week for the overview and chapters 1–2; then one week each for chapters 3–7, 8–11, 12–16, 17–18, and 19–20; and a final week for chapters 21–22 and the "Big Picture" summary.

➤ 2 KINGS: *7 weeks* — one week for the overview and chapters 1–2; then one week each for chapters 3–4, 5–7, 8–11, 12–17, and 18–20; and a final week for chapters 21–25 and the "Big Picture" summary.

➤ 1 CHRONICLES: *6 weeks* — one week for the overview and chapters 1–9; then one week each for chapters 10–12, 13–16, 17–21, and 22–27; and a final week for chapters 28–29 and the "Big Picture" summary.

➤ 2 CHRONICLES: *8 weeks* — one week for the overview and chapters 1–5; then one week each for chapters 6–9, 10–13, 14–16, 17–22, 23–28, and 29–33; and a final week for chapters 34–36 and the "Big Picture" summary.

➤ EZRA: *4 weeks* — one week for the overview and chapters 1–3; then one week each for chapters 4–6, and 7–8; and a final week for chapters 9–10 and the "Big Picture" summary.

➤ NEHEMIAH: *6 weeks* — one week for the overview and chapters 1–2; then one week each for chapters 3–4, 5–6, 7–8, and 9–10; and a final week for chapters 11–13 and the "Big Picture" summary.

➤ ESTHER: *3 weeks* — one week for the overview and chapters 1–2; one week for chapters 3–7; and a final week for chapters 8–10 and the "Big Picture" summary.

➤ JOB: *13 weeks* — one week for the overview and chapters 1–2; then one week each for chapters 3–5, 6–7, 8–10, 11–14, 15–19, 20–24, 25–28, 29–31, 32–37, 38–39, and 40–41; and a final week for chapter 42 and the "Big Picture" summary.

➤ PSALMS: *36 weeks* — one week for the overview and Psalms 1–5; then one week each for chapters 6–10, 11–16, 17–18, 19–22, 23–27, 28–32, 33–35, 36–38, 39–41; 42–45, 46–50, 51–54, 55–59, 60–65, 66–68, 69–72, 73–75, 76–78, 79–82, 83–86, 87–89, 90–94, 95–101, 102–104, 105–106, 107–109, 110–114, 115–118, 119:1–88, 119:89–176, 120–129, 130–136, 137–140, and 141–145; and a final week for Psalms 146–150 and the "Big Picture" summary.

➤ PROVERBS: *13 weeks* — one week for the overview and chapters 1–2; then one week each for chapters 3–4, 5–7, 8–9, 10–11, 12–13, 14–15,

16–18, 19–21, 22–24, 25–26, and 27–29; and a final week for chapters 30–31 and the "Big Picture" summary.

➤ ECCLESIASTES: *4 weeks* — one week for the overview and chapters 1–3; then one week each for chapters 4–6 and 7–10; and a final week for chapters 11–12 and the "Big Picture" summary.

➤ SONG OF SOLOMON: *2 weeks* — one week for the overview and chapters 1–4; then a second week for chapters 5–8 and the "Big Picture" summary.

➤ ISAIAH: *21 weeks* — one week for the overview and chapters 1–2; then one week each for chapters 3–4, 5–6, 7–9, 10–12, 13–18, 19–23, 24–27, 28–33, 34–35, 36–39, 40–41, 42–43, 44–45, 46–48, 49–50, 51–53, 54–57, 58–60, and 61–64; and a final week for chapters 65–66 and the "Big Picture" summary.

➤ JEREMIAH: *14 weeks* — one week for the overview and chapters 1–5; then one week each for chapters 6–10, 11–15, 16–20, 21–24, 25–29, 30–31, 32–33, 34–36, 37–38, 39–43, 44–45, and 46–49; and a final week for chapters 50–51 and the "Big Picture" summary.

➤ LAMENTATIONS: *2 weeks* — one week for the overview and chapters 1–2; then a second week for chapters 3–5 and the "Big Picture" summary.

➤ EZEKIEL: *9 weeks* — one week for the overview and chapters 1–9; then one week each for chapters 10–17, 18–24, 25–28, 29–32, 33–34, 35–39, and 40–44; and a final week for chapters 45–48 and the "Big Picture" summary.

➤ DANIEL: *6 weeks* — one week for the overview and chapters 1–2; then one week each for chapters 3–4, 5–6, 7–8, and 9–10; and a final week for chapters 11–12 and the "Big Picture" summary.

➤ HOSEA: *4 weeks* — one week for the overview and chapters 1–3; then one week each for chapters 4–7 and 8–10; and a final week for chapters 11–14 and the "Big Picture" summary.

➤ JOEL: *1 week.*

➤ AMOS: *3 weeks* — one week for the overview and chapters 1–2; one week for chapters 3–6; and a final week for chapters 7–9 and the "Big Picture" summary.

➤ OBADIAH: *1 week.*

➤ JONAH: *2 weeks* — one week for the overview and chapters 1–2; then a second week for chapters 3–4 and the "Big Picture" summary.

➤ MICAH: *3 weeks* — one week for the overview and chapters 1–2; one week for chapters 3–5; and a final week for chapters 6–7 and the "Big Picture" summary.

➤ NAHUM: *1 week.*

➤ HABAKKUK: *1 week.*

➤ ZEPHANIAH: *1 week.*

➤ HAGGAI: *1 week.*

➤ ZECHARIAH: *4 weeks* — one week for the overview and chapters 1–4; then one week each for chapters 5–8 and 9–11; and a final week for chapters 12–14 and the "Big Picture" summary.

➤ MALACHI: *2 weeks* — one week for the overview and chapters 1–2; then a second week for chapters 3–4 and the "Big Picture" summary.

➤ ENTIRE OLD TESTAMENT: *281 weeks.*